OPERATION
ALACRITY

D1714562

T21644

OPERATION
ALACRITY

THE AZORES
AND THE
WAR IN THE
ATLANTIC

NORMAN HERZ

NAVAL INSTITUTE PRESS

Annapolis, Maryland

Naval Institute Press
291 Wood Road
Annapolis, MD 21402

© 2004 by Norman Herz
All rights reserved. No part of this book may be reproduced or
utilized in any form or by any means, electronic or mechanical,
including photocopying and recording, or by any information
storage and retrieval system, without permission in writing
from the publisher.

Library of Congress Cataloging-in-Publication Data
Herz, Norman, 1923–
Operation Alacrity : the Azores and the war in the Atlantic /
Norman Herz.
    p. cm.
Includes bibliographical references and index.
ISBN 1-59114-364-0 (hardcover : alk. paper)
1. World War, 1939–1945—Portugal. 2. World War, 1939–1945—
Azores. 3. World War, 1939–1945—Campaigns—Atlantic
Ocean. 4. Azores—Strategic aspects. 5. Azores—History,
Military—20th century. 6. Portugal—Foreign relations—United
States. 7. Portugal—Foreign relations—Great Britain. 8. United
States—Foreign relations—Portugal. 9. Great Britain—Foreign
relations—Portugal. 10. Military bases—Azores. I. Title.
D754.P8H47 2003
940.53′4699—dc21

                                                    2003011181

Printed in the United States of America on acid-free paper ∞
 11 10 09 08 07 06 05 04   9 8 7 6 5 4 3 2
First printing

To Christine

CONTENTS

PREFACE AND ACKNOWLEDGMENTS

During the last Great War the 928th Engineers and the 96th Seabees sailed to the Azores Islands to carry out an operation drawn up by the Combined Chiefs of Staff of England and the United States (CCS), and approved by their commanders-in-chief Winston Churchill and Franklin Delano Roosevelt. What made the operation, called "Alacrity" by Churchill, unique was the reluctant involvement of Portugal, a neutral power and possessor of the Islands. What made the operation important was to provide air cover for Allied convoys' "black hole" of the Atlantic, and to get to the Azores before the Germans did.

Secrecy had to be maintained during the operation and for many years after the war. The servicemen who carried out Alacrity had no idea of the scheming, planning, and negotiating that had gone on before they sailed from America. When they left they fully expected to end up somewhere in the Mediterranean Theater and the shooting war, not on an island in the middle of the Atlantic Ocean, a place that few even knew existed. Although no information about the high-level meetings or diplomatic maneuvering was ever revealed to the Task Force nor even the name or rationale for the operation, each man soon understood why he was in the Azores and the strategic importance of the job that had to be done.

I took part in the operation as an engineer corporal and in trying to learn more about the mission was surprised to find it conspicuously missing in most official and unofficial histories of World War II or even in descriptions of the Battle of the Atlantic, where it played such a critical role. Reading through the literature, the Azores was sometimes mentioned cursorily, but rarely was any information given on the background or the consequences of Operation Alacrity. Only by delving into the mine of declassified secret information on World War II was the complete story finally revealed. For this, I am deeply indebted to Dr. James H. Guill and to the government historians and archivists for their assistance in uncovering the many once-secret State Department, Joint Chiefs of Staff, and Army and Navy records. Dr. Guill, a leading authority on the history of the Azores, gave me access to his extensive file of declassified documents on the Lajes Air Base.

Sally Kuisel of Civilian Records, Gibson Smith and Ken Schlesinger of Modern Military Records of the U.S. National Archives, and Dr. Jim Dunn of the U.S. Army Corps of Engineers Office of History were especially helpful. A very large debt of gratitude is owed to Carol Marsh, Staff Historian, Naval Construction Battalion Center, for diligently uncovering the Navy's and especially the Seabees' contributions towards the success of the Operation. I must also acknowledge the generous assistance by my family: to my son Jonathan Herz for logistical help in our nation's capital, and to my wife Christine for her constant moral support and encouragement throughout the long years of research and writing. Thanks to all these fine people the story of Operation Alacrity can be told.

CHRONOLOGY

8 MARCH 1916	Portugal declares war on Germany and enters World War I on the side of the Allies.
5 JULY 1932	Salazar becomes prime minister of Portugal, a post he holds until 25 September 1966.
1 SEPTEMBER 1939	Germany invades Poland and annexes Danzig; England and France give Hitler an ultimatum to desist.
3 SEPTEMBER 1939	England and France declare war on Germany. Start of limited activity (*Sitzkrieg*) on Western Front.
4 SEPTEMBER 1939	The United States modifies its neutrality stance allowing "cash and carry" purchases of arms by belligerents, a policy favoring England and France.
17 DECEMBER 1939	Disabled German pocket battleship *Admiral Graf Spee* scuttled off Montevideo, Uruguay. Still no activity on the Western Front.
10 MAY 1940	Nazis invade Netherlands, Belgium, and Luxembourg. Chamberlain, architect of appeasement, resigns as England's prime minister; Churchill takes over.
26 MAY–3 JUNE 1940	Dunkerque evacuation—about 350,000 out of 400,000 Allied soldiers rescued from Belgium by British civilian and naval craft.

22 JUNE 1940	France surrenders and signs armistice with Germany at Compiègne.
10 JULY 1940	Start of 114-day Battle of Britain as Luftwaffe bombs southeast England.
17 APRIL 1941	Germans launch attacks in Balkans. Yugoslavia surrenders; General Mihajlovic continues guerrilla warfare; Marshal Tito leads left-wing guerrillas.
27 APRIL 1941	German tanks enter Athens; remnants of British Army quit Greece.
27 MAY 1941	Sinking the *Bismarck* effectively ends the argument for big ships versus U-boats.
21 JUNE 1941	Operation Barbarossa, Germany invades Russia.
7 JULY 1941	U.S. Marines relieve British forces in Iceland.
14 AUGUST 1941	Atlantic Charter—Roosevelt and Churchill agree on war aims.
7 DECEMBER 1941	Japanese attack Pearl Harbor, Philippines, and Guam; Pacific fleet crippled; United States and England declare war on Japan.
11 DECEMBER 1941	Germany and Italy declare war on the United States; Congress declares war on them.
15 FEBRUARY 1942	British surrender Singapore to Japanese.
9 APRIL 1942	U.S. forces on Bataan Peninsula in Philippines surrender.
12 JUNE 1942	Eight Nazi saboteurs land by U-boat on Long Island but are quickly captured.
11 AUGUST 1942	Pierre Laval, prime minister of Vichy France declares that "the hour of liberation for France is the hour when Germany wins the war."
18 OCTOBER 1942	Operation Torch, convoys sail from England and the United States to North Africa.
23 OCTOBER 1942	Start of Battle of El Alamein, high water mark of German invasion of Egypt.

4 NOVEMBER 1942	Axis forces retreat from El Alamein in a major victory for British commanded by General Bernard Montgomery.
8 NOVEMBER 1942	Operation Torch, Allied landings in French northwest Africa at Oran and Algiers; thirty-five thousand U.S. troops led by General Patton land at Casablanca in Morocco.
18 JANUARY 1943	Soviets announce the German blockade of Leningrad is broken.
2 FEBRUARY 1943	General Paulus surrenders the German Sixth Army at Stalingrad. Turning point of the war in Russia.
5 APRIL 1943	The 928th Engineer Aviation Regiment, Headquarters and Services Company activated at the Richmond Virginia Army Air Base.
12 MAY 1943	Last remnants of German Afrika Korps surrender in Tunisia on Cape Bon.
15–18 MAY 1943	Trident Conference in Washington. Allied strategy for Azores approved.
1 JUNE 1943	The 96th Naval Construction Battalion (NCB) activated at the Naval Construction Center, Camp Peary, Williamsburg, Virginia.
25 JULY 1943	Mussolini deposed; General Badoglio named Italian premier.
11–30 AUGUST 1943	First Quebec Conference. Roosevelt and Churchill agree that England should enter the Azores with permission of Portugal, followed by the United States two weeks later.
18 AUGUST 1943	Portugal signs agreement giving England the use of bases in the Azores.
3 SEPTEMBER 1943	Allied troops land on Italian mainland after conquest of Sicily.
8 SEPTEMBER 1943	Italy surrenders, terms are "unconditional surrender."
10 SEPTEMBER 1943	German army occupies Rome.

1 OCTOBER 1943	A combined British force commanded by Air Vice Marshal G. R. Bromet sails to the Azores from Liverpool.
12 OCTOBER 1943	Churchill announces agreement on Azores to Parliament.
25 OCTOBER 1943	Kennan gives Portugal American assurances to respect its sovereignty.
5 NOVEMBER 1943	Overseas alert to 928th Engineer Aviation Regiment (EAR).
22–26 NOVEMBER 1943	Cairo Conference—Roosevelt, Churchill, and Chiang Kai-Shek pledge defeat of Japan.
28 NOVEMBER– 1 DECEMBER 1943	Tehran Conference—Roosevelt, Churchill, and Stalin agree on invasion plans for Europe.
18 DECEMBER 1943	Provisional agreement allowing the United States to use Lagens air base.
24 DECEMBER 1943	928th EAR heads to POE (Port of Embarkation), Hampton Roads, Virginia to prepare to sail to the Azores.
31 DECEMBER 1943	96th NCB departs Davisville, Rhode Island POE for Azores; advance party flies ahead.
9 JANUARY 1944	96th Naval Construction Battalion arrives Terceira.
17 JANUARY 1944	928th Engineer Aviation Regiment arrives Terceira.
22 JANUARY 1944	U.S. and British troops land at Anzio on the western Italian coast.
27 JANUARY 1944	Allies start siege of Monte Cassino, Italy.
4 JUNE 1944	Allied troops enter Rome.
5 JUNE 1944	U-boats sink the Portuguese merchant ship *Serpa Pinto* in mid-Atlantic prompting Salazar to embargo all tungsten shipments to Germany.
6 JUNE 1944	D-Day, Allied landings in Normandy.
27 JUNE 1944	Cherbourg and its U-boat pens captured by the United States. U-boats moved to Norway.

20 JULY 1944	Hitler wounded in bomb plot.
25 AUGUST 1944	Paris liberated by Allies.
11 SEPTEMBER 1944	Second Quebec Conference between Roosevelt and Churchill.
12 SEPTEMBER 1944	U.S. troops enter Germany near Trier.
13 OCTOBER 1944	Athens liberated by Allies.
20 OCTOBER 1944	The United States invades the Philippines.
28 NOVEMBER 1944	Agreement for American construction of the Santa Maria air base.
16 DECEMBER 1944	Germans launch counteroffensive in Belgium (Battle of the Bulge).
22 JANUARY 1945	Russian army reaches the Oder River on a thirty-five-mile front.
28 JANUARY 1945	Allied supplies, much flown in via the Azores, reach China over the newly reopened Burma Road.
4–11 FEBRUARY 1945	Yalta Agreement signed by Roosevelt, Churchill, and Stalin.
7 FEBRUARY 1945	Ardennes salient eliminated, end of Battle of the Bulge and last German offensive of the war.
7 MARCH 1945	U.S. First Army crosses Rhine at Remagen where Germans fail to destroy bridge.
12 APRIL 1945	Death of President Roosevelt, Harry Truman inaugurated as president.
25 APRIL 1945	U.S. and Russian troops meet at Torgau on the Elbe River.
1 MAY 1945	Admiral Dönitz takes command in Germany; suicide of Hitler announced.
2 MAY 1945	Berlin falls to Allies.
7 MAY 1945	Germany signs unconditional surrender at Rheims; V-E day declared following day.
6 August 1945	The United States drops atomic bomb on Hiroshima.
14 August 1945	Japan agrees to surrender; V-J Day declared on following day.

OPERATION
ALACRITY

ONE

THE BLACK HOLE
IN THE ATLANTIC

Liberty and democracy in the world were more seriously in
danger a few years ago than at any time since they were
overwhelmed in the last days of the Athenian democracy.
Our whole democratic civilization twice hung by a thread
during the recent war—once during the summer of 1940 after
Dunkirk and the fall of France, when Britain even with her
Navy might have failed to repulse a full-scale German attack
across the Channel, and again during 1942, when German
submarines were sinking three Allied merchant vessels for
every one constructed.

CORDELL HULL, *Memoirs*

The year 1944 dawned with the United States already at war for more
than two years. In an event not noted by history books, the 96th Navy
Construction Battalion (the "Seabees") sailed across the Atlantic from
Rhode Island and the 928th Engineer Aviation Battalion (EAR) left
Hampton Roads, Virginia. Both outfits were ignorant of each other's
existence or where they were going but they were soon to join up on a
secret mission—"Operation Alacrity"—planned by the Allied Chiefs of
Staff with the collaboration of their leaders, President Roosevelt and
Prime Minister Churchill.

The story of World War II has been told many times through its
more famous operations, including the United Nations's[1] victories of
Overlord (the Normandy invasion and the liberation of Europe), and
Torch (the landings in North Africa and the capture of Germany's crack
Afrika Korps). For the Axis powers there were the debacles of Opera-
tion Barbarossa (the Russian invasion decimating the *Wehrmacht*) and

Sea Lion (the aborted invasion of England that annihilated the *Luftwaffe*). These operations determined the course of the war, involved millions of men at a cost of hundreds of thousands of dead, wounded, missing, or captured.

In addition to these major operations, there were many smaller operations that, although not celebrated as great landmarks on the road to victory, nevertheless were important milestones. Some of them have also been well described, but others have been ignored or kept secret far too long. Alacrity is one of these, first formulated by Churchill to get an air base in the Azores Islands before the Germans got there first.

Operation Alacrity was smaller in scale, not nearly as dramatic— and definitely not bloody—as were the big operations, but still played a crucial role in making the Allied victory possible. Its amphibious landings were unheralded, without a shot being fired, in a spot unknown to most of the world. Another difference between Alacrity and other World World II operations was that it involved Portugal, a neutral power and owner of the Azores, which made diplomatic maneuvering necessary. As far as anyone can tell, besides canceling out Germany's "tonnage war" and helping to bring victory in the Battle of the Atlantic, Alacrity hardly hurt anyone or anything except for a number of sunken U-boats and giving the prime minister of Portugal many sleepless nights.

Each world power wanted the Azores and had its own ideas on how to do it. Operation Alacrity was Churchill's, Roosevelt had Task Force Gray and Operation Lifebelt, and Operation Felix/*Projekt Amerika* was Hitler's. Each side knew of the other's plans and each had the same goal in mind: to occupy the strategically located Azores Archipelago by fair means or foul, by diplomacy, intimidation, or armed invasion. For the Allies, controlling the islands with their strategic position in the middle of the Atlantic Ocean meant protecting the important convoy routes of the central Atlantic. Failing to control them left a giant "black hole" in the Azores Gap for convoys headed to the Mediterranean and England, a gauntlet with U-boat wolf packs ready to turn the route into a shooting gallery of Allied troop and supply ships. If an invasion of Europe was to take place, the Azores Gap had to have air cover. Only an Allied airfield in the mid-Atlantic could provide that cover.

For Germany the Azores represented a base for U-boat operations and air bases needed for *Projekt Amerika*—a *Luftwaffe* bombing campaign of the United States's East Coast cities. With a base for provisioning in the middle of the Atlantic, U-boats would not waste so many days and precious diesel fuel sailing out of and returning to submarine pens in France. Their time in action would be almost unlimited. Equally important was the fact that the greatest chance of being sunk anywhere was in the Bay of Biscay, which had to be traversed to reach the open sea. The Royal Air Force (RAF) took advantage of the compact targets formed in the narrow gauntlet through which the submarines passed. Once out of the pens and safely through the gauntlet, U-boat commanders tried to stay at sea as long as possible, postponing the day when a return run had to be made through the RAF death trap.

A problem for all these planned operations was that Portugal, strictly neutral, had no desire to get involved in a conflict between the great powers, firmly believing that "when an elephant sneezes a mouse dies of pneumonia." To stay out of the war, Portuguese Prime Minister Salazar wanted neither side to use his territory as a base for offensive operations.

After the war broke out, the Allies established air bases in Labrador, Greenland, and Iceland to provide protection for convoys crossing the North Atlantic, a major step in the battle against the U-boats. Any submarine operating within about five hundred miles of the new bases found that their major concern was survival—there was a good chance they would be detected by aircraft, hunted down, and attacked—not hunting merchant vessels. Although the northern Atlantic route between the United States and Europe became safer for convoys, air cover was far out of reach for the central and southern ocean routes that had to be followed to supply operations in North Africa and the Mediterranean. Without the fear of attack from land-based aircraft, U-boats patrolled freely, hunting Allied convoys with less to worry about than their brethren sailing in the north. Protecting central Atlantic shipping routes from the United States to Gibraltar became critical; Operation Alacrity was given the highest priority.

Alacrity involved top-level decisions that had been discussed and finalized at the meetings between Churchill, Roosevelt, and Charles de Gaulle in Casablanca. Liberating Europe was the eventual goal, but first the Atlantic had to be made safe for Allied convoys. Step one would be to counter the German U-boat menace. If aircraft were based in the Azores Islands, the "black hole" would be covered, and the entire northern Atlantic would be within range of air protection. The Azores had to be occupied; Churchill's Operation Alacrity was accepted as the Allied approach. The Joint Chiefs of Staff knew about Operation Felix and that Hitler wanted the Azores for a U-boat base and to carry out his ambitious *Projekt Amerika*. Alacrity had to be successful, for if the Germans got to the Azores first, the Battle of the Atlantic might be lost.

When Operation Overlord was being planned it became clear that bases in the Azores would solve two critical problems: first, convoy traffic would be protected against U-boats; second, a mid-Atlantic airport was needed for ferrying aircraft and for air transport. Flying from Washington, D.C., to London or the Mediterranean meant puddle-jumping: Miami–the Caribbean–Natal, Brazil–Dakar, French West Africa–Marrakech, Morocco–London which, lacking a better alternative, was especially necessary in the winter months. The route was time-consuming and wasteful of personnel, aviation fuel, and aircraft but the northern route via Labrador—Greenland–Iceland—had severe drawbacks: the North Atlantic suffered from bad weather in the winter, and the strong tail winds leaving North America became a fierce westerly head wind returning. In addition, the northern route was a lengthy detour for North African and Mediterranean traffic. With a base in the Azores, an easy nonstop flight from the United States or London, every transatlantic round trip could be made efficiently via the central Atlantic.

Because Portugal was unwilling to allow any of the belligerents to establish bases in the Azores, Winston Churchill—always resourceful and mindful of history—resorted to a diplomatic maneuver; he called on the Treaty of Eternal Friendship signed in 1373 between England and Portugal. The gambit worked: the treaty was the wedge that allowed the Lagens[2] air base to be built on the island of Terceira.

When the Joint Chiefs geared up for the Operation, the 928th EAR and the 96th Seabees were charged with the jobs of building the air base and improving the port facilities of the island. Following standard military procedure, nobody taking part in the Operation, certainly no one below the command level, knew anything about the discussions and planning that led to their being sent to the Azores. When the GIs arrived at the port of embarkation, they fully expected to be on their way to Tunisia or Sicily, where the war was actually being fought. But the big United Nations's operations to save the world from Hitler needed some help from small Operation Alacrity, so they went to the Azores instead.

The secrecy surrounding Alacrity was pervasive as well as long-lived. In August 1944—after the Operation was well under way and the Lagens air base was fully functional—a few key enlisted men, myself included, each received commendations from Brigadier General Cyrus R. Smith, Commander, Military Air Transport Command. The letter of commendation only stated that each "had contributed to the success of the mission," leaving the world completely unenlightened with not the vaguest hint of exactly where or what "the mission" was all about.

The exhaustive and authoritative history of the Army Air Force in World War II by Wesley Craven and James Cate describes the history of the Air Force and the important role played by the Aviation Engineers. However, their discussion only covers the activities of the 19th, 21st, and 38th EAR plus fifty-four different Engineer Aviation Battalions (EAB) and three Engineer Aviation Brigades, with not even a hint about the existence of the 928th. The 801st EAB, the sole battalion of the regiment, is mentioned, but only for its role along with twenty-five other EABs in building heavy bomber bases on Okinawa. The Craven and Cate book does admit the 801st was in the Azores but leaves out any details: "the 801st EAB had spent most of the war on the Azores. It had the unusual opportunity of comparing the hurricane endured there with the great typhoon of October 1945 on Okinawa."[3] Lundeberg's exhaustive treatise on U.S. antisubmarine Operations in the Atlantic also noted the lack of published information on the Azores operation, pointing out that in Craven and Cate "the Azorean story is a startling omission."[4]

A visit to the Office of the Historian of the U.S. Army Corps of Engineers at Fort Belvoir, Virginia, shed no more light but was revealing for what was not there. In the files of the Historian, "The Narrative History of the 928th Engineer Aviation Regiment" begins: "The unit having completed its overseas mission returned to the United States 10 March 1945 . . . for 30-day recuperation leave and furlough while en route from the Port of Entry [Hampton Roads, Virginia], to Geiger Field, Washington."

Not a word of what "its overseas mission" had been, where it took place, or why. It was clear that the mission was too secret to entrust to the Office of the Engineer Historian. Together with its lone battalion, the public history of the 928th began with its scheduled departure for Okinawa.

The Navy was less hesitant about describing publicly the Seabees' role in the operation. The Seabee web site gives a thumbnail history of the 96th NCB including a tantalizing two-sentence description of its arrival, departure, and role on Terceira.[5] At the Seabee Historians Office at Port Hueneme, California, the complete war records of the

96th are kept, describing when they were organized to their deployment in the Azores, followed by assignment in the South Pacific, and finally ending the war building an air base in China.

Buried away in the U.S. National Archives and declassified fifteen to twenty-five years after the end of World War II, the events that led up to the movement of the 928th EAR to Geiger Field and the mysterious "overseas mission" were revealed. Complete in five large boxes are the Joint Chiefs, CCS, and the COS files, and two boxes of State Department records with enough information to piece together the story of the Azores bases.[6] Revealed are the military decisions and dip-lomatic maneuvering, the adventures, misadventures, and accomplishments that led to the Engineers and Seabees being sent to the Azores.

This book is based primarily on those documents, as well as official publications and other declassified documents of the United States, England, Germany, and Portugal, and augmented by my own personal experiences as a corporal in S-3 (Plans and Operations) of the 928th EAR Headquarters and Service Company.

Geology and Geography of the Islands

The Azores Archipelago (in Portuguese *Arquipélago dos Açores*) shares the distinction with Iceland and five islands in the South Atlantic—Ascension, Saint Helena, Tristan da Cunha, Gough, and Bouvet—of sitting exactly on the Mid-Atlantic Ridge. These islands are composed of purely volcanic and oceanic material without the foundation of continental rock found in other Atlantic islands, such as the Canary Islands and the Cape Verde Islands, which rose from the margins of Africa. What makes the archipelago unique, however, is that it bestrides the major east-west shipping routes of the North Atlantic and lies almost midway between Europe and North America, facts which have earned it an unsought role in world geopolitics.

The Azores have a total land area of 910 square miles (2,355 square kilometers), or slightly less than Rhode Island (which, coincidentally, may have the largest population in the world of Azoreans and their descendants outside of the homeland). They consist of nine islands located at about 37°40' N and 25°31' W stretching over 373 miles (600 kilometers) from Corvo in the northwest to Santa Maria in the southeast and geographically fall into three groups: an eastern one of Santa Maria and São Miguel; a central with Terceira, São Jorge, Pico, Faial, and

Population and Area of the Azores Islands, 1996

ISLAND	AREA KM²	POPULATION
Santa Maria	97.2	6,030
São Miguel	746.8	130,140
Terceira	402.2	56,780
Graciosa	61.2	4,960
São Jorge	245.8	10,300
Pico	447.7	14,930
Faial	173.1	14,750
Flores	141.7	4,430
Corvo	17.1	300

Graciosa; and Corvo and Flores in the west. Santa Maria, closest to Europe, is about 930 miles (1,500 kilometers) from Lisbon; Flores, the farthest—and considered by some geographers to be the westernmost point of Europe—is 1,100 miles (1,770 kilometers) from Labrador and 2,240 miles (3,600 kilometers) from the East Coast of the United States.[7] For strategic reasons in World War II, President Roosevelt called the Azores the easternmost point of North America rather than the western-most of Europe and rallied his own geographers to argue the point. Geo-logically, at any rate, Roosevelt was 22 percent correct: the two west-ernmost islands lie west of the Mid-Atlantic Ridge axis which marks the boundary of the North American Plate, but the other seven extend 344 miles (550 kilometers) east of the Ridge. Those seven islands are just north of the Gibraltar-Azores Fracture Zone, which separates Europe from Africa, so they are part of the European tectonic plate. The western two islands, however, are unequivocally on the North American plate.

In 1941 the total population of the Azores was estimated at 287,000; in 1996, largely through emigration to the United States and mainland Portugal, the number had dropped to 242,620.[8] About half, 125,000 in 1941 and 130,140 in 1995, live on São Miguel, the largest island, with nineteen thousand residing in Ponta Delgada, the capital and largest city of the archipelago. Angra do Heroïsmo, capital of the island of Terceira, with about twelve thousand is the second city of Azores, and only five other towns on all the other islands number more than six thousand. The two Allied airfields that are the subject of this book are on Terceira and Santa Maria. The air base on Terceira, called Lagens by the Allies in World War II and Lajes in Portuguese today, is now a NATO base and considered an essential linchpin connecting flights of the Military and

Naval Air Transport Commands from the United States to Europe, the Middle East, and Central Asia.

The weather on the islands is controlled largely by the "Azores high," a band of high pressure (about 1025 millibars) that extends from the Mediterranean westward towards Bermuda. The band moves north from April through August, centering over the Azores, ensuring mild summer weather for the islands. In the fall of 2001, however, the Azores high was unusually strong and persistent through the fall extending its influence over eastern North America (it might have caused the jet stream to shift northward resulting in record warm temperatures in October and November).[9]

The high pressure keeps storms and hurricanes away from the central Atlantic but unfortunately the pleasant weather does not last: the Azores high disappears in the fall allowing tropical storm systems— anticyclones—to hit the islands. The anticyclones develop off the African coast and move across the equatorial Atlantic towards North America where they turn north, then east and southeast in the direction of the Azores. Nearly one-third of seasonal Atlantic anticyclones reach the islands, mostly during September and October, but one or two also arrive in winter, especially during the months of January and February. Christopher Columbus was unlucky enough to encounter one when he visited Santa Maria in February 1493 on his way home from discovering the New World. In January 1944, 450 years later, Navy Seabees and Army Engineers arrived on Terceira in time to have a supply ship wrecked by another fierce anticyclone.

Temperatures year round are moderate with a maximum of about 82 degrees Fahrenheit (28 degrees Centigrade) in August and a minimum of 57 degrees Fahrenheit (14 degrees Centigrade) in February. Average annual rainfall in the archipelago increases to the northwest: in Flores it reaches 54.8 inches (139.1 centimeters); in Horta, on Faial, site of an Allied naval support station, 47.9 inches (121.7 centimeters); at Angra do Heroísmo, Terceira, 34.8 inches (88.3 centimeters); in São Miguel 28.7 inches (72.8 centimeters); and in Santa Maria only 25.7 inches (65.2 centimeters).

The topography of all the islands is controlled by their volcanic origin, and only Santa Maria has extensive marine sedimentary deposits as well as volcanic rocks, a definite advantage for World War II runway construction. Typical features are shores lined with rock debris flanking mostly inactive volcanic cones and calderas that rise to impressive heights. Pico Alto on the island of Pico is the highest of the entire archipelago, rising to a height of 7,713 feet (2,351 meters)—one of the nineteen peaks above one thousand meters (3,280 feet), twelve of which are on Pico. This conventional elevation, however, only measures the part of the island peaks that is above sea level. Taking into account their rise from deep ocean basins more than four thousand meters below sea level, the Azores crests would rank among the highest mountains of earth, higher for instance than the 4,807-meter Mont Blanc, the highest peak of western Europe.

To retrace the earliest history of the archipelago, we must go back some two hundred million years when all the continents were joined together in one big super-continent called Pangaea, and the dinosaurs of Mongolia could wander over to Arizona without getting their feet wet, if they had the mind to do so. Approximately 180 million years ago the gigantic continental plate started to break up, North America moved away from Europe making room for the nascent Atlantic by a process called Sea Floor Spreading, a critical part of the theory of Plate Tectonics. Ever since the initial break the plates have kept moving apart as the line of the rift became the Mid-Atlantic Ridge and new volcanic material continually rose up from the earth's mantle to fill in the ever-expanding fracture. As the American Plate moved west and the Old World east, the rift grew wider leaving the continents where we see them today with the ocean filling in the space created between the plates. The two sides of the Atlantic move apart at about the same rate that fingernails grow, averaging from a half to one inch (one to three centimeters) a year, only a snail's pace compared to the Pacific where the spreading rate is up to five or six inches (twelve to fifteen centimeters). But over geological time measured in millions of years or even historic time measured in centuries, the snail's wanderings become significant: the Vikings had seventy-five feet less to travel crossing to the New World than today's flight from Labrador to Norway and even Columbus's voyage to the New World was forty feet shorter than if he left Cadiz now.

The Azores Archipelago formed exactly at the point where the Gibraltar-Azores Fracture Zone dead-ends on the Mid-Atlantic Ridge. The point of intersection of these two major tectonic features may lie over a "hot spot" or thermal mantle plume which rises from deep within the earth's mantle, passes through the earth's crust and feeds the intense volcanism which gave rise to the islands. The Gibraltar-Azores Fracture Zone is the western end of the world's longest fracture zone, which starts in the Himalayas, goes through northern Iran and

Turkey into the Mediterranean passing through the Gibraltar gap and out into the Atlantic where it ends on the Mid-Atlantic Ridge. The junction of these two dynamic crustal boundaries makes for an unstable tectonic environment responsible for volcanic eruptions, powerful earthquakes, and an unsettling history of environmental disasters for as long as the Azores have been inhabited.

The oldest volcanic rocks are found on Santa Maria and date the birth of the islands at mid-Miocene 5.5 million years. As the volcanoes grew their eruptions coalesced forming the archipelago, seven of which are geologically young (less than seven hundred thousand years old). Volcanic activity has been more or less continuous throughout the history of the Azores, feeding the growth of the original islands and creating new ones.

The western group of islands of the Azores, lying on the relatively tectonically quiet North American Plate, is increasingly separated from the other islands by sea-floor spreading along the Mid-Atlantic Ridge. On the eastern side of the Mid-Atlantic Ridge the story is different; the Gibraltar-Azores Fracture Zone and its Mediterranean extension are active tectonically and responsible for damaging earthquakes and active volcanoes all along their length. Movement on the Gibraltar-Azores Fracture Zone is not sea floor spreading but rather faulting. Stresses are built up along the fault from Gibraltar to the Azores as the European Plate slides easterly against the African Plate, causing severe earthquakes whenever segments of the fault which had been hung up break free and release great amounts of energy.

Since human habitation began in the Azores, the Gibraltar-Azores Fracture Zone has been responsible for many devastating earthquakes. Two such with a Richter magnitude of 8 occurred in February 1969 and May 1975. In 1980 a major earthquake hit São Jorge and Terceira doing extensive damage to Angra do Heroïsmo. But even more destructive, in fact the most destructive earthquake ever to hit Western Europe in historic times, occurred on All Saints Day, 1 November 1755, when Lisbon was destroyed by a combination of an earthquake and tsunami.[10] The event, described by Voltaire in *Candide,* resulted in a huge loss of life, with more than sixty thousand casualties, and property damage estimated at fifty million dollars, an enormous sum for the time and for such a small country.

Volcanic systems today are most active on São Miguel, Terceira, Faial, Pico, and São Jorge, with São Miguel, the largest and most heavily populated island, suffering the greatest amount of damage from vol-

canic events. In 1444 the first settlers to arrive described a huge structure dominating the island, a graceful volcanic mountain similar to
those on Pico and much like Mount Saint Helens (in the state of Washington) before it erupted and blew out its cone.[11] That same year the
Furnas volcano blew its top in a spectacular and frightening eruption
and then subsided into what became the huge five-by-seven kilometers
caldera. Although the scene appears peaceful enough today, twenty-
two active hot springs in the valley of Furnas are a constant reminder of
the potential dangers posed by the magma chambers that could erupt
again at any time.

The Allied air base at Lajes on Terceira was built in the shadow of a
large caldera. The Furnas eruption took place on the flank of a caldera
of an apparently inactive volcano and the same scenario can be repeated on Terceira. The Lagens site was selected because it was the best
place on the island to build an air base, being relatively flat with a fairly
good approach for landings and takeoffs and long enough to accommodate a runway. No thought could be given to choosing a tectonically
safe site, free of the possibility of an eruption or earthquake—such sites
do not exist on the island.

Terceira has had its tectonic problems, but they were not nearly as
violent as those of São Miguel. On 22 November 1760 inside the same
caldera whose eastern rim overlooks Lagens Field, eruptions took place
when Pico Gordo of the Serra de Santa Bárbara exploded forming three
lava flows. Eruptions from the vent of Pico Gordo continued into 1761
resulting in building up five new volcanic cones. No other eruptions
occurred on the island during the time of human habitation, but several
destructive undersea eruptions took place just to the north and south,
one of which in 1902 destroying an undersea communication cable. On
New Year's Day, 1980, the most destructive earthquake recorded since
the catastrophe of 1522 occurred with an undersea epicenter about
twenty-five miles west of Terceira.[12] Damage was extensive on the
island as well as on São Jorge and Graciosa with sixty persons killed,
over five thousand homes and thirty-two churches demolished, and
more than twenty-one thousand left homeless.

In the four hundred year period from 1560 until 1960, the archipelago averaged five and a half destructive volcanic eruptions per century
or more than one every twenty years. Despite the ever-present danger
from earthquakes and volcanic activity, Azoreans peacefully go about
their everyday lives. Although whaling has been outlawed, the fishing
remains good, and where soils have developed by weathering of the

volcanic rocks they are fertile and suitable for farming. There are no extremes of temperature and, except for the occasional anticyclone, the most serious problem affecting the quality of life has not been natural disasters but the diminutive size of the islands. Because of the rugged volcanic topography and outcropping lava flows on each island, the total area available for habitation and farming is severely restricted. Each succeeding generation finds fewer opportunities for farming or industry at home, so large-scale emigration of entire families takes place, principally to mainland Portugal, Brazil, Massachusetts, Rhode Island, California, and Hawaii.

To select a site for an airfield the Allied Chiefs had to consider the following factors.

THE WESTERN AZORES

Flores and Corvo are the closest to North America of all the Azorean Islands so flying time from the United States would be kept to a minimum. Being west of the Mid-Atlantic Ridge and on the quiescent North American plate also meant they were the most tectonically stable of the archipelago and would not suffer any damaging earthquakes or volcanic eruptions. However, easily outweighing those virtues was the fact that they were the most northerly islands, with miserable flying weather throughout the year. During the year they were the last to gain the protection of the Azores high and the first to lose it, so for weeks at a time they could be plagued with storms and anticyclones, making flying conditions the worst imaginable.

THE CENTRAL AZORES

Of the five islands of the central group, Terceira and Faial stood out as most desirable. Weather conditions were much better than in the northern group and one could learn to live with the tectonic activity as long as one did not build near any active volcanoes or faults. Faial had the best natural port in the archipelago and was the farthest west of the Central group, making it a favorite of the Navy. An airport on the island could supplement the naval base, creating a double-barreled threat to the U-boats.

Terceira already had a grassy airstrip (*aerovaca* in Portuguese), where grazing cows competed with aircraft. The presence of a landing strip was promising, and a grass field would facilitate the construction of a larger facility to support heavy aircraft traffic. In addition, the relatively large size and population of the island suggested that it could provide a labor force, commercial enterprises, and farms to help support the base.

THE SOUTHERN AZORES

The British were interested in São Miguel for an air base. The largest island with the biggest city and population had the best developed infrastructure of the entire archipelago. The only truly functioning air base in the Azores was on the island and could be expanded to accommodate Allied aircraft. However, it was a Portuguese Air Force base and there was little chance it could be shared with the Allies. Even if it could be arranged, São Miguel's violent tectonic history made it the riskiest place to build a large air base.

Santa Maria, the farthest island of all from the United States, had advantages that more than compensated for the extra three hundred miles of flying distance: first, the best year-round weather of all the islands; second, extensive sedimentary rock cover that was easy to excavate and use for airport construction; and third, the fact that it was the most tectonically quiet of the eastern group.

These were the physical facts that made it easier to select an airfield site. What the Allies quickly discovered was that the only serious problems were first, dealing with Portuguese Prime Minister Salazar; second, that negotiations for the Azores air bases would be interminable and difficult; and that, third, they would provide their leaders with some of the worst headaches of the war.

A Little History

Early in the war Prime Minister Dr. António Salazar, mindful of the sad state of preparation of Portugal's armed forces, turned to England—his country's most ancient and durable ally—for assistance. There was a great danger, he felt, that Germany would launch an invasion of the Iberian Peninsula and attack Portugal who was, after all, historically pro-British but sadly unprepared for modern warfare. However, if her armies were better trained and equipped with arms and aircraft and if

England would promise to defend the country in case of an invasion, then Germany might be discouraged from attacking. England and Portugal were bound by a treaty of mutual assistance, the Treaty of Windsor (1373), that forged the oldest alliance still in force today between any two countries. England was at war with Germany, Portugal felt threatened by Germany, and the time appeared propitious, so Salazar sent a secret delegation of high military officials to London in early 1941 to initiate discrete discussions regarding mutual assistance. Did England require assistance from his country according to the guidelines of the Treaty of Windsor? If so, could England provide modern aircraft and arms and training to help make the Portuguese army a first class fighting force? Then she could both defend herself should Germany attack and also afford meaningful assistance to England.

The Treaty of Windsor has been in force continuously since 1373 (except for the sixty-year lapse starting in 1580 when Spain occupied Portugal). In 1826 Lord Canning described the uniqueness of the Anglo-Portuguese alliance:

> Among the alliances by which at different periods of our history this country has been connected with the other nations of Europe, none is so ancient in origin and so precise in obligation, none has continued so long and been so faithfully observed, of none is the memory so intimately interwoven with the most brilliant records of our triumphs as that by which Great Britain is connected with Portugal. . . . While Great Britain has an arm to raise, it must be raised against the efforts of any power that should attempt forcibly to control the choice and fetter the independence of Portugal.[13]

The origins of the alliance actually go back more than two hundred years before the signing of the treaty. In the first half of the eighth century, the Moors invaded and occupied the entire Iberian Peninsula. In 1139 Afonso Henriques assumed the title of king of Portugal (*Porto Cale*, derived from the northern city of Porto) and attempted to extend his control south to Lisbon. He appealed as a Christian king for help to free his kingdom from the Moslem Moors. English and Flemish soldiers bound for the Second Crusade in 1147 stopped off long enough to help Afonso drive out the Moors, seize Lisbon, and establish his new kingdom. Many of the Crusaders liked the country so well that when the fighting was over they decided to settle down there. Having been raised in the generally miserable climate of the British Isles, the sunny skies, warm seas, and fertile green pastures of this new land were too much of a temptation to resist. Grapes could be grown easily and delicious wines produced, something that was definitely missing back home. Besides, the expatriate Britons who had helped liberate the country were looked on with favor by the new king who offered them land and titles to induce them to stay and settle down.

Cordial relations between the two nations grew, commerce prospered, and large numbers of English continued to settle in Portugal culminating in the treaty of signed at Windsor Palace. Nearly six centuries later when Churchill invoked the treaty to justify British occupation of the Azores, he quoted Article III to Parliament which provided for one party to "furnish, supply and send succor to the requiring party for the protection of the Kingdom menaced."[14]

The Azores were reputedly discovered about 1427 by Diogo de Senill, a pilot in the service of the king of Portugal.[15] However, the islands had been depicted on older maps and as early as 1154 on a globe made by Sherif Mohamed al Edrisi for Roger, king of Sicily. Edrisi spotted nine islands in the Atlantic and named one of them "Raca," after a species of eagle living there. Nothing much resulted from Edrisi's globe or from Senill's discovery, because in 1431 Prince Henry the Navigator sent Gonçalo Velho Cabral, one of his most trusted sea captains, out into the Atlantic to find the islands, but all he came up with were a group of low lying rocks which he named the Formigas ("the Ants"), probably reflecting his disgust and disappointment as head of the expedition.[16] Henry would not accept the report as final, so the following year he sent Cabral out again with instructions to look harder. On 14 August 1432, only fifteen miles from the Formigas, he found an island, which he named Santa Maria. This was the first of the archipelago to be officially discovered; by 1450 all the islands of the eastern and central groups had been located. A few years later the last two, Corvo and Flores, were discovered, completing the entire archipelago.

Henry sought settlers for the Azores Islands, and many Flemish families immigrated, bringing their trade skills, especially weaving and business enterprises to the new lands.[17] An appealing factor for the Flemish weavers was the fact that woad (*Isatus tinctoria*), an important source of blue dye, grew there in abundance. The first head or captain-donatory of Terceira, Jácome de Bruges, was Flemish and responsible for organizing the two main settlements of the island, Angra,[18] and Praia.

By the end of the fifteenth century all the islands were inhabited, and trade with Portugal became well established. Soon after they were settled, the Azores played an important role in the history of European exploration of the New World. Many great voyages either embarked from the islands or called on their way, including Columbus returning from his voyage of discovery. But even before Columbus set sail, Alvaro Martins Homem and João Vaz Corte-Real may have already landed in Newfoundland. João Fernandes, whose title was *labrador* or landowner in the Azores, sailed to Greenland and later served as navigator for John Cabot. A 1534 map shows Labrador already named after Fernandes "because he who gave the direction was a labrador of the Azores, they gave it that name."[19]

As mentioned above, the only period in history when the Treaty of Eternal Friendship effectively lapsed was from 1580 until 1640 when Spain occupied Portugal. Phillip II of Spain, taking advantage of a dearth of legal successors, claimed the throne and sent in an army under the Duke of Alba to back up his claim. The country quickly submitted to Spanish rule, except for the Azores, which did not recognize the Spanish pretender. Phillip found this intolerable and to convince the islanders of their errors he sent out a fleet to blast them into submission. This was the first time that an unwanted foreign army attempted to land in the islands: the next was in January 1944 when the U.S. Seabees and Engineers arrived uninvited.

In this first battle of the Azores the Spaniards were led by the distinguished captain Don Pedro Valdez (who would help found St. Augustine, Florida, in 1565). Included in his company was one of Spain's greatest writers, Lope de Vega who, luckier than most, lived to tell about the debacle. Valdez commanded a fleet of ten ships that landed on 25 July 1581 in the Bay of Salga, present-day Praia da Vitória, which was, from his perspective at sea, undefended.

Two thousand Spanish troops disembarked and started to sack the town. By noon, the battle had reached a stalemate; the Spaniards were dug in and the islanders could make no progress in the face of artillery and superior firepower. From the hilltops overlooking the battlefield, Father Pedra, an Augustine monk and a principal leader of the resistance forces, knew that the most ferocious bulls of the entire archipelago were bred on Terceira. He ordered the farmers to bring in quickly every fierce bull they had. About a thousand were brought in. Directed by musket shots and loud screaming, they were made to charge downhill in the direction of the heavily armored Spaniards, closely followed by the locals sporting an odd assortment of weapons, including pitch-forks, sickles, and antique blunderbusses. With the bulls and the un-orthodox weapons and tactics of the islanders, the Spaniards were panic-stricken. Defending their homes had given the Terceirenses all the courage they needed to make up what they lacked in armament.

The stalemate became a rout. The Spaniards' retreat to the beach was pure chaos. Many fell prey to a bull's horn or pitchfork spike or had trouble getting through the marsh with their heavy armor. Most of the invaders perished; those who did not die in the attack drowned trying to return to the galleons. Only five hundred survived the trip back to Cadiz. It was not until two years later that Phillip II tried another land-ing on Terceira, this time successfully.[20]

With the Spanish occupation of Portugal, the English felt free to act as "reprisal pirates." Many distinguished noblemen became privateers with a mission to highjack Spanish treasure ships returning from the New World. To protect the precious cargoes, in 1555 the great Spanish admiral, Don Alvaro de Bazan, developed the first convoy system, and from 1560, armed escorts were regulated by another great admiral, Don Pedro Menendez de Aviles, who designed the first frigate. The armed convoy was now mandatory for all returning cargo ships.

In the organization of a Spanish convoy the galleons carrying the most valuable cargo sailed in the middle surrounded by armed escorts. Outside this tight inner circle were smaller ships, loaded with less valuable cargo and sitting ducks for the reprisal pirates who came up to the convoy at dusk, boarded a ship on the perimeter and made off with either the cargo or the entire ship before any of the lumbering armed escorts could reach the scene. The Allies copied the convoy system in World War I and England did so soon after the outbreak of World War II.

All predators in the Atlantic—sixteenth- and seventeenth-century reprisal pirates highjacking Spanish treasure and U-boats of World Wars I and II chasing Allied convoys—found the Azores a happy hunting ground. Because the most important transoceanic currents pass by the Azores, they became an ideal place for cargo ships—as well as their hunters—to pick up supplies or just to rendezvous. But because of the vile weather for much of the year and a shortage of good harbors, the islands are also a graveyard for the hunters and the hunted. The anchor-age at Angra, despite being one of the largest in the Azores and much used by Spanish treasure ships, is not an ideal place for a ship to put in. The seabed of the harbor consists of volcanic boulders and detritus with a steep drop-off of hundreds of feet close to shore. The port opens to the south and affords no protection against the fierce southerly winds that rise up frequently. Sailing vessels attempting to anchor were forced to luff up and haul in close inshore under conditions that would be a nightmare even for modern yachtsmen. The lesson that the waters of the Azores were treacherous, a true ships' graveyard, was not lost on the Joint Chiefs in World War II when they decided that in addition to building an air base, a Seabee Battalion would be needed to construct port facilities.

The United States has had close relations with the Azores since before the War of Independence. One of the first consulates of the new nation was established on São Miguel, to represent U.S. interests, especially whaling.[21] New England whaling ships would regularly head for the Azores, right up to World War I, both to pick up a crew and to hunt whales. Two out of every three sperm whales caught in the world's oceans were harpooned in the waters around the Azores. The contact with New England whalers eventually led to a major emigration of Azorean families to the same ports from where their ships had sailed.

In World War I, on 23 November 1914, Portugal declared war on Germany, honoring the Windsor Treaty.[22] On 4 July 1917, a German U-boat surfaced in the harbor of Ponta Delgada and fired on the city—the first time since the days of the Spanish occupation that an enemy bombed any of the islands. The submarine was driven off by the supply ship USS *Orion*, which had been sent—with five escort destroyers—to establish an Allied naval station in the Azores. In World War I, in contrast with World War II, Portugal cooperated closely with the Allies, England and the United States, giving them access to the ports of Horta and Ponta Delgada for antisubmarine warfare and as a safe harbor for ship repair, provisioning, and refueling of convoys.

Germany had long had designs on the Azores.[23] A highlight of the 1897–98 *Winterarbeiten* (winter war games) of the German Admiralty was a discussion of invasion strategies of the United States and selection of possible landing sites in Chesapeake Bay, Cape Cod, and Long Island as a prelude to an attack on New York City. Naval bases in the Azores would be used to provision the invasion fleet. In World War I, in December 1916 Admiral von Holtzendorff presented the Navy's comprehensive war aims program, including the need to establish naval bases at either Dakar in French West Africa or in the Cape Verde and Azores Islands to serve for U-boat operations. The fact that the Azores were perfectly sited for U-boat operations in the Atlantic and to launch an attack against the United States was also not lost on Hitler and his admirals in World War II.

TWO

THE WAR BEGINS:
PORTUGAL OFFERS
SUCCOR, 1930–1940

> Few statesmen have lived as obscurely as Dr. António de
> Oliveira Salazar. His personal life has always been withdrawn,
> his public appearances few. His speeches, during his public life,
> were sometimes hard to interpret, harder still to translate. His
> distaste for the personality cult has restricted him to a speech
> or two a year, an occasional interview with a foreign journalist.
> Very few people have taken a meal with him, or addressed him
> by his Christian name.
>
> HUGH KAY, "Salazar and Modern Portugal"

Churchill's description of Russia as an enigma wrapped in a riddle
aptly describes Dr. António de Oliveira Salazar, prime minister of Portugal as well. Throughout the war Salazar was frustratingly difficult
for the Allies to deal with. Anthony Eden, Churchill's able foreign
minister, who was driven to the point of despair many times negotiating with Salazar, spoke of "conduct incomprehensible in an ally." As a
confirmed neutral but friend of England, his prime concern was to
maintain a diplomatic pose of proper behavior and not give the Germans an excuse to invade his country. With the world at war, with
England's and his own nation's existence at stake, he consistently
stuck to the literal wording in treaties, asking point blank each time
how the Treaty of Eternal Friendship of 1373 applied. The way he saw
it the Treaty was unclear because both nations were threatened by
Germany, and Portugal, being the weaker party, could easily be overrun with little chance that any "succor" from England would arrive in
time to do any good. Of course, the treaty could not foresee the eventuality that other dangers besides an invading army might exist, and

that predatory submarines might some day range up and down the Atlantic threatening England's very existence. England, the party more seriously threatened, could legitimately request "succor" from Portugal in two distinct ways: first, to allow RAF bases in the Azores Islands to counter the U-boat menace and help keep her Atlantic lifeline open, and second, for Portugal to stop selling Germany tungsten, a metal necessary to harden steel and for lamp filaments. Salazar, ever wary, would not admit either request until it was clear that Germany was not going to win the war.

Salazar became prime minister in 1932 as head of the *Partido da União Nacional*, the National Unity Party.[1] In a national plebiscite the following year the party won 59 percent of the vote and immediately inaugurated an authoritarian form of government with Salazar as prime minister, a post he held until 1968. His regime was constantly criticized by the western press for its close friendship with Francisco Franco, dictator of neighboring fascist Spain, who had come to power in a bloody civil war. However, the Iberian alliance was felt to be necessary and in both countries' interest, given that each was strongly Catholic and anticommunist: both had an overwhelming fear of a communist takeover.

Throughout the war years Salazar walked a tightrope, acting outwardly neutral to justify his refusal to grant the Germans U-boat bases in the Azores although still trading with them and being careful not to antagonize Hitler. At the same time he denied repeated requests from the Allies who needed an air base in the Azores to protect convoys from U-boats and to serve as a way station for transatlantic air routes. When the CCS planned the invasions of Europe and North Africa, Azores bases were considered crucial to the success of both operations but Salazar had to be convinced to allow the Allies in the Azores. His attitude towards Hitler and Germany could best be characterized as reserved, whereas his sympathies towards Churchill and England were unwaveringly friendly.

The Portuguese admired England most of all the European nations, although the friendship could be strained at times, especially if Salazar suspected a double cross in the making. When Prime Minister Chamberlain gave away the store to Hitler at Munich in September 1938, handing over Czechoslovakia, turning a blind eye to Germany's rearming, and blithely declaring "peace in our time" only one year before World War II broke out, reports came back to Lisbon that England put more on Hitler's plate than had been made public. When Lord Halifax went to Berlin in November 1937 to discuss their territorial demands, the Germans expected him to offer Portugal's African colonies in lieu of England's returning Tanganyika. (In the Treaty of Versailles after World War I, England had seized the German African colonies including Tanganyika, the one they considered their prize possession, and now Hitler felt that payback time had arrived.) The English plan according to reports reaching Lisbon was to placate Germany with the quid pro quo, "we keep Tanganyika, and you get Mozambique." Although this deal was denied by England, its mere possibility made Salazar suspicious that Churchill might have hidden motives when he proposed raising the Union Jack in the Azores and the Cape Verde Islands.[2]

Germany could not afford to bully Portugal over the Azores when she also needed a steady supply of tungsten. Because the British Navy had blockaded the continent, tungsten had to be obtained on the continent: Portugal, Sweden, and Spain were the only suppliers that could ship the metal overland to Germany. Portuguese production was the most important by far—three thousand tons a year, whereas the Swedish was only three hundred tons. To the dismay of the Allies Salazar insisted that trade with Germany was important to maintain his country's neutrality and incidentally not damage its economy or antagonize the Nazis and he continued to ship tungsten.[3]

Negotiations over the tungsten shipments dragged on for longer than the discussions on air bases and were just as contentious. During the darkest period of the war, Salazar signed an agreement on 24 January 1942, awarding Germany export licenses for twenty-eight hundred tons a year. The German ambassador had promised Salazar sixty thousand tons of finished steel, so this might have been a quid pro quo. Shipments were completely stopped only when it became clear that Germany was not going to win the war.

Despite his professed neutrality, Salazar was the sole leader of a European country who felt that England would eventually triumph but only after a long and bloody conflict. A U.S. journalist, Henry J. Taylor, reported that Salazar told him privately

> As early as Hitler's attack on Poland in 1939 and even after France fell . . . he foresaw a very long struggle and the war ending in an Allied victory, instead of a short war and a German peace. He was convinced that England would stand . . . that the

United States would come in and that victory would go to us. I found not another continental European leader who then agreed with him.[4]

A few days before the war broke out Germany promised to respect the integrity of Portugal but only on condition that it remained scrupulously neutral. A neutral Portugal also suited England because it had neither the resources nor the desire to help defend the country should Germany invade. A German occupation would mean U-boats operating out of bases in Portugal whose coastline juts far out into the Atlantic, a consequence too horrible to contemplate. So when Salazar, early in the war, consulted with England on what was expected of him, Churchill agreed to help modernize the Portuguese army but urged him to stay out of the war.

Just to be ready for any eventuality after the war broke out, during 1940–41 Salazar doubled the size of the Portuguese army from forty thousand to eighty thousand. Because of the threat to the Azores, when the Allies arrived in late 1943 they found the islands garrisoned by forty thousand Portuguese troops. In reinforcing the islands, Salazar also managed a massive diplomatic triumph—the Allies were sure this had been done to defend against a possible German assault and the Germans, who had also pressured Salazar to reinforce the Azores, were sure it was to resist an Allied landing.

Salazar had other worries besides German aggression and English duplicity; he also had to be wary of his Spanish neighbor. On 17 March 1939 Salazar and Franco signed an Iberian pact, a treaty of nonagression, which reiterated the bonds of friendship that tied Portugal and Spain together. But at the outbreak of the war Franco also signed the Anti-Comintern pact aligning Spain on the side of the Axis Powers. Even if Spain ostensibly remained cordial to Portugal, England feared she would be hard pressed to deny her new ally the right to cross the Pyrenees, march through the country, seize Gibraltar, and invade Portugal.

Hitler's interest in occupying Portugal's Atlantic islands grew steadily after the conquest of France. From Norway's North Cape on the Arctic Ocean to France's Biarritz in the Bay of Biscay, the European Atlantic coast now afforded many safe havens for German naval operations. The Azores operation could be carried out with troop-carrying U-boat fleets sailing from several southern French ports preceded by VLR aircraft bombardment and paratroop attack.

Washington Prepares

During the winter of 1938–39, at the same time that Germany was marching into Czechoslovakia, the American Joint Planning Committee of the Joint Chiefs of Staff was given this problem: determine "the various practicable courses of action open to the military and naval forces of the United States in the event of (a) violation of the Monroe Doctrine by one of more of the Fascist powers, and (b) a simultaneous attempt to expand Japanese influence in the Philippines."[5] Next the Planning Commission was asked to study what courses of action were open to the United States in the event of an Axis attack.[6] The proposed plans were given the code names Rainbow 1 to 4 for the defense of the Western Hemisphere and the Pacific. In the event that England and France were at war with Germany and Italy (and possibly also with Japan), it was assumed that the United States would become involved as a major participant.

When France surrendered—and England was expected to fall soon after—the defense of the Western Hemisphere would rest on the shoulders of the United States and Canada.[7] The Pacific fleet should be pulled back to Hawaii and Alaska; the Atlantic fleet withdrawn to the Caribbean; and South America defended as far south as the bulge of Brazil. When England did not fall, it became clear that eventually America would join her as an active ally in the war. A new Rainbow 5 was needed to set strategy and to provide a basis for discussions with the British General Staff, referred to as the ABC-1 agreements. The aims of Rainbow 5 were "to secure the Western Hemisphere from European or Asiatic political or military penetration, maintain the security of the United Kingdom, and . . . ensure the ultimate security of the British Commonwealth of Nations."[8] ABC-1 was worked out by the CCS meeting in Washington between January and the end of March 1941. The United States would not come into the war until Pearl Harbor nine months later but the grand strategy of Rainbow 5 laid out the steps necessary to achieve an Allied victory:

1. Economic pressure against the Axis powers.
2. A sustained air offensive against Germany.
3. Early elimination of Italy as an Axis partner.
4. Air, land, and naval raids and minor offensives against Axis military strength.

5. Support of neutrals, allies, and associates of the United States and England and people in occupied territories in resistance to the Axis Powers.
6. Building up forces for an eventual offensive against Germany.
7. Capture positions from which to launch an eventual offensive.

The U.S. Army and Navy were assigned certain tasks including

1. protect Allied sea communications;
2. prevent the extension of European or Asiatic military powers into the Western Hemisphere; and
3. protect outlying military base areas and islands of strategic importance against land, air, or seaborne attack.

The Azores Archipelago figured prominently in the first and third of these tasks, and also fit in the second if it could be considered geographically a part of the Western Hemisphere.

The Allies and the Azores

Churchill's war cabinet laid down explicit guidelines for relations with Portugal: under no circumstance would Portugal be encouraged to declare war, her neutrality must be preserved at all costs, but an Allied air base was needed in the Azores. If diplomatic negotiations failed and Portugal would not recognize the primacy of the 1373 treaty, the islands would be invaded.

It was expected that the British would occupy the Azores first (and possibly also the Cape Verde Islands), but if circumstances required, a U.S. naval task force (including Marines) might be called on to assist or to carry out either operation. The U.S. Joint Chiefs thought that the British would probably occupy the Cape Verdes and leave the Azores for the U.S. Marines. The Army would eventually relieve the Marines in the Azores as well as the British garrisons in Iceland and the British Caribbean islands. The task force for the operation to capture and occupy the Azores was code-named Gray.

While the joint planning was taking place in Washington, Western Europe was being overrun by the Nazi *blitzkrieg.* President Roosevelt was afraid that Americans were too complacent and that sentiments encouraging isolationism rather than preparedness had been nurtured by events in Europe. Neither the people nor Congress seemed to appreciate the great dangers faced by the nation; its very existence was at stake. The United States could no longer take comfort in the large oceans on either side for protection. In a message to Congress, the president highlighted the new facts of geography and modern technology to bring home the message that the nation was in great danger:[9]

> The American people must recast their thinking about national protection. Motorized armies can now sweep through enemy territories at the rate of 200 miles a day. Parachute troops are dropped from airplanes . . . We have seen the treacherous use of the "fifth column"[10] by which persons supposed to be peaceful visitors were actually part of an enemy unit of occupation . . . The element of surprise . . . had become more dangerous because of the amazing speed with which modern equipment can reach and attack the enemy's country . . .
>
> The Atlantic and Pacific Oceans were reasonably adequate defensive barriers when fleets under sail could move at an average speed of 5 miles an hour. Even then by a sudden foray it was possible for an opponent actually to burn our National Capitol.[11] Later the oceans still gave strength to our defense when fleets and convoys propelled by steam could sail the oceans at 15 or 20 miles an hour.
>
> But the new element—air navigation—steps up the speed of possible attack to 200 to 300 miles an hour. Furthermore it brings the new possibilities of the use of nearer bases from which an attack . . . on the American Continents could be made. From the fiords of Greenland it is 4 hours by air to Newfoundland; . . . and only 6 hours to New England.
>
> The Azores are only 2,000 miles from parts of our eastern seaboard, and if Bermuda fell into hostile hands it is a matter of less than 3 hours for modern bombers to reach our shores . . . The islands off the West Coast of Africa are only 1,500 miles from Brazil. Modern planes starting from the Cape Verde Islands can be over Brazil in seven hours. And Pará, Brazil is but four flying hours to Caracas, Venezuela; and Venezuela but two and a half hours to Cuba and the Canal Zone; and Cuba and the Canal

Zone are two and a quarter hours to Tampico, Mexico; and Tampico is two and a quarter hours to St. Louis, Kansas City, and Omaha.

In the speech the president justified his policy of remaining diplomatically neutral but factually committed to defend the Western Hemisphere against a plausible German attack. The country was to be aligned militarily with England, and in the name of self-defense would take whatever actions it deemed necessary. In adding the need to allow a preemptive strike anywhere, he set U.S. policy towards the neutral countries including Portugal and her Atlantic islands for the rest of the war:

> A defense which makes no effective effort to destroy the lines of supplies and communications of the enemy will lose. An effective defense, by its very nature, requires the equipment to attack an aggressor on his route before he can establish strong bases within the territory of American vital interests.[12]

He would eventually define the territory of U.S. interests as the entire Western Hemisphere, including Danish Greenland and Iceland and the Portuguese Azores.

Barely two weeks after rescuing the remains of the British army from the continent, and only ten days after the U.S. Joint Chiefs approved Rainbow 4, on 17 June 1940 Churchill sent a personal minute to the first lord of the Admiralty, A. V. Alexander, ordering him to draw up plans to seize the Canary Islands (code *Bugle*), the Cape Verdes (code *Shrapnel*), and the Azores (code *Alloy*). These operations would be carried out if Spain declared war and attempted to invade Gibraltar or if Germany invaded the Iberian Peninsular for the same purpose.[13] Operation Felix was the code name for the German operation but to succeed it required Franco to allow the transfer of armed troops through Spain. Intelligence about Felix made Churchill apprehensive but he had no need to be worried, at least for the time being—Franco, ever wary of Hitler's motives, was not convinced that Felix was in his country's best interests.

Berlin Plans, June–July

With Western Europe conquered, the German High Command started planning its next campaign. The Navy had prepared an invasion scheme against England dating back to November 1939 but Hitler, in a meeting on 20 June 1940, felt that it was unnecessary: air attacks and a naval blockade would be enough to defeat the British.[14] Hitler suggested occupying Iceland (Operation *Ikarus*) but the C-in-C Navy, OKM, argued that it would be impossible to maintain supply lines over that great distance against the British Navy. The High Command admitted the one glaring weakness in the German war machine—the Navy was ineffective and outgunned against England; it had to be built up; shipyards had to be given a high priority for critical materials.[15] The decision to call off Ikarus was also influenced by fact that the British-Canadian occupation of Iceland, which began on 10 May, meant a strong Allied force was already in place by the end of June.

Because the Navy lacked the resources to invade Iceland or blockade England, Hitler and the High Command decided that next they would launch an all-out campaign against England. On 2 July the first directive for Operation Sea Lion (*Seelöwe*), the invasion of England, was issued. However, before tackling Sea Lion, the German naval staff asked for more bases in the Atlantic and repeated the need to build up a fleet, from submarines to battleships, that could challenge the Allies on the high seas.[16] To assure control of the Atlantic Ocean would require German occupation of the European–North African coast from Norway's North Cape south to at least Morocco or preferably Dakar. An important part of the scenario called for the establishment of air and marine bases in the Atlantic islands by occupying Iceland or the Azores (or both) as well as the Canary and Cape Verde Islands. Taking over the islands would be done as part of Operation Felix or as independent operations. Although the OKM presented these plans enthusiastically on 21 June and 11 July 1940 and suggested that a U-boat blockade should be given the chance to starve England into submission and avert the need for an invasion. Hitler was reluctant hold up the operation against England or to initiate any action against the Atlantic islands. He did however agree to increase the steel quota for ship construction.

 The final decision had been made and on 16 July 1940 the German High Command issued the directive for the invasion of England. On 2 August Air Marshall Hermann Goering announced his plan of attack,

"Eagle Day," beginning with massive air strikes which would completely destroy British air power and open the way for a land invasion. The Battle of Britain began with 700 British fighter planes opposing 1,200 German bombers, 700 single-engine fighters, and 250 twin-engine fighters.

Churchill must have worried about the discussions going on in Berlin and he certainly knew that the German war machine was ready to start its next campaign of aggression. The paramount question in his mind was where and when, with possible attacks against England, Gibraltar, or the Atlantic islands known to be real threats. The Allied occupation of Iceland circumvented any Axis designs on the northern Atlantic; to protect the middle Atlantic, on 7 July Churchill ordered the Chiefs of Staff to prepare a Royal Marine Brigade for operations against the Portuguese islands: the operation against the Azores was code-named Accordion, against the Cape Verdes was Sackbut.[17] Neither operation had to be carried out when the Germans revealed their next move: the Luftwaffe began its massive air assault on England. The German High Command Staff was enthusiastically preparing for an amphibious crossing of the English Channel and invasion of England.

But by September, the invasion was called off for at least two good reasons, one based on hard facts and another on questionable intelligence. First, the RAF was making mincemeat out of the Luftwaffe, which was obvious to everyone—even to Goering, who had been fabricating numbers showing high RAF kills and negligible German losses. Second, faulty intelligence supplied by the *Abwehr*, Admiral Wilhelm Canaris's Foreign Intelligence Department, stated that the large, well-armed British Army and Navy was prepared to take on the invaders and could easily overwhelm an amphibious ground force.

Goering had been boasting as late as the end of August that his Luftwaffe operations were successful, that 2,669 of his operational aircraft had destroyed 1,115 of the RAF at a cost of only 467 German planes. When fact finally caught up with fiction, it became clear that phase one of the invasion, the air war to bomb England into oblivion and destroy the RAF, had not gone according to plan. The unexpectedly spirited defense put up by the RAF, the clear superiority of British Spitfires over the German Messerschmidts, and the staggering losses of the Luftwaffe in each raid—185 German aircraft were shot down on 15 September alone—showed that despite Goering's blustering Germany did not have command of the skies. There was no other choice left to Hitler and his generals than to cancel the invasion.[18]

Another good reason to call off the invasion was the disconcerting report filed by Admiral Canaris on the state of anti-invasion preparations in England. The Canaris memorandum to the OKM dated 5 September was based on the report of an Abwehr agent who had allegedly seen the fortifications on the south coast, exactly where the invasion force was going to land. The report stated that the area Tunbridge Wells to Beachy Head was distinguished by a special labyrinth of defenses so well camouflaged that an observer looking straight at them would not see anything extraordinary. A better reason for the disappearing labyrinth was its nonexistence outside of the agent's fertile imagination. Based on the report, German Intelligence calculated the size of the British forces at 1,640,000 men: an overestimate by several orders of magnitude.

This was not the first or the last time that Admiral Canaris's Abwehr was found wanting. RAF intelligence sources called the admiral the best unconscious double agent in the business and some believed he was actually in the pay of the English. The truth was that Canaris was very much against Hitler, who he felt was destroying Germany and did everything he could to make sure the Nazis did not win the war.[19] Towards the end of war he was an important player in the failed plot to assassinate Hitler and was condemned with his co-conspirators to face a firing squad. Admiral Karl Dönitz complained that the German High Command had received no information on the vast preparations taken by the Allies for what became a surprise landing in North Africa, a failure that eventually led to the loss of the entire Afrika Korps. In addition to the failure of intelligence in North Africa, Dönitz added that at no time during the entire war did the U-boat Command ever receive a single piece of useful information about the enemy.[20]

24 JULY: LONDON

In a personal minute to Lord Halifax, Churchill suggested the Admiralty should examine what immediate action England might take against Spain in the event of their moving against Gibraltar, while at the same time emphasizing to the government the dangers to which they would be exposed if they made such a move.[21] Three days earlier, during a meeting with his staff, Hitler had suggested that England's refusal to surrender or at least negotiate terms to end the war would change quickly if she were confronted with a political front that included

Spain, Russia, and Italy.[22] Wooing Franco would be no great problem, he felt, especially if Gibraltar could be promised as bait. Churchill suspected such a maneuver was brewing, but if Spain could be convinced not to join Operation Felix, Gibraltar would be saved and England's lifeline through the Mediterranean preserved. Better to disabuse Spain and abort Operation Felix before any wheels were set in motion.

Churchill still wanted access to the Azores and reiterated his earlier recommendation to seize the islands even if Spain made no move against Gibraltar:

> Must we always wait until a disaster has occurred? I do not think it follows that our occupation temporarily, and to forestall the enemy, of the Azores would necessarily precipitate German intervention in Spain and Portugal. It might have the reverse effect. The fact that we had an alternative fueling base to Gibraltar might tell against German insistence that we should be attacked or anyhow reduce German incentive to have us attacked. Moreover once we have an alternative base to Gibraltar, how much do we care if the Peninsula is overrun or not?[23]

JULY: BERLIN AND LISBON

Hitler's information on Portuguese attitudes and feelings towards Germany were based on Admiral Canaris's Intelligence Service reports and by the German embassies in Iberia.[24] Both the German minister to Portugal, Baron Oswald von Hoyningen-Hüne, and the ambassador to Spain, Eberhard von Stohrer, collected most of their information from influential fascist sympathizers who expressed private wishful thinking more often than actual facts. In 1940, while a Portuguese military mission was in London and talks were proceeding on mutual defense, von Stohrer was proud to report to Berlin that "Dr. Salazar was firmly determined to repel most sharply an encroachment on the part of England" and that "Salazar fully realized that the reorganization of Europe, with the more or less complete exclusion of England, was imminent."

Joachim von Ribbentrop, German foreign minister, completely believed the cheerful wishful-thinking-intelligence and sent a long telegram to von Stohrer detailing all the clever moves the German High Command had in store for Iberia with instructions to help speed up

Portugal's cooperation, considering that Spain's was a foregone conclusion: "If a military alliance between Portugal and Spain were concluded, which would entail the detachment of Portugal from England and possibly the final denunciation of the Anglo-Portuguese Alliance, this would definitely be in the German interest."[25]

8 AUGUST: MADRID

Franco presented his list of conditions to Ambassador von Stohrer, which Hitler would have to meet before Spain would join the Axis as a full-fledged military partner. Hitler considered the terms extortion, but Franco had been encouraged by Admiral Canaris to be hard-nosed with his demands because, he confided, Germany was planning Operation Barbarossa, and Spain had nothing to fear because invading Russia would tie down just about all the Nazi forces.[26] Operation Felix could not happen before Russia had first been taken care of. Franco had four conditions for his country to become an Axis partner:

1. Gibraltar and French Morocco had to be promised as spoils of war.
2. Germany must supply military assistance needed to modernize the Spanish army.
3. Germany must provide wheat and oil to bolster Spain's lagging economy.
4. Spain would not commit its own forces to the war until Nazi armies had landed on the English coast in a full-scale invasion, a condition that Hitler considered the most outrageous of all.[27]

12 AUGUST: THE AZORES'S "BLACK HOLE"

As if to dramatize the importance of establishing bases in the Azores, the Italian submarine *Malaspina* under Commander Leoni sunk the British merchant ship *Fame* in waters just east of São Miguel.[28] Three days later Commander Cohausz of the German U-boat UA[29] sank the merchant ship *Aspasia* near where the *Fame* had gone down. Two additional ships were torpedoed by Italian submarines in August around the Azores. The submarines were taking advantage of the lack of air protection in the circle around the Azores, named the "black hole" by mariners and far out of range of Allied air bases. The "black hole" was a zone in the Atlantic through which Allied shipping could pass only at great risk.

12 AUGUST: AZORES

Prime Minister Salazar was wary with the Axis submarine offensive around the Azores and was afraid that it might be signaling an attempt to take over the islands by force. Hoping to convince any would-be invader that the country was prepared to defend its territories, he sent off a large force that included all of Portugal's Gladiator II fighter planes to the Azores.[30] Fifteen Gladiator IIs and five Junkers Ju-52 bombers went to São Miguel and fifteen Gladiator IIs to Terceira. Except for São Miguel, hard-surfaced runways did not exist on the islands so aircraft used suitable meadows converted into grassy landing strips and re-named airfields, the horrific *aerovacas* ("air-cows") where the planes competed with grazing cattle. The landing strip on Terceira, Achada, was eleven hundred meters long by two to three hundred meters wide bordered on two sides with high peaks and with only a 270-degree access. Fighting deadly cross winds that could set their planes on a collision course against mountains or guarding against wandering cows that appeared out of nowhere helped the Portuguese pilots develop a fatalistic streak that fit well with the national temperament.

24 AUGUST: BERLIN

Großadmiral Erich Raeder, concerned that the Allied were planning to seize the Atlantic Islands as well as North Africa, proposed to occupy all the Atlantic islands, the Spanish Canaries and the Portuguese Azores and Cape Verdes as soon as possible.[31] Raeder was emphatic in pointing out the importance of the operation that should not be of "secondary importance" but "one of the main blows against Britain." Hitler approved the operation but did nothing to implement it.

On this same day Marshall Henri-Philippe Pétain, leader of Vichy France, committed his government to support Germany against the Allies. This meant, at a minimum, that German armed forces could use unoccupied France for transit to the Iberian Peninsula, ready to cross the Pyrenees whenever Franco gave his approval.[32]

Roosevelt took Pétain's commitment seriously and warned him against supporting any German operations against England. On 25 August the president began discussions with his Chiefs of Staff to occupy the French Caribbean islands as well as the Azores soon, before the Germans established themselves in either place. With German bases in the Caribbean and mid-Atlantic, the United States and all maritime commerce would be in great danger. Given the sorry state of her defense forces it would be impossible to drive the Germans out once they were established anywhere.

I SEPTEMBER: LONDON

Churchill was growing ever more impatient at the operational inactivity and what he considered a lack of imagination on the part of his War Cabinet.[33] None of his suggestions for action against the Atlantic Islands had been seriously considered so he tried another tack, moving into North Africa rather than Dakar, another operation that had been rejected. The War Cabinet was unhappy with this new suggestion and warned that not enough forces were available for a large-scale operation, but if they had to endorse some kind of offensive action they would prefer to skip Africa altogether and instead head to the Azores. Given the comparatively low amount of resources and manpower required, an operation in the Atlantic Ocean against Portugal rather than one on land against Germany was preferable. At this point Churchill was pleased to hear that his Cabinet would approve of any kind of offensive operation.

26 SEPTEMBER:
SOISSONS, OCCUPIED FRANCE AT
FÜHRER HEADQUARTERS

Admiral Raeder reported to Hitler at 1700 hours, just before Operation Sea Lion was called off, that an operation against the Azores was still necessary, but emphasized that the Navy should first be given the resources to carry out such an operation.[34] The time was long overdue to build up the fleet. Once a powerful *Kriegsmarine* was ready, seizing not only the Azores but also the strategic Cape Verde Islands would be feasible. The Cape Verdes would make a perfect base for attacks on north-south convoys sailing to or from England to southern Africa and India just as the Azores would serve against east-west convoys to the Americas. Once in control of the islands, Germany could completely dominate ship traffic in the central Atlantic and convince the United States to stop sacrificing her merchant marine on suicide supply missions to

England. Turning the Atlantic into a ships' graveyard would have the added benefit of convincing the United States to stay out of the war and perhaps even abandoning her ally England. But if the United States should enter the war, it was even more important for Germany to have a powerful fleet and Atlantic bases to meet the new threat. Without an adequate fleet Germany could do nothing if the United States attempted to extend the war into the Atlantic, as she has been threatening, occupying every island in the ocean—the Canaries, the Cape Verdes, the Azores, and Greenland—and even venture into Africa to seize Dakar. The Führer agreed that the islands might easily be taken by the Luftwaffe in surprise attacks, but they could be held only by troops and material transported by a strong navy, strong enough to challenge the British and U.S. fleets. There was no question that the Kriegsmarine had to be built up. If England was cut off from supplies it would only be a matter of time before she would have to admit defeat. It was clear that the fleet was not being built up as quickly as promised; the shipyards were not getting all the strategic materials needed; and that Hitler had given the Atlantic islands a low priority.

An operation against the Azores would need at least the tacit approval of Spain. Because Spain was a fellow fascist power and supposedly sympathetic to the Axis cause, plus the fact that the fortunes of war were running strongly in favor of Germany, Franco might approve an operation against Portuguese territory, especially one that would hasten an Axis victory. A surprise air- and submarine-borne attack on the Azores would be followed up by landing large numbers of troops and material transported by the Navy. Such a plan should be done soon, at least before the United States came into the war which the German General Staff was convinced would happen sooner rather than later.

Operation Felix now called for an aerial attack on Gibraltar by planes based in France beginning 10 January 1941 with artillery bombardment from German guns secretly emplaced in nearby Spanish bases.[35] This would also have the effect of driving away any British naval support. About three weeks later, German ground forces would arrive to spearhead a ground attack: two divisions coming through Spain, one armored and one motorized, would cross the Strait into French Morocco and seize control of the Atlantic littoral. Three more divisions would head to the Portuguese border where they would be in a position to invade the country and counterattack a possible British landing. Germany would then occupy Gibraltar and effectively close the Straits to British naval traffic. Because other countries besides Germany had strong interests in the operation, including Spain which had its own designs on Gibraltar, France whose North African colonies were being occupied, and Italy who relished the idea of taking over French North Africa after the war, Hitler resolved to effect a "reconciliation of conflicting French, Italian, and Spanish interests in Africa . . . only by a gigantic fraud."[36] An operation against the Azores was left to brew for a bit longer while the Navy was given more time to build up its resources.

27 SEPTEMBER: BERLIN

The Tripartite Pact, whose primary purpose was to keep the United States out of the war, was signed by Germany, Italy, and Japan. The Axis Powers felt that the United States would remain neutral if threatened by a two-front war in the Atlantic and the Pacific, which would immediately follow the start of a conflict with any one of the three.[37] Hitler assured Japanese Foreign Minister Matsuoka that Germany would declare war if a Japan–U.S. conflict started, regardless of who started it, even though the Pact only called for mutual assistance in the event of an attack by the United States.[38] Hitler assured Matsuoka that he did not seek a conflict with the United States but the possibility had already figured into his calculations. Germany was going to make sure that no Americans could ever land in Europe; the U-boats and Luftwaffe would guarantee it.

OCTOBER

In late 1940 signs pointed to an impending German drive to the southwest, in conjunction with Italy's effort to conquer Greece and crush British power in the eastern Mediterranean and with the collaboration, at least passively, of Vichy France. If successful, the way to the Near East and Africa would be open.[39]

When Japan, with its large and powerful fleet joined the Axis, the United States was forced to concentrate large naval forces in the Pacific. Under Rainbow 4, the United States defended the Alaska-Hawaii-Panama triangle, but if a threat appeared from the east, the United States would have to move quickly, seizing the Azores at the first indication of a German advance into Spain and Portugal and occupy airfields in northeast Brazil. If the worst happened and the British fleet was destroyed then within three months, the United States must occupy all Atlantic outpost positions from Bahia in Brazil to Greenland. To occupy the Azores, the Joint Chiefs would allow one reinforced army division plus a naval squadron including an aircraft carrier.[40] To implement Rainbow 4, the United States needed a minimum force of 1.4 million to defend the entire Western Hemisphere north of Brazil.

23 OCTOBER:
HENDAYE, FRENCH-SPANISH FRONTIER

Hitler had approved planning for Operation Felix on 24 August and now had to convince Franco to go along. All his previous face-to-face meetings with world leaders had been successful and the Führer felt sure that this meeting would be the same; after all, none of them withstood his power of intimidation. The two dictators met at Hendaye on the border between Spain and German-occupied France, but the occasion proved to be a first for the Führer. Franco was not at all like the weak-kneed leaders of Western Europe, but a hard bargainer, suspicious of Hitler's sincerity, not easily intimidated, and maintaining his country's rights over the demands of the Axis. He asked for heavy weapons to build up his armed forces and refused to back off from his demands for Gibraltar and large slices of French North Africa as the price for collaborating. If Germany agreed to these conditions Spain would contribute to Felix and allow more than token "volunteers" to serve with the Axis forces.

Franco's demands were diametrically at odds with Hitler's view of Spain as a vassal state, supplying Germany's war effort with raw materials and men, and with its economy managed from Berlin. Franco's expansionist desires and his implied condition to be treated as an equal were firmly rejected. Hitler later remarked on the meeting that he would rather visit the dentist than go through another round of negotiations with the Spaniard.[41] For his part Franco grew deeply suspicious and more determined than ever not to grant the Nazis bases on Spanish soil nor allow them passage through the country. Although the German High Command acknowledged these obvious facts, Hitler steadfastly refused to understand that Franco would not willingly swap British control over Gibraltar for German. He had his own sights set on the Big Rock and suspected that judging by recent history once in Spain German troops might just stay.

On 12 November the German General Staff completed plans for Operation Felix, which now called for the Wehrmacht to march through Spain with or without Franco's approval. However, in January 1941 the operation had to be postponed, but not canceled, because British successes against the Italian army were threatening to turn North Africa into an Allied enclave. If French North Africa fell to England there was a good possibility that France would switch sides, and, given a hostile Iberia, the OKM felt that the attack on Gibraltar was doomed before it started. The German expedition would be isolated, confronted by a strong Anglo-French army with unfriendly Spanish forces at their back. Operation Felix was put on a back burner as higher priority opportunities unfolded elsewhere—North Africa, Russia, the Balkans, and Italy.

The one operation that appealed most to Hitler and the OKW was an invasion of Russia, Operation Barbarossa.[42] The High Command was sure that the Russians—badly trained, poorly led, and weakly armed—could be disposed of in a maximum of three months. So confident were the Nazis of success that they actually started to cut back arms production before the invasion so that more resources and industry could be devoted to the production of consumer goods. Hitler liked the idea of a Russian invasion: after all, he was elected on a promise to save the world from an invidious communist menace.

To placate the admirals, Hitler and the General Staff agreed on 26 October to give a high priority to building up Germany's sea power, and that once Russia was taken care of an operation against the Azores would be next. The policy to enhance the fleet was finally put into effect when production in all war industries—except marine—was cut back. Submarine shipyards were granted more labor and raw materials and were to work around the clock. But not for long—as things turned out, ship production did not reach the promised level, raw materials needed for submarine construction remained in short supply, and a sufficiently large labor force for the shipyards never materialized. To which can be added, the *Amerika* bomber project was proving a dismal failure. In what was already a familiar litany, despite promises, the fleet was again short-changed as preparations for an invasion of Russia became the new highest priority. Throughout the war Hitler provided lip service to the admirals, but his heart was always set on land battles rather than sinking ships.

In meetings with the OKW and the OKM, Hitler kept repeating that he had not forgotten the Atlantic islands and was still interested in plans to occupy the Azores "with an eye to the future war with America." He fully expected such a war would break out soon.

4 NOVEMBER:
HITLER MEETING WITH OKW
AND OKM IN BERLIN

Hitler raised the subject of an operation against Gibraltar. Despite the lack of results at the Hendaye meeting, he was sure that Franco, if pressed, would enter the war on Germany's side, assuring free passage across Iberia. The three armored infantry divisions were now prepared and waiting expectantly on the other side of the Pyrenees for the green light to cross into Iberia. However, the OKW had lost his enthusiasm for the operation and raised three serious objections: first, was Franco really ready to take his country to war?; second, even as a passive ally would Spain allow fully armed German troops to cross her territory for any reason?; and third, which was the most obvious although not discussed, Franco might have his own ideas on who should control Gibraltar. Assuming the British were driven out, and it was not clear that this operation could force their departure, Franco's first choice for a new landlord would be Spain, certainly not Germany.

Hitler asked if Gibraltar was too tough a nut to crack, then what about the Cape Verde Islands? They were a Portuguese colony, sitting out in the Atlantic just 385 miles (620 kilometers) west of Dakar off the coast of Senegal, and would provide an excellent base for U-boat operations in the South Atlantic. Merchant marine traffic between England and the African colonies and India was heavy in this part of the Atlantic. The OKM was unenthusiastic about that operation and expressed his strong reservations. First, the operation would depend on cooperation from the French in nearby West Africa—but they could not be counted on to give strong support. Dakar was a hotbed for the Free French forces so if anything, they would try to sabotage the operation. A large commitment was required from the German Navy, which still did not have the resources to spare given its other assigned duties: patrolling the Norwegian coast awaiting a possible British invasion and pursuing the war against Allied convoys. Hitler had always assumed, fed by false intelligence, that the British planned an operation to free Norway and so ordered the Navy to maintain a strong defensive force there, even at the cost of depleting units needed for other operations. The order was an albatross hung around the neck of the Kriegsmarine, and fulfilling it meant that it was permanently undermanned where ships were most needed.

The OKM was not keen about launching an operation against any Portuguese territory at that time. The consequences might be disastrous for Germany: "it would be better to desist from occupying the Cape Verdes and from taking immediate military steps against Portugal . . . Any German military action against Portugal would afford the British the possibility of occupying the Portuguese colonies of Madeira, the Cape Verdes and the Azores." Given the superiority of their fleet, there was little question that the British would be quick to land in force on any of the islands under the pretext of coming to the aid of their ancient ally. The Navy's immediate priority was still to build up its own resources rather than a commitment to spread the war to Iberia and the Atlantic islands.[43]

14 NOVEMBER: BERLIN

Hitler had hinted in previous meetings and finally revealed to the OKM the important role he had in mind for the Azores islands. The tactical reason for a base in the Atlantic: "the Azores provided the only possibility for carrying out aerial attacks from a land base against the United States" which would force it to "build up its nonexistent antiaircraft defense instead of helping England in this matter" and incidentally "cut down on the amount of war materials being shipped to England."[44]

The Führer's plan was simple: "to attack America in case it entered the war, with a modern Messerschmidt bomber (still on the drawing boards), a model capable of a 12,600 km operational range." Hitler ordered "immediate inquiry" into the harbor facilities of the Azores to select a site where airplane and heavy machinery parts could be shipped. Officers of the Navy and Luftwaffe are to be sent to the Azores, presumably covertly, to carry out this study. Admiral Raeder described the venture as a "very risky operation, but which can succeed with luck."[45]

The *Amerika* bomber, as well as the other VLR German bombers built during the war, was a saga of disaster. Not one of the several VLR class aircraft with the range capable of attacking the United States and returning proved operationally successful. The *Amerika*, a four-engine

Messerschmidt Me-264 with a range of nine thousand miles, could carry a four-thousand-pound bomb load but the first one built was only ready in December 1942, a year after Pearl Harbor, and as it turned out was the only one ever finished.

In 1940–41, Germany's VLR bombers included a few models of the Focke-Wulf 200C, the so-called Lufthansa four-engine "Condor" with a range of twenty-five hundred miles. Another was the four-engine Heinkel He-177 with a range of thirty-four hundred miles and a payload of 13,200 pounds but did not offer better prospects for carrying out VLR bombing missions. Over a period of three years, 1,446 were built, but 50 were lost in initial test flights, and by January 1944 only 35 were ready for an aerial assault on London.

Thanks to meddling by senior *Reichswehr* (German Army) generals, aircraft designers faced an almost insurmountable problem. The ground generals remembered the fantastic success of the Stuka dive-bombers that, by creating havoc on cities and on the ill-prepared and demoralized Polish and French troops, paved the way to easy German victories. But a year later, when the British had built up their own air force based on the newly designed Spitfire Marine fighter, the cumbersome, slow-flying German dive-bombers were shot out of the skies. Generals Hans Jeschonnek and Ernst Udet demanded that all German bombers, even ones designed for strategic long-range operations, must be capable of releasing their bomb loads on a steep dive. Although it is hard to imagine any situation where a large four-engine bomber would be asked to carry out a dive-bombing attack, many years were wasted attempting to design a VLR bomber fuselage sufficiently strong enough to withstand the stress of a high dive.[46]

I DECEMBER: LONDON

The prime minister, worried about Hitler's next move, ordered the War Cabinet to make plans to launch operations Brisk and Shrapnel against the Azores and Cape Verdes and "hot foot upon it."[47] Both should be ready to go at forty-eight-hours notice from 3 or 4 December. Operation Counterpoise, seizure of Cueta, the North African port opposite Gibraltar, should be ready early that week. "I take it as settled" that "Workshop," the operation against Pantellaria, "moves forward leaving here the 18th." He was very pleased that a base was established at Suda Bay in Crete, one that "made an enormous change in the Eastern Mediterranean."[48]

Churchill felt that the war could be lost if the Germans were allowed to control the Atlantic. If Hitler took over Iberia and extended German bases to the Portuguese islands, convoys would be open to attack from both U-boats and the Luftwaffe anywhere in the Atlantic. As if to dramatize the new danger, an England-bound convoy was attacked by French-based German VLR bombers off the Azores resulting in the loss of five ships.[49]

7 DECEMBER:
WINSTON CHURCHILL LETTER TO
FRANKLIN ROOSEVELT

In a fifteen-page letter, Churchill expressed his fears on the direction the war was taking. He was constantly worried about the enormous losses merchant fleets were suffering, that shipping was being sunk at a greater rate than at any other time in either world war. He saw no possibility of victory over the Axis Powers unless the Battle of the Atlantic was won first:

> The decision for 1941 lies upon the seas; unless we can establish our ability to feed this island, to import munitions of all kinds which we need, unless we can move our armies to the various theaters where Hitler and his confederate Mussolini must be met, and maintain them there and do all this with the assurance of being able to carry it on till the spirit of the continental dictators is broken, we may fall by the way and the time needed by the United States to complete her defensive preparations may not be forthcoming.[50] It is therefore in shipping and in the power to transport across the oceans, particularly the Atlantic Ocean, that in 1941 the crunch of the whole war will be found.[51]

In order to win over the large Irish-American population to the Allied cause, Churchill promised to promote a future union of Northern Ireland and Ireland. He asked the United States to pressure the government of Ireland to show its solidarity with the democracies of the English-speaking world and give up its role as an avowed neutral. For all practical purposes remaining neutral was equivalent to being pro-Nazi. Antisubmarine bases in Ireland would go a long way toward making the eastern Atlantic safer for North American convoys.

The prime minister made a strong appeal for a method whereby

England could receive supplies from the United States without paying cash. This request provided the kernel for Lend-Lease Act the following year: the United States would provide aid, including some aged destroyers, in return for leases of bases on British possessions and dominions.

27 DECEMBER: BERLIN

Admiral Raeder was not happy with Operation Barbarossa and was skeptical about its chances for quick success, especially starting it before England was defeated. But Hitler was determined to attack Russia, all the more so after an especially frustrating meeting with Foreign Secretary Molotov in November. He drew a long north-south border along the Ural Mountains on the large globe in his Berchtesgaden retreat, which would be the eastern limit of German occupation and enough to bring the communists to their knees.

For the Kriegsmarine there were far more important operations to worry about than Russia. Raeder complained that the Italians had proven to be a big disappointment not only on land, but also in the Mediterranean where promised control by the combined Axis fleets never materialized. The best way to establish a secure position in the Mediterranean would be by controlling Gibraltar. The admiral enumerated the many benefits of taking over Gibraltar including: protect Italy; safeguard the western Mediterranean; secure supply lines from North Africa to Spain, France, and Germany; eliminate an important link in the British convoy system; close the sea route to Malta and Alexandria; and restrict the freedom of the British Mediterranean fleet. The strategic reasons for Operation Felix now were more necessary than ever.

Hitler agreed with the arguments to take over Gibraltar but said that Franco was proving inflexible. England promised food to Spain and he refused to compromise because food was in short supply over the entire European continent, and Germany was in no position to hand any over to Spain. Besides Spain did not need it as badly as the Fatherland. Hitler was sure that the British promise was a fraud and that he would try again to influence Franco but through the foreign minister via the Spanish ambassador to Berlin, having no desire to meet anytime soon with the Spanish dictator.

Raeder repeated his argument that England could be brought to her knees purely by the U-boat, that Operation Sea Lion never was necessary. Attacks on convoys could disrupt transatlantic traffic and prevent supplies from America from ever reaching England. First, however, submarine construction would have to be stepped up, for despite repeated promises the shipyards were turning out only twelve to eighteen ships monthly. Why could not production be increased to at least the level achieved in World War I when twenty to thirty submarines were produced each month?

Hitler, whose thoughts were only on the new Eastern Front, promised to try to improve the supply of materials to the shipyards but the highest priority was to the Army, which must be made sufficiently strong "to eliminate at all costs the last enemy remaining on the continent." After that would be the Luftwaffe and the Navy.[52]

29 DECEMBER: PRESIDENT ROOSEVELT'S FIRESIDE CHAT

As his last Fireside Chat of the year to the American people, Roosevelt underscored the threat posed by the Axis in the oceans east and west and that the country's very survival hung in the balance. Isolation from the rest of the world was no longer a viable option. He compared this crisis to the economic one he faced eight years earlier, when banks were failing and unemployment was universal:

> I had before my eyes the picture of all those Americans with whom I was talking. I saw the workmen in the mills, the mines, the factories; the girl behind the counter; the small shopkeeper; the farmer doing his spring plowing; the widows and the old men wondering about their life's savings . . . America met the issue of 1933 with courage and realism. We face this new crisis—the new threat to the security of our Nation—with the same courage and realism. Never before since Jamestown and Plymouth Rock has our American civilization been in such danger as now.[53]

He reminded the nation that the axis powers had signed an agreement in Berlin on 27 September warning the United States not to interfere in the expansionist programs of any of the three, or they would unite in an ultimate action against the country. Hitler laid down the gauntlet earlier in the month: "There are two worlds that stand opposed to each other . . . With this world we cannot ever reconcile ourselves . . . I can beat any other power in the world."

Roosevelt, acknowledging the United States's debt to England in this crisis, asked:

> Does anyone seriously believe that we need to fear attack while a free Britain remains our most powerful naval neighbor in the Atlantic? Does anyone seriously believe, on the other hand that we could rest easy if the Axis powers were our neighbor there? ... The width of these oceans is not what it was in the days of clipper ships. At one point between Africa and Brazil the distance is less than from Washington to Denver—five hours for the latest type of bomber. And at the north of the Pacific Ocean, America and Asia almost touch each other. Even today we have planes which could fly from the British Isles to New England and back without refueling. And the range of the modern bomber is ever being increased.[54]

Thus, 1940 was a year with lots of activity and scheming but nothing happening to Portugal or its Atlantic islands. England, Germany, and the United States staked out arguments for seizing the Azores but took no action. Roosevelt also made it plain that the United States had a definite interest in the outcome of the war and that it was essential to make certain that England triumphed over the Axis. He justified sending England all the material the United States could muster to support that goal, and acting under the powers granted by the Monroe Doctrine, the United States would protect the entire Western Hemisphere. It was also clear that he was going to shove the boundaries of the hemisphere eastward to cover the Atlantic islands considered critical for the defense of the country. The development of VLR aircraft had in fact shrunk the world's dimensions and hemispheric boundaries were no longer an academic exercise.

The coming year 1941 held promise for U.S. action in the Atlantic, whether or not the country remained neutral. Roosevelt was playing geographic roulette with rules allegedly set by the Monroe Doctrine: Greenland, Iceland, and the Azores were about to join the Western Hemisphere.

THREE

THE VIEW FROM WASHINGTON, JANUARY–MAY 1941

Somewhat less speculative (the *Marschplan* [plan of advance] called for an invasion of America by 100,000 men based out of Puerto Rico or Provincetown, Massachusetts), the commander in chief U-boats was aware, were current plans for a Luftwaffe bomber offensive against American coastal cities. The plans had been under serious consideration by Hitler since at least 22 May 1941 when Naval Staff minutes of a Hitler conference recorded in italics: "Führer seeks the occupation of [the Azores] in order to deploy long-range bombers against the United States."

MICHAEL GANNON, *Operation Drumbeat*

With the war raging in Europe and Asia, the United States had to play a difficult diplomatic game towards the belligerent powers. Until the attack on Pearl Harbor the United States was theoretically neutral and a large block of public opinion in the country was all for staying that way. The America First movement, supported by such distinguished persons as Charles Lindbergh (an unabashed admirer of Hitler) and Henry Ford (an avowed anti-Semite), was especially powerful. In many parts of the Midwest isolationist congressmen had been elected thanks to their support of the movement. Despite pervasive isolationist sentiment, President Roosevelt decided the Axis was a threat to the entire free world and he felt it our duty to support England, which was fighting not only a war of survival but also was our proxy against the Nazis. This he did in every way possible short of declaring war, with the support of the Congress when he could get it or by presidential decree when he could not. Cordell Hull, Roosevelt's secretary of state, stated the United States's policy towards the belligerents:

> As the year of war, 1941, dawned, we intensified our diplomatic and material assistance to the Allies throughout the world. Wherever it was possible, whether in Vichy France, Latin America, the Balkans, Africa, the Atlantic islands, or the Far East, to bolster the Allies either by exerting our influence or pressure or by furnishing concrete aid, we were quick and wholehearted in making the necessary moves.
>
> Our position toward the conflict was clear. We were convinced that an Allied victory was possible and we were determined to do everything we could to bring it about, short of actually sending an expeditionary force. . . . We were equally convinced than an Axis victory would present a mortal danger to the United States. Those nations that supported the Allies could count on our friendship, those that supported the Axis on our opposition. We were acting no longer under the precepts of neutrality, but under those of self-defense.[1]

In response to Churchill's desperate appeal for material assistance, Roosevelt acted on his own moving the country closer to a state of war with Germany. On 2 September 1940 he signed an agreement swapping fifty destroyers with England in return for ninety-nine-year leases on naval bases stretching from Newfoundland to British Guiana. The German naval staff declared this to be "an openly hostile act by the United States against Germany."[2] The exchange of destroyers—needed for England's survival—for naval bases for which an alleged neutral had no clear use foreshadowed "imminent close cooperation between the USA and Great Britain." From that point, the United States's support of the British cause shifted from covert to open. In 1941 the United States's abandoned its official policy of "nonbelligerency" for undeclared war against Germany.

The Germans were correct: this would be the first of many "openly hostile acts." In February 1941 the U.S. and British chiefs of staff held a joint secret meeting to plan an American-British Grand Strategy (ABC) for either of two eventualities: U.S. nonbelligerent support or joining England as a fighting ally.[3] The A-B staff agreed that Germany was the predominant member of the Axis powers so consequently the Atlantic and Europe were to be the decisive theater of conflict.

Early in 1941 Roosevelt convinced Congress to pass the Lend-Lease Act, which provided for the transfer of war supplies, including food, machinery, and services to nations whose defense was considered vital to the defense of the United States. Congress gave the president power to sell, transfer, lend, or lease such war materials. The president was to set the terms for aid; repayment was to be "in kind or property, or any other direct or indirect benefit which the President deems satisfactory."[4] Harry L. Hopkins was appointed in March to administer the act.

8 January: Lisbon

London decided that the time was ripe to strengthen ties with Portugal. The first step was to replace the ineffective Ambassador Sir Walford Selby with Sir Ronald Coleman, until then British ambassador to France, and just the man to energize the moribund "pleasant but ineffective Embassy of tradition."[5] He took over a new office building to find enough places for the vastly expanded staff of one hundred while at the same time sent many of Selby's cronies back to London. Coleman was the perfect man to insure that Allied—or at least British—interests would be well represented to the Portuguese government. Meanwhile, the United States did not even have an embassy but a legation with much lower diplomatic status, headed not by a prestigious ambassador but a minister, with rank among the lowest of the entire foreign diplomatic corps in Lisbon. Measured by effectiveness, the U.S. minister—Burt Fish—was on a par with Selby.

20 January: Berlin

Hitler's reaction to Roosevelt's belligerent actions was unexpected; he was overjoyed and assured Mussolini that the United States posed no great danger to the Axis even if she entered the war.[6] Two weeks later, on 3 February, he admitted to the Japanese Ambassador Kurusu that Germany and the United States were destined to remain enemies for at least one or two centuries.

February–March: Lisbon and London

Salazar was confident that with the British control of the seas the Germans could not mount an invasion of any of the Portugal's Atlantic islands. Besides, because Admiral Canaris was passing secret high-level German plans and decisions to Franco, who was almost certainly leaking them to Salazar, the German admirals' veto of an Azores invasion must have been known in Lisbon.[7]

In February Salazar appointed Brigadier Godinho to organize and command the defenses of the Azores.[8] Godinho, who saw combat as an infantry captain in Flanders in World War I, had seen enough to worry that the Germans were considering an invasion; otherwise how to explain the fact that U-boats were operating openly around the Azores, coming close enough to be seen from land? A supply submarine, a *milchkuhen* ("milk-cow"), spent much of the time stationed just west of Faial where it might have been picking up provisions from an *Ettapendienst* agent working in Horta. (The *Ettapendienst* was a secret world-wide supply service set up to maintain the U-boat fleet.)[9] Godinho was prepared to resist an invasion but he knew his forces would be overwhelmed if the Germans came with enough air- and sea-borne strength.

With German armies roaming up and down the European continent, and Operation Felix, which called for an invasion of Iberia and a takeover of the Atlantic islands, still on a back burner, Salazar decided to send a delegation to London to discuss mutual defense and to request heavy weapons and aircraft to modernize his own armed forces.[10] They could not successfully defend the country against a determined German invasion, but making it appear that the cost of victory would be high might be all that was needed. Hitler, after all, was marshalling his forces for more important operations—to attack Russia and to beef up the collapsing Italians in North Africa—so he would avoid any new, potentially costly operation. Peace in Portugal might be preserved simply by appearances—showing the will to resist and having armed forces to back it up.

The arrival of a Portuguese military mission to London could not have come at a worse time, with memories still fresh of the evacuation of the entire British army from the European continent less than a year earlier. This was not a good time to be talking about military cooperation but, given the long history of friendship and the 1373 treaty of alliance, the mission could not be dismissed out of hand. Considering the Germans had taken over most of Western Europe despite the hapless efforts of England, options to defend Portugal were limited and would probably be as ineffective as they had been elsewhere.

When Prime Minister Salazar's uninvited high-level military delegation arrived in London in early March, the British had no other choice than to quickly organize a staff team to meet with them and roll out the welcome mat. The Portuguese mission was led by Staff Colonel J. F. de Barros Rodrigues and included Lieutenant Colonel Craveiro Lopes, later commander-in-chief of the Army and president of Portugal. Lieutenant Colonel G. A. Fenton was head of the British delegation that included Wing Commander Roland Vintras (later air commodore and director of RAF Intelligence Operations.)

Guidelines from the highest level were passed down to the British delegation: the meetings should not produce any meaningful results, the only goals were to "socialize and procrastinate" at least until the War Cabinet figured out exactly what the Portuguese policy should be. The delegation was ordered to be circumspect. It could not afford to alienate their ancient allies nor could it promise any dispersion of England's meager military resources to rearm them. For their part, the Portuguese, cognizant of England's desperate situation, had arrived with low expectations. Nobody on either side at the meetings was prepared to propose any concrete steps for the defense of anything. Colonel Fenton had no ready answer for the inevitable question from Colonel Rodrigues: did England want Portugal to declare war against Germany or not? In the best British waffling tradition, Colonel Fenton answered "Yes and no," which confused everybody and demonstrated that the true guidelines for the meetings were to make no commitments or at least to keep them as ambiguous as possible. The official Portuguese translator was stumped and asked Commander Vintras, "What does that mean?" Vintras could not immediately come up with a satisfactory translation—although he promised he would work on it.

The meetings did have one important result: the Portuguese agreed to make a complete topographic and engineering survey of the Azores to help the RAF plan an air base. Salazar later approved the survey but his delegation had little success in obtaining anything but vague promises for armaments from the British. England's priority was to rearm itself, so in lieu of arms and aircraft the suggestion was made that if the Germans attacked Portugal, the government should immediately move to the Azores courtesy of the British who would provide a fleet to transport everyone from Lisbon. A substantial part of the Portuguese army could go along with the government or be sent ahead and only token resistance put up against the invasion. Salazar accepted this advice and immediately began to reinforce the island garrisons.

Major Humberto Delgado was placed in charge of the operation to survey the Azores and set out to work immediately. The full agreement appeared harmless; it was hoped that it did not appear threatening enough to provoke a German invasion of Portugal because no British officer was to go to the islands and the Portuguese would be in complete charge of the operation, presumably building a civilian air base.

Major Delgado went about his assignment diligently making frequent trips to the Azores and occasional visits to London bringing along the maps and engineering data needed to plan the air base. Over the many months that the collaboration went on, the Germans never got wind of it, nor did they suspect the real reason for Delgado's many trips. His cover was chaperoning groups of junior Portuguese Air Force officers to England for flight training. On one of the trips, a suspicious incident occurred at the Portuguese Embassy, alerting Delgado to the possibility that the Germans were trying to learn if he was up to something more serious than keeping second lieutenants out of trouble in London.

While working in his office one day at the Portuguese embassy in London, Delgado placed an envelope in his left-hand pocket containing documents relating to the Azores operations, including the plans for a military airfield. In his right-hand pocket he had another envelope containing thirty-six one-hundred-escudo notes. Seeing an important-looking document sticking out of Delgado's right pocket and not realizing that two envelopes were involved, someone stole the envelope. Shortly after this incident a typist in the Embassy was arrested as a German spy and condemned to death, a sentence later commuted to life imprisonment. If it was the typist who lifted the envelope, he got an unexpected windfall but missed a hot intelligence scoop that might have earned him a promotion from Berlin. The plans for a British air base in the Azores were still secure and the Germans continued to accept the idea that Delgado was only chaperoning young pilots.

Major Delgado did an excellent job reconnoitering the Azores Archipelago, preparing maps so that the best sites for airfields could be chosen and reporting all this both to his government and to the British. His reports were referred to as "Delgado's Blue Reports," numbered sequentially, and it was number two that the German spy missed when he rifled Delgado's right pocket. Armed with the reports, Terceira was selected for the airfield. Delgado immediately set out to supervise construction of a graded, packed-dirt airstrip with hired local laborers and engineers and with occasional covert visits from RAF officers checking on its progress. The modus operandi was simple: armed with detailed maps of Terceira, Delgado would discuss details of the construction with RAF officers in London, outlining each step on the maps: land acquisition, building construction, and grading the landing strip. With the discussion finished, Delgado would return to Lisbon, hop on a small plane, and fly to the Azores to supervise the next steps. As the airfield progressed he briefed his superior generals in Lisbon, and then returned to London to chaperone another bunch of officers. The reasons for the frequent triangular trips—London–Lisbon–Terceira—were never explained to his curious colleagues or to anyone in England not privy to the operation. Best of all, the Germans never had any idea what was going on until the dirt strip changed into an RAF air base a year and a half later.

5 March: U.S. Consulate, Ponta Delgada

The State Department had two listening posts in the Azores: consulates in the capital of the archipelago, Ponta Delgada on São Miguel, and at Horta on Faial, a transatlantic cable station and the largest and best port of all the islands. On 5 March, Leonard G. Dawson, U.S. consul at Ponta Delgada, sent Secretary Hull an alarming eight-page dispatch on what he perceived as a deteriorating state of affairs.[11] Dawson's dispatch turned out to be a wake-up call to Washington:

1. Military Officers in the Government of the Azores—almost the entire government of the Azores has been militarized. . . .
2. Azoreans Have Little Part in the Government—the officers almost all came in recent months from mainland Portugal. . . .
3. Fears of a German Seizure of the Azores—residents sympathetic to the Allies have expressed alarm over the possibility of a German landing in the islands with aid expected from German residents and Nazi sympathizers. . . . A German task force aided or not opposed by the army could seize all the islands with relative ease. Many people were fearful that the reported presence of German surface raiders in the nearby waters was an indication that German forces would attempt to land within the next few weeks or months. . . .

Two other bits of evidence that made the consul feel that a German landing was imminent were first, that the German residents were compiling lists of British sympathizers, and second the oft-repeated allegation that the British were preparing an invasion of the islands, both acts similar to those which preceded invasions of other neutral countries.

4. Possibilities of a German Landing—many people expressed surprise that no U.S. naval units were cruising in the waters of the Azores to discourage German raiders from landing. That a U.S. naval force "would be welcomed by the unofficial population there is little doubt."[12]

5. Protection against Landings from the Sea—Ponta Delgada has a battery completed in August 1940, the only such defense against an attack from the sea.

6. Troops in the Azores—about twelve hundred troops are garrisoned at Ponta Delgada, and an additional thirteen hundred were expected to arrive shortly from the continent. Other garrisons were already in place on Terceira and Faial.

7. Pro-German Elements of the Population—the consul heard from a "well informed source" that a large proportion of the Portuguese Legion and the youth organization, the *Mocidade Portuguesa*, as well as many army officers were Nazi sympathizers. However, the overwhelming majority of the population was friendly towards the Allies, especially the middle classes, farmers and workers but they have little influence and no power under the present political system.

8. Pro-U.S. Elements of the Population—many people could be counted on for support. So many have lived in the United States, or receive financial aid from there and have friends or relatives in the United States, that their sympathies lie with our country. In fact, one hears the hope that a U.S. naval base would be established in Ponta Delgada, as was done in the last war, not only to prevent a German landing but also to bring a return of the prosperity they knew at that time.

9. Current Rumors—one rumor based on wishful thinking was that a fleet of fourteen U.S. naval vessels was on its way to establish a naval base at Ponta Delgada. Others concerned (1) anti-British propaganda handed down from Lisbon and (2) the sentiments of Portuguese soldiers: A corporal told a local resident that the army officers met to determine what measures

could be taken in the event of an invasion. Although the officers resolved that an attempt by America "would be resisted
with all the force available," the corporal added that if the
Americans came, he and a number of his fellow soldiers
would take to the hills, leaving only the officers to do the
fighting. Before the military took over the governance of the
islands, the local Civil Governor asked the central government to recruit troops stationed in the Azores locally, to
help relieve unemployment. The request was denied, "on the
ground that the people here are of questionable loyalty, the
statement being made that they would constitute a large
American fifth column."[13]

Dawson's memorandum electrified official Washington. No longer was
this an academic exercise; there was a real danger that the Germans
might invade the Azores helped by a fifth column and a sympathetic
army. Clearly the time for discussion was over; action had to be taken
sooner rather than later to prevent this from happening. The talks held
by the Combined Chiefs of Staff were now elevated from the status of
a war game—"let's assume"—to the more serious one of operations
planning.

March: Washington, D.C.

Following passage of the Lend-Lease Act on 11 March, U.S. actions
grew bolder and even more overt leaving no question in the minds of
the German General Staff that the United States was committed to the
defense of England:[14]

> 24 March: England permitted to repair her ships in U.S. ports.

> 27 March: ABC-1 Staff Agreement that priorities be given to the
> Atlantic rather than the Pacific if America entered the
> war.[15] The Azores and other Atlantic islands were to
> remain the basic responsibility of England although
> America could assist in the occupation of both the
> Azores and Cape Verdes.

> 30 March: All German, Italian, and Danish shipping in U.S.
> harbors was put under "protective custody."

Shortly after Washington suggested it to the American republics, Mexico, Costa Rica, Venezuela, Peru, and Ecuador also seized Axis ships in their ports and every Latin American country backed the action except Argentina. As a result Germany lost a total of twelve ships totaling sixty thousand tons all interned for the duration of the war.

April: The United States Goes to Greenland

On 10 April the State Department announced the signing of an agreement by the secretary of state and the Danish minister to Washington, Henrik de Kauffmann.[16] The United States recognized Ambassador de Kauffmann as the legitimate representative of the Danish government even though the German-controlled Danish government did not, so the agreement was not acceptable to Copenhagen, not that that was any concern in Washington:

> The agreement recognizes that as a result of the present European war there is danger that Greenland may be converted into a point of aggression against nations of the American Continent, and accepts the responsibility on behalf of the United States of assisting Greenland in the maintenance of its present status.
> The agreement, after explicitly recognizing Danish sovereignty over Greenland, proceeds to grant to the United States the right to locate and construct airplane landing fields and facilities for the defense of Greenland and for the defense of the American Continent . . . The circumstances leading up to the agreement are as follows. On April 9, 1940 the German Army invaded and occupied Denmark, and that occupation continues. . . . This invasion at once raised questions as to the status of Greenland, which has been recognized as being within the area of the Monroe Doctrine. The Government of the United States announces its policy of maintenance of the status quo in the Western Hemisphere.
> On May 3, 1940 the Greenland Councils, meeting at Godhavn, adopted a resolution in the name of the people of Greenland reaffirming their allegiance to King Christian X of Denmark, and expressed their hope that so long as Greenland remained cut off from the mother country, the Government of

the United States would . . . assure the needs of the population of Greenland.[17]

The announcement described the menacing actions taken by the Germans clearly foreboding an invasion. In the summer of 1940 three ships sailing from occupied Norway arrived off the coast of Greenland ostensibly for commercial or scientific purposes but were actually collecting meteorological information. These parties were eventually cleared out but in the late fall of the year, German reconnaissance aircraft appeared over East Greenland. Then on 27 March a German bomber flew over the eastern coast followed the next day by another warplane, making it clear that they were reconnoitering in preparation for a military operation. "Under these circumstance it appeared that further steps for the defense of Greenland were necessary to bring Greenland within the system of hemispheric defense envisaged by the Act of Habana" signed on 25 July 1940 and which declared that "any attempt on the part of a non-American state against the integrity . . . or independence of an American state should be considered an act of aggression, and that they would cooperate in defense against any such aggression."[18]

Ambassador de Kauffmann agreed to just about everything the United States asked for: building air bases in Greenland under the authority of the Monroe Doctrine and the 1940 Act of Havana, and later gave his approval for a repeat in Iceland.[19] On 5 April Roosevelt authorized five million dollars for the construction of the air bases, just one day before the German invasion of Yugoslavia.

8–9 April: Azores Gap

In late March Admiral Dönitz dispatched his son-in-law, Günter Hessler, Germany's greatest U-boat commander of the war, to patrol in the Azores Gap where in two days he sank four ships.[20] The carnage was continued by other German and Italian U-boat skippers so by the end of the year submarines had sunk twenty-four more Allied ships within the Azores Gap.

April–May: Washington, D.C.

On 10 April U.S. naval patrols in the Atlantic were ordered to guard the sea lanes west of the 26 degrees west meridian but to extend their protected zone eastward to include the east coast of Greenland and all of the Azores.[21]

Reaction came quickly from the Danish-German government. On 14 April, it ordered the immediate recall of their minister in Washington. Secretary of State Cordell Hull dismissed the order, "We consider this to be the true representation of Denmark"[22] and invited de Kauffmann to stay on. The Danes, as reported by U.S. representatives in Copenhagen, were elated, although diplomatic protests continued to arrive in Washington from the Quisling Danish Foreign Office.

By the spring of 1941, Washington knew of Hitler's plans for an operation against the Azores, but because Germany was occupied with campaigns in eastern and southern Europe as well as North Africa, invasion was not considered imminent. The United States made it clear that it would prevent any occupation of the Azores under the pretext of safeguarding the Western Hemisphere, while the Portuguese, for their part, watched nervously as each of the big powers hatched schemes "to protect" their islands. Portugal was still determined to remain neutral and had no desire for anyone to protect them from an invasion by somebody else. President Salazar was afraid that if the United States declared the Cape Verdes and the Azores part of the Western Hemisphere they would be occupied for their protection as were Greenland and Iceland. If the United States occupied the Azores, Germany might use that as a pretext to invade the homeland to protect it from a similar fate. Why couldn't everyone just stop worrying about protecting Portugal and get on with their own private war?

In order to quell Salazar's fears that the United States had plans to bring the war to the Atlantic Islands, Cordell Hull assured him that such rumors were false that the United States did not intend to occupy the Azores to keep them from falling into German hands:

> I assured the Portuguese Minister on April 18, 1941, that the reports were without foundation. Nevertheless, if Germany made a move to occupy the Azores, we were prepared to occupy them and the President gave instructions to this effect to Admiral Stark, Chief of Naval Operations on May 22, 1941. . . . We were in agreement with Britain that we would occupy the

Azores if Hitler tried to seize them. Vargas[23] was approached to see if Brazil would send a token force since that would have a beneficial effect on Portuguese public opinion.[24]

11 April: Washington, D.C.

Eight months before the United States's actual entry into the war, Roosevelt decided to redefine the boundary of the earth's hemispheres from a geographic or historical viewpoint to a political one ending up at some point east of the Mid-Atlantic Ridge. The geologically accepted divide between the Eastern and Western Hemispheres was the Mid-Atlantic Ridge discovered during the 1872–76 voyage of the HMS *Challenger*, the first scientific oceanography expedition. The ridge runs through both Iceland and the Azores Archipelago, so geologically, at any rate, Roosevelt had some sort of argument, but unfortunately the ridge was not as well defined in 1941 as it is today. However, geography was against him—because of ties to their mother countries and being closer to Europe, they were considered part of the Eastern Hemisphere.

Roosevelt cabled Churchill, code-named "the Former Naval Person" in his dispatches, advising him that for political reasons the United States was taking these actions unilaterally and not after diplomatic negotiations. The United States's so-called security zone was to be extended to a line covering all North Atlantic waters west of about 25 degrees west longitude. Aircraft and naval vessels working from Greenland, Newfoundland, Nova Scotia, the United States, Bermuda, and the West Indies—with a possible extension later to Brazil—would be utilized to patrol the new security zone. British intelligence was to notify the United States of the movement of any convoys so that patrol units could seek out any planes or ships of "aggressor nations . . . when located in our patrol area, but thought it advisable to make no public announcement about this new policy, either from the American or the British sides. . . . I may decide to issue necessary naval operations orders and let time bring out the existence of the new patrol area." He suggested that convoys transit as much as possible in the far northern Atlantic where some protection was afforded by land based aircraft stationed along the ocean rim from Newfoundland to Greenland and Iceland later in the year.[25]

When Roosevelt extended Atlantic patrols to 25 degrees west longitude he effectively placed Greenland and the Azores in the Western

Hemisphere and into that half of the world President Monroe committed the United States to defend. Roosevelt realized that he had stretched the hemispheric boundaries beyond Monroe's original conception but justified his action on 27 May 1941 when he asserted the need to defend the "island outposts of the New World," insisting that the Azores were vital to the "ultimate safety of the continental United States."[26]

President James Monroe enunciated his Doctrine, a cornerstone of U.S. foreign policy, in his annual message to Congress on 2 December 1823. Declaring the Old and New Worlds had different systems and must remain distinct spheres, Monroe made four basic points:

1. The United States would not interfere in the internal affairs of or the wars between European powers.
2. The United States recognized and would not interfere with existing colonies and dependencies in the Western Hemisphere.
3. The Western Hemisphere was closed to future colonization.
4. Any attempt by a European power to oppress or control any nation in the Western Hemisphere would be viewed as a hostile act against the United States.

Roosevelt, feeling a need to legitimize his action, asked Isaiah Bowman, president of Johns Hopkins University and a distinguished geographer, for a detailed analysis of Western Hemispheric boundaries.[27] Bowman's report of 19 May warned of the pitfalls trying to define the hemisphere by a line of longitude but reassured the president that "cartographic convenience" could be based on historical precedent. He traced the history of thinking about hemispheric approaches and showed that a 25-degree longitude line was a good 5 degrees west of the conventional hemispheric limits shown in modern atlases. Bowman went on to assure Roosevelt that Greenland as well as Iceland, though perhaps on the wrong side of the 25-degree line, could be considered part of the Western Hemisphere but that the Azores posed a serious problem. The islands were well within Roosevelt's geographic boundary—the 28-degree longitude line ran right through the middle of the group—but in their case the geographic and historical literature preferred to place them in the Old World. Bowman warned Roosevelt that because of abundant contrary opinions, a European coalition could make its own claim to the Azores. Roosevelt thanked Bowman for his report and decided to put the Azores in the Western Hemisphere anyway; the physical boundary would take precedence over geography and history. He would present his decision to the American people in a Fireside Chat on 27 May.

Drawing boundaries in the Atlantic Ocean was nothing new. Roosevelt was merely following the precedent set in 1493 by Pope Alexander VI, who issued bulls setting up a line of demarcation running from the North Pole to the South Pole, one hundred leagues (three hundred miles) west of the Cape Verde Islands. Spain was given exclusive rights to the region west of the line; Portuguese voyages were to keep to the east; the Azores were safely on the Portuguese side but the entire New World was Spanish.

Was the Pope biased? After all, he was Spanish, born Rodrigo de Borja y Doms in Aragon to the Spanish side of the Borgia family. The *Encyclopedia Britannica*, trying to be kind—an admittedly difficult task, given the sordid facts of his life—describes him not as corrupt as depicted by Machiavelli. In a classic case of damning with faint praise, the encyclopedia admits that Alexander VI holds a high place on the list of the so-called bad popes. In a blessing or otherwise, depending on your point of view, he is credited by his actions to have contributed substantially to the development of the Protestant Reformation. One of his illegitimate children was the equally infamous Lucrezia Borgia, with whom he allegedly had an incestuous relationship. All in all, not the ideal spiritual leader that the two leading Catholic world powers should completely trust to patch up their differences.[28]

The Spanish rulers Ferdinand and Isabella were pleased that the Pope supported their claims and discouraged the Portuguese and other rival claimants. After all, the New World had recently been discovered by Columbus sailing under their flag even though he had received all his navigational training at Prince Henry's school in Portugal. The Cape Verde line was not acceptable to King João II of Portugal because he had hopes of carving out his own empire in the west. If the pope's line were upheld, Portuguese caravels would not even have sufficient sailing room for their African voyages. And for the crucial question: did Portugal know, or at least suspect, that Brazil was waiting to be officially discovered only seven years later?

Portugal's unhappiness led to another diplomatic meeting the following year, on 7 June 1494, at Tordesillas in northwestern Spain. The Spanish and Portuguese ambassadors reaffirmed the principals of the papal division, but moved the line itself 370 leagues (1,100 miles) west of the Cape Verde Islands, or between 48 and 49 degrees west of Green-wich. A new pope, Julius II, sanctioned the change in 1506 but by then the new line had already become de facto when Portugal claimed Brazil after its discovery by Pedro Álvares Cabral in 1500.

Roosevelt had no papal bull to fall back on, but he could quote the 1823 Monroe Doctrine which, like Tordesillas, received a mixed reception from the European powers. England, our staunchest ally, recognized the Doctrine, but Germany, in many public statements over the years, made it clear that our right to meddle in the affairs of a country on either side of the Atlantic was not sanctioned by any recognized international law, that we could not intervene unilaterally whenever we felt that a Western Hemisphere nation was threatened.

10 April: Hull to Lisbon

With the State Department still worried that the Germans might attempt to invade the Atlantic islands, Cordell Hull asked Bert Fish to make it clear to Salazar that the United States did not "intend to stand by on the sidelines but that on the contrary we do intend to play our part in resistance against the forces of aggression."[29] If that statement was designed to make the Portuguese feel more at ease, it not only failed miserably but frightened them into thinking that the United States had something more sinister in mind than just defending the Azores.

18 April: Washington, D.C.

Salazar was growing unhappier each day with insistent rumors coming out of Washington that Roosevelt had made up his mind about placing the Azores in the western hemisphere and thus into the sphere of protection of the United States. Portugal's Ambassador Bianchi presented Salazar's concerns to the secretary of state who attempted to calm Portuguese sensitivities, informing the ambassador that such reports were completely untrue; that as he had stated, the United States would not occupy the islands unless the Germans made a move against them. To allow the United States some "wiggle room," exactly what was meant by that remark was not made clear: would it be merely a threat or an actual invasion of mainland Portugal or the Atlantic islands? Not answered was the critical issue: exactly what kind of move by the Germans would be considered threatening enough to provoke a U.S. occupation of the islands? Bianchi left his audience with Hull as much in the dark as ever, which was probably just how the secretary of state wanted it.[30]

23 April: Former Naval Person to Roosevelt

Churchill answered Roosevelt's cable of 11 April with his assessment of the war in the Atlantic. U-boats had been driven away from the British Isles thanks to the gift of destroyers from the United States and he guessed that the area west of 35 degrees west longitude and south of Greenland would be the next danger zone. VLR air patrols from U.S. bases in Greenland were necessary to counter this new threat.

Another area which was giving much trouble to England-bound convoys was bounded by Freetown in Africa, north to the Cape Verdes and west to the Azores. Convoys could not be routed very far to the west of the triangle—owing to the endurance of the vessels on this run—unless they lightened their cargo load and took on extra fuel, a costly and inefficient process. Escorts for convoys were inadequate; air reconnaissance from U.S. carriers was desperately needed because it could cover the area for some distance in advance of and around the convoys.

The prime minister added an alarming note for Roosevelt alone—he and his naval staff were worried about the increasing pressure put on Spain and Portugal by Germany. The Iberian nations could collapse at any time and Germany would gain control of Gibraltar. It was not necessary to move a large force through Spain; only a few thousand artillerists and technicians could gain control of the batteries commanding the Gibraltar anchorage. German agents had already done "some of their usual penetration into Tangier, and thus both sides of the straits might quickly pass into the hands of expert hostile gunners."[31]

If Spain were to give way or be attacked, two expeditions that had been held in readiness in England would be dispatched, one to an island in the Azores quickly followed by a landing on a second isle and another operation to the Cape Verdes. These operations would take eight days from the time the signal was given but, unfortunately, England did not have the resources, given her other tasks in the war, to maintain a continuous watch on the situation. Churchill proposed a simple solution to defuse the threat: a U.S. naval squadron should make a friendly cruise and visit the islands as soon as possible. "This would probably warn Nazi raiders off and would keep the place warm for us as well as giving us invaluable information."[32]

24 April: Washington, D.C.

Isolationist sentiment was still strong in the country with many of its advocates in Congress arguing that no viable threat to the country existed from either the wars in Europe or the Pacific. The motto of the America First party, and echoed (strangely enough) by the American Communist Party, was that it made no difference who won the war— England or Germany. Cordell Hull, fully cognizant of real threats across the oceans, that Germany's Projekt Amerika nullified the safety net provided by the Atlantic, felt this attitude was intolerable. Hull and Roosevelt were trying to convince the U.S. public that the Battle of the Atlantic was vital to the security of the nation, and, that for our own good, we had no choice but to play an active role. In his speech to the American Society of International Law, of which he was president, Hull warned:

> Some among us . . . contend that our country need not resist until armed forces of an invader shall have crossed the boundary line of this hemisphere. But this merely means that there would be no resistance by the hemisphere . . . until the invading countries had acquired complete control of the other four continents and of the high seas, and thus had obtained every possible strategic advantage, reducing us to the corresponding disadvantage of a severely handicapped defense. This is an utterly shortsighted and extremely dangerous view.[33]

1 May: Roosevelt to Former Naval Person

Portugal was not keen about a "Friendly Visit" from a U.S. squadron to the Azores or the Cape Verdes, in fact strongly protested against the mere suggestion of such a visit. The next best option was to visit the Spanish Canary Islands, which the U.S. ambassador reported had a good chance to be approved but with an added stipulation that made it impossible—no fuel could be taken on locally or in Spain. Any hope of "showing the colors" was effectively ruled out.

Roosevelt assured Churchill that the new naval patrols would extend just to the west of both the Azores and the Cape Verde Islands, but neither planes nor ships would get too close to the islands themselves. Roosevelt thought it important that no English force be sent to either place unless it was certain that a German attack was imminent upon Portugal or the Azores. To avoid being "hoist with his own petard," Roosevelt wanted the prime minister to make it clear to Portugal that if the Allies should occupy the Azores it would be solely for the purposes of British defense and only for the duration of the war. In other words, England would restore the islands to Portuguese sovereignty after the war "if Portugal is restored as an independent nation. The reason I suggest this is that as you know, most of the Azores are in Western Hemisphere under my longitudinal map reading."[34] Following Roosevelt's interpretation of the Monroe Doctrine, even England had to be careful about trespassing in the Western Hemisphere.

3 May, Midnight: Roosevelt from Former Naval Person

Churchill thanked Roosevelt for his support: "no temporary reverses, however heavy, can shake your resolution to support us until we gain the final victory." However the prime minister was upset with the president's admonition to take no action until it was clear that the Nazis were moving upon Portugal or Spain or the Atlantic islands. German "tourists" had already infiltrated and were gathering intelligence, the same step taken before the invasions of Holland, Denmark, Greece, and everywhere else in Western Europe. The fear in which both Portugal and Spain held Germany kept them from officially taking any action against the infiltration of the islands "lest worse befall them at home." England had made no decision as yet but the prime minister felt sure that Roosevelt "would not wish to prescribe our remaining passive, if we feel we have to act in advance" of the conditions set by the president, that is if Portugal is attacked or England gets word of an imminent invasion of the Azores or Cape Verdes.

If England did move against the Azores, she will declare that they are occupied only for defensive purposes and will be restored to Portuguese sovereignty at the close of the war. The United States should stand guarantor for the execution of the agreement, that England has no desire to add to her territory, only to preserve her own life (and incidentally that of the United States).[35]

6 May: American Blustering and Portuguese Reaction

The distinguished *New York Herald-Tribune* political commentator, Walter Lippmann, suggested that with or without Portuguese consent, we should not allow the Germans to occupy the Azores. Senator Claude Pepper of Florida issued a call-to-arms from the floor of the Senate: that the United States should declare a national emergency and take more aggressive action abroad, that the Nazis should not be allowed into the Western Hemisphere, and that we should immediately move troops and take over the Azores lock, stock, and barrel.[36] He said we should occupy "those points of vantage from which monsters are preparing to attack us. In that category I include Greenland, Iceland, the Azores, the Cape Verde Islands, the Canary Islands and Dakar."[37] Pepper was a member of the Senate Foreign Relations Committee and had made pronouncements in the past that were followed by U.S. policy decisions; consequently his words were widely publicized and always taken seriously. Berlin, at least outwardly, dismissed his statements as "amateurish" but Lisbon worried about them. When Pepper's speech was followed by Roosevelt's extension of the Monroe Doctrine three weeks later, Portugal became truly alarmed. They had a long-standing treaty with the British that legitimized mutual defense but, lacking any similar agreement with the United States, U.S. involvement would only complicate their status vis-à-vis Germany. This had been clearly pointed out when Colonel, later major general, Robert Olds, head of the Air Transport Command desperately searching for a shorter route to England than Brazil–South Atlantic–Dakar, requested landing privileges in the Azores for U.S. military aircraft.[38] Salazar turned down the request.

President Salazar protested to the United States, reaffirming Portuguese neutrality and asking the British for help to get us to stop making provocative statements. Portugal would defend its own territory against any attacker and challenged the right of the United States to define threats against itself while disregarding the sovereignty of other nations. Secretary of State Hull disavowed Pepper's remarks, reaffirming U.S. respect for Portuguese neutrality, and Roosevelt smoothed out the relations with a personal exchange of notes with Salazar in July.

7 May: Ambassador Cárdenas to the Secretary of State

The U.S. newspapers report of Senator Pepper's suggestion to seize the Canary Islands reverberated in Madrid. The Spanish ambassador in Washington was told to inquire whether or not these statements represented official government opinion. Ambassador Cárdenas asked the secretary of state "to be good enough to undo the bad impression that the incident has produced, at the same time clarifying the viewpoint of the American Government."[39]

There is no record of the secretary of state's response. Whether it was written or verbal, presumably it did the trick and calmed down the Spanish government. The United States had no designs on the Canary Islands, which, in any case, would play no role in safeguarding transatlantic shipping lines to England but were needed to protect the north-south routes around Africa. The Portuguese islands, most especially the Azores, were the chief preoccupation of Roosevelt and the Joint Chiefs, necessary to cover the dreaded "black hole."

9 May: Washington, D.C., and Lisbon

Senator Pepper's speech set in motion a great brouhaha that refused to disappear. João Antonio de Bianchi, Portugal's ambassador to Washington, was the next to call on the secretary of state. The Portuguese government he insisted had received no requests by any belligerent power to use any ports, bases, coasts, or islands, that his government had taken measures for the defense of the island groups in the Atlantic, and that his government would resist any attack that might be directed against them. Bianchi was happy to accept from Hull, on behalf of the Portuguese government, the declaration that Senator Pepper's views "in no way correspond to the feeling of complete respect for Portuguese sovereignty by the United States Government."[40]

Hull added in a press conference that there was nothing new in the

United States's friendly relations with Portugal; although members of other branches of the government could state their individual and unofficial views, such statements did not represent the official policy of the U.S. government. Hull sent this information to Fish to use as he thought desirable.

Fish responded with a copy of the official statement made by Salazar, which was almost identical to the protest presented by the Portuguese ambassador.[41] There is no record of Fish personally meeting with Salazar to explain U.S. policy, which was not surprising given that much of his time in Lisbon was spent avoiding Salazar and making as few official contacts with the Portuguese government as he could.[42]

18 May: Sinking the Bismarck

Sinking of the *Bismarck* effectively ended the argument for the big ships favored by Hitler and a few of his old line admirals versus U-boats and support vessels promoted by OKM Raeder. The *Bismarck* had been holed up in a Norwegian fjord and was ordered out into the Atlantic to see if it could inflict more damage to Allied shipping than the submarines did. Although it was ordered to avoid a fight and to attack merchant ships, the *Bismarck* encountered and engaged the British battleship HMS *Hood*, which it sank in a fierce twenty-four minute battle.[43] A combined British air-sea force was quickly organized to pursue and sink the *Bismarck*, which it effectively did nine days after she left safe harbor, sending to the bottom all but 110 of her crew of 2,000.

Hitler's preference was for the warships because of their impressive size and noble appearance and courageously facing the enemy head-on rather than the cowardly U-boats, which relied on ambush as their favorite tactic. Pocket battleships such as the *Bismarck*, *Tirpitz*, and the *Graf Spee* were big, heavily armored, and fearful looking on the high seas, but much more valuable for public relations than anything practical. Each of them ended their careers either blockaded in continental ports or sunk at sea. When the *Bismarck* went down, so did the argument for the big ships. Despite the psychological terror they spread through the world's oceans, by the time the war ended surface raiders had accounted for only 6.1 percent of Allied shipping whereas 70 percent were sunk by U-boats and the rest by mines or aircraft. There was no reason to delay the decision any longer: U-boat construction was to receive a top priority in the German war industry and no more large capital ships would be launched.

23 May: Lisbon to London to Washington, D.C.

The British had pressed Salazar to answer what Portugal's response would be if the Germans attacked or even threatened to attack the homeland or any of the Atlantic islands. Months earlier they had urged him to plan to move the government to the Azores, to send the bulk of the armed forces there as well, and that the British fleet would help with the move. He had been putting off an answer for as long as he could, but now when a bona fide German threat appeared he finally responded. Salazar's written documents always took long to translate, and even worse, his style of writing, conditioned by years of training in academia and the church, made whatever he said open to several interpretations.

The British Foreign Office, taking the most liberal approach they could to Salazar's response, felt that it was possible to reach some arrangement regarding the Atlantic islands. If their interpretation was correct, then it would be best for the United States not to try its own hand at intimidation or worse, an armed invasion of the Azores. Halifax urged Hull not to send a representative to Lisbon to negotiate at this critical time, that such an arrival would promote "rumours and give an opportunity to the Germans for mischievous propaganda. Under the circumstances, the British Government's view . . . is that it would be better to hold American influence in reserve for the moment."[44]

The British attitude towards Portugal throughout most of the war was tempered by the treaty of 1373, and so as allies they could discuss mutual defense legitimately without upsetting the Axis. On the other hand, because the United States was entering the scene with no proper credentials, any action it took could be interpreted as aggression. This became a major cause of disagreement between the British and the Joint Chiefs, who were sure their Allies were deliberately keeping the Azores for themselves and did not want any Americans on what they considered their turf.

During the winter and spring of 1941 as England's military fortunes steadily deteriorated, the United States moved towards direct participation through "measures short of war" in the Atlantic. The Wehrmacht appeared unstoppable; every new campaign in Europe and North Africa brought Germany closer to world conquest. The Balkans and Libya were invaded and occupied in April with almost the same ease that Western Europe had fallen only a year earlier. On 15 May Marshal Pétain announced that, bowing to Hitler's demand, his government would henceforth collaborate with Germany. The United States immediately protested and seized the eleven French ships in U.S. ports, including the *Normandie*. Intelligence reports out of Vichy revealed the principal reason behind the German demand: the Wehrmacht, planning a new campaign headed to the southwest, was about to start moving troops south through France to Mediterranean ports and to the Pyrenees border with Spain. German troops would be ready to march through Spain with one task force to attack Gibraltar and another to spearhead an invasion of Portugal. A third force would move through southern France to Marseilles, cross the Mediterranean to Algeria and Morocco, march through French North Africa with Pétain's approval and close the pincers on Gibraltar from the south. French North Africa would become a German enclave. These movements would implement Operation Felix, the conquest of Gibraltar and the Iberian Peninsula, and for good measure Northwest Africa and the Atlantic islands.

A German move to the southwest in Europe and into Northwest and West Africa was viewed as a threat to the United States. First, commerce in the Atlantic Ocean would be threatened as U-boats could sail from anywhere on the European coast, from North Cape in Norway to Faro, the southern tip of Portugal, as well as from North African ports. German air and U-boat bases on the Atlantic islands could deliver the coup de grâce to England's lifeline to the United States. Roosevelt and Churchill resolved this would not happen; occupying the Azores would give them the base needed to prevent Germany from controlling the Atlantic.

FOUR

THE UNITED STATES GOES TO WAR, MAY–DECEMBER 1941

The intensifying of the German efforts to cut off supplies reaching the British Isles . . . might lead the Germans to attempt to sieze these islands . . . from which such a large part of the routes to the Brisith Isles could be patrolled by airplanes based on the islands. Once established . . . it would be hard to dislodge an occupying force, and such a large force would be necessary to effect a dislodgement that it is not considered possible that it could effect a landing in the face of air attacks from bases on the islands. In other words, if the Germans could once establish themselves here, they could hardly be driven out, and they could effectively attack sea transport over a wide area of the Atlantic from here.

LEONARD G. DAWSON,
American consul, Ponta Delgada,
to secretary of state,
5 March 1941

By 1941 Germany appeared to be well on its way to establishing the "Thousand-Year Reich." Its armies were invincible. Less than two years after starting World War II the German blitzkrieg had proven unstoppable, overrunning most of Europe seemingly with little effort. Remarkably enough, this was accomplished without straining the German economy. Four million men had been drafted into the armed forces without the country suffering a manpower shortage. To take up the slack in industrial production the work week was lengthened and more than three million slave laborers were brought into the Third Reich, prisoners of war and foreign "volunteers" from the conquered European nations. Additional raw material now available from the occupied lands and neutral countries, such as steel from Sweden and wolframite—an ore of tungsten—from Spain and Portugal, actually resulted in an 11 percent increase in Germany's national production.

The High Command, convinced of its invincibility and having cut its teeth on Poland, France, Holland, Belgium, Luxembourg, Denmark, and Norway, was itching get going on another big operation, a blitzkrieg that would be a giant step towards the goal of world conquest. Because the attack on England had to be aborted, Operation Barbarossa, the campaign against Russia, was promoted by the Wehrmacht as the next step to reach that goal. Hitler, who relished the idea of occupying Russia and gaining possession of its vast stores of raw material, and incidentally getting rid of the communist menace once and for all, found the arguments for Barbarossa most appealing. However, also on the agenda was Operation Felix/*Projekt Amerika,* proposed by the OKM as an alternative to another land war. Conquest of Russia might not be as simple as imagined; the outcome of such an operation was not certain. Admiral Raeder, accompanied by Admiral Dönitz, head of the U-boat fleet (*Befehlshaber der U-boote*), argued for the Navy that England could not be beaten by air but was slowly being strangled by sea. The U-boat war against shipping was continuing unabated with little apparently that the Allies could do about turning it around. By the end of the year 2.1 million tons of shipping would be sunk. U-boat production was increasing, from 65 in July 1941 to 198 in September and to more than 230 by December. Merchant ships were being sunk at a faster clip than they could be replaced while at the same time the submarine fleet was actually growing. England was completely dependent on its marine supply routes for food, raw materials, and war supplies. With U-boat control of the seas and disruption of her supplies, England would be quickly starved into submission.[1]

The Allies could protect ship convoys with escorts, either armed merchantmen or warships, and air support. Of these, air support was the most efficient in keeping the shipping lanes clear of U-boats but air bases existed only on the northern rim of the Atlantic and convoys could be protected only within five or six hundred miles of shore. U-boats preferred to cruise on the surface where their speed was higher than underwater and their ability to visually detect merchant ships greatly enhanced but where they were also most vulnerable to air attack. The popular IXC U-boat was capable of speeds of 18.3 knots on the surface and a maximum submerged speed of only 7.3 knots which could be kept up for only one hour. Normal surface cruising speed was ten knots allowing a range of 16,300 miles; submerged the cruising speed was two to four knots with a range of 128 to 63 miles, respectively. Until the invention of the *schnorchel*, U-boats had to surface periodically to air out accumulated diesel fumes and to charge their batteries. A U-boat airing itself out was a sitting duck for aircraft on a submarine hunt. The Germans took a long time to figure out that the Allies' new radar enabled planes to sneak up on U-boats that relied, for the most part, on visual observation. The likelihood of being attacked and sunk on patrol in the northern waters of the Atlantic made U-boat captains prefer to seek targets elsewhere.[2]

For merchant ships sailing more than five hundred miles outside of the normal range of Allied air bases in Newfoundland, Greenland, England, the United States, and, later in the year, Iceland, there was no guarantee of security. The vast "black hole" in the middle of the Atlantic centered around the Azores, where U-boats picked off isolated merchantmen or formed "wolf packs" sprawled out in a long picket line over shipping routes, lying in wait to ambush convoys headed to Europe and the Mediterranean. Admiral Dönitz argued that cutting England's supply line by increasing the rate of attrition of merchant ships was a simpler path to victory than any ground operation. The rewards from beating England in the Atlantic were higher, less risky, more economical in resources, with a lower loss of manpower than invading Russia. To win the war in the Atlantic, Admiral Dönitz figured he had to sink 600,000–750,000 tons of shipping per month for a year, something that could be accomplished with a fleet of three hundred operational U-boats. Now that the *Bismarck* had been sunk, the argument for the noble pocket battleship versus the sneaky U-boat had been resolved.

Back in the United States, only four months before Pearl Harbor, Roosevelt waged a bitter battle with Congress to sustain the Selective Service Act. War was raging all over the world, the Japanese were on the verge of controlling eastern Asia, and the Axis powers had conquered most of Western Europe. When the vote in Congress was finally taken in August 1941, the result was a bare 203–202 victory to continue the civilian draft and maintain the strength of the armed forces. Japan had invaded southeast Asia three weeks before the vote was taken, and on 22 June Germany started Operation Barbarossa in what appeared would be an easy conquest of Russia.

By fall Hitler had given Washington much cause for worry. His armies attacked Yugoslavia and Greece and the war against Russia appeared almost won. The blitzkrieg seemed unstoppable. There was no question that more aggression was planned in Berlin, including against

Portugal and her Atlantic islands, which would threaten the security of the United States. The United States lacked a functioning overseas intelligence network so there were no reliable sources of information, mostly educated guesswork. So-called intelligence fed to Washington was basically gossip picked up at social events or items read in local newspapers by the embassy staff. Except for electronic intercepts, neither the British nor the Germans had much better systems, and each country generally made policy without reliable information on what the others were planning. If Portugal was about to be invaded by Germany, then a preemptive U.S. strike against the Azores was a fitting response. However, if the Germans had no such plans, then seizing the Azores might precipitate their invading mainland Portugal. Interesting enough, the German High Command, with no hard information on Allied plans, decided to invade Portugal only if the Americans first landed in the Azores.[3]

May–June: Island Hopping in the Atlantic

The Portuguese Atlantic islands stood high on the agenda at the ABC-1 meeting in early January, the first called between the Allied Chiefs of Staff to choose "the best methods by which the armed forces of the United States and the British Commonwealth can defeat Germany and the powers allied with her, should the United States be compelled to resort to war."[4] It was agreed that they fell within the British sphere of responsibility and British forces should be earmarked to occupy the Cape Verdes and the Azores if the Germans made a move against Spain and Portugal such as crossing the Pyrenees in force. ABC-1 was signed on 27 March and ruled out involvement of U.S. ground forces any earlier than September, but if needed the Navy could give assistance in the Atlantic. The Army had not anticipated involvement in any kind of shooting operation until it was properly prepared, that being sometime after September—especially if the United States went to war. The Joint Chiefs had given little thought to invading any Atlantic islands; they had been operating on the basis of Roosevelt's statement of 11 March, which set the defense of England and Greece as his highest priorities.[5]

But Churchill, afraid of a possible German move and lacking the manpower to protect the entire Atlantic from Iceland to the Cape Verdes, asked Roosevelt if the United States could at least assume responsibility for the Azores. On 1 May Roosevelt warned him that as a neutral the United States could not cooperate with England in any operation aimed at preventing Germany from seizing the Azores or the Cape Verdes; the definition of neutrality had already been stretched to the limit. Although Roosevelt decided against taking military action in the Portuguese Atlantic islands, he did take the first steps towards discouraging German aggression against them.

On 22 May he instructed Admiral H. R. Star, chief of Naval Operations, to have the Navy patrol the Atlantic west of a mid-ocean line at 26 degrees West longitude but stretched a bit east to include all of Greenland and the Azores. On 27 May three battleships augmented the forces on patrol. Unsurprisingly, by September the Navy was drawn into a shooting war with the U-boats.[6]

Germany responded angrily to Roosevelt's action. Full of righteous indignation, Admiral Dönitz exclaimed that "no justification of any sort will be found anywhere in international law either for thus extending a security zone or for putting it to the uses to which it was thus arbitrarily put."[7]

On the next day, 23 May, Roosevelt had a change of heart, cabled Churchill that U.S. troops could occupy the Azores before the Germans tried to do so, and ordered the Joint Chiefs to prepare Task Force Gray to be readied in a month to seize the islands. He had received a report of 7 May from the War Plans Division that rated the archipelago number two, right after Dakar, in their list of "areas of urgency." Iceland was down in sixteenth spot, so from the standpoint of national defense sending troops to the Azores made more sense than sending them north to Iceland. The president resolved the dilemma posed by the Neutrality Act—which forbade the use of U.S. armed forces outside the western hemisphere while the country was not at war—by declaring that the Azores were in the Western Hemisphere, and therefore subject to U.S. protection.[8]

Task Force Gray and Operation Lifebelt—also called Lifeline—would join with Churchill's Operation Alacrity, with the avowed aim of heading off Germany's expansion south and west from occupied France. However, the Joint Chiefs were surprised and unhappy at the order from the president to prepare an expedition to go anywhere before the Army was prepared, especially sending one out to the Azores where it would be isolated in the mid-Atlantic. Of course, as with all armies since Alexander the Great marched into India with his Macedonians and Greeks, the Joint Chiefs had already prepared a book full of plans for any conceivable operation. There were plans for many different operations—some serious, others fantasies—but no one expected to implement any of them on short notice, especially with the country theoretically at peace. The Azores, together with a number of obscure places on earth, were already in the book but were not considered viable operations before the country was prepared for war. In addition to the advantages of each exercise, pages of objections listed unintended consequences that might follow if any were actually attempted, and for the Azores enough negatives were listed to keep them from being taken too seriously.

The arguments were cogent and until then kept Roosevelt from going ahead: such an operation was well beyond the resources of this country with its small peacetime army; even if landing against Portuguese opposition and an occupation of the islands was successful, logistical support and defending the islands against German air power would be difficult. The islands were indefensible against air assault, especially if Germany occupied Portugal and then flew from bases in Europe only 870 miles (1,400 kilometers) to the easternmost island, Santa Maria, one of the prime sites selected for an Allied base. With U.S. provocation as an excuse, Germany would invade Portugal and establish air bases there. Being only a few hours flying time away, devastating air attacks and enemy paratroop landings in the Azores were all but certain.

The Joint Chiefs actually were not as worried about the Azores as they were about a possible German invasion of the Western Hemisphere from an African base, a fact they had recognized when Dakar was placed first on the list of "areas of urgency." Hitler might decide to take advantage of Pétain's offer of cooperation and move his forces south to French West Africa with the idea of striking against northeast Brazil, across the narrowest part of the Atlantic. If the Germans attempted to gain this closest access to the Western Hemisphere, the Azores were too far north to effectively prevent the operation.

But now the commander-in-chief had given orders that an expedition to the Azores would take place, and that it would start with a deadline of 22 June. General George C. Marshall, head of the Combined Chiefs of Staff, protested strongly against any U.S. operation far out in the Atlantic. He argued that the Army would have to commit its best troops, of which there were precious few at the time, virtually all of its small arms ammunition with little hope of rapid replenishment, and much of its sparse equipment to a remote area where the whole task force could easily be isolated by an unlucky naval reversal. The general reminded Roosevelt that the country was not yet at war and added that there were legislative restrictions on sending troops outside the Western Hemisphere in peacetime. Despite Isaiah Bowman, there were many in Congress who did not buy his definition of where to draw the boundary between the hemispheres, choosing to rely on tradition, which put the Azores squarely in the Eastern. Marshall would not permit sending any troops outside the United States who were not completely trained and equipped to meet a first class enemy. The odds were good that the Germans would have arrived first as airborne paratroopers while the Americans were still chugging their way across the Atlantic in a slow convoy.[9]

The lack of airfields in the Azores ruled out the use of air transport, so the operation would have to be completely by ship. A large convoy dispatched from the States could not be kept secret for long; every U-boat in the Atlantic would be out on the prowl. Finally, there was the unknown question of what kind of reception to expect from the Portuguese Army when the task force arrived. Much of the Army had already been moved from the mainland to discourage any country from attempting to take over the islands.

Only forty thousand U.S. troops were considered ready for any overseas operation in May, but it would have been almost impossible to put together a balanced force for Task Force Gray given the Army's serious deficiencies in specialized troops. Moving the Task Force to the Azores was another major problem; the Army Transport Service had only twenty-six ships, all fully engaged in routine ferrying service mostly in the Pacific.[10]

Nevertheless, the president ordered an expedition to the Azores and to have it ready to go in a month. Faithful to its orders, by the end of May the Joint Chiefs worked out the constitution of the invasion force: the First Army and the First Marine Divisions were to form the nucleus of a task force of about twenty-eight thousand under Navy command with the Marines in charge of the landing. Three of the twelve battalions to land on D-day were to be contributed by the Army, which would also have reserve forces of eleven thousand available for a total of twenty-five thousand troops.[11] To make the operation more acceptable to Portugal, Roosevelt revealed that Brazil might supply a token force to accompany the Americans.[12]

Availability of troops was not the only problem; there were serious logistical questions as well. The lack of U.S. preparedness became known when an attempt was made to requisition ammunition for the expedition. Even given the absolute minimum allowable for assault elements and adding only partial allowances for follow-up forces would completely exhaust all stocks of many critical types of anti-aircraft and antitank ammunition, for example, 3-inch anti-aircraft and 37-mm antitank shells, and actually exceed both the stocks and anticipated production until 1 October of 50-caliber anti-aircraft shells. The ammunition allowance requested for the Azores expedition had to be slashed on average by half. Not only would the nation's stocks be depleted, but according to the production schedules some critical types could not be restocked for at least several months.

The shortage of shipping also added to the disarray. Puerto Rico was considered the ideal place for landing rehearsals but because not enough ships were available to haul everyone and their gear down together in one trip, it would just barely be possible to schedule one round trip before the target date. So instead of a full-scale major landing rehearsal, separate small Army-Marine landings were held along the East Coast. Forty-one troop transport and cargo ships were needed for the initial movement to the Azores, but the Armed Services had only twenty-nine available. The Navy wanted to commandeer six of the Army's newest large troop transports despite the fact that two of them had been designated for the Pacific to rush troops to Hawaii or Alaska in case of war. The Maritime Commission would have to find an additional twelve for the operation plus fourteen more to make up for the ships removed from normal military transport service. If Operation Lifeline had been carried out and the Japanese had attacked Pearl Harbor then and not seven months later, the United States would have been in an even more helpless situation to defend itself; reinforcing garrisons in Hawaii and the Aleutians would have been impossible.[13]

The failure to mount even a small-scale invasion of the Azores was damning evidence that the United States was not prepared for war. We could not mount an operation involving a force of just twenty-eight thousand; we had neither the landing vessels nor enough ammunition to pull off an effective invasion against a poorly equipped Portuguese army. On the positive side, for the United States it dramatized the need to prepare for global warfare, to construct landing craft and transport vessels, to build up its arms and armament, to be ready to fight a two-ocean war with amphibious operations the norm.

The U.S. declaration that it would "defend" the Azores worried Salazar more than Germany's or England's intentions because both countries kept tight-lipped about their own plans for the islands. He had always assumed that England would not attempt to occupy the islands forcibly, that the British would negotiate as they were doing and justify their request by invoking the 1373 treaty. Moreover, given England's control of the seas, the odds of a German attack on the Azores he felt were remote. He did have good reason to worry about the United States, however. Despite Roosevelt denying any aggressive intent to Salazar, an Azores operation was being readied, exactly what Senator Pepper had demanded on the Senate floor.

On 4 June the president approved the plan drawn up for Operation Lifeline due to start on 22 June under overall Navy command. Then, only three days later, he ordered the armed services to raise a force of "about seventy-five thousand" for an operation to Iceland to relieve the British. That one was scheduled to start a month later.

General Marshall had great misgivings about the Azores adventure and now with the president adding Iceland to the armed forces burden he was doubly upset. He argued strongly with the president and finally talked him out of having two overseas missions going at the same time. At this early stage of the United States's preparedness it was much too risky; if one operation had to be chosen, going to Iceland rather than the Azores made better military and logistical sense. Iceland was already functioning as an ally under British control with fully operating airfield and marine port facilities, so all we had to do was send the personnel and material by air and sea and move in. The shortage of arms and munitions would not be a problem; this was a peaceful operation.

Churchill was to get at least one of his wishes. The British force stationed in Iceland was replaced by a large detachment of U.S. Marines. Churchill was elated: "I am much encouraged by your marines taking over that cold place and I hope that once the first installment has arrived you will give full publicity to it. It would give us hope to face the long haul that lies ahead. It would also produce the best effects in Spain, Vichy France, and Turkey."[14]

Going to Iceland proved even simpler diplomatically than getting into Greenland. As early as 24 December 1940, the Icelandic Foreign Office wanted to know what our reaction would be if the Althing (Parliament) asked for U.S. protection. The country was worried about a possible German occupation especially because Iceland was then a dependency of Denmark, which was occupied by the Nazis. On 7 May 1941, British Ambassador Halifax reported to the secretary of state that German air and submarine activity around Iceland had increased and that the threat of an invasion was becoming very real. On 17 May the

Althing voted to dissolve the union with Denmark. With an independent Iceland, there were no diplomatic problems such as with Greenland, the United States could legally deal directly with Reykjavik, and
the Nazi-controlled government in Copenhagen could not do anything
about it. Moreover, as a neutral the United States was not committing
any aggression, just honoring a request by an independent neutral country for our protection.[15]

Despite things finally looking up for air support for convoys in the
northern Atlantic, U-boat operations were threatening to win Admiral
Dönitz's tonnage war. During the first six months of 1941, three million tons of Allied shipping was sunk, a figure much greater than the
shipyards could replace. The existence of the "black hole" in the mid-
Atlantic without air protection would have to be confronted sooner
rather than later. But if the dangerous central Atlantic routes could not
be protected, convoys would have to favor the North, staying within
range of air protection afforded by the new Allied bases in Greenland
and Iceland. With generally bad weather and floating icebergs, especially during the winter months, the North Atlantic was not the ideal
for year-round routing, and almost useless for Mediterranean-bound
convoys. The large "black hole" of the Azores Gap would remain festering until the Allies could get that needed base on the Mid-Atlantic
Ridge.

21 May: SS Robin Moor Torpedoed

A German U-boat attacked and sunk an unarmed U.S. cargo ship, the
Robin Moor, in the South Atlantic. Cordell Hull protested:

> The sinking was atrocious because the German submarine com-
> mander knew from the Robin Moor markings, flag, and the
> statements of her crew that she was American, en route from
> New York to Capetown, with a general cargo none of which was
> war materials. The crew and passengers were forced to put out
> in small boats many hundreds of miles from shore.[16]

Roosevelt sent a message to Congress that the sinking was meant
as a warning that the United States could only use the seas with Nazi
consent. However, Hitler had not authorized the attack and in fact
issued orders to avoid such incidents against U.S. ships. Plans for Bar-

barossa were moving ahead and Hitler did not want any more *Robin Moor* problems with the United States at this point. No punishment was considered against the captain of the U-boat and, in fact, Hitler agreed with the OKM that where the United States was concerned "firm measures are always more effective than apparent yielding." Because the Nazis were expecting to go to war with Uncle Sam soon, there was no point worrying about diplomatic niceties.[17]

22 May: The Berghof, Hitler's Mountain Retreat

Hitler met with the OKM on the same day that Roosevelt declared both Iceland and the Azores were in the Western Hemisphere and fell therefore under the sphere of protection of the United States. Neither Germany nor any other European power except England, who did not get around to it until 1903, ever recognized the right of the United States to declare such a "sphere of protection." Certainly no international court of justice would ever uphold rights based on the unilateral declaration of one nation and not negotiated by a treaty between nations. Germany would not respect the Monroe Doctrine and reserved the right to take whatever steps it deemed necessary in its own defense.[18]

The OKM proposed going more aggressively against the Azores as an important step to win the war in the Atlantic and to do it before the Allies, who had been threatening for so long, got there first. Germany should try to coax Portugal, ostensibly neutral, into allowing it to build naval and air bases on the islands or, should persuasion fail, take them over by force. U-boats could bring in supplies and troops; paratroops would fly in by VLR aircraft. An advanced base for U-boat operations would seal the fate of any ship foolish enough to try to sail from North America to England or to the Mediterranean via the central Atlantic. In addition to cutting its critical lifeline to the United States, England would lose contact with its African and Asian colonies and its sources for foodstuffs and war material. England would be starved into submission; it could easily be conquered without need for a cross-Channel amphibious operation. Moreover, it should not be too difficult to take over the Azores Islands.

The OKW and some admirals did not buy this argument. They agreed that a small number of combat forces transported by submarines and aircraft could invade the islands, and that the initial occupation would be relatively easy to accomplish especially if the only resistance was from local Portuguese army garrisons. But supplying and reinforcing the invasion and the occupation troops in the face of British and probable U.S. counterattacks would be almost impossible. All German naval forces would have to be committed to the Azores operation and forced to cease operations elsewhere in the Atlantic, including protecting the Norwegian coast against a possible British invasion. Moreover, even if the Azores were in German hands Allied convoys could still make it across the ocean unmolested following the northern route.

Hitler decided to put all future discussion on the Azores and *Projekt Amerika* on hold, promising they were postponed but not forgotten. He agreed with the OKW's assessment that they could be taken easily but could not be held in the face of British and U.S. counterattacks and that the Navy's main task that summer of 1941 must be to disrupt British supply lines. He insisted, however, that he still favored *Projekt Amerika* and eventually occupying the Azores in order to have an advanced base to attack the United States.

Admiral Raeder accepted the hyperbole on *Amerika* at face value— the VLR bomber on the drawing board would be capable of flying the twenty-five hundred mile round trip from the Azores to New York City with a full bomb load. The Americans were certainly not prepared to defend themselves against aerial bombardment. *Amerika* bombers should throw enough terror into the country that, according to German intelligence, was not keen about entering the war. A bombing campaign should be effective enough to swing public opinion against involvement in the war as an ally of England. If that were not enough, then the United States could be invaded by forces based in the Azores immediately following the bombing campaign. Accomplishing this before the United States mobilized its resources and manpower was a worthwhile goal; giving the country too much time to prepare for war was foolish because it could become too strong an opponent to dispose of easily.

In addition to the bombing campaign, U-boats could spend more time in U.S. waters attacking coastwise shipping. By sailing from bases in the middle of the Atlantic rather than from pens on the coast of France, the U-boats would shave over two thousand miles off a round trip just to get to the United States and arrive with enough diesel fuel to spend at least one extra operational week.

The Kriegsmarine Command should have known better, that the devastating bombing campaign would probably never come off given the aircraft industry's dismal record with other VLR bombers. The *Amerika* bomber was never submitted to an operational test, which was just as well because every other VLR model fabricated by German industry was a failure.

Admiral Raeder and Admiral Dönitz, who succeeded him as OKM, both felt that if the *Projekt* could be carried out successfully, then both the United States and England would have no choice but to sue for peace. Russia, isolated and weak, would then be completely intimidated and follow suit. The nightmare of a communist takeover of Germany and Western Europe would be gone forever with a minimal cost in lives and materiel.

Hitler rejected the Navy's arguments and made his decision: Germany would go ahead with Operation Barbarossa; the invasion of Russia would start that year and require the full resources of the Reich. Some generals were skeptical about the alleged ease of conquering the communists but as ground and air soldiers they much preferred a campaign on European soil to any Navy-sponsored operation on the Atlantic. Besides, they had guessed incorrectly before when Hitler ignored their opinions and took over Holland, Belgium, Luxembourg, and France in only a few weeks. Hitler also liked the idea of invading Russia, succeeding where Napoleon failed, and spending Christmas in Moscow. Russia was to be invaded and *Projekt Amerika* shelved until the fall when the conquest of Russia was expected to be successfully concluded. On 22 June 1941 Operation Barbarossa began with a blitzkrieg against Russia. By the end of the summer, as Hitler had predicted, it was going very well.

Raeder stated in his memoirs, "the Führer is still in favor of occupying the Azores, the occasion may arise by autumn." Autumn came and went with no invasion of the Azores; the war in Russia was becoming progressively more difficult. Later than the fall of 1941 was already too late; the United States was in the war as a shooting ally of England by the end of the year. As for Dönitz's calculations on how the submarines could win the war: the highest tonnage loss of Allied shipping was a little over five hundred thousand tons per month in 1941 and the number of operational U-boats in the Atlantic was barely much more than two hundred in mid-1942 with only a fraction of that on patrol at any one time. Hitler's meddling insured that despite increased production, but not as much as promised, Dönitz would never have the force he needed to win the Battle of the Atlantic.[19]

In the last half of the year, an average of twenty boats per month entered service. A U-boat normally required four months for training and breakdown cruises between commissioning and starting patrol operations, so the OKM was counting on an increase of twenty boats per month starting in 1942. However, with bad weather that winter, the Baltic Sea where the crews received their training froze over, and work in the shipyards was forced to slow down. As a result for the period January–March an average of only thirteen U-boats per month entered service and for April–June the figure sank to ten. The promised twenty new boats per month never materialized.

For Dönitz low submarine production was only half the sad story. Of the sixty-nine U-boats that actually entered service in the first half of 1942, twenty-six (40 percent) were diverted to patrol Norwegian waters and two went to the Mediterranean. Twelve boats had been lost in the Atlantic, so the sixty-nine new U-boats represented only an increase of twenty-nine devoted to the war on shipping. The total number of operating boats in the Atlantic was 101. Of these an average of fifty-nine were at sea at any one time with forty-one in port refitting. Of the fifty-nine actually at sea, only nineteen were actively engaged in operations with the rest either en route or returning from operational zones. Considering the damage done to Allied shipping by only nineteen U-boats, if Hitler had given Dönitz the submarines he was promised, the war might have gone the way the admiral predicted.

27 May: Roosevelt's Fireside Chat and Its Consequences

Roosevelt decided to declare a National Emergency and warn the nation of the threats posed by the dangerous turn of events in the war. Instead of making the announcement in a speech before Congress, he would do it in a radio address to the entire nation as one of his Fireside Chats to give it the widest immediate publicity possible. Secretary of War Stimson unsuccessfully tried to talk Roosevelt out of emphasizing the importance of the Azores, which he thought would be waving a red flag at the Germans and might just challenge them to try to seize the islands first.

The Fireside Chat made for high drama as not only millions listened glued to their radios at home, but it was also relayed over loud speakers for the seventeen thousand spectators who had come to see a baseball game at the New York Giants's Polo Grounds. The president explained how critical it was for the nation's security to control the Atlantic approaches, that this was now a turning point in our attitude in the war, and for our own survival we would have to confront the Axis more actively. Although no specific actions were proposed, the "island outposts of the New World," especially the Azores, were highlighted in the speech as being vital for the "ultimate safety of the continental United States." Now he was taking the green light offered by Isaiah Bowman and rejecting a line of longitude to define the hemispheres.[20]

29 May: Former Naval Person to the President

Churchill "cordially welcomed" Roosevelt's agreement to take over Iceland which relieved a British division urgently needed to defend against possible German threats elsewhere. The prime minister added that it would have a morale effect on the occupied nations and the neutrals beyond its military importance. Now that Germany was put off from an Iceland adventure, the War Cabinet turned its concern to Hitler's intentions about Iberia and the Atlantic Islands. Churchill saw the likelihood that German air bases would be established in southern Spain or in Spanish or French North Africa, which would render the Gibraltar harbor unusable. Given England's military resources, it would be impossible to resist such a move; however, the loss of Gibraltar could be mitigated to a large extent by occupying the Atlantic islands.[21]

Although the British could not provide an army to defend either mainland Portugal or Spain, they would support guerrilla movements. Meanwhile, they were going to offer Portugal arms, especially anti-aircraft, to defend the islands and encourage the government to withdraw to the Azores if the Nazis overran the country. Such a move had a great historical precedent; when Napoleon invaded Portugal 140 years earlier, the Portuguese royal court packed up and left for Brazil where it stayed for the duration.[22] If the possibility of moving to the Azores was raised and Salazar accepted the protection of England, Churchill would ask for the cooperation of the United States, details to be worked out between the Foreign Office and the State Department. But whatever Salazar decided, collaboration with a U.S. token force was welcomed before, during, or after the occupation of the islands which Churchill thought could be turned over completely to the U.S. force, "as a matter of mutual war convenience" as was done in Iceland.

In addition to the Azores, Churchill proposed that the United States take over Dakar in West Africa and pointed out that the surest method for an invasion force would be to land tanks on nearby beaches from specially constructed vessels. He suggested immediate consultation between U.S. and British military staffs to lay out a workable plan and have it ready if circumstances required, in other words, German occupation or neutralizing of Gibraltar. This was still seven months before the United States became an active partner in the shooting war, but interestingly enough the prime minister's suggestion, added to the Task Force Gray fiasco, helped convince the Joint Chiefs to start designing and constructing tank and personnel landing craft. When the country got into the shooting war, amphibious landing craft were available and put to good use in many operations from the Mediterranean to Normandy and through to the Pacific.

30 May: Ambassador Bianchi Visits the State Department

Ambassador Bianchi presented an official protest from Dr. Salazar to the secretary of state. The leader of Portugal was highly incensed over U.S. insensitivity to his country's sovereignty and penned a protest in his own unique obfuscating prose. Although the meaning of each line might be hard to decipher, the tone of the entire letter was clear: Portugal would resist with force any attempt by the United States to occupy her territories allegedly to protect them against a potential German aggression. Salazar's letter is a good example of the problems translators found in almost all of his pronouncements, and why they generally were open to more than one interpretation. Because the original Portuguese was so contorted and hard to understand, the translators had to be forgiven, they were doing their best. In the second paragraph of his protest there is one long line:

> The Portuguese Government would not feel justified in addressing itself to the Government of the United States to refer to an address made by the Chief Executive of the Great American Nation to its citizens were it not for the fact that it contains direct references to Portuguese territories which, coupled with some of the theses set forth by President Roosevelt, and unaccompanied by any express mention of respect for the complete and centuries old sovereignty of Portugal over these territories,

are open to diverse interpretations and, therefore could not surprise the Portuguese people.[23]

The original letter, even in its original language, as typical of all of
Salazar's writings, was no easier to fathom for Portuguese speakers.
Hull answered the note the following day saying that he could not
"undertake to say a single word orally in reply . . . but that I would give
it my early attention."[24]

In addition to leaving the note with Hull, Bianchi emphasized the
fear felt by his government that Hitler would use the Fireside Chat as an
excuse for taking over the Azores and the Cape Verdes and perhaps
worse, invading Portugal. This was exactly what Secretary of War Stimson had warned Roosevelt might happen. Hull offered no excuses for
Roosevelt's speech but only pointed out that Hitler had found excuses
for invading some fifteen European countries, always after solemnly dis-
claiming any intention to attack them. He asserted a policy of neutrality
for each intended victim until he was ready to pounce on them. Germany was on a march of world conquest moving across Europe and the
Mediterranean, and each country still swearing its neutrality should
realize its imminent danger of being attacked whenever Hitler felt ready
to do so.

Finally on 10 June Hull answered categorically denying that the
United States had any aggressive designs on either the Azores or the
Cape Verdes. The Portuguese were unimpressed and still felt threatened
by many newspaper articles that expressed the contrary and that were
widely quoted in the German and Italian press. The fear in Lisbon was
that the Axis might be preparing to invade the country and the Azores to
"protect" them from a U.S. occupation. Later in June, when Germany
chose invading Russia instead of heading into Iberia, the Allies felt the
pressure was off; the Nazis would have their hands full for at least the
next few months. Unfortunately for the Allies, Salazar did not feel relieved at all.[25]

On 13 June Ambassador Bianchi requested another interview with
the secretary to deliver Salazar's reaction to the denial that the United
States planned to seize any Portuguese territory. The critical statement
in Salazar's complaint reads: "The Portuguese Government . . . can not
but regret that, in the presence of a precise request for clarification . . .
and involving the concrete revendication [sic] of the sovereign rights of
a friendly power, the Government of the United States of America
should not have gone beyond a generical [sic] and vague declaration

which did not even refer individually to the very country in question, and failed to assert whether or not they maintained the former declaration made by the Secretary of State."[26]

One thing is clear from the note: Salazar must have been close to the boiling point when he wrote it. However, Sumner Welles, the undersecretary of state who met with Bianchi at the State Department, was if anything cool and collected and was, like his boss Cordell Hull, more exasperated than angry with the Portuguese. From the State Department's point of view, Salazar was ignoring the fact that war was raging outside Portugal's borders and the very existence of all nations, neutral or otherwise, hung in the balance. Welles pointed out that the statements and declarations in Secretary Hull's note "could not have been clearer nor more specific, and it was consequently difficult for me to understand what was implied by the Portuguese Government when it used the phrase 'a generical and vague declaration.'" For the past nine years[27] the American government had scrupulously respected "the independence and integrity of other peoples, and a policy of non-aggression and of non-intervention."[28] Welles then delivered the coup de grâce to the protest asserting that "the policy of this Government . . . was based on the principle of self-defense and that no interpretation could legitimately [conclude that this] was a policy of aggression."[29]

Bianchi must have felt the wind leave his sails. He admitted that he knew all this and that most people in his government also knew it and trusted the United States, but many influential people in Portugal—in the press, in politics, in the armed forces, in commerce—were pro-German. They twisted every statement or newspaper article coming out of the United States to stir up fear that the Americans were planning an aggression against the Atlantic islands. To calm the situation he asked that more categorical assurances be given. Welles only answered that he would give further consideration to the minister's note and would advise him later of the conclusions reached by his government.

A month later, on 15 July, the German propaganda machine went into action denouncing Secretary Welles's statement, which did "not in the German view in any way contribute to clarifying the international atmosphere which is being disturbed by certain threats from across the ocean relating to the positions of European countries in the Atlantic regions." The Germans self-righteously complained that "the concept of international relations being based on treaties is in the process of being superseded" and that "Roosevelt places the right of self defense before all other considerations apparently including respect for existing constitutional and international rights . . . with a view to the occupation of any given area . . . that this formula of self-defense means that there is an intention whenever necessary to ignore the sovereign rights of other countries without scruple . . . and in the case of Portugal it means . . . an undermining of the assurances given by the White House to the Portuguese Government." It is amazing to see the United States denounced by the Nazis for what was established Nazi policy.[30]

May–June: Task Force Gray

After canceling the Azores operation, the Army's portion of Task Force Gray was kept intact and told it was headed "for action in Iceland, the Cape Verdes, or elsewhere."[31] Having been assembled for an operation in the middle of the Atlantic, the Task Force was now ordered to repack for a colder climate. The personal effect of high-level decisions and changes of plans on the troops who actually carry out the operations is rarely considered. In the case of Task Force Gray, the saga for the GIs stationed at Camp Stewart, Georgia, going on and off overseas alert, packing and unpacking, disposing of personal property such as automobiles, was recorded as a postscript from the Commanding Officer:

> In May a secret letter was received. . . . The unit was to be part of a task force, then forming, and was to draw its cold-weather clothing. But soon a new order came. The unit was now assigned to task Force Gray and was to prepare for tropical service. For the next two weeks, the troops were busy packing equipment, turning in cold-weather clothing, drawing tropical clothing, and requisitioning personnel. With all equipment packed and crated and, for the most part, loaded on trucks, the regiment waited for movement orders which never came. About July 1 the unit learned that the task force had been disbanded, three days later that it had been reconstituted.[32]

When the final decision was made, Task Force Gray was diverted at the very last minute to Iceland, where it was welcome, rather than to the Azores and an unknown reception. To restore himself in the good graces of Salazar, just in case he had gotten wind of the planned invasion, Roosevelt assured the leader of Portugal that we stood ready to aid in the defense of his country and its possessions "should your government express to me its belief that such aggression is imminent." Salazar answered on 29 July thanking Roosevelt for his offer of assistance but reminded him that England was still his paramount ally. Portugal however might request some defense material from the United States if it could not be obtained from England.

4 June: British Embassy, Washington, D.C.

The number two people of the State Department, Undersecretary Sumner Welles, and the British Embassy, Chargé d'Affaires Neville M. Butler, met to discuss the state of affairs regarding the Azores. Butler made these points: On 17 May, Welles informed the British ambassador that President Roosevelt was thinking of asking Salazar if he would welcome U.S. and British assistance in moving his government to and defending the Azores in the event of a German attack of the mainland. A week later, on 24 May, Halifax replied that British authorities had sounded out Salazar regarding the intentions of the Portuguese government if Germany should attack. Salazar's response seemed to hold out the possibility of an agreement regarding the Azores. Under the circumstances, the British thought the United States should not send any emissary to Lisbon to discuss the Azores independently for the time being, and that Halifax would keep Hull closely informed on the progress of discussions with the Portuguese.

On 28 May President Roosevelt told Halifax that he was anxious to reach a complete understanding with Churchill in regards to joint action in the Azores and the Cape Verdes in the event of Germany invading Spain or Portugal. Salazar should be induced to invite the protection of the United States and England for the Atlantic islands if a German action made this necessary. Roosevelt envisioned the British taking action immediately with the United States subsequently assuming the defense of the islands, relieving the British forces. Roosevelt thought it important that Salazar himself invite the U.S. government to take such action.

Churchill answered Roosevelt on 30 May explaining that should the Germans take steps to render Gibraltar unusable by the British Fleet or be obviously about to take such steps, the British were prepared to send expeditionary forces to occupy the Canary and Cape Verde Islands and one of the islands in the Azores, and would welcome the collaboration of a U.S. task force at any time—before, during, or after the occupation. If it were so desired, the defense of the islands could be turned over to the Americans. Because discussions were well under way between the British and Salazar over the eventuality of a withdrawal of the Portuguese government to the Azores, it would be best for the U.S. government not to approach the Portuguese until they had first agreed to the idea of transferring their government.

The progress of discussions between the British and Portuguese was summarized:

Last March secret military conversations took place on the subject of the defense of Portugal. The accepted hypothesis then was that Spain would resist any German attempt to cross the Pyrenees and invade Iberia. Portugal would be offered limited supplies of war materials and steps would be taken to defend the Atlantic islands. A provisional timetable was worked out for the dispatch of a British force to Portugal, but no firm commitment to send such a force was made. The Portuguese government took immediate steps to reinforce the Atlantic islands but on 21 May they said they disagreed with the accepted hypothesis on two points: first, that Spain not only would not resist a German invasion of her country, but that she might join in an attack on Portugal, and second that the British underestimated the scale and speed of the possible German attack. The memorandum also explained that no appeal for help from Portugal could be made until Portugal itself was invaded and by then any assistance would come too late.

On 30 May the British admitted the Portuguese scenario was possible and that in such circumstances, no British force could arrive in time to be of any assistance. Unfortunately, owing to commitments elsewhere, it was impossible to substantially improve the program for supplying war materiel agreed to in March and clearly there was no way to provide assistance early enough or on a large enough scale to be effective in helping to defend the mainland. However, if the nation was threatened the best policy would be to transfer the government to the Azores and only offer token resistance on the mainland. If the Portuguese agreed to accept this course, British authorities could help in a transfer to the Azores, facilitate the early delivery and installation of anti-aircraft defenses, train the necessary personnel and develop new airfields, furnish local naval defense equipment with personnel, and provide coast defense guns as well as install them in the Cape Verde Islands. Finally, the British government suggested that a plan of action should be agreed upon to go into effect in the event of a German threat to the country.

In revealing this information to the State Department, the British Embassy asked that it be kept highly confidential and that under no circumstances should any of it be disclosed to the Portuguese government. From the account given of the conversations between the Portuguese and British governments it was clear that the object of the British was the same as that of the president, in other words, to defend the Atlantic islands only at the invitation of the Portuguese government. The position had been compromised when on 30 May the Portuguese ambassador protested to Anthony Eden statements made by President Roosevelt and private individuals that the United States should take over the Azores or the Cape Verde Islands. There was a feeling in Portugal that the United States was planning some aggressive action against the islands. The ambassador's note went on to state that Portugal had no political commitments with the United States and had to consider any U.S. action which ignored Portuguese sovereignty over the islands—even if based on a presumption of a German intent to occupy the islands—as an act of aggression "from which the logical reactions would naturally follow." The ambassador urged that this unfortunate situation which had arisen between his country and the United States should be resolved soon "and that any steps should be avoided which might still further complicate matters or disturb Portuguese public opinion."[33]

Eden replied that the Portuguese should feel that the safety of the islands had been strengthened by the president's speech. The ambassador did not agree with this interpretation and added that the Portuguese people could not accept such a detached view. Furthermore, unless care was taken, the Germans might use the incident for their own propaganda purposes. Because Portugal was allied with England and had no political commitments with the United States, Eden felt that they should do all the negotiating, and any possibility of U.S. intervention should be kept in the background at least for the time being.

18 June: Churchill to Roosevelt

British Intelligence kept reporting that the Germans were gearing up to start a big operation, with one good possibility being against Portugal and the Azores. Frustrated by the lack of progress in dealing with Salazar, Churchill proposed to change from a watch and wait stance to action before the Germans had a chance to strike first:

The British Government desired to know whether the Government of the United States would be prepared immediately to undertake joint staff conversations with the British Government to agree upon plans covering the occupation of the Azores, such plans to be contingent upon the unwillingness of the Prime Minister of Portugal to request assistance of the British and United States Governments in the defense of the independence and integrity of those islands.[34]

The State Department records do not show an answer to Churchill's request. However, three days later Hitler ended the suspense when he revealed where the operation would be—not into Iberia but an all-out invasion of Russia. The pressure was off the free-world's leaders to take immediate action in the Atlantic. There was no need to worry about the Germans seizing the Azores and disrupting marine traffic. Strong action by the Allies was no longer necessary, at least for the time being, and now the job was to convince Salazar by diplomatic means that concession was "an offer he couldn't refuse" and allow the bases to be built.

22 June: Barbarossa

Operation Barbarossa started in the early dawn—two million German soldiers crossed the Russian border with 2,770 aircraft providing air cover. This was to be an important step in Hitler's plans for world conquest as he revealed to his war cabinet:

1. defeat of the Soviet Union in three or four months,
2. followed by a three pronged attack (a) through Bulgaria and Turkey into Syria, Iraq, and the Persian Gulf, (b) through the Caucasus into Iran, and (c) through Libya into Egypt. Afghanistan becomes German by this scenario threatening British India.
3. Japanese attack through the Malay Peninsula and Burma threatening India. Japan must follow this route to avoid the Philippines and possibly provoking the United States into war.
4. Conquest of Gibraltar, Northwest Africa, and presumably the Atlantic islands to achieve an "offensive stance against America."[35]

These ambitious plans to bring Europe and Asia under the control of the Axis powers were preconditioned on "all continental European problems" being solved in 1941 because the United States was expected to be in a position to intervene the following year. Because there was no immediate danger of a German move to the Azores, Roosevelt agreed with General Marshall to disband the task force, but insisted that planning for an eventual Azores expedition should continue.[36]

7 July: Iceland and Washington, D.C.

U.S. Navy forces arrived in Iceland with the Marine Corps First Brigade relieving the British. The occupation of Greenland and Iceland was backed by U.S. Naval Task Force 19, made up of four battleships, thirteen destroyers, and eight supply ships or more than the entire German fleet in the Atlantic. The northern convoy route to England was made more secure, VLR bomber aircraft would now protect shipping.

Roosevelt thought this might be the proper time to restore harmonious relations with Portugal. He wrote Churchill that he planned to write a personal note "couched in a very friendly and informal tone which will make clear to Dr. Salazar that this Government has never had the slightest intention of encroachment in any form upon Portuguese sovereignty over the Azores or the other Portuguese colonial possessions . . . that this Government will be prepared to take such action as may be required to assist Portugal in the event that Germany undertakes any aggressive move against the Azores."[37]

If the United States had carried out Operation Lifebelt before Hitler decided to go into Russia, would Germany have put Barbarossa on a back burner instead of Operation Felix and invaded the Iberian Peninsula? Our good ally England would have found itself in an untenable position saddled with, or at least making a pretense of, defending Portugal. The entire Iberian Peninsula including Gibraltar would have fallen into German hands, as well as most probably North Africa, but the Azores would be Allied controlled and the "black hole" in the Atlantic covered. All this might not have changed the outcome of the war, but one certain consequence would have been the United States's going to war earlier.

8 July: Berlin

Hitler wanted to react forcibly to the occupation of Iceland but realistically he could do nothing because any operation to dislodge U.S. troops would stand little chance of success. The Kriegsmarine and Luftwaffe would have to transport and supply an invading German force traveling over hostile North Atlantic waters controlled by the Royal Navy, an impossible task given the limited resources and needs for both services elsewhere. But the Azores were another matter. The German Navy had not given up its idea of establishing bases on the Azores and was ready to "react strongly against any American action against the islands."

Despite his professed shock that the United States, a neutral, should have taken such a belligerent stand against Germany, Hitler told the OKW and the OKM to avoid any direct confrontation while operations were going ahead on the Russian front. This was not the time to antagonize the United States: unrestricted submarine warfare against U.S. shipping must be postponed.

9 July: OKM Navy and the Führer in Wolfsschanze

With the U.S. patrol force out in strength and in numbers far greater than the entire German fleet, the OKM considered the United States to be virtually at war with Germany. The U.S. naval route to England (Newfoundland–Greenland–Iceland) had effectively checkmated Germany's "tonnage war." Raeder thought the United States's action in occupying Iceland only the first step in going to the Azores, Dakar, and the Cape Verdes. He asked for a formal declaration of war but Hitler did not want to provoke the United States, at least not then, adding that "he would never call a submarine commander to account if he torpedoes an American ship by mistake."[38]

Raeder warned that in this connection no guarantee could be given, that a naval commander on wartime patrol should not be held responsible for a mistake. Hitler's answer according to the transcription of the meeting must have been very simple and direct: "The Führer agrees."[39]

German newspapers denounced our occupation of Iceland. Headlines read: "Invasion of Iceland; Roosevelt provokes war; Stab-in-the-back attempt by the U.S. president against Europe; Arm-in-arm with

Bolshevik mass murderers; Roosevelt has irrevocably torn up the Monroe Doctrine."[40]

The Germans were satisfied that the pressure they were putting on Portugal to remain neutral was really working. Portugal was sending troops to the Azores to reinforce the small garrison stationed there, ostensibly to defend the islands against an invasion, but from whom? Germany thought the Allies who in turn were sure it was against the Germans. Portuguese President António Carmona made high profile visits to view the Azores defenses in July and August; Salazar flattered the Germans by describing the visit as Portugal's "contribution to the defense of Europe."[41]

14 July: President Roosevelt to Dr. Salazar

Roosevelt turned on all of his irresistible charm in his letter to Salazar. He flattered the prime minister with assurances that he was writing him an entirely personal and informal letter in the belief that in this way he could put an end to the regrettable misunderstandings that had arisen between the two governments. Never mind the twenty-five thousand men of Task Force Gray packing and repacking, swapping the tropical gear thought proper for an invasion of the Azores (somebody should have checked *National Geographic*) to the warm woolies needed for Iceland. With the pressure off thanks to Hitler's commitment to a Russian invasion this was a good time for the United States to work its way into Salazar's good graces. Just to make sure that Hitler did not change his mind about invading the Azores, Acting Secretary of State Sumner Welles issued a warning that Portuguese sovereignty over the islands must be maintained inviolate or U.S. intervention might follow.[42]

Roosevelt insisted that the United States consistently upheld the right of Portuguese sovereign control over her territories, although the State Department waffled on this commitment over the next two years. Roosevelt blamed the troubles on the press "in false reports deliberately circulated by propaganda emanating from governments which have desired to impair the traditional relations between our two countries." If ever the Portuguese government felt threatened, the United States stood ready to come to its defense, reinforced with troops from Brazil, a UN ally.

Ending on a pull-the-heartstrings note, Roosevelt wrote he felt "particularly chagrined" that his attitude towards Portuguese sovereignty should be impugned. After all, he knew about the Azores first hand from a visit in World War I and still had fond memories of the islands. On 4 July 1917 a German submarine surfaced in Ponta Delgada harbor, São Miguel, and fired on the city. Portugal was already at war with Germany and asked for our assistance to defend the islands. The USS *Orion* arrived to drive off the submarine and became the first ship in a newly established supply base, which eventually held six ships, including a repair ship and submarine-killers. Ponta Delgada was the first foreign controlled military base ever built in the Azores, but it was instituted at the request of Portugal when both countries were allies. The president visited the Azores in his role as assistant secretary of the Navy to check the bases made available to U.S. ships—the port of Horta as a fueling base and Ponta Delgada as a naval base. As soon as the war was over, the U.S. forces were withdrawn "without the slightest detriment to the sovereign jurisdiction of the Portuguese government."

Salazar answered two weeks later, again in one of his special rambling messages that went on and on but did leave a distinct impression of understanding and joy with the continued friendship between the two nations. The final word that Roosevelt's letter truly did accomplish its goals was reported by the British ambassador to Washington relaying the good news from the British ambassador in Lisbon who had spoken directly to Dr. Salazar. The Portuguese leader felt "great satisfaction and pleasure with the letter which the president had sent him. The British government felt that the president's letter had completely removed the misunderstandings which had occurred and had greatly facilitated the British policy in Portugal."[43]

25 July: OKM Navy and the Führer in Wolfsschanze

It was obvious that Hitler had given much thought to the possibility of U.S. involvement in the war and of occupying the Portuguese and Spanish islands.[44] "After the eastern campaign I reserve for myself the right to take severe action against the United States . . . As soon as the United States occupies Portuguese or Spanish Islands, I will march into Spain. From there I will bring tank and infantry divisions into North

Africa in order to secure this area." Three armored divisions waiting
north of the Pyrenees could march into the Iberian Peninsula and
invade Portugal, just as soon as Spain accorded Germany transit rights.

Raeder repeated his need for air reconnaissance by the Luftwaffe,
never implemented by Air Marshall Goering despite promises to do so.
The Luftwaffe considered flying reconnaissance over the Atlantic and
searching out merchant ships for U-boats an inferior task because it did
not show immediate results: no enemy planes shot down, no bombs
dropped over British cities, no medals. Reconnaissance service lacked
glory and did nothing to promote the careers of Luftwaffe pilots who
would much rather be taking on Spitfires. The Führer's solution: he
will see to it that decorations are given to reconnaissance pilots.[45]

10–15 August:
Placentia Bay, Newfoundland

One of the most important meetings of modern times took place when
the two allied leaders met secretly in Newfoundland to formulate and
sign the Atlantic Charter. Accompanied only by their chief military and
diplomatic advisers, Prime Minister Churchill arrived on the British
battleship *Prince of Wales* and President Roosevelt on the U.S. cruiser
Augusta. They declared their countries sought no new territory; their
only goal in victory was the destruction of Nazi and fascist oppression in
Europe.[46]

The statement of aims of the Allies would become the cornerstone
of the United Nations: the right of peoples to choose their own form of
government; no aggrandizement; no territorial changes opposed by the
peoples concerned; access to trade and raw materials; improved labor
standards, economic advancement, and social security; international
security; freedom of the seas; and disarmament.

Eventually the discussion came around to the Azores. Roosevelt
and Churchill agreed that Salazar's letter had given permission to
occupy the islands in case Germany attacked Portugal. Churchill did
not want to wait for the aggression and urged Roosevelt to join him
in Operation Pilgrim, that to avert the German threat to the Iberian
peninsula the British would seize the Canary Islands and the Americans would provide protective occupation of the Azores. Churchill
wanted to go ahead with Pilgrim in mid-September but Roosevelt
would commit his part only if and when requested to do so by Portugal.

Although denied by Portugal, Roosevelt maintained that a request for U.S. protection in the event of a German invasion had already been received.[47]

Churchill agreed to seek a formal invitation from Salazar for Pilgrim while at the same time the British military staff was ordered to work with General Marshall and his staff on plans to occupy the Azores. The Joint Chiefs left Newfoundland with the impression that Operation Pilgrim was a firm commitment, and that the Azores were now on a front burner.

After returning to Washington, Roosevelt had second thoughts about Operation Pilgrim. He felt that without a direct German threat or an invitation from Salazar, there was no need to mount an operation against the islands. It was clear that Russia was going to be a greater problem for Germany than originally thought, and the last thing Hitler wanted was to start a risky military venture in the Atlantic with his armies bogged down in the east. Roosevelt urged Churchill to call off his Canary Islands operation as well, to wait for some sign of provocation from the Nazis. Churchill reluctantly agreed to wait. Allied anxiety about a German move across the Pyrenees into Iberia faded by the end of the year as Hitler withdrew large forces from southern France, transferring them to the Russian front.

September

Hitler always had a soft spot in his heart for the only other people he considered to be on a racial par to the Germans—the Anglo-Saxons of the British Isles. Having called off a cross-channel assault, he still seriously believed that the British reciprocated with the same warm feelings towards the Germans. He was willing to extend a guarantee to England to retain her colonies in return for recognition of German hegemony on the continent and return of Germany's African colonies. The two would divide up France's possessions and join together against the United States: "I will not live to see it, but I am happy for the German people [Volk] that it will some day witness how Germany and England united will line up against America."[48]

30 November

Despite the growing problems with the Russian campaign, the OKW finished the planning for Operation Felix and worked out a detailed timetable. The date to start the operation was left open pending Franco's approval. The immediate tasks of the German Navy were to defend Gibraltar after it had been conquered; assist in the occupation and defense of the Canaries; and occupy the ports of Vigo, Ferrol, Cadiz, and Malaga. Then on 11 December, Field Marshall Wilhelm Keitel ordered Felix canceled "as the political conditions no longer obtain."[49]

Franco was refusing to go along with the operation, making it too costly in men and materiel to go through Spain against opposition, attack Gibraltar with unfriendly forces in front and behind, and mount an amphibious invasion against the Canary Islands. Besides, the Eastern Campaign, which was supposed to be over by fall, demanded all the manpower that Germany could muster.[50]

7 December: Pearl Harbor

The Japanese attack on Pearl Harbor took not only President Roosevelt by surprise but also Hitler and his General Staff. Roosevelt asked Congress to declare war against Japan—which it did immediately. The idea of carrying out an air carrier strike over three thousand miles of open ocean and annihilating a battle fleet was a new concept in modern warfare, equally bold as anything the Germans had done on the ground in their lightning conquest of Europe. That Japan had gone to war against the United States was more or less expected, but the timing and overwhelming success of the Pearl Harbor operation was positive proof to Germany that the United States was, first, incompetent; second, woefully unprepared for war even though every person on earth knew that war would come to the United States sooner or later; and third, that Americans had no heart for warfare.

11 December: Reactions to Pearl Harbor

Soon after the declaration of war against Japan, Germany and Italy came to the aid of their ally and declared war on the United States. The Nazis never did have a high opinion of the capabilities of U.S. society, which they considered mongrelized, and were convinced that a change in status from simple animosity to belligerency would not make any difference in the outcome of the war. U.S. armed forces were technologically inferior to every one in Europe—after all, it was reported that the basic infantry weapon was still the single-shot breech loading Enfield rifle (used in World War I) and even more laughable, due to the shortage of even these outmoded guns, draftees were training with wooden models. It would take the United States months or even years to mobilize its war industry and to properly equip and train its armed forces. How could the United States ever be made ready to wage a two-ocean war against the technologically superior and battle-hardened troops of the Axis powers? If Germany had any questions about our fighting abilities, the Pearl Harbor disaster was all the proof needed that the United States would never be a decisive factor in the outcome of the war.

There was an added advantage to a Japan–United States war. The German General Staff knew that our first priority would be to fight the Japanese in the Pacific, that all resources would go west to where our principal interests lay. Having a state of war with the United States but no active engagements for several years would definitely serve Germany's interests.

But the Germans were wrong in underestimating the United States's will and capability to fight. The United States mobilized and trained its armed forces more quickly than the Axis thought possible. Industry was retooled for defense, and guns and "Liberty Ships" were rolling out of Henry Kaiser's California shipyards faster than the U-boats could sink them. Antisubmarine defenses were eventually organized and strengthened. Despite German denigration, U.S. material support and armed forces were the decisive factor in the war. With war supplies arriving in massive amounts England was saved and Russia, with U.S. manufactured arms, was more than a match for Hitler's no longer irresistible forces. The tide of the war was slowly changing; victory for the Axis was no longer such a sure thing.

With the United States in the war, *Projekt Amerika* became even more important for the Germans but "the cat was out of the bag" and word of the proposed operation was no longer secret. Washington already knew that Admiral Raeder had reassured his admirals on the eve of the Russian invasion that the Führer still was in favor of occupying the Azores but it would have to wait until autumn.[51]

After Germany declared war on the United States there was no longer any need for niceties. Unrestricted submarine warfare began with a vengeance, and caught the country completely unprepared. Torpedoing of U.S. ships in American coastal waters reached an intolerably high level at the start of war, called the worst naval defeat in U.S. history, and certainly the most disgraceful phase of the Battle of the Atlantic.[52]

12 December: Berlin

Admiral Raeder briefed Hitler and the General Staff, stating that the situation in the Atlantic would be eased by Japan's intervention. U.S. battleships and cargo would be transferred to the Pacific, putting greater strain on British transport ships and cutting down on protection of convoys. This called for intensified U-boat warfare. The pocket battleships *Scharnhorst* and *Gneisenau* would patrol for targets in the Atlantic as well. The situation could be improved if Germany moved into French West Africa and seized the port of Dakar.

The Führer asked:

1. Does the OKM believe the enemy will in the near future occupy the Azores, the Cape Verdes and attack Dakar to win back the prestige that was lost in the Pacific?
2. Will the United States and England abandon their military campaigns in East Asia for a time in order to crush Germany and Italy first?

The OKM Navy did not believe such steps were imminent. The United States would, he felt, concentrate all her strength in the Pacific and could not withdraw her fleet without being exposed to further Japanese attacks.

Raeder complained that the Navy's basic supply of oil was slashed 50 percent, a serious handicap for it to remain an effective fighting force. Hitler explained that Romania, Germany's principal source of petroleum, had been temporarily cut off because they were demanding payment in gold. He promised to straighten the situation out.[53]

16 December: Lisbon

Salazar appealed to Churchill for military aid, pointing out as especially serious the lack of fighter aircraft in mainland Portugal, because all thirty Gladiators had been sent to the Azores.[54] Despite the facts that Operation Felix had been called off, which he might not have known, and the Russians stopping the *Panzer* armies short of Moscow and Leningrad, he still felt the threat of a German invasion of the Atlantic islands and the mother country was strong. England had stored sixteen Curtiss Mohawk IV fighter aircraft originally sent by the United States to aid France and now they were transferred to Portugal. Although the Mohawks were a vast improvement over the Gladiators, they still could not compete with the aircraft being flown by the Germans and the Allies. However, England, at least, had fulfilled her promise to modernize Portugal's armed forces, bringing the capabilities of the Air Force closer to the 1940s than they ever had been before.

The British were also actively pursuing confidential talks with Portugal regarding its role in the war. The results were summarized in a memorandum from the British ambassador in Washington to the State Department. First, Portugal did not want to abandon its neutral status —except, of course, if Germany invaded. However, the Portuguese government did agree to collaborate with England and in July plans were elaborated for the Atlantic islands. As a result of these discussions the British Foreign Office considered preparations for Anglo-Portuguese cooperation in the Atlantic Islands were well advanced.[55]

22 December: Washington, D.C.

Churchill landed at Hampton Roads, Virginia, after a ten-day Atlantic crossing. With both democracies at war, it was essential to consult, set priorities, coordinate individual efforts, and make sure that all tasks were directed to the same war aims. Churchill was flown immediately to Washington where he spent the next three weeks as Roosevelt's guest in the White House. The meeting, known as the Arcadia Conference, was the first of several held by the two leaders through the course of the war.[56]

The two got along well. Churchill and Roosevelt saw eye-to-eye on just about everything for, as the prime minister wrote to his wife after his first several days in the White House, "All is very good indeed; and my plans are going through. The Americans are magnificent in their breadth of view."[57]

With no time to waste, their first meeting took place the evening Churchill arrived. The prime minister was accompanied by Lords

Beaverbrook and Halifax; with the president were Cordell Hull, Sumner Welles, and Harry Hopkins. The first item discussed dealt with Germany's next move if either the Wehrmacht conquered or became bogged down in Russia. All agreed that if Russia was beaten then the Nazis might next start Operation Felix. They knew that Felix was shelved but could be revived if the Wehrmacht overcame the unexpectedly stiff Russian resistance.[58]

The success of the British forces in Libya over the Axis opened up the prospect of the Allies "joining hands" with Free French forces in Northwest Africa. This possibility alone might be good enough reason for Hitler to revive Felix despite what happened in Russia: a chance to outflank the British and gain control of Morocco and Gibraltar. To prevent this eventuality, it was agreed that the first combined Allied operation would be to land in Morocco, that it was "vital to forestall the Germans in North West Africa and in the Atlantic Islands." The decision was made that the first U.S. Expeditionary Force of World War II would land in North Africa.

The Combined Chiefs of Staff had one more good reason, beyond an antisubmarine base, to covet the Azores. The Allies agreed that the eventual liberation of the European continent would begin with landings in North Africa and go on to Italy and eventually France. The Azores would be necessary as a mid-Atlantic air base for direct flights for transport planes rather than their following the longer and more costly northern route via Greenland–Iceland or the southern Brazil–Africa route resulting in a considerable savings in time, aviation fuel, and personnel. Admiral William D. Leahy, Roosevelt's chief of staff, calculated that over a period of six months (November 1943–April 1944), if the route via the Azores was in full operation:

1. approximately 51.5 million gallons of high octane aviation fuel would be saved, enough to support fifty-four hundred heavy bomber sorties per month over the same period, or the equivalent of one month's consumption by the combined operations of the RAF and the USAAF (United States Army Air Force) in and from England;

2. savings in engine hours of each bomber ferried to England sufficient to permit six or more additional combat missions before engine overhaul;

3. release of approximately 150 transport aircraft for service in India-China-Burma or other theaters where they are urgently needed;

4. fifteen thousand trained ground personnel released for duty in the combat zones.

The fuel required for the indirect routes was being taken from the USAAF Training Program, which had to be curtailed as a result. The flow of replacement combat crews to theaters of operation was reduced substantially and the United States's combat effectiveness was suffering. The Joint Chiefs now had strong arguments for the need to get into the Azores by any means, hopefully diplomatic, but failing that by outright invasion.[59]

24 December: Washington, D.C.

U.S. newspapers had been reporting details of the historic meeting between Roosevelt and Churchill, not omitting the expressed need for air bases in the Azores. Salazar was upset once more and had the Portuguese ambassador deliver another protest. Giving Roosevelt the benefit of the doubt, he blamed the reports on a campaign in the press to influence public opinion and pressure the government into seizing the Azores and Cape Verdes.[60]

With the United States at war and its very existence at stake, Undersecretary of State Sumner Welles saw no need to be overly diplomatic with Ambassador Bianchi. First of all he maintained, most of the vicious rumors that circulated worldwide were initiated in Berlin, intended to rattle both the Allies and any remaining neutral powers. If Portugal was upset with press reports, it should direct its anger not at the United States but to Berlin. The United States fully respected Portugal's desire to remain out of the war but scores of other nations which, "by trusting to their neutrality and by trusting to the tenets of international law, had one after the other made it possible for Hitler to occupy them, to ravage them and to place their peoples in a state of abject slavery." Ending on an upbeat, which seemed a little out of place after his stern lecture to the ambassador, Welles added that nothing he said should "be regarded as having been said in an unfriendly spirit, but . . . the best kind of friendship at this moment was to speak frankly." The time for polite diplomacy was finished; Washington's foreign policy had gone to war.[61]

31 December: Washington, D.C.

At the Arcadia Conference the CCS mapped out a master plan for the war, the U.S.–British Grand Strategy (A-B2). When they had met earlier in February discussions were only general with many alternative scenarios laid on the table because the United States, although supporting England in her war efforts, was not yet a fighting partner. With the United States no longer ostensibly neutral the wraps were off; at A-B2 there were no limits, the United States and England were fighting allies. The Combined Chiefs could define a grand strategy for fighting and winning the war.

First, it was agreed that the statement at A-B1 that Germany was the predominant member of the Axis powers still held, the Nazis were the prime enemy, and their defeat would be the key to eventual victory. Once Germany was defeated, the collapse of Italy and Japan must follow. A cardinal principal of A-B strategy was the use of minimum forces in other theaters only to safeguard Allied vital interests so that the major effort could be devoted to operations against Germany. Steps to be taken in 1942 included:

1. Maintenance of Communications.
2. Part I listed the main sea routes which must be secured: the United States to England followed by the Pacific and Panama Canal, the Atlantic and U.S. coastal traffic, and ending with "open up and secure the Mediterranean route."
3. Part II listed the main air routes to be secured, mostly flights from the United States including two routes to England. The first, via Newfoundland, Greenland, and Iceland, was already established or being built. The second that had to be established was via the Azores and considered essential to support operations in North Africa, the Mediterranean, and the eventual landings in France. The Allies agreed that the Atlantic islands were essential to pursue the war against Germany, and that in addition to Greenland and Iceland, the Azores had to be taken over.[62]

U.S. policy towards Portugal and the Azores during 1941 was inconlsistent, but not as inconsistent as Churchill's. Roosevelt resisted the prime minister's frequent urging to make a preemptive move, feeling that in the long run such an action might provoke Germany into invading Iberia. Churchill's attitudes towards the Azores changed frequently, from doing nothing at the start of the year to taking over the islands himself, or having the United States do it, or do it jointly, and finally back to restraint at the end of the year. Salazar had to play the most complicated game of all, balancing his country's existence between the warring powers, showing a pleasant face to each, not antagonizing anyone, and making both Germany and England feel that Portugal was at least sympathetically on their side.

For the Axis he showed off his solidarity with Spain and flattery for its military successes. With the British, he swore to abide by the treaty of perpetual friendship and alliance then already over five hundred years old. With the United States, he lectured on the sovereignty and importance of neutrality for his country. General Marshall and Roosevelt took seriously Salazar's promise to defend his country against an invasion by anyone as they monitored Portuguese troop reinforcements to the Azores and agreed that a forced landing might be costly.

Much as they may have wanted to, Hitler and the High Command had too many fish to fry to give the Azores a high priority. The Navy wanted the Azores to give it a commanding position in the Atlantic and a simpler way to beat England than an amphibious Channel crossing. The admirals might have been correct, but we will never know thanks to Hitler, who listened to the OKW rather than the OKM. Franco's refusal to go along with Operation Felix certainly reinforced Hitler's decision to go ahead with Barbarossa. We can only wonder how differently the war might have gone if the German Army had switched priorities and crossed the Pyrenees first, and put off fording the Vistula River. If that had happened, with the United States's commitment to keep the Nazis out of the Azores, the United States might have gone to war much earlier than Pearl Harbor.

The year ended with lots of smoke and many high-level conferences, with threats to seize the Azores but no action taken by anyone. At the end of the year, only six U-boats were on Atlantic patrol, all near the archipelago. It was a master game of "chicken" and fear of unintended consequences. England was in no position to confront Germany in Iberia and Hitler was afraid that any German force sent to the Azores would be isolated by superior Allied naval strength. The year of 1941 was one for watchful waiting trying to fathom what the other side was going to do and doing nothing in the meantime. As regards the Azores the order of the day was, again, watchful waiting.[63]

FIVE

THE U-BOATS'
HAPPY WAR, 1942

> For six or seven months the U-boats ravaged American waters
> almost uncontrolled, and in fact almost brought us to the
> disaster of an indefinite prolongation of the war.
>
> WINSTON CHURCHILL, *The Second World War*

Soon after a state of war was declared, Admiral Dönitz ordered the first
group of U-boats to head for U.S. waters. They arrived to find the
United States not only completely unprepared but with no contingency
plans to counter what should have been an expected assault on shipping. German submarines openly attacked oil tankers and anything
else afloat without fear of reprisal. No more formality of waiting until a
ship was out in the open sea. Dönitz knew that his large U-boats, the
1,050-ton IXB and the 1,120-ton IXC could make the round trip over the
three thousand miles of open Atlantic from the new French base at
Lorient to New York Harbor and arrive with enough diesel fuel to do
one or two weeks worth of marauding. The IXB would have enough
fuel for six or seven days, whereas the larger IXC had fifteen days, supply before returning to France. If the U-boats and their supply subs, the
milchkuhen, had sailed from Flores, the westernmost island of the
Azores, at least one additional week would be added for operations in
U.S. waters. Transatlantic distances to Newfoundland would have been
shaved to eleven hundred miles and about twenty-two hundred miles
to the United States's East Coast.[1]

Dönitz's attack on U.S. shipping, Operation *Paukenschlag* (Drumbeat), proved devastating. The U-boat offensive, which lasted from January to July 1942, found a shooting gallery—unprotected U.S. ships were
sitting ducks for torpedo or surface attack as the submarines roamed

Principal U-Boats of the German Navy in World War II

TYPE	SURFACE DISPLACEMENT (TONS)	RANGE (NAUTICAL MILES) AT SPEED (KNOTS)	MAXIMUM SPEED (KNOTS)
I	862	6,700 (12 sf*), 80 (4 uw**)	17.7 sf, 8.2 uw
VIIB	753	8,700 (10 sf), 6,500 (12 sf), 72 (4 uw)	17.2 sf, 8.0 uw
IXC	1,120	13,450 (10 sf), 11,000 (12 sf), 63 (4 uw)	18.2 sf, 7.3 uw
IXD2	1,612	31,500 (10 sf), 23,700 (12 sf), 57 (4 uw)	19.2 sf, 6.9 uw
XXI	1,621	15,500 (10 sf), 11,150 (12 sf), 285 (6 uw)	15.5 sf, 17.5 uw
XXIII	232	1,350 (9 sf), 175 (4 uw)	9.5 sf, 12.5 uw

Source: Dönitz, *Memoirs: Ten Years and Twenty Days,* 479.
* sf = surface
** uw = underwater

unmolested up and down the East Coast. Approximately four hundred cargo ships were sunk in this unheralded period of battle, one that has been called an "Atlantic Pearl Harbor" except that in terms of ships and men lost it was much worse than Pearl Harbor.[2]

Although the U-boats were having a field day off the United States's East Coast, the story was different on the other side of the Atlantic. By 1 January, only six U-boats remained on patrol in the Atlantic, all near the Azores and well out of range of Allied land bases. The British, who had been fighting U-boats for over two years and developed the technology and tactics to keep them in check, had plenty of good advice to give to the U.S. admirals, if they had been asked. This is one of the war's greatest mysteries and might be explained by acute anglophobia by the Joint Chiefs—not the first or the last time in the war that communication failed between the two United Nations powers. Admiral Roskill of the Royal Navy wrote:

> While the enemy was achieving enormous, and one may feel largely avoidable, destruction in the west, three thousand miles

away to the east his experiences were very different. British anti-submarine tactics and weapons, both surface and air, were improving rapidly, and, unknown to the enemy, radar had arrived in a form capable of being fitted in escort vessels and aircraft. The activities of our aircraft over the Bay of Biscay transit routes and the counter-blows of our air and surface convoy escorts were causing the enemy serious losses and much anxiety. The surface escort of Convoy OS18 sank U-82 on February 6, that of the troop convoy WS17 dealt similarly with U-587 in March, and in April U-252 was destroyed by the escort of GG82.[3]

13 February: Berlin

The OKM reported good results in the war in the Atlantic but pointed out again that submarine construction had not yet received a high priority. Workmen were drafted from the shipyards, not enough material was consigned to U-boat construction, which fell to sixteen to seventeen per month, a number entirely inadequate to maintain the strength of the fleet and inflict maximum damage on the Allies. Churchill, Raeder pointed out, spoke time and time again of destruction of shipping being his greatest worry and unless controlled could be the principal factor in losing the war. With England and the United States building seven million tons of merchant ships this year, the Axis powers must sink a monthly total of six hundred thousand tons to offset the increased production. Hitler listened sympathetically but promised nothing. For the first quarter of the year, the monthly steel quota was cut from 170,000 tons to 153,000 tons and then even lower in the second quarter to 150,000. All work on cruisers and larger ships was canceled. U-boat construction was not increased. The war in Russia was demanding more and more of Germany's resources.[4]

17 February: Seville, Spain

In a meeting of the Iberian dictators, Franco warned Salazar that any landing of Allied forces in Portugal would be considered an act of aggression and Spain would be forced to take whatever steps were necessary in her own defense. At the time, Franco was convinced the Axis was going to win the war and obviate the need for a German operation against Portugal. His warning was merely frosting on the cake, taking the opportunity to show Salazar who was really in charge in Iberia. Salazar was already frightened of the prospect of a German invasion, so Franco's adding more threats did nothing to calm down the Portuguese prime minister.

Salazar now had more to worry about. He needed to be scrupulously neutral, for if the Germans did not invade Portugal then he might expect their supernumeraries, the Spaniards, to show up instead. It was no wonder he felt it necessary to behave properly negotiating with England over the Azores bases, to fall back on the excuse of international law and the 1373 treaty of mutual friendship and assistance to justify any concession. His much preferred modus operandi was inaction—do nothing that might antagonize his bullying neighbor or the barbarian Nazis. He could negotiate endlessly with England, with whom he was treaty-bound, but he could find no legal justification to even discuss cooperation with the United States.

The meeting in Seville ended on an upbeat; the two leaders pledged a meaningless alliance of mutual defense to come to each other's aid in the event of aggression. Salazar remarked after the meeting to a U.S. journalist that "Spain will turn back from a ghastly, incalculable mistake," so at least one important consequence of the meeting was not reported to the press. Salazar apparently convinced Franco to remain neutral, to play down his cozy relationship with the Axis, and to start thinking about the possibility that the Allies might win. Operation Torch, the Allied landings, and conquest of North Africa, which came later in the year, finally convinced Franco that his Iberian neighbor was on the right track, and that he had better start convincing the world that he too was completely neutral or at least not pro-Axis.

29 March: São Miguel, Azores

High-flying aircraft passed over the Azores, too high for identification but according to the U.S. Consul at Ponta Delgada "one heard by me about 6 A.M. March 27 sounded like a German motor."[5] The planes were later identified by the Portuguese military as a VLR Ju-92 gathering reconnaissance information needed for an operation against the islands. Although the operation never took place, the flights had long-lasting repercussions in Lisbon, as well as Washington and London. For the Allies it was clear that the Germans were still thinking of invading the Azores, so it might be time to take some decisive action of their own to prevent the U-boat bases from becoming a reality and fulfilling Churchill's biggest nightmare.

Portuguese authorities in the Azores were upset by the high-flying aircraft, although they were not certain of their nationality. Air space had been violated, and something had to be done to show they were still in command. The military governor of São Miguel island transmitted an order to the civil governor of Ponta Delgada dated 29 March which was passed on to Mr. Dawson, the U.S. consul who in turn re-layed it to the Department of State:

> 1. All foreigners without exception are required to concentrate themselves on the football field of the local high school following any firing or signal of three shots fired by artillery. . . .
> 2. All foreigners including consular officers found outside the concentration field one hour after the beginning of the concentration will be considered spies and will be executed. . . .
> 3. Any foreigner who . . . is unable to present himself in the concentration camp must . . . consider himself a prisoner in the place where he is.[6]

Dawson pointed out to the governor that in case of emergency he was expected by recognized international custom to remain in the consulate to protect or to destroy codes, confidential correspondence, and the like. Before he could comply with the order from the Portuguese authorities he was requesting instructions from Washington.

Two days later the local government ordered all foreigners residing on the island outside of the capital to establish their residence within the city by 4 April or suffer imprisonment or deportation. Because there were few citizens of any country besides the United States living on the island, the order primarily affected the ninety-four registered U.S. citizens and hundreds more born in the United States who could claim citizenship. The order was issued at the request of "the military authorities due to fear of fifth column activities in the event of an invasion attempt."[7]

The State Department ordered Ambassador Bert Fish to convey the U.S. government's strong protest immediately to the Portuguese Foreign Office. Fish said he tried his best, but the foreign minister was out of town for Easter and when he returned to Lisbon he seemed to be "indisposed." Finally, a week after he started trying, Fish succeeded in seeing Costa Carneiro, chief of the political section, who was sympathetic and implied that "there had been an excess of zeal on the part of the insular authorities." Asked for an explanation why such severe measures had been applied in the Azores, Costa Carneiro said he knew of no specific reason "except that spring is the season when new campaigns are launched."[8]

On 13 April former Minister of War General Passos e Sousa arrived in Ponta Delgada for the express purpose of investigating the conduct of the military commander. After his arrival military censorship was established for all incoming and outgoing correspondence. Although the order as regards the U.S. consul was rescinded, the remainder of the commander's troublesome order was not. However the situation on São Miguel became calmer as news circulated that the military commander responsible for the orders was to be recalled because, it was strongly suggested, he was mentally unbalanced.

From this incident it was clear that by diplomatic stalling tactics and leaving the orders intact against a possible "fifth column" in the Azores, both aimed principally against Americans, Salazar was afraid that the United States posed a serious threat of invasion. From discussions going on in Washington, he had a lot to worry about.[9]

17 April: State Department

A Mr. Codoner, attached to the U.S. Consulate in Ponta Delgada, presented a disquieting verbal report to the State Department on his return to the United States:

1. The governing authorities, the wealthy class . . . and army officers are, or appear to be, pro-axis. There are 22,000 troops on the island of São Miguel, shortly to be increased to 25,000. . . . The large majority of the people are pro-ally and especially pro-American.

2. There is much friction . . . between civilians and soldiers primarily because living costs have gone up and life generally has become more difficult. The secondary reasons for the friction are:

that the soldiers have brought with them a large
increase in the prevalence of contagious diseases. The
soldiers . . . are only favored by the female population, to
the additional annoyance of the civilian males. The
soldiers resent their enforced sojourn in the Islands and
their morale is generally very low. They are billeted in
barns and stables, and wherever in fact roofs are available.

The feeling (of both the islanders and the soldiers) is
that these troops have been brought there to defend the
islands against the United States.

3. Preparations have been made to receive the Portuguese
   Government in an emergency.
4. The economic "octopus" of the Island, Sr. Vasco Bensaude
   is believed to be pro-British. The chief engineer of the
   municipal power plant is German as is the controller of the
   breakwater.
5. An unexplained delivery of silver bullion to the Azores from
   New York shipped on the S.S. *Villa Franca* took place in
   March. There was also talk of a delivery of gold from
   Portugal on the S.S. *Serpa Pinto*. Presumably these
   shipments were brought in to finance a government-in-exile,
   in case of an emergency on the mainland.[10]

Before leaving the Azores, Codoner was asked by the consul to warn
the State Department that the entire consulate staff were virtual prisoners in Ponta Delgada. Because they could not go outside the limits of
this small town, Dawson considered they were as good as interned. The
Germans, however, came and went freely, which meant the travel ban
effectively applied only to the British and Americans.

Because Americans and British not connected with their consulates
were being expelled from the island, Dawson asked, "Are there any restrictions on the many Portuguese citizens in the United States, particularly the many consular officers there?" Someone high up in State
marked two bold lines in the margin next to the question—was it
Welles or Hull?—as a reminder to find the answer.[11]

Other annoyances continued: no action had been taken by local officials to extend Dawson's permit for his car; only one letter from the
United States had been received since January even though other foreign mail was carried regularly from Brazil. Another problem was with
the fifteen hundred persons of dual Portuguese-American nationality

on the island. The authorities wanted to call up all men between the ages of twenty and twenty-one for military service, including Americans. Many of the young men were born in the United States and protested against serving in the Portuguese army. The civil governor responded by ordering those claiming U.S. citizenship to leave the island by October or else they would be considered Portuguese nationals.

Codoner also brought with him a secret document entitled "Germans in the Azores," which listed about thirty German nationals in residence, two specifically named as the most dangerous. First on the list was a Mr. Dompie, allegedly the Nazi paymaster in Ponta Delgada, who regularly received checks from both the United States and Germany. He had recently purchased or rented a large estate near the town. The other person was an Oscar Neppach, considered to be the chief Nazi spy in the Azores, who worked as a commission merchant most probably for the Etappendienst.[12] Other potential danger spots were the municipal electrical works whose chief engineer was German, and the breakwater that was being constructed by a German engineering firm.

The German government wanted to replace their consul——born in the Azores to a German father and Portuguese mother whose loyalty was in doubt——with an experienced diplomat, the former consul general in Manila. The new consul was appointed presumably to upgrade the consulate but also to get along better with Neppach than the incumbent. He had, however, one serious problem——there was no way to leave Europe to assume his post.

It was clear that people in power in the Azores were sympathetic to the Axis, and equally bad, German agents were in positions where they could do great damage. A fifth column was in place to either assist a German takeover or to sabotage an Allied landing.

13–14 May:
Führer Headquarters, Wolfsschanze

Admiral Dönitz presented a special report on the situation in the Atlantic at a meeting with Hitler, the OKW, the OKM, Reichsminister Albert Speer, and other dignitaries:

> the greater part of American tankers is used in coastal traffic, transporting oil from the oil region to the industrial area. From

January 15 to May 10, 1942, we sank 112 tankers or a total of 927,000 tons. Every tanker we sink not only means one tanker less for carrying oil but also represents a direct set-back to America's shipbuilding programme. Therefore it seems to me that the destruction of these American oil supply vessels is of greatest importance to us.

I do not believe that the race between the enemy shipbuilding programme and the submarine sinkings is in any way hopeless. The total tonnage the enemy can build will be about 8,200,000 tons in 1942 and about 10,400,000 tons in 1943. That would mean that we would have to sink approximately 700,000 tons per month in order to offset new constructions; only what is in excess of this amount would constitute a decrease in enemy tonnage. However, we are already sinking these 700,000 tons per month now. . . . Moreover the construction figures quoted are the maximum . . . mentioned by enemy propaganda as the goal of the shipbuilding programme. Our experts doubt that this goal can be reached and consider that the enemy can build only about 5,000,000 in 1942. That would mean that only about 400,000 to 500,000 tons would have to be sunk per month in order to present any increase. Anything above that number cuts into the basic tonnage of the enemy.

The daily average [of ships sunk by each submarine in American waters] amounted to 209 tons in January, 378 tons in February, 409 tons in March, and 412 tons in April. Everything points to the fact that the Americans are making strenuous efforts to prevent the large number of sinkings. They have organized a considerable air defense and are likewise using destroyers and patrol craft off the coast. However, all these are manned by inexperienced crews and do not constitute a serious threat at present. In any case, the submarines with their greater experience in warfare are mastering these countermeasures. The American fliers see nothing, the destroyers and patrol vessels are traveling too fast most of the time even to locate the submarines or they are not persistent enough in their pursuit with depth charges. In anticipation of the expected decrease in traffic due to convoys, it is planned to mine Chesapeake Bay, Delaware Bay, and New York Harbor. Up to now, with heavy traffic it is more economic to use torpedoes.[13]

This was the "happy time" for German U-boats who were astounded to see tankers and freighters cruising up and down the East Coast, neither in convoy nor with any armed protection and silhouetted with brilliant back lighting on shore. Admiral Ernest J. King, chief of Naval Operations, refused to recognize that ships were safer traveling in convoys than sailing alone and ignored the experience of England, which had already learned how to counter near-shore U-boat attacks. For the first half of the year, tankers were being sunk at a rate of 3.5 percent of the country's total oil-carrying capacity each month. The loss was frightening, and without any hope of improvement as long as Admiral King held out against the use of convoys. General Dwight Eisenhower, then chief of the Army's War Plans Division wrote in his diary that King was "the antithesis of cooperation, a deliberately rude person . . . a mental bully . . . One thing that might help win this war is to get someone to shoot King."[14] For all the war years, between 1939 and 1945, 1,584 ships—including 318 stragglers—were lost in convoy compared to 2,482 independent ships lost including 367 detached from convoys. Compared to the actual numbers at sea, losses to independent ships were twice that of the convoyed ships. One independent ship was lost for every 148 sailed (0.66 percent), but only one convoyed ship was lost for every 296 sailed (0.33 percent).[15]

A few months later protective measures were finally started. Convoys were organized, with England and Canada sharing the responsibility for their protection. Hitler's conviction that Norway had to be protected probably saved the U.S. merchant marine from complete destruction. The number of U-boats available at any one time was small and ordering Dönitz to keep many of them on routine guard duty saved Admiral King the embarrassment of explaining how he managed to loose the country's entire merchant fleet. On 1 February only sixteen U-boats were stationed in the Atlantic: seven protecting Norway, three just west of Gibraltar looking out for an Allied invasion, and only six on offensive operations in U.S. waters. U.S. industry also saved the country from a desperate situation, for despite German predictions U.S. shipyards turned out ships faster than Dönitz's submarines could sink them, and eventually it was losses of U-boats, instead of Allied merchant shipping, that became unsustainable.[16]

Late May

British intelligence broke the Abwehr Enigma cipher in December 1941 and by late spring the entire German order of battle and plan of operations in the Iberian Peninsula was known. German headquarters in Madrid had approximately twenty officers supervising stations in eleven Spanish cities, including Algeciras, where shipping in Gibraltar could be easily monitored. A training school for agents was run at Barcelona with German instructors and some stations were managed entirely by Spaniards. German clandestine operations could flourish in Spain given that Franco had signed on as a silent partner with the Axis.

Abwehr headquarters in Lisbon was much smaller, with outstations in the Azores, the Canaries, and the Portuguese African colonies. Many agents were recruited from the fishing fleet and among merchant seamen, some of whom also served as couriers and supplied weather reports. In July, the Royal Navy arrested two Spanish trawlers passing on shipping and weather information to the Germans, and in November a Portuguese trawler was apprehended radioing to the Germans and found to be on course to meet a large convoy headed to Torch.

In March the Portuguese protested the clandestine activities of the Special Operations Executive (SOE: the British equivalent to the United States's Office of Strategic Services [OSS]) in Portugal. In response, the Foreign Office sent Salazar a lengthy dossier prepared by the Secret Intelligence Service (SIS) with evidence of the Abwehr's subversive activities. The dossier named the head of the Lisbon office and several important subordinates, showed evidence of recruiting Portuguese stevedores for sabotage operations, and also named Portuguese police officers and other officials in the colonies who were under German control. Salazar agreed that it was his country's duty to arrest any citizens known to be working for a belligerent but took no action, even in September when the SIS provided copies of correspondence between the Abwehr and its agents in Angola, Madeira, and the Azores. Finally in December the Portuguese head of the ring and his associates were arrested, breaking up the courier system. However, Salazar refused to take any action against the Abwehr, such as declaring its agents persona non grata and expelling them from the country.[17]

15 June: Führer Headquarters, the Berghof

Admiral Raeder reported on a meeting with Hitler, the OKW, General Jodl, Admiral Theodor Krancke (Commander-in-Chief West Group), and Captain Karl-Jesko von Puttkamer (Hitler's aide-de-camp): "1) Permission was granted to attack Brazilian shipping and ports starting in August. 2) An operational group of subs should be ready to react quickly in case enemy should strike at Azores, Madeira or Cape Verde. The eight U-boats now patrolling convoy lanes from the U.S. via Azores could be alerted."[18]

Hitler's order, passed down to Dönitz to assign U-boats to guard against Allied landings in an as yet unknown Atlantic island, was not received kindly. The admiral had been chafing for over a year at the unfulfilled promises to increase the U-boat fleet, to have the Luftwaffe carry out reconnaissance for U-boat operations, for Hitler to do more to promote submarine warfare. The order received on 21 June was the last straw; the fleet was already stretched to the limit. In all the world's oceans there were then a total of only fifty-nine German U-boats on patrol at any one time, carrying out what was supposedly their first priority—the war on Allied shipping—and Hitler's high priority guarding the Norwegian coast. Those fifty-nine were responsible for the massive damage inflicted on shipping, so Dönitz could only imagine what a fleet ten times that size could do. Because the number of U-boats in the Atlantic was minimal, the admiral insisted that none were available to waste their time on guard duty, that none could be withdrawn from Atlantic patrol to await a landing that might or might not happen.[19]

In June U-boats sank 145 ships in the Atlantic, 96 in July, 108 in August, and merchant raiders sunk or captured an additional 16 ships in the same period. The June losses were the highest for any one month of the war.

23 July: London and Lisbon

Thanks to Major Delgado's efforts, by July 1942 the RAF considered the Lagens airfield ready and wanted to move in to start operations. Something had to be done about the carnage inflicted by the wolf packs in the mid-Atlantic if England was to survive. On 23 July, Foreign Secretary Anthony Eden told the British ambassador in Lisbon to request formal permission for the RAF to land on Terceira and take over the new base but the response was that the plan was being amended and the RAF could not move in as yet. This was not acceptable to Churchill but President Salazar, still afraid of Hitler's reaction to such a bold move, pointed out that under the treaty Portugal, not England, was the country that was supposed to ask for "succor."[20]

Also influencing Salazar's decision was the fact that at that time things were not going well for the Allies. Earlier in the year on 15 February Japanese forces captured Singapore and on 9 April U.S. forces surrendered on the Bataan Peninsula in the Philippines. German armies were in complete control of the Balkans and rolling through Russia. It would not be until November that the Allies took the initiative by landing in North Africa and only in February of the following year that Russian armies stymied the German advance at Stalingrad. But for now, discretion being the better part of valor, Salazar would delay his decision until there was no longer a question which side was going to win the war.

29 June: Rio de Janeiro

Air routes to Europe from the United States were following either a northern course, via Newfoundland–Greenland–Iceland or via Bahamas–Brazil–Dakar, which although much longer had generally good weather year round. The airfields of northeast Brazil were proving inadequate for the heavy volume of traffic so pressure was brought on Brazil to allow the United States to construct larger facilities and longer air strips. In a tactic that was to be repeated later with Portugal, Brazilian authorities would allow works to improve facilities at Recife, Natal, Maceió, and Bahia if they were carried out by Panair do Brasil, a subsidiary of Pan American World Airways (Pan Am). The United States would have full use of the bases for the duration of the war on condition that all land acquired remain vested in the Brazilian government and all buildings and "tangible results of our program" be donated to Brazil at the conclusion of hostilities. Involving Panair at least on paper maintained a semblance of neutrality for the country although at the same time Brazil ignored U.S. armed forces involvement in constructing the bases.[21]

August: Azores Gap

The Admiralty watched with anxiety as each month Intelligence reported great increases in the number of U-boats on Atlantic patrol. In January there were twenty-two, in May sixty-one, and at the beginning of August the number reached eighty-six due in part to the withdrawal of boats from the U.S. coast. Submarines withdrawn from the western Atlantic were repositioned between Gibraltar and the Azores, operating either singly or in wolf packs. From 5–10 August a pack of eighteen U-boats fought the first of a new round of battles against convoy SC-94, sinking eleven of its thirty-three ships, sending fifty-three thousand tons of merchant shipping to the bottom.

During August and September U-boats located twenty-one of the sixty-three convoys that sailed, made sustained attacks on seven of them and sank a total of forty-three ships. During this time the number sunk in the Atlantic was still less than on the North American seaboard, where U-boats continued to find soft spots in the Caribbean and St. Lawrence. During October, however, the number of U-boats in the Atlantic reached just over 100 and the total monthly sinkings exceeded half a million tons for the first time. The U-boat menace had to be contained or Churchill's prophecy that the war could be lost in the Atlantic might come true.[22]

22 August: Rio de Janeiro

Brazil declared war on Germany in response to U-boats torpedoing five passenger vessels twenty miles off the coast of Sergipe on 12–16 August. The ships were plying between local Brazilian ports carrying, among others, pilgrims on their way to a Eucharistic Congress in São Paulo. Prior to this atrocity, with many lives lost, U-boats had already sunk thirteen Brazilian ships. Brazil was the first Latin American country to declare war on the Axis, and was shortly followed by most of the others, with the notable exception of Argentina. Brazil, however, was the only one to actually go to war, sending troops to fight with the United Nations in Italy.[23]

26 August: Führer Headquarters, Wehrwolf

The mood was upbeat at Hitler's meeting with his admirals. The U-boat offensive along the United States's East Coast had proven devastating and lasted much longer than expected thanks to inept U.S. leadership. First, the jurisdictional dispute on who was in charge of the operation, the Army or Navy Air Corps, had to be resolved. Next was Admiral King's refusal to ask the British for pointers on training pilots and skippers in antisubmarine warfare or organizing convoys. These problems had been resolved, however, and U.S. countermeasures were becoming effective so change was called for. Attacks on convoys by one or two U-boat groups in the northern and middle parts of the North Atlantic should yield favorable results as long as the attack stayed beyond the range of aircraft protection. The U-boat losses up to 24 August were serious but still sustainable if new boats were produced and crews could be found:[24]

1. Total U-boats in operation since beginning of the war: 304
2. Total lost since beginning of the war: 105
3. Average monthly loss: 2.9 percent
4. Average monthly loss to number in operation: 4.9 percent
5. Total loss of operating personnel each year: 38 percent

As Allied air cover in the northern Atlantic became better organized and more deadly for the U-boats, Dönitz continued to shift operations to the central Atlantic around the Azores Gap. During the year forty-eight Allied ships were sunk in the Gap as he stepped up the wolf pack patrols.

Blücher, an especially notorious wolf pack of seven boats, was dispatched from France to the Azores Gap. The boats left their pens singly and sailed through the Bay of Biscay with orders to rendezvous near the eastern end of São Miguel. To increase the likelihood of encountering a convoy, the standard procedure for wolf packs was to spread out on a patrol line, stationing the boats in a long row about ten to twenty miles apart across shipping lanes. Once a convoy was spotted, word was quickly passed up and down the line for the U-boats to converge and start the attack. Because advance intelligence on convoy sailings was rare, the U-boats had to rely on such chance encounters to find targets.[25]

From a point starting about thirty miles from the eastern edge of São Miguel, the Blücher U-boats stationed themselves in an east-west picket line stretching in the direction of Lisbon and directly across north-south shipping lanes. On 17 August the British convoy SL-118, which had formed up near Freetown in Sierra Leone and was heading home to England, was sighted by the easternmost U-boat. The convoy consisted of thirty-three merchant ships, an armed merchant cruiser, the auxiliary cruiser *Cheshire*, a passenger liner, and four corvettes.

Four U-boats reached the convoy and attacked. The attack continued for the next two days and only broke off when the convoy came within air range of B-24 Liberator bombers based in Cornwall, England. The wolf packs knew they were no match for the bombers, so as soon as the planes appeared the pack split up, either scurrying back to their pens in France or returned to the Azores Gap, well out of aircraft range. Before they broke off however, four ships had been sunk and the *Cheshire* was severely damaged.

22 September: Horta, Faial Island, Azores

Apparently inspired by the macho blustering of the commander of São Miguel, the military commander of Horta decided it was his turn to twist Uncle Sam's beard. He issued an order that if he declared a state of alarm on the island, no foreigners, including consular representatives, would be allowed to leave a certain specified locality for any reason whatsoever. Furthermore, during the state of alarm all telegraphic equipment—including the cable equipment of the Western Union and Commercial Cable Companies—must be turned over to the Portuguese Legion. In addition to being an important naval port and a terminal for Pan Am transatlantic flights, Horta was an important way station for transatlantic cables and anyone controlling the offices could disrupt the cable service. A brief disruption could have disastrous consequences for Allied communications if the U.S. managers of the company were ordered to disconnect the cables and evacuate their offices. A state of alarm had been declared the previous week for an air raid exercise and U.S. Consul Douglass was afraid that another one might be declared again at any time. He transmitted this information both to the State Department and to the U.S. Embassy in Lisbon.[26]

By now the State Department had had enough and on 9 October

Acting Secretary Sumner Welles ordered Ambassador Fish to clear the matter up at once with the highest authorities in the Portuguese government. The problems raised earlier in Ponta Delgada had never been resolved and the State Department's patience had worn thin. Fish was told to obtain a relaxation of the restrictions on the movements of our consular officials and the restriction requiring foreigners to reside in specific localities, which appeared only to apply to U.S. citizens of Portuguese antecedents. (They had to opt for Portuguese citizenship in order to keep their houses and farms.) Welles emphasized that "it is obviously distasteful to this Government that its citizens should be thus forced to alienate themselves and adopt another allegiance." Finally, the decision of the local authorities to take over the station was a violation of U.S. property rights and must be brought forcibly to the attention of the Portuguese government, asking it to furnish "assurances that American property rights will in all events be respected."[27]

Ambassador Fish did not respond to Washington until two weeks later. He had consulted with Douglass, who advised him that the U.S. citizens living in the interior of Faial were all dual-nationality cases. Because of that, Fish was reluctant to protest to the Portuguese authorities. In his last correspondence of record to the State Department he went on to say that he "reopened with the Foreign Office the general question of the restrictions established in the Azores and has communicated our Government's desires as instructed but has not pressed the point."[28]

Fish had been appointed to Lisbon, considered a plush, little-to-worry-about post, perhaps as a political favor to Claude Pepper, the powerful U.S. Senator from Florida, but events in the war had transformed it into one of the most critical diplomatic spots on earth. The United States's habit of rewarding politicians and political party benefactors with ambassadorships and sending career State Department personnel as ambassadors to the tough countries had come home to roost. We had a pussycat for an ambassador when the job called for a lion. Portuguese officials did not take Ambassador Fish seriously and he had never made a serious effort to establish close relations with Prime Minister Salazar, who could have resolved disputes with a telephone call.

The situation was finally salvaged when George Kennan, just returned from internment in Germany where he had served in the embassy, was dispatched to Lisbon as first secretary. The following year Burt Fish died and Kennan assumed the duties of counselor of legation, the United States's de facto ambassador to Portugal. He proved to be the right person for this critical position, someone who would act forcibly with all the power of the United States behind him and was not afraid to negotiate with anyone from the prime minister on down.

28 September: The Reich Chancellery, Berlin

Dönitz report to Hitler: increased number of U-boats makes it easier to locate the enemy. Convoys travel direct route on the Great Circle but are strongly protected making it difficult for submarines to approach. The great menace for the submarines today however is aircraft. Allied air bases have forced us to push attacks against convoys towards the middle of the Atlantic and away from airfields.[29]

October

Planning for the Allied landings in North Africa, Operation Torch, was moving ahead as D-day approached. However, reports from British Intelligence were no cause for elation—the number of U-boats had reached an unprecedented high. All submarines had been withdrawn from U.S. waters and were registering pronounced successes against Allied convoys. The new Enigma code for U-boats had not been broken so Intelligence had to rely on less reliable sources for information. It was assumed that the Germans knew that a big operation was impending because they started flying daily reconnaissance missions at the end of September over England's southwestern ports and Gibraltar. The first sea lord had good reasons to warn Churchill "the U-boats might well prove menacing" to "the most valuable convoys ever to leave these shores."[30] Despite the lack of deciphered information from the U-boat codes, the Operational Intelligence Center of the Admiralty (OIC) could still make reliable estimates of the numbers of U-boats at sea. On 2 November when convoys were approaching Gibraltar, there were actually 212 in service; the OIC guessed 228, but the correct figure for the North Atlantic was 94, as well as the 42 between Iceland and the Azores. The Germans were preparing to stop Operation Torch by unleashing carnage at sea.[31]

Elsewhere this was the month when the Axis lost the initiative in the war. On the Russian Front the once-invincible Wehrmacht found itself stalled as the Red Army mounted its epic defense of Stalingrad. Malta, a key to transport across the Mediterranean, was holding out against massive air attacks and the threat of invasion. In Egypt, General Bernard Montgomery's Eighth Army stopped General Erwin Rommel's Afrika Korps's advance to the Suez Canal at the great battle of El Alamein. On 23 October the tide turned when the Eighth Army went over to the offensive after the victory, and by 22 November the Germans had given up all their gains in Egypt, retreating over five hundred miles back to Benghazi in Libya where the offensive began. Soon Rommel would have more worries of impending disaster; not only the Eighth Army to his east but Allied armies were about to land behind his back in French North Africa.

At sea, the story was different. The tonnage war of Admiral Dönitz was going well with massive losses of Allied shipping compared to sustainable losses of U-boats. To take full advantage of the "black hole," Dönitz devised a new strategy. In the North Atlantic U-boats were discouraged from operating too close to land but because no patrols could fly within the Azores Gap, it became the new "happy hunting ground":

> From October 1942 onwards there were always two U-boat groups permanently available in the North Atlantic for operations against convoys. They were disposed in two patrol lines, one in the eastern Atlantic and one in the western. The task of the eastern group was to gain contact with west-bound convoys while the western group intercepted eastern convoys before either type of convoy entered "the U-boat zone of operations," that area in mid-Atlantic which could not be reached by land-based aircraft.

Once spotted, the convoy was attacked as soon as it entered into the zone of operations.[32]

14 October: U.S. Consulate, Horta, Faial

Scott Lyon, vice consul in Horta, sent a seven-page memo to the State Department regarding the military situation in the Azores based on his return trip from Lisbon on the Portuguese passenger ship SS *Carvalho Araujo*. The ship departed on 23 September, and although it made several ports before reaching Faial, he was allowed ashore only on Madeira and São Miguel. Despite being restricted to shipboard he still managed to obtain much information about the disposition of Portuguese defenses in the Azores.

In the port of Angra on Terceira, Lyon attended a dinner on board the ship during which a Portuguese infantry colonel discussed the situation on the island. He complained that a general rather than a mere colonel should be in charge, especially because there were more troops on Terceira than São Miguel. The colonel either forgot the presence of the American at the table, or more probably, assumed that he did not understand Portuguese. Lyon learned the exact designation of the outfits stationed on the island, including the numbers of the regiments of infantry, artillery, engineers, medical, and aviation, which he reported along with detail on forts; guns, their emplacements and fields of fire; and barbed wire obstructions on the beach. The report also identified several potential beachheads for amphibious landings.[33]

The following year, on 22 May 1943, Edward Anderson, U.S. consul at Horta, reported his observations on "The Military Situation in the Azores," made on a similar trip between the islands. As was the case with Scott, he was not allowed to debark until he reached his destination, but from what he observed, the state of readiness of Portuguese forces had not changed in the interim.

18 October–8 November: North Africa

Operation Torch: convoys started to depart from England and the United States on 18 October and landed on 8 November in French Northwest Africa almost unopposed. At Casablanca, thirty-five thousand troops led by General George Patton landed after sailing directly from North America. British forces under General Fredendall at Oran and General Ryder at Algiers came ashore having sailed from England through the Straits of Gibraltar unmolested. German plans to ambush the convoys outside the Straits with a heavy submarine attack completely failed thanks to a British Intelligence gambit. Two special units had been formed within British Military Intelligence (MI-5): one code named "Ultra," which relied on information obtained from deciphering German top secret signals via the Enigma coding machine, and the "Twenty Committee"—better known as "XX" (the double cross) for counterespionage operations. The special role of the Twenty Committee was to "leak" misinformation on Allied plans to German intelligence. Abwehr agents were fed misinformation, which they forwarded to Berlin, material calculated to mask the actual Allied landing areas. Admiral Dönitz was told the Allied landing would take place at Dakar, and so stationed his U-boats at Freetown and the Cape Verde Islands. After the landings began some two thousand miles north in North Africa, and the largest convoys were already in the Mediterranean, he rushed his submarines to the western approaches to Gibraltar where they sank ten merchant ships, four transports, and five warships. But because the Allies were expecting the attack and were prepared for it, providing both good air- and seaborne protection, the U-boat fleet paid a high price: eight German and one Italian U-boats sunk and nineteen damaged. Getting into the Mediterranean was a major problem for the submarines because of British defenses and an underwater chain fence, so any large-scale attack on Allied convoys had to take place outside the Straits.

German intelligence agents had been openly monitoring ship movements through Gibraltar from their offices in Algeciras, just across the bay from the Rock itself. However, by the time they saw the Allied convoy passing into the Mediterranean and not headed down the African coast it was already too late to do anything. Even then, thanks to the Double Cross, the Abwehr's guesses as to where the convoy was headed were not even close to the mark. Possible landing spots mentioned were Malta to reinforce the garrison, Egypt to join the battle at El Alamein, and the Aegean Sea to start a new campaign in Greece. With their head start, the British troops were safely ashore long before the U-boats made it to Gibraltar from Dakar.[34]

In addition to their observation post at Algeciras, the Axis had agents in and around the Azores to report on convoys headed to the Mediterranean from the United States. In fact British Intelligence learned that the Italian consul at Ponta Delgada reported to the Italian naval attaché in Lisbon on 5 November that a large U.S. convoy had passed the Azores bound for Africa. At the end of October the Kriegsmarine heard from their own agents that a large U.S. convoy was headed to Africa, probably the same one spotted by the Italians, but thanks to the XX system they thought it was headed to Dakar. The "Large American Convoy," of course, was General Patton and his army on their way to Torch, the first of what would be many cross-Atlantic troop movements.[35]

Now the pincer movement was set in motion: the Afrika Korps would be trapped in Tunisia with Anglo–U.S. armies to the west and the British Eighth Army advancing from Libya to the east. Rommel's army would be encircled with no possibility of escape. The end would come on 12 May the following year when Italy's Marshall Messe and Germany's General von Arnim surrendered with a quarter million men, the last survivors of Hitler's scheme to capture the Suez Canal.

Hitler was in his private railway car on 7 November on his way to Munich to celebrate the anniversary of the 1923 Beer Hall Putsch when he received news that an Allied fleet was entering the Mediterranean. General Jodl, Hitler's chief of staff, consulted the intelligence files filled with XX misinformation and concluded that the Allied convoy was headed for Malta.

The Double Cross operation was good practice for MI-5. It had succeeded beyond anyone's expectations and was as well done as their later, more celebrated, success in the deception for Operation Overlord. Allied landings were on the beaches of Normandy and Brittany but thanks to XX Hitler was convinced that the real attack would come farther north at Pas de Calais, where much of the German army dug in awaiting the attack that never came.

19 November: Führer Headquarters, the Berghof

C-in-C Navy meeting with Hitler and the OKW on the status of naval operations: "The Führer wants light naval forces to be sent to Norway and desires Norway to be heavily stocked with supplies, since all available reports lead him to fear that the enemy will attempt an invasion during the Arctic night."[36]

C-in-C Navy was more worried about the U-boat supply situation than Norway. The Allies had stepped up their aerial surveillance in the Bay of Biscay, "apparently interested in out-bound tankers which he suspects of being submarine supply ships."[37] Three of five blockade runners had to return to harbor because of damage from Allied aircraft.

Admiral Raeder emphasized the importance of holding on to Tunisia, which he felt was a critical position in the Mediterranean. The submarine fleet in the Mediterranean must be maintained at twenty-four ships—five were lost recently and needed to be replaced. Fifty-seven submarines and two submarine tankers were operating in the

Atlantic. Of them, twenty-five were west of Gibraltar waiting to attack ships entering the Mediterranean. Twelve were stationed between the Azores and the Iberian Peninsula–Straits of Gibraltar. Raeder noted that attacks on convoys were especially successful at this time, that the U-boats were being used to "exploit the weakness of the enemy escort forces and to inflict the largest possible losses on enemy shipping." Many of the escort warships had been diverted to the Mediterranean leaving less protection for the convoys.[38]

The U.S. occupation of Iceland still weighed on Hitler's mind as well as the fact that the Azores Archipelago was not yet under German control. He ordered the Navy to build transport submarines immediately because "he has again taken up the idea of a sudden invasion [of Iceland] and establishment of air base there."[39] The OKM promised to look into the matter.

Hitler now appeared to depart more and more from reality and imagined the war as going according to his wishes. U.S. forces were in Iceland in great numbers, well armed, with fully functioning air and naval bases. Transporting a large enough number of troops via the yet-to-be-built troop-carrying submarines and overcoming Allied resistance was not a realistic possibility. Even if the units could be dispatched from Germany, only a small number of submarines would make it through the Allied blockade of aircraft, mines, and destroyers. The troops that survived the voyage could expect a devastating reception from a well-armed and entrenched force when they attempted to land.[40]

11 December: Lisbon

At 9:30 P.M. the British ambassador, Sir Ronald Campbell, asked for an immediate audience with Salazar, who was usually in bed by that hour but agreed to meet him at 1 A.M. Salazar was afraid that the Allies were about to invade the Azores with the help of the maps his officers had given the RAF. Campbell quickly disabused him; the reason for the meeting was Churchill's desire for Portugal to be the first country to be told of the combined Anglo-American landings in Tunisia just beginning. The operation was a great success and would hasten the Axis defeat in North Africa, sealing the fate of the Afrika Korps. Soon there would no longer be any reason for Portugal to worry if she agreed to honor the 1373 Treaty of Eternal Friendship.

24 December: The OKM Report to Hitler

The Führer would not let up on his Norway fixation. He was afraid that the invasion could come in January, the time of maximum Arctic nights when anti-aircraft defenses would be useless because of the darkness. Stationed in Norway at the time were five battleships and nine destroyers, which the OKM must have thought could be put to better use elsewhere.

Other serious problems confronted the Kriegsmarine besides standing Norwegian guard duty: first, the critical fuel oil shortage because of a reduced delivery of Romanian oil in the winter months; second, U-boats were being lost at a greater rate than new ones were built. During the month of November fifteen submarines were lost but only eleven were replaced. The rate of loss was far in excess of the monthly average of 3.8 submarines for the war as a whole.

That evening C-in-C Navy had a private dinner with Hitler during which he brought up the "Iberian question." Raeder could see many advantages for the Navy if Spain and Portugal, along with their Atlantic islands, were occupied. He thought that if Germany did not act first, there was a good possibility that the Allies might step in themselves. Naval bases in Iberia would allow intensification of submarine warfare, ease blockade running for German bound cargo, and neutralize the imminent Allied occupation of all of North Africa. Germany must be prepared to seize Spain and Portugal and integrate both into the Nazi economic sphere. Hitler agreed with Raeder, especially over the benefits that would accrue by occupying Iberia, but for the time being he wanted to await the results of new negotiations going on with Spain. He expected a certain Spanish general, Munoz Grande, to bring home a favorable agreement that would allow German forces into the country.[41]

The year 1942, which started out on such a high note for the Wehrmacht and Axis ambitions for world conquest, was ending badly for Germany. The tide had turned in favor of the Allies in Russia, North Africa, and the South Pacific; the offensive advantage was lost to the Axis armies who were now falling back everywhere. The story, however, was different at sea where more than six and half million tons of Allied shipping had been sunk, largely by U-boats. This was the most successful year of the entire war for the submarine fleet. Dönitz argued constantly—and he thought convincingly—to Hitler and the OKW that the war could be won at sea. Cutting her lifeline, England would have no other alternative than to surrender. At each meeting with Hitler, promises were made to allocate more war material for U-boat construction, improve radar and communication technology, and assign VLR reconnaissance to support U-boat patrol operations, but they remained largely unfulfilled.

In the early months of the year, Allied merchant shipping was lost at twice the output of the shipyards whereas U-boat losses were only half the number of new boats coming into service—forty per month.[42] An official British Admiralty report stated that "We are consuming three-quarters million tons more than we are importing. In two months we could not meet our requirements if this continued."[43] Hitler and the OKW did not appreciate that if Germany could win the Battle of the Atlantic, despite the pounding her armies were taking in Europe and North Africa, she might have a chance to win the war.

Dönitz never gave up hope of occupying the Azores. Operating in the Azores Gap far outside the range of Allied VLR aircraft bases, the U-boat fleet was achieving its greatest success. In 1942 forty-eight Allied ships were sunk in the Gap, and if Dönitz could establish a port in the islands to service and supply U-boats that number could go up by orders of magnitude. By the end of the year, twenty-five U-boats were on patrol between Iceland and Newfoundland but forty in the Biscay–Gibraltar–Azores area where the rewards were highest in terms of Allied tonnage sunk versus U-boat losses.[44]

SIX

THE TRIDENT CONFERENCE, JANUARY–JULY 1943

The Combined Chiefs of Staff had no difficulty in reaching
agreement on a number of other points, such as the
prosecution of the U-boat war, the bombing of Germany, and
the occupation of the Azores. The last-named was a delicate
problem. Both the Americans and ourselves were anxious to
have a base on that island [*sic*] for operating the long-range
aircraft which were employed in giving cover to our convoys
and dealing with the U-boats, but there seemed little hope that
Portugal would grant this concession of her own free will.
It was therefore agreed that the British should mount a small
expedition to capture the island at an early date, it being
understood that this must be done without the use of violence.
It is easy for high authority to make that sort of stipulation,
but the unfortunate commander may easily find his attempts
at seduction are unavailing and be compelled to have recourse
to rape.

GEN. LORD HASTINGS ISMAY, 17 May 1943

On 8 November 1942 the puppet French government of Laval and
Pétain broke relations with the United States over the Allied landings
in French North Africa but both Portugal and Spain quickly sent messages assuring that they would remain neutral and continue to maintain friendly relations. As events unfolded in 1943 it became apparent
to Salazar that the chances of a German invasion of Portugal were
becoming increasingly remote. After the Allied victories of El Alamein
and Operation Torch, plus the speedy liberation of Sicily and the landings in Italy, Franco made it known that the Wehrmacht would not be

welcome in Spain. If the Germans wanted to mount an invasion of Portugal it would have to be via the sea but with large Allied navies in the Atlantic, that possibility was even more remote.[1]

The tonnage war in 1942, however, was a bleak one for the Allies. They lost 6,266,000 tons of shipping, and by year's end the number of operational U-boats had increased from 91 to 212. If victory was to be achieved the Allies had to control the sea. U.S. troops sent to join the invasion force to liberate Europe would never arrive; troopships would meet the same fate that awaited cargo ships—death on the high seas from U-boat wolf packs.[2]

As the year 1943 began, U-boat sinkings rose from 203,128 tons in January to 359,328 in February to an astounding 627,377 in March when U-boat strength had risen to 240 submarines. In March the greatest convoy battle of the war was fought when twenty U-boats attacked two convoys that had merged: a total of seventy-seven ships. Twenty-one ships totaling 141,000 tons were sunk with a loss of only one U-boat. This was a bleak time when it seemed that the Allies were close to losing the war in the Atlantic. The battle was saved by two unrelated factors: victory in North Africa and a new technology.

The battle for North Africa was going well. The Afrika Korps was on the run, cut off from supplies from mainland Europe by the Allied blockade in the Mediterranean, and outflanked both to the east and the west. Adding to its misery was the fact that Italian allies were surrendering in droves at the first sight of a U.S. or British infantryman. For the first time in the west Axis armies were outnumbered by United Nations forces. With the battle going so well, the Allied general staff agreed to free some VLR Liberator bombers from North Africa to join the Battle of the Atlantic where they were desperately needed. The new type XXI U-boat had a maximum underwater speed of 17.5 knots, but if attacked it could achieve almost perfect silence and still maintain an underwater cruising speed of 5.5 knots. One unexpected shortcoming of the new design that prevented the XXIs from becoming invincible killers was the tell-tail plume of smoke left by the schnorchel that could easily be spotted from the air.[3] Captain S. W. Roskill noted that "in the early spring of 1943 we had a very narrow escape from defeat in the Atlantic; and that, had we suffered such a defeat, history would have judged that the main cause had been the lack of two more squadrons of VLR aircraft for convoy escort duties."[4] Winston Churchill confessed that "The only thing that ever really frightened me during the war was the U-boat peril."[5]

At the end of March twenty aircraft were transferred from North Africa to the Atlantic Theater followed by forty-one additional planes during the first two weeks of April. Land-based aircraft were the single best antidote for U-boats, spotting them from great distances and attacking long before the submarines had any idea that they had been detected. The Liberators were stationed at air bases in the North Atlantic, closing much of the large gap south of Greenland and north of the Azores. As the number of aircraft increased and the patrols grew more deadly, U-boat captains stayed farther and farther away from the North Atlantic rim and sought safety in the Azores Gap. In addition to VLR aircraft, destroyers and aircraft carrier escorts (CVE) were released to beef up the warships on convoy duty.

Between February and March 1942, the Allies developed new types of radar, an ultra-short 3-cm and a short 10-cm wavelength, with a greater range and that allowed for deeper sensing into the sea than the old 1.5-cm equipment used by both sides. It took Dönitz a long time to realize that his U-boats could now be detected without knowing that they had been spotted. Although German scientists assured him that radar was not capable of penetrating deeply into the sea, the U-boat captains knew better because submerged submarines that once were considered safe in the ocean depths were now routinely attacked by VLR aircraft. The admiral of U-boats noted:

> We now know that when these three boats (U-82, U-587, and U-252) were destroyed between February and April 1942, the British were using the new short-wave radar location device for the first time. The new short-wave radar locating apparatus could locate a target at long range and with far greater accuracy than the long-wave device which had hitherto been used, and about which we knew. The position of a U-boat could therefore be pinpointed as soon as it appeared over the horizon, both at night and in poor visibility by day. This meant that in most cases by day and always at night, the U-boat would be "seen" before it itself could "see."[6]

Losses to shipping fell to 327,943 tons in April, 264,852 in May, and 95,753 tons in June. Except for July and September 1943 and March 1944 monthly losses never again exceeded one hundred thousand tons. The Allies had gone on the offensive in the Atlantic; U-boats were now attacked not only at sea, but also in transit to and from the Bay of Biscay. The first sea lord reported the pleasant news to the cabinet's emergency Anti-U-Boat Warfare Committee that whereas in November 1942 U-boats were being destroyed at only one-third the rate that new ones were constructed, by February 1943 the numbers were almost equal: twenty-three destroyed versus twenty-five constructed. From the miniscule number sunk previously, U-boat losses rose to fifty-six in April and May. The Battle of the Atlantic was now going against Germany but the "black hole" around the Azores was still there.[7]

6 January: In the Azores Gap

U-515, on its second cruise in the Atlantic (7 November 1942 to 6 January 1943 between Gibraltar and the Azores), sunk the 10,850-ton Royal Navy destroyer depot ship HMS *Hecla* with 279 lives lost out of a crew of 847 and the 18,743 ton passenger liner troop ship Ceramic with only one survivor out of 656.[8]

6 January: Rio de Janeiro

Roosevelt started the slow waltz to induce Brazil to sign on with his plan for a joint occupation of the Azores. Roosevelt felt that Salazar might accept an Allied presence in the Azores if it was proposed by President Getúlio Vargas of Brazil, a fellow Portuguese-speaking national leader, rather than by any high-powered delegation of English-speaking diplomats. But the plan had to be kept secret even from Vargas until Roosevelt could spring it on him at the right time and place. The State Department found out about Roosevelt's scheme when Jefferson Caffery, the U.S. ambassador to Brazil, reported that Oswaldo Aranha, the Brazilian minister for Foreign Affairs, was told by Carlos Martins, Brazil's ambassador to the United States, that President Roosevelt had asked him to invite President Vargas "to meet him in Trinidad," the date and time not specified. President Vargas said he would be glad to do so.[9]

On 8 January, when Roosevelt heard Vargas's positive response, he quickly tried to defuse any idea that important joint policy would be discussed. Roosevelt sent Sumner Welles a short memo stating that he merely said "that if I went to the West Indies this Winter I hope much President Vargas would meet me in some central location like Trinidad. Nothing further." Roosevelt then had to prepare for the Casablanca meeting with Churchill where he would discuss the idea of enlisting Brazil to help obtain an air base in the Azores.[10]

14–24 January: Casablanca

Churchill, Roosevelt, and their staffs met at Casablanca in the residential suburb of Anfa to set priorities for future Allied operations. There was general agreement that the war in the Atlantic was the first priority leading to the goal of unconditional surrender by the Axis. The Final Memorandum entitled "Conduct of the War in 1943" contains the declaration: "The defeat of the U-boat must remain a first charge on the resources of the United Nations."

Both leaders agreed to the necessity of establishing air bases in the Azores to cover the "black hole." Roosevelt suggested his Brazilian plan because it appeared that Salazar would not accept either the Americans or the British. Brazil had declared war on Germany and in so doing became one of the United Nations, so it was perfectly legitimate to have Brazilian troops act as surrogates for an Anglo-American operation. President Vargas could try to convince Salazar to let Brazilian troops protect the islands so that Portuguese forces could return to the mainland where they would be needed in case the Germans invaded.[11]

11–30 January: Hitler Headquarters, Wolfsschanze

In a series of meetings Hitler viciously attacked Großadmiral Raeder, citing the failure of naval tactics in every war since 1864 and blaming it largely on the constitution of Germany's Navy. His bad mood was brought on by the failure on 31 December of a force led by two heavy cruisers to advance and attack an Allied convoy bound for Russia.

The Royal Navy Arctic convoy screen was led by Captain R. St. V. Sherbrooke in the HMS *Winslowe;* the German force was made up of the heavy cruisers *Hipper* and *Lützow* and six destroyers. The Royal Navy ships repulsed the attack, damaging the *Hipper,* and succeeded in bringing the convoy into Murmansk intact. The German admiral broke off the engagement when he mistook the two British cruisers coming to the assistance of the convoy as the vanguard of a larger battle squadron.

Following orders, the German admiral quit the attack rather than risk the destruction of his task force to a superior British squadron. Because of its small numbers, German skippers had been told that self-preservation was their first priority rather than fighting it out when they found themselves outgunned.[12]

The news of the failed attack on the Arctic convoy was not passed on immediately to Hitler's headquarters; worse, he heard the news about the "Battle of the Barents Sea" in a BBC broadcast. At the meeting on 11 January, after attacking the leadership of the Navy, Hitler concluded with a threat to scrap all the big ships of the fleet. Raeder had already experienced Hitler's displeasure over the recent setbacks against Allied convoys and warships and saw no other recourse but to resign as OKM, a position he had held since 1928, in order to preserve the integrity of the naval arm. He told Dönitz that he intended to tender his resignation and to propose either him or Admiral Carls, a senior admiral, as his successor. Did he feel fit enough to assume the job, if so, to let Raeder know within twenty-four hours.

Dönitz telephoned back that as far as his health was concerned, he felt able to assume command of the Navy. Raeder then submitted both Carls and Dönitz's names as his possible successors and suggested that if Hitler wished to emphasize the fact that the U-boat arm was now of primary importance, "the choice of Dönitz would be fully justified."[13] Hitler chose Dönitz over the more senior Carls. He also must have felt some satisfaction that choosing a flag officer of submarines would pay off some of his grievances against the more senior officers of the capital ships.

If a new organization and strategy was required, then Dönitz was the obvious choice as OKM. Now he would have complete freedom to operate without asking authority each time from the *Seekriegsleitung*, the Naval War staff. He could stop sharing the Navy's limited resources with the large ocean raiders beloved by senior admirals but proven to be a strategic disaster. The large ships were wasteful of strategic materials, and tied up ship maintenance personnel and trained crews that he felt could more productively serve the submarine fleet. The argument over which strategy was superior, one based on unlimited U-boat warfare against Allied convoys or of large warships operating as commercial raiders was now moot. From now on no more beautiful heavily armed and armored large battle cruisers; U-boats would carry on the battle against enemy shipping. He would step up production and promote the development of radical new technology and designs that would make torpedoes more accurate and U-boats faster with a greater range.

Dönitz's argument against the battleships was persuasive, but he had a willing audience in Hitler. It was folly to think that Germany could wage a naval war against the two largest marine powers on earth, England and the United States, for there was no way that a German fleet could ever attain the strength to challenge either one, let alone their combined fleets. Forget about challenging Allied battleships when the U-boats did the job that had to be done—cut the lifeline to England with no need to confront the behemoths:

> We are in conflict with the two strongest maritime powers in the world who dominate the Atlantic, the decisive Theater of the war at sea. . . . Very soon, as the result of enemy counter-measures, our surface vessels will find themselves compelled to abandon their offensive . . . in favor of the purely defensive role of avoiding battle with superior enemy forces. . . .
>
> Only the U-boat, therefore, is capable of remaining for any length of time and fighting in sea areas in which the enemy is predominant, since it alone can still carry out its operations without at the same time being compelled to accept the risk of battle against superior enemy forces. An increase in the number of enemy battleships and cruisers in these waters, far from constituting any addition to the dangers to which the U-boats are exposed, is regarded, on the contrary as a welcome addition to the targets for which they are always searching.[14]

Then in the coup de grâce to his admirals' visions of a fleet of giant ships, Dönitz added they would also be useless for amphibious operations such as the invasion of the Azores, "If it be also accepted that it is equally not possible to employ these ships for other purposes, such as the seizure and occupation of groups of islands, the inevitable and only logical conclusion must be that they are no longer of major importance to the prosecution of the war as a whole."

With Dönitz as head of the U-boat fleet and OKM of the German Navy, with carte blanche from Hitler, he could implement new tactics immediately, order high priority research to design new devices, such as acoustical torpedoes and improved radar, and increase U-boat production. No more pleading with an unsympathetic Naval War staff.

Churchill now had even more reason to fear the U-boats could turn the tide of battle against the Allies, but luckily, despite lip service from Hitler and his new position of power, Dönitz still did not have the full backing of the German war machine. He was never allocated the amount of steel needed to increase U-boat production and had to contend with Field Marshall Goering, who refused to order Luftwaffe reconnaissance for submarines and Admiral Canaris, who throughout the entire war (perhaps deliberately) supplied only useless or misleading intelligence to the U-boat command.

26 January: Rio de Janeiro

After the Casablanca meeting Roosevelt resumed the Brazilian-Azores caper, now with Churchill's endorsement. Ambassador Caffery reported to the secretary of state that Foreign Minister Oswaldo Aranha showed him "telegrams this morning giving very interesting and graphic descriptions of North African Conferences [the Casablanca meeting] and concluded with the statement "I leave this morning with Oswaldo's boss [Vargas] to meet you know whom [FDR]. I should be back Friday."[15]

29 January: Natal, Brazil

Now the two presidents would get to discuss the plan that might work to get into the Azores. First Caffery briefed President Roosevelt from his perspective as U.S. ambassador to Brazil and with information gleaned from a ten-page letter of advice from Foreign Secretary Aranha to President Vargas shown to him by Aranha. Caffery told Roosevelt that in his opinion Vargas would agree to join the Azores caper.

There were actually two good reasons to enlist Brazilian aid. In addition to the obvious one of getting the air bases, there was another one that could not be revealed to Vargas. Brazil had declared war on Germany and was itching to get involved in the ground war in the Mediterranean. The CCS had no desire to have any troops they considered poorly trained and inadequately armed on the battlefield—they might, in fact, turn out to be a serious detriment to the conduct of battle. The problem could be easily resolved without hurting any Brazilian feelings if the divisions were sent instead to the Azores and Madeira to relieve the Portuguese garrisons who would then return to Portugal. Caffery thought there was a good chance that Vargas would agree.

President Roosevelt began his conversation with President Vargas by describing the course of the war in great detail. For the postwar, he felt that the French possessions in Africa, especially Dakar, the closest point of the African continent to Brazil, should be held in some sort of trusteeship administered by three commissioners, one American, one Brazilian, and a third from another country. This was definitely the icing on the cake and the idea of having some control over Dakar, within easy round-trip bomber range of Brazil, appealed to Vargas.

Roosevelt suggested that it was time for Brazil to join the United Nations in the war effort. Vargas indicated that he would take steps to become an active member of the United Nations but he added, ". . . this might be an opportune moment to say again that we need equipment from you for our military, naval and air force." And as for the Azores, Vargas agreed to suggest it to Salazar but again on the same condition: "We cannot send troops to the Portuguese Islands unless you furnish adequate equipment for them."

After the meeting, the two presidents made an inspection of the U.S. and Brazilian establishments around Natal and judged the airfield to be one of the finest in the world. Caffery reported both presidents were delighted with the events of the day, President Vargas especially so according to Aranha "that he has rarely seen him so pleased with anything." Roosevelt's gambit to enlist Brazil in an Azores operation was off to a brilliant start. The next step might be more difficult—convincing Salazar. Caffery's report to the secretary of state concluded "the meeting was eminently successful from all points of view."[16]

22 February: London

In July 1942 England made the first of many strong representations to Portugal for permission to build air bases in the Azores but to no visible effect. Months rolled by and permission was not forthcoming. For Churchill and his war cabinet patience was running out, so discussion now was to find ways to hasten a favorable decision out of Salazar. First Sea Lord Admiral Dudley Pound prepared a detailed memorandum on the use of aircraft to protect convoys, pointing out the need to use the

Portuguese Atlantic islands. The memorandum was later accepted by the CCS at the Trident Meeting on 15 May as the basis for strategic planning in the war in the Atlantic.[17]

The memorandum pointed out that the mounting tide of Allied successes probably eliminated any threat of a German invasion of the Iberian Peninsula, a fact that even Dr. Salazar must realize. The 1373 treaty called for either party to aid the other party in case of war as long as such assistance can be provided without great injury to his country. Early in the war when Portugal offered to come to the aid of England, she was informed that it would be best to maintain her neutrality. Now, England changed her opinion as recent developments in the war proved the Allies could master the Axis on land, in the sea, and in the air, but a full offensive on the U-boats was still necessary to achieve final victory. Dr. Salazar must recognize this and should grant the needed facilities in the Azores.

By now the British War Cabinet discovered that without being fully informed, the United States was toying with a strategy to use Brazil and perhaps also South Africa to get into the Azores. The British thought the rationale was ludicrous; there was no way that Brazilian troops would make Allied occupation of the Azores any more acceptable to the Portuguese or palatable to the Spaniards. Realistically, the only approach that made any sense was for England to invoke the Treaty of Eternal Friendship of 1373, but knowing that Salazar was a stickler for legalities, it would be necessary to quote the exact chapter and verse. The Portuguese government would then be honor bound to acquiesce to the request.

The first task for the British War Cabinet was to find the chapter and verse to quote to Salazar. This unexpectedly became a problem when it was discovered that nobody knew the actual provisions of the treaty and worse, nobody seemed to know where to find the document itself. The War Cabinet started with a request to the Foreign Office to produce either the original or an authentic copy. The Foreign Office informed the Cabinet that the treaty could not be found, that the original was probably buried deep in the archives of the British Museum, but that they might have an English translation, however, if they did, it unfortunately would be deeply buried in the Foreign Office archives. With almost six hundred years of British history intervening since the signing of the treaty, fighting many wars, decapitating a king, changing the state religion and suffering many other calamities, the Foreign Office might be forgiven for losing track of a 1373 treaty. After the Foreign Office failed to come up with it, RAF Group Captain—later Air Commodore—Vintras was put on the trail to find the missing treaty.

Two days after starting the search, Vintras discovered two important sections. His memoirs do not reveal where he found these precious pieces of text, but they provided sufficient ammunition for the cabinet to decide on a course of action. Vintras sent this memorandum to the director of plans of the War Cabinet:

D. of Plans   MOST SECRET

I will let you have the full text of the Anglo-Portuguese Treaty of 16th of June 1373, when and if I get hold of a copy. Meanwhile, here are two extracts. I hope that the latter part of Article 3 can be said to have applied to more recent Anglo-Portuguese Collaboration!

Article 1 of the Treaty says that the Kings of England and Portugal and their successors "shall henceforth reciprocally be friends to friends, and enemies to enemies, and shall assist, maintain and uphold each other mutually by sea and by land against all men that may live or die . . . (a later protocol allowed two exceptions: the Pope and Good King Wenceslas).

Article says that "if the kingdom, lands, dominions, or places of the other party should happen to be infested, oppressed, or invaded by sea or by land by enemies, persecutors, or rivals, or if these enemies should at least purpose, prepare or in any manner appear anxious to infest, oppress, or invade," and if the threatened party applies by letter or trusty messengers "for assistance or succor of troops, archers, slingers, ships, galleys sufficiently armed for war, *or any other kind of defense* . . . then shall the said party so required bona fide furnish, supply and send the said succor . . . whenever such party shall *without great injury to his country* be able to spare a certain proportion, . . . at the cost, expense, and pay of the party requiring, to be strictly estimated by four military men of experience or able and discreet members of the legal profession . . . ; it being understood throughout these proceedings no duplicity and unfairness shall appear, but that the straight path of equitable dealing and benignity shall be pursued."

R. E. Vintras, Group Captain
Cabinet War Room Annex   February 24th 1943[18]

Churchill now had all the ammunition he needed. Delays and excuses were no longer acceptable—Portugal must come to the aid of their most ancient ally.

1 March: Washington Convoy Conference

The U-boats' wolf-pack tactics were taking a terrible toll on ships, inflicting great damage by bold attacks on convoys sailing outside the range of VLR aircraft. Strong antisubmarine measures were needed but action was hampered by the lack of a unified leadership not only between the Allies, but also between the U.S. Armed Services. Disagreement over the primary function of aircraft between the Army Air Corps and the Navy was one major stumbling block. The Air Corps motto was "Search, Strike, Sink!" and labeled the Navy strategy of only supporting convoys "purely defensive." Moreover, Admiral King had depleted the fleet in the Atlantic to reinforce the Pacific which, despite the president's views, he considered to be the primary theater of war. Worried naval officers including Captain Richard W. Bates, impatient with the rare sinking of submarines, warned Admiral Stark in January that unless hunter-killer groups were organized, the number of U-boats might so increase as to overwhelm convoys. The British had been through much of this in the first years of the war, but it was hard to convince King to seek their advice on strategies to counter the submarine menace.

Eventually when King had been converted to the wisdom of protected convoys, and accepted the fact that the U.S. fleet could not do it alone, he convened a conference at the request of Vice Admiral Percy W. Welles, chief of the Canadian Naval Staff. A system had to be devised for escort protection in the North Atlantic, coordinated with the British and Canadians to stop the blood-letting: merchant tonnage lost in February 1943 reached 359,328 tons and during the first twenty days of March the horrendous total of 536,643 tons. The crisis, which was unparalleled in the war, could no longer be ignored.

The Air Force argued that protecting convoys should not be the primary role of aircraft but rather hunting U-boats. Admiral King, however, carried the day with a resolution that the first task of the fleets was to protect convoys and as he insisted "the defeat of the U-boat is not of itself the goal we seek." Admiral Noble, former commander in chief, Britain's Western Approaches, pointed out that the strategy of protecting convoys in itself would lead to the destruction of U-boats and added that "The submarine menace, to my mind, is becoming every day more and more an air problem." The problems in the air were first, the disagreement in the U.S. services on what was the chain of command and which service had what responsibilities, and second, the lack of air protection over the Azores Gap. The first problem was solvable; the second would have to wait.[19]

It was agreed at the conference that England and Canada should take complete control of the North Atlantic convoy system and Admiral Roland W. Brainard's Task Force 24 would do escort duty in the Central Atlantic and Caribbean–South Atlantic protecting the routes followed by tankers between England and the West Indies. Two hundred fifty-five VLR aircraft were promised by the Americans and would be delivered to airfields by July for antisubmarine patrol duty.

The conference ended on 12 March having achieved a workable geographic division of responsibility and leaving each command to solve the problem of antisubmarine warfare as it thought best. Two months later, as the Atlantic Fleet began receiving long-awaited escort carriers and destroyer escorts, Admiral King established the Tenth Fleet within COMINCH headquarters to coordinate U.S. antisubmarine activities, but not until 10 June did the Air Force and Navy finally come to terms on their individual responsibilities. In a bit of "horse trading," the Air Force agreed to withdraw from antisubmarine warfare and exchange its antisubmarine-rigged B-24 Liberator bombers for an equal number of unmodified B-24s from the Navy. The agreement was accepted on 9 July and implemented by 1 September. Each side got what it wanted: the Navy assumed complete responsibility for VLR-based antisubmarine operations and the Army Air Force "really wanted to turn it over to the Navy and let them do their own work."[20]

4 March: Atlantic Ocean, Azores Region

The infamous U-515 under Lieutenant Commander Henke, on its third cruise northwest of the Azores, sunk the cargo ship *California Star*, 10,657 tons with fifty out of seventy-four crewmen lost.[21]

16 March: London

Three weeks after receiving Vintras's report and with the justification found in the 1373 treaty requiring "succor" from Portugal, Churchill ordered his staff into action, sending this memo to General Sir Hastings Ismay for the COS:

> Sir Orme Sargent
>
> 1. The sinkings in the South Atlantic bring the question of the Azores again to the fore. You know how keen the President [Roosevelt] is on establishing Allied Control there. It seems hardly likely that at this moment such an event could bring the Germans down upon Spain. Now that Mr. Eden is in Washington is the moment for this matter to be discussed over there.
> 2. The Foreign Office should furnish the Chiefs of Staff and me today with a paper showing shortly the political considerations and any pledges we may have given.
>
> [initialed] W. S. C. 16.3.43[22]

The COS decided that all dealings must be directly with the Portuguese and not with either the Americans or Brazilians. But instead of resolutely following an aggressive course of action, neither the COS or the Foreign Office did anything in the month that followed. The COS felt they had to wait until the last Axis troops were completely cleaned out of North Africa so that there would be no danger of an invasion of Iberia. General Ismay did not want to approach Portugal "until we have cleared the Tunisian tip" even though it was obvious that the remnants of the German army in North Africa had enough to do just staying alive, let alone plan an invasion of Iberia. By March the Allies were mopping up the remnants of the Afrika Korps and their Italian allies, but it was not until 12 May that the war actually ended in North Africa when the last of the German army surrendered on Cape Bon. If an excuse was needed to procrastinate and not take any action against the Portuguese Atlantic islands, waiting to clear the Axis armies out of Africa had been good enough.

5 April: Mitchel Field, New York

A decision was made by the powers-that-be that Operation Lifebelt would take place sooner rather than later, so units needed to be trained and made ready to sail whenever the order came through to build the air base. On this day General Order No. 26 was issued by Headquarters Army Air Forces, Eastern Defense Command, to activate the 928th EAR (less three battalions) on 10 April at the Army Air Base, Richmond, Virginia. Barely two months later, on 12 June at Camp Peary in Williamsburg, Virginia, the Azores team was completed when the 96th NCB was activated. It is more than a coincidence that the Trident Conference was sandwiched between these two events. The CCS met with Churchill and Roosevelt with the Azores a leading item on the agenda.[23]

Lt. Col. Arthur H. Kemp, author of the *History of the 928th Engineer Aviation Regiment (Less Three Battalions)* and eventually commanding officer, is the source for most of the information on the regiment. His secret report is in the U.S. National Archives, with not even a copy in the Office of the Historian, U.S. Army Corps of Engineers, where the official history of the 928th begins with their return to the United States from "overseas": "The unit having completed its overseas mission returned to the United States 10 March 1945." The regiment was one of the first to be redeployed from the European Theater through the United States to the Pacific, thanks to flying from the Azores air base which it had constructed. The regiment ended the war on Okinawa but that is another story.[24]

The first item in Kemp's history is the activation and a statement of the function of the regiment: "the supervision of training and operations of battalions which may be assigned to it by higher authority." Although no further information can be found in the National Archives other than Colonel Kemp's history, it is clear that the decision to activate the 928th EAR and the 96th NCB and for them to construct an air base in the Azores was made at a very high level. The 96th and the 928th would train themselves and then await orders to head out to Operation Lifeline.

Lieutenant Colonel Kemp was so certain that the regiment's secret pre-Pacific operation had been a great success that he took the liberty to end his report on a whimsical unmilitary note: "The unit embarked 16 July 1945 at Seattle, Washington. Japan's sudden surrender (that the 928th Engineer Aviation Regiment was en route is not to be overlooked as a contributing factor) entailed a two-week layover at Saipan."

Personnel assigned to the 928th were selected with care and with more attention paid to their professional engineering and construction skills than military attributes. Immediately upon activation at the Richmond Army Air Base, the 928th, with its officers and enlisted men acting as instructors, took over control of the officer's school at the base to give advanced training to newly commissioned Corps of Engineers officers.

The Richmond Air Base was an important center during the war for training aviation engineers—a uniquely American invention. European armies left air-base construction in the hands of "technicians," either conscripted civilians or engineers assigned to the ground forces, but with little input or control from the Air Force beyond its request for an airfield at a particular site. When the European war broke out General Hap Arnold, commander of the Army Air Corps, negotiated with the chief of engineers to form special engineer units to work directly with his Air Corps. The original idea was that small groups of skilled construction and engineering troops trained intimately with air units would be easily available to build and patch up airfields damaged by bombing, camouflage them, and if necessary defend them. They were prepared to accompany task forces and build airfields in support of operations in forward areas, answering primarily to the Air Force and only secondarily to the Corps of Engineers.[25]

In June 1940, soon after the German invasion of Poland, the Corps of Engineers accepted the Air Corps proposal. The Corps organized the first self-contained Aviation Engineer battalions consisting of 27 officers and 761 men, equipped with much of the heavy equipment typically used in civilian airport construction. On 4 June 1940, the newly reactivated 21st Engineers (General Services) Regiment, which had a proud history in the St. Mihiel and Meuse-Argonne offensives of World War I, was redesignated the 21st Engineers (Aviation) Regiment at Fort Benning, Georgia, and thus became the parent unit of the aviation engineers.

When the United States entered the war, some engineer aviation battalions were already overseas and went to work immediately. The units had been organized and equipped well enough to function independently, carrying out missions in every theater throughout the war. At their peak, in February 1945, the Aviation Engineers numbered 117,851 officers and men.

11 April: Führer's Berghof near Berchtesgaden

The OKM reported nineteen U-boats sunk in February, fifteen in March and sixteen (to date) in April. Submarine warfare was more difficult as the new Allied tactics were starting to pay off, and the ratio of enemy ships sunk to U-boats destroyed was becoming unfavorable. Germany was losing the one strategy that could win the Battle of the Atlantic—sinking ships faster than the enemy could build them. Dönitz pleaded for an increased allocation of thirty thousand tons of steel to the shipyards to boost construction to twenty-seven boats per month. Hitler agreed and authorized the increased allocation.

There was general agreement that Operation Gisela, successor-apparent to Operation Felix and the occupation of Iberia, was possible only with the consent of Spain. Considering the turn of events, and with only limited German forces available for the operation, cooperation was absolutely essential to have any chance of success. But it was unlikely that Franco would cooperate with Germany, who he must perceive as losing the war.[26]

13 April: Richmond Air Base, Virginia

Lieutenant Nathan D. Jaffe appointed company commander of Headquarters and Services Company 928th Engineer Aviation Regiment which consisted of 19 officers and 257 enlisted men.

A month later, on 25 May, Jaffe, by then a captain, was relieved and 1st Lieutenant Harris M. Gitlin assumed command, which to judge by the illustrated company history, improved company morale. Gitlin was promoted to captain and remained company commander throughout the operations in the Azores.[27]

17 April: North Atlantic

Captured U-boat crew members, who only two months earlier were defiant and felt it only a matter of time before they were liberated by a victorious Germany, had now lost their bravado and were expressing pessimism about the ultimate victory promised by the Führer: Hermann

Klotsch, *Obsteuermann* (navigator) on U-175, captured 17 April 1943 after his boat was sunk by U.S. Coast Guard Cutter *Spencer:*

"Things look very bad for us. The boats are being sunk one after the other."

A navigator from Regensburg talking to another captured U-boat crew member: "If things go wrong, Adolf [Hitler] will go to Switzerland."

"No he'll do himself in. Herrmann [Goering] will go to his daughter who is married and living in Sweden. Himmler will put on a fig leaf and go to Africa."[28]

17 April: Newfoundland

The ATC (Air Transport Command), under increasing pressure to expedite supplies and personnel to North Africa and the Mediterranean, decided to try flying nonstop from Newfoundland to Marrakech in North Africa. The first flight to attempt this twenty-six hundred mile stretch was a C-54 under contract to American Airlines, piloted by John F. Davidson, with a cargo load of 4,705 pounds and carrying two passengers, including Brigadier General Benjamin F. Giles commander of the ATC North Atlantic wing. Giles wanted especially to fly over the Azores and get a good look at the islands but unfortunately they were completely blanketed by clouds when the plane passed over them. The C-54 reached Marrakech in fourteen hours with barely an hour and a half fuel supply left but showed that the new route was feasible, at least in an easterly direction. Returning the same way was impossible because of prevailing westerly winds so planes from North Africa had to return by the South Atlantic route.[29]

Eighteen hours after the C-54 left Newfoundland, a B-24 with auxiliary bomb-bay fuel tanks installed departed on the same route arriving in Marrakech in fifteen hours. Ferrying of four-engine bombers to the Mediterranean was thus shown to be feasible but would be easier if aircraft could fly both east and west using a base in the Azores.

25 April: London

Group Captain Vintras had been informed by his Portuguese counterparts that the landing strip on the island of Terceira in the Azores could be operational by the summer. This was indeed good news; it was critical to reach an agreement soon and for the Royal Navy and the RAF to occupy the base as soon as it was ready, or preferably before. Unfortunately the Chiefs of Staff and the Foreign Office were still procrastinating on what should be the next step, so another memorandum was needed to shake them up. Captain Charles Lambe, Admiralty Director of Plans, had his fill of frustration and wrote on 25 April to the Chief of the Naval Staff:

FIRST SEA LORD   MOST SECRET

Atlantic Islands

[1.] I understand that the present situation regarding the Portuguese Atlantic Islands is as follows:—

(a) The Chiefs of Staff deferred decisions until C.I.G.S. was satisfied regarding German inability to invade Spain.

(b) C.I.G.S. now appears to be reasonably satisfied regarding this.

(c) Brigadier Hollis has informed the Foreign Office that the Chiefs of Staff do not now envisage action regarding Portuguese islands in the near future.

(d) As a result of (c) Sir Ronald Campbell has now gone back to Portugal *and no further preparations are being made by the Foreign Office for an approach to Dr. Salazar* [emphasis in originals]. . . .

2. We in the Joint Planning Staff gather from talks with Sir Ronald Campbell that the prospects of obtaining the use of the Azores were *by no means hopeless.*

3. If it is still the intention of the Chiefs of Staff to press for such action immediately the Germans are thrown out of Tunisia, I think they should recommend to the War Cabinet that the preparations should be completed as soon as possible.[30]

General Sir Alan Brooke, chief of the Imperial General Staff, was one of the principal impediments to taking action. His overworked imagination nursed a nightmare that the German Army had a "Mass of Maneuver"—renamed by the Joint Intelligence Staff the "Mass of Manure"—which could sweep down through Spain and Portugal at a moment's notice and compromise all Allied operations in the Mediterranean.

This despite the general knowledge that Operation Gisela had been written off as completely beyond the Reichswehr's limited resources.

With no action on the part of the War Cabinet or Foreign Office, consequently with no pressure applied to Portugal, Churchill decided he could wait no longer. Until the screws were put to him, Salazar would do what he was so adept at doing—temporizing. Forceful action was required if a base was to be established in the Azores. Portugal had to be told that England's patience was worn thin, and military action would be taken if diplomatic negotiations did not produce favorable results.

28 April: Cable to Secretary of State, Washington, D.C.

Robert D. Murphy transmitted an agreement by the Mediterranean Air Command to consider the proposal of Aero-Portuguesa to operate a direct service between Lisbon and French Morocco. In return the Command wanted the Portuguese government to permit transatlantic planes operated by a civilian air line to use the Azores for refueling. From May to October the route would be Gander–Azores–northwest Africa and in the winter months New York–Bermuda–Azores–Africa. If the airports needed improvement to bear the increased traffic, the U.S. government would be willing to take care of the problem. It was clear from Murphy's cable that U.S. officials in the Mediterranean had no idea that negotiations to obtain bases in the Azores were ongoing.[31]

12 May: North Africa and Europe

Surrounded on all sides in Tunisia and with an Allied blockade of the sea, the much-vaunted Afrika Korps witnessed a total collapse when its last remnants plus the Italian armies surrendered en masse on Cape Bon. Now that the war in North Africa was won, and the threat to Portugal no longer imminent, pressure on Dr. Salazar could be more relentless.

Hitler had plenty of other things to worry about besides Iberia. Foremost, of course, was the loss of the Afrika Korps, but in addition, as he complained to his High Command, was being saddled with Italy. Italy was disintegrating rapidly, army desertions were high, and morale was at rock bottom. It was clear to Mussolini that the Allies would invade Sicily followed by Italy next, but Hitler was completely taken in once again by British Intelligence. The military problem of where the Allies would next strike was still unsolved. While Dönitz was in Italy, an Allied order had been discovered and shown to Hitler, pointing to Sardinia and the Peloponnesus as the next Allied objective.[32] One thing was certain: if the Allies invaded Sicily, the Italian army would switch sides in a heartbeat, and the Germans would have to invade and occupy their former partner.

15–18 May: The Trident Conference, Washington, D.C.

One purpose of the Trident conference was to work out a strategy regarding the Azores. The prime minister and his War Cabinet arrived on the *Queen Mary*, which could easily outrun any U-boat, and given the protection afforded by the British fleet escort, was less perilous than traveling by air. Churchill was especially pleased to be in Washington with military leaders who thought as he did and away from his unadventurous War Cabinet in London. The military people respected only action; to the politicians in London the only solution to any problem was to negotiate ad infinitum ad nauseum. Surrounded by people who thought alike, the two leaders of the world's greatest democracies could talk about the use of force if necessary to get an air base in the Azores. It was no secret that Roosevelt enthusiastically favored immediate action and that Churchill did not need much arm-twisting to go along with him.[33]

On 7 May, while en route to Washington, the British Chiefs of Staff Committee, General A. F. Brooke, Admiral Dudley Pound, and Air Chief Marshall C. Portal prepared a detailed report for consideration at the meeting based on Admiral Pound's memorandum of 22 February to the War Cabinet. The U.S. Secret and British Most Secret report "Use of Portuguese Atlantic Islands" subsequently became the keystone for Allied policy dealing with Portugal:

> Experience has shown that so long as we can keep even a single aircraft with a convoy during the greater part of each day, the operation of U-boats is greatly hampered. In order to obtain maximum air protection at the present time, it is necessary for our

convoys to follow a route which not only suffers from the disadvantages of bad weather and ice, but which inevitably becomes known to the enemy. If we take a southerly route at the present time we have to forego a considerable measure of air protection. If we had both a northerly and southerly route which had equal air protection it would be a great advantage and consequently facilities in the Portuguese Atlantic Islands would be of outstanding value in shortening the war by convincing the enemy he has lost the Battle of the Atlantic.

The memorandum went on to list the facilities needed for operating VLR aircraft and for fuelling naval escorts, including Terceira for aircraft and Faial for naval escorts. Increased air cover would allow

much greater scope for evasive routing, for example, when U-boats were concentrated in northern waters, North Atlantic convoys could be routed via the Azores instead of always having to follow the Iceland route. Without the Azores we shall always be moving on the outside of the circle while the enemy operates inside it. Air forces there would be centrally placed to cover all varieties of the U-boat campaign against the North Atlantic and Mediterranean theaters.

We could increase our harassing action against U-boats not only when on passage to and from the Biscay bases, but also while resting, refueling and recharging their batteries in mid-ocean where hitherto they have been practically immune from interference by aircraft. New detection and attacking devices, which are expected to come into service this Spring, would enhance the effect of such action.

The memo ended with the warning that it might be necessary to

undertake new commitments in order to induce Portugal to give us the facilities in question. The extent of that price and the character of those commitments will depend upon our, and still more important the Portuguese, estimate of the way in which the Axis is likely to react to the transaction. Although we cannot be certain of it, strong reasons can be advanced for thinking that Germany will not, in fact, attack the Iberian Peninsula. . . . If we assume the worse case, i.e. that the Axis Powers . . . make war upon Portugal and attack her metropolitan overseas territory . . . the commitments which Portugal would require us to undertake . . . would probably include . . . the defense of Portugal against land and air attack . . .

To fulfil a guarantee to go to the assistance of Portugal against [an] attack we should have to earmark and prepare now between 9 and 11 divisions and some 20 squadrons of aircraft, and hold this force in readiness together with their shipping. This course could only be followed at the expense of HUSKY[34] and other future operations in the Mediterranean. Even·if this could be done, there would be no certainty that we could protect more than a portion of Portuguese territory. . . .

If we take the risk of provoking a German invasion of the Iberian Peninsula . . . we may well find that we shall be left without a footing in the Peninsula, except at Gibraltar itself. A base in the Azores would be of particular value during the winter, when the weather in the north frequently interferes with flying. From this aspect, therefore, it is desirable to make our approach to the Portuguese sufficiently early to allow the bases to be in full working order by the autumn. A particularly favourable moment to open negotiations is now when victory in Tunis is in sight. The Portuguese are less likely to make high demands for protection and the Spaniards are more likely to resist German pressure.

Having regard to the fact that we consider Germany is unlikely to invade the Iberian Peninsula, and the tremendous benefits we would gain from the use of the Island . . . we feel the risk is acceptable. We therefore recommend that the War Cabinet should authorise an approach to the Portuguese Government now, but no guarantee should be given, and every endeavour should be made to persuade the Portuguese that no threat exists.

/s/ A. F. Brooke,

> Dudley Pound,
> C. Portal.
> S.S. Queen Mary, 7 May 1943.

The U.S. Joint Chiefs enthusiastically endorsed the report and presented it to Roosevelt and Churchill to adopt as official Allied policy.[35]

Proposals for action came with lightning speed. First, Admiral King suggested that England take the initiative, seize the Azores, and build an antisubmarine base to insure the safety of transatlantic convoys and communications. Next, President Roosevelt recommended sending a whole division plus four hundred anti-aircraft guns and fourteen squadrons of fighter aircraft to the Azores. Churchill cabled his War Cabinet in London that he was going to discuss a combined front with the United States against Salazar and that they would present with an ultimatum to allow Allied occupation of the islands or else face the use of force.[36]

The CCS approved the plan for a British invasion but then gave in to the War Cabinet pleading to first wait and see if ongoing negotiations failed. Every diplomatic approach should be exhausted before resorting to force for after all an invasion of the Azores would be in violation of England's treaties with Portugal, its most reliable ally and friend in Europe. Moreover, the argument was moot: no landing craft were available; every vessel in and around Europe had been committed months before for the coming invasions of Sicily and Italy. The CCS wanted to earmark three landing craft LSA (LSI-L) for amphibious landings in the Azores but this was vetoed because the invasion of Sicily starting on 10 July would require the use of every landing craft afloat in the European and Mediterranean theaters. Sicily was to be quickly followed by landings on mainland Italy and the loss of even three landing craft would compromise both operations.[37]

Roosevelt and Churchill confronted the problem by suggesting that a full-scale invasion of the Iberian Peninsula might be a worthy substitute for Italy. For the military, German-Spanish resistance to an Allied landing followed by a full-fledged Peninsula war was a strategic nightmare to be avoided at any cost. Napoleon had learned the hard way to avoid making war in Iberia when his armies met their first critical defeat at the hands of Lord Wellington and the combined Anglo-Portuguese forces. The lesson was not lost on the CCS.

The conference culminated in approval of a position paper calling for action; this year alone four U.S. convoys headed to the North African–Mediterranean Theater suffered losses to the U-boats. All the convoys had to sail through the Azores Gap and across most of the Atlantic without the protection of VLR bombers.[38]

One hundred vessels sailed each month to the Mediterranean Theater and to England from the United States through the "black hole"

U.S. Convoys to North Africa Lost to U-Boat Attacks, January–April 1943

CONVOY	PORT OF EMBARKATION	SAILING DATE	ARRIVAL DATE	SHIPS ARRIVED (TONNAGE)	SHIPS LOST (TONNAGE)
UGS-4	New York	13 Jan	31 Jan	34 cargo, 2 tanker (316,500)	4 (6,700)
UGS-5	New York, Hampton Roads	7 Feb	19 Feb	36 cargo, 5 tanker (363,500)	1 (7,900)
UGS-6	New York, Hampton Roads	4 Mar	21 Mar	34 cargo, 2 tanker (329,500)	5 (39,000)
UGS-7	New York, Hampton Roads, Baltimore, Boston	1 Apr	19 Apr	31 cargo, 10 tanker (310,000)	3 (29,900)

Source: Leighton and Coakley, *The United States Army in World War II*, 485.

and an additional one hundred sailed from the Caribbean and South America. Protection of convoys in the central Atlantic was essential to sustain Allied operations in the Mediterranean and to keep the buildup for Overlord on schedule. The memorandum read:

THE COMBINED CHIEFS OF STAFF
WASHINGTON
18 May 1943
MEMORANDUM FOR THE PRESIDENT AND PRIME MINISTER:
Subject: Use of Portuguese Atlantic Islands.

The Combined Chiefs of Staff are agreed as to the tremendous benefits which the United Nations would gain from the earliest possible use of the Azores Islands. They recommend that the Portuguese Government should be approached at once on this subject, but that no guarantee should be given and that every endeavor should be made to persuade the Portuguese that no threat exists. They consider that Germany is unlikely to invade the Iberian Peninsula if the Azores Islands are so used, and that the risk is acceptable.

In submitting this recommendation the Combined Chiefs of Staff propose that while the diplomatic approach is being made forces should be prepared for the prompt seizure and use of the Azores if diplomacy fails. Plans are therefore being prepared and will be submitted, showing the earliest date for their execution and how, it at all, they will affect operations now in view.

A. F. Brooke,	William D. Leahy,
General,	Admiral, U.S. Navy,
Chief of the Imperial	Chief of Staff to the
General Staff.	Commander in Chief of
	the Army and Navy.[39]

Before any military action was taken, two distinguished and powerful advisers convinced the world leaders to calm down, Roosevelt by General Marshall and Churchill by Eden who asked the prime minister not to take such an extreme step but to wait until he returned to London to discuss the alternatives with the cabinet. Churchill reluctantly agreed, induced to wait and hear his cabinet's side after reading Eden's cable:

> His Majesty's Ambassador in Lisbon . . . thought there was a chance of Salazar giving us what we want. Salazar's temperament being what it is he is less likely to give way to an ultimatum. We feel it would be better to invoke the Alliance and state our case. If he rejects that he will have shown that the Alliance is of little value. We should then be in a better moral position than if we, without any approach, suddenly threatened to seize the territory of an Ally.[40]

Because no landing craft were available, the Azores expedition was called off. Eden won this time. He knew that when Churchill left for Trident, the fleet admirals, RAF air marshals, and army generals would press for an invasion of the Azores. Eden was also afraid that Roosevelt might just go ahead with a Brazil–U.S. task force if he felt frustrated by a British veto. Although Trident did not lead to an armed invasion of the Azores, it did result in increased diplomatic pressure on Portugal, and convinced Salazar that the patience of the Allies had worn thin. But if enough landing craft had been available, how would history have explained the only aggression by the Allies in World War II against a neutral country?

21 May: Berlin

Admiral Dönitz withdrew his U-boats from the North Atlantic where he acknowledged that Germany suffered a serious although, he thought, temporary defeat. He was confident that German science would soon provide the means to counter the Allied technical advantage, notably the superior radar, and design a class of super-submarines. To win the war, the U-boats would have to return to the North Atlantic and prevent the United States's bottomless source of supplies and manpower from reaching Europe. A German radio broadcast publicly acknowledged that "the U-boats have been temporarily thwarted by new Allied defensive measures."[41] However, through all this, the size of the U-boat fleet was increasing. On 31 May the OIC figured 240 U-boats in service, an increase of 66 since September 1942 despite the great losses they suffered in the interval. In June the number was 226 with another 208 waiting in the Baltic.[42]

According to a decrypt of a telegram from the Japanese ambassador in Berlin of an interview with Dönitz, Germany expected to resume "effective U-boat warfare" at the end of August.[43] Meanwhile, in order to preserve the fleet, Dönitz decided to move the U-boats out of range of Allied airfields and ordered the sixteen boats on patrol in the north Atlantic to form a new group, *Trutz* (Defiance), and operate southwest of the Azores with the task of intercepting convoys bound from the United States to Gibraltar. Most of the U-boats still in their pens in Bay of Biscay ports were dispatched to other more distant waters. If Dönitz's prediction was true, with a larger and faster U-boat fleet equipped with better anti-aircraft guns, improved radar search receivers, and schnorchels, the balance might tilt in favor of the submarines. Meeting with his technical experts from the Naval High Command, all agreed upon the following measures which would give the Allies plenty to worry about:[44]

1. U-boats to be equipped with search-receivers which would determine if they were being detected and radar gear, notwithstanding the limited range of the current model.
2. An investigation to see if it would be possible to insulate a U-boat against radio location. Although the enemy emitted his signals he would obtain no echo because the signals would be absorbed by the U-boat.

In an effort to boost sagging morale Dönitz sent his personal message to the U-boat fleet:

> Whoever is of the opinion that offensive action against convoys is no longer possible is a weakling and not a true U-boat commander. The battle in the Atlantic is becoming harder, but it is the decisive factor in this war. Be conscious of your great responsibility and be quite certain that you will have to answer for your deeds.[45]

On 31 May Hitler tried his hand at boosting morale in the U-boat fleet explaining why it had to keep up the unequal battle in the Atlantic:

> There can be no talk of a let-up in the U-boat war. The Atlantic is my first line of defense in the West. And even if I have to fight a defensive battle there, that is preferable to waiting to defend myself on the coast of Europe. The enemy forces tied down by our U-boats are tremendous, even though the losses by us are no longer great. I cannot afford to release these forces by discontinuing the U-boat war."[46]

June: U.S. Ministry, Lisbon

While diplomats and military brass were consumed in Washington, London, and Berlin devising strategies to fight the war in the Atlantic, the U.S. Embassy in Portugal was headed by an acting ambassador.[47] The United States was fortunate that he happened to be George Kennan, one of the most brilliant diplomats of the twentieth century who in 1943 became the de facto ambassador when Ambassador Burt Fish unexpectedly died. Kennan had been carrying out most of the duties of ambassador since he arrived the year before because Fish was reluctant to meet with Salazar, a man he thought too smart for him to deal with. Kennan ascribed Fish's refusal to seek an interview with Salazar to a healthy respect bordering on fear: "Ah ain't goin' down there and get mah backsides kicked around," he told Kennan. 'He's too smaht for me.'"

Kennan thought Fish's lack of vision and inactivity as not only unsatisfactory, but considering the unknown course the war might take,

dangerous. He was certain it was critical to define our wartime relationship with Portugal, and the sooner the better. The country was
expected to remain neutral, but any new developments in the direction
of the war would introduce more problems in the relations. It was
absolutely essential to establish some reasonable understanding between the United States and Portugal and it would take a strong man to
do it. Kennan was exactly that person. As he described the circumstances around his appointment:

> This was to be my formal position and I was to have all the nor-
> mal duties and responsibilities that went with it. But in addition
> to this I was asked, privately and informally, to take the lead in
> trying to straighten out the dreadful confusions which our vari-
> ous intelligence people had created, among themselves and with
> the British, in their efforts to insert themselves into the already
> seething cauldron of espionage and counterespionage that war-
> time Lisbon constituted.

Kennan learned informally that the British were secretly negotiating to
acquire an air base in the Azores and later discovered that the U.S. military wanted one of their own, more ample than the British base. Plans
for the liberation of Europe called for a dramatic increase in the volume of transatlantic air traffic much of which would be routed via the
Azores.[48]

Kennan appreciated the fact that getting U.S. troops into the Azores
was not going to be a simple task. Neither the State Department nor
(especially) the Joint Chiefs had the patience to resolve the problem
peacefully, and much of his time was to be spent fighting an ongoing
battle against the schemes coming out of Washington. Many in Washington appeared to be indifferent about English reaction if we invaded
Portuguese territory and were not worried about fouling up the negotiations which were about to begin.

Churchill had been won over to the diplomatic route and was planning to invoke the 1373 treaty. Negotiations would go slowly and
painfully, but the general feeling in the War Cabinet was that the
United States should just wait and "get in the back door" after the
British first arrived in the Azores. The United States should not bring
pressure independently on Portugal nor take the rash step of invading
the Azores because that would certainly compromise the negotiations,
which appeared to be finally on track. In any event the situation would

have been a great embarrassment and difficult to explain: the Portuguese and their English allies were bound by the 1373 treaty and would, theoretically, fight together against Americans.

One horrendous idea—that mercifully was shot down—was a brainstorm of General "Wild Bill" Donovan, chief of the Office of Special Services (OSS), who was planning his own private covert operation in Azores. The OSS assumed:

1. The inhabitants of the Azores could be made to rise up "spontaneously" in a massive revolt against Portuguese authority, a drive for independence, which would be popularly supported on all the islands.
2. Salazar was a dangerous Fascist, a good friend of Mussolini, and in league with the enemy. If not overtly, he at least covertly supported Germany. The OSS felt there was a real danger that if asked by Hitler, Salazar would welcome German occupation of the Azores.[49]

Kennan, backed up by the British ambassador to Portugal, reacted strongly and succeeded in having the plan squelched. The OSS's premises for the operation were completely wrong, based on wishful thinking coupled with ignorance of the situation in the islands. This and other schemes for a U.S. invasion and occupation of the Azores ignored some salient facts. People from the Azores were proud to be part of Portugal and to have played an important role in Portuguese history. Never had they shown any evidence that they wanted independence from the mother country. Although the islands are now autonomous and have their own legislature, the locals invariably insist "Sou Português das Ilhas" ("I'm Portuguese first then from the Islands"). It was true that Portugal was totalitarian, but the people appeared to respect their leader Salazar who, like them, was politically conservative and deeply religious.

Kennan learned that a stumbling block in the negotiations with Salazar was the United States's refusal to guarantee the territorial integrity of Portugal. Why should Salazar let us in the Azores if he had no guarantee that we would ever leave? Despite Roosevelt's statement in his earlier personal letter that the United States would recognize Portuguese sovereignty, the State Department thought that the guarantee could be withheld as a quid pro quo for the Azores bases. Kennan, on the other hand, felt that giving the guarantee would alleviate Portuguese fears that we planned to permanently occupy the islands and might convince them to approve the bases now. He was all for cutting the Gordian knot but did not know that a more influential voice, that of John Winant, U.S. ambassador to London, was behind the idea of withholding the guarantee as a means of putting pressure on the Portuguese.[50]

The State Department, confronted with three different approaches on how to get in the Azores—two diplomatic ones from Kennan and Winant plus the undiplomatic one from the Joint Chiefs to go to war with Portugal—did what it did so well: vacillate. It let Winant pass his ideas along to Churchill but also told Kennan to extend assurances to Salazar, and no one told him that his action was contradictory to that of our ambassador in London.

Roosevelt let Churchill know that a U.S. force of ten thousand men could be sent at a moment's notice to start work on an air base. The prime minister was pleased but the War Cabinet was horrified and convinced him to calm Washington down. First, such a large U.S. force would be a needless duplication of the British forces that were scheduled to go to the Azores once an agreement went through. Second, headway had finally been made with Salazar who was about to agree to the British bases. Finally, Salazar wanted to keep the Americans out of the picture for two good reasons: first, that once in the Azores they would stay; second, how to explain it to Germany.

1 June: Williamsburg, Virginia

As per orders from Navy Headquarters the 96th "Seabee" Battalion was organized at the Naval Construction Training Center, Camp Peary, Williamsburg, Virginia, under the command of Lieutenant Commander E. H. Honnen. In a few days officers and drafts of men began arriving, most of them just out of basic training but almost all skilled in the construction trades. The cruise book of the 96th describes the first days:

> Those were busy days. Medical records had to be checked, and all those who had not been previously inoculated were given treatments[51] . . . Then there were those experience cards for 1,100 men . . . organization charts . . . war bonds . . . and miscellaneous details which, coupled with three of the hottest, most sultry days yet experienced that summer in Virginia, made the

week an unpleasant memory. However, the newness of the job, the contrast with routine "boot" work, and the sincere desire of everyone to "get going" as soon as possible, all contributed sufficient impetus to cope with the job at hand.

June 12th saw the Battalion "shoving off" for Davisville, Rhode Island.

The decision to activate the 96th Seabees and the 928th EAR must have been made at a high level. The Army Engineers could handle many of the construction projects at Lagens relating to the airfield, such as improving the landing strip and erecting buildings, but some tasks would require Seabee talents. Considering the need for ship traffic to supply the base, port facilities would have to be improved. A submarine pipeline to offload tankers and fuel storage tanks for aviation fuel were needed; quarters and service facilities for the expected Navy antisubmarine squadron had to be built. All this called for the Seabees.[52]

The Seabees were organized in March 1942 and arose out of the civilian construction workers who were doing the bulk of the Navy's overseas construction work when the war broke out. By international law, as civilians these workers could not be armed, had no way to defend themselves, and had to rely on the Navy for protection. Rear Admiral Ben Moreell, chief of the Bureau of Yards and Docks, realized that as civilian employees they had no place in a combat zone so asked for and received the "OK" to form them into military units that could defend themselves against attack and hold and defend the construction site. The need for such an organization was dramatized when naval civilian construction workers were trapped on Wake Island at the outbreak of war. They could not be evacuated and despite the legal protection afforded by international convention as noncombatants, they were all eventually shot by the Japanese.[53]

Once organized, the Seabee Battalions immediately went to work building airstrips to support island invasions in the Pacific but were eventually represented in every theater. When Operation Overlord began they went on to their most famous construction project of World War II, building an artificial harbor in Normandy following the landings. But right now the 96th NCB was about to take part in a supersecret operation and were no more enlightened about it than their cohorts in the 928th EAR.

27 June: Atlantic Theater

The U-boats were taking a beating in the North Atlantic from VLR air-craft on the Newfoundland–Greenland–Iceland route and from the much improved convoy escorts. In the month only ten Allied merchant ships were sunk against a loss of sixteen U-boats. U-boat losses had risen from about 13 percent of those at sea to 30 percent, a rate the Ger-man Navy could not sustain. At least operations around the Azores Gap did not have VLR bombers to contend with so Dönitz ordered wolf pack Trutz to move directly to the west of the Azores. Trutz was a six-teen boat patrol force which had been operating in the North Atlantic and now would form a barrier along the forty-third meridian, about 750 miles west by south of Faial. Being far from Allied bombers should make life more sustainable for the submarines.[54]

Unfortunately for Trutz, its moves were well known to British Intelligence, thanks to decrypted Enigma messages. The escort-carrier *Bogue* was sent to protect two threatened convoys that had to pass through the Azores Gap. Excellent intelligence gave the *Bogue* a great advantage over the wolf pack—it had a good idea of its exact strength and disposition. The first convoy was successfully diverted so it would not pass anywhere near the pack. On 4 June the second convoy steamed through a gap opened up in the heart of the wolf pack by *Bogue*'s air-craft. The aircraft surprised the U-boats who had no idea their position was known; three submarines were attacked and one was sunk. During the next four weeks the wolf pack's patrol area was shifted several times, but each time new movement orders went out, British Intelli-gence read them as fast as the U-boat captains could decrypt them. Convoys were rerouted as Trutz changed positions with the result that not one target sighting was made by the U-boats during the entire period of patrol. Finally at the beginning of July, west of Cape São Vicente off the southwest tip of Portugal, the wolf pack suffered its last indignity—another surprise air attack and the loss of three more sub-marines. Trutz was ordered home and no more U-boat packs would be sent out until September.[55]

Two other serious problems that plagued Admiral Dönitz were first, the great losses U-boats suffered just leaving their pens in France and sailing through the Bay of Biscay to reach the open ocean, and second, the Allies targeting the milchkuhen that allowed U-boats to stay out longer on patrol. In the year ending May 1943, the milchkuhen had refueled 170 U-boats headed for distant waters and 220 operating against convoys, and had done so without being disturbed, although three were sunk while on passage. At the beginning of June, nine supply U-boats were available and three more became operational by the end of the year. However, ten were sunk by then, no less than four during 13–20 June.

An important part of the campaign was for U.S. escort-carrier task forces to hunt the supply U-boats in their favorite rendezvous spots. There was a serious problem that both the British and U.S. commands had to resolve: if the operation was too successful, then German fears would be aroused that their codes were broken, but this did not happen. On 12 June aircraft from the *Bogue*, working on information from Enigma, surprised the supply U-boat U-118 at its rendezvous point about four hundred miles southwest of Faial, 30°49′ N, 33°49′ W and sunk it as well as two other submarines that were followed from the rendezvous. The loss of U-118 forced a recall of some operational U-boats and a delay of others in reaching distant patrol areas. The success of this operation convinced the Joint Chiefs to exploit Enigma even more in the campaign against German refueling operations. Dönitz complained to Hitler that

> we are facing the greatest crisis in submarine warfare, since the enemy by means of new location devices . . . makes fighting impossible, and is causing us heavy losses (15–17 submarines a month). . . . Furthermore at the present time the only outward route for submarines is a narrow lane in the Bay of Biscay. This passage is so difficult that it now takes a submarine ten days to get through.[56]

Hitler agreed that the losses were too high, that something had to be done but rejected the OKM's suggestion that "the occupation of Spain, including Gibraltar would be the best strategic solution. This would constitute an attack against the flank of the Anglo-Saxon offensive, the Axis would regain the initiative, a radical change would take place in the Mediterranean, and submarine warfare could be given much broader basis." Hitler's response was that first-class German troops would be needed, that they were not available and further, in his first admission that Spain was not on the side of the Axis, "since they are the only real tough Latin people, and would carry on guerrilla warfare in our rear." This appeared to be the last word on Operation Gisela, an admission that it was too late in the war to think about invading Spain and Portugal.[57]

8 July: Führer Conference at Wolfsschanze

The OKM reported that

1. Professor Messerschmidt developed a new six-engine aircraft with a range of 17,000 km and which possesses very strong armament and high speed. Hitler has given up the idea of bombing the U.S. because the few aircraft that would make it there would only arouse the American will to resist. However, these machines can be used for reconnaissance.
2. Submarines transferred from the North Atlantic to new areas of patrol where antisubmarine measures are not so strong. However our losses are high in the exit lanes against the Strait of Shetland and the Bay of Biscay where the enemy is directing his main efforts.
3. New efficient radar will be ready end of July to give warning and a flash fix of position of the radar source. Speer is producing the subs but the Navy does not have crews to man them. Needs 262,000 young men by autumn 1944 but the Führer thinks the figure too high, men are not available. OKW will supply 10,000 technicians of age group 1925 (18 years old) and 20–25,000 recruited by the SS from occupied territories.[58]

18 July: Gulfport, Mississippi

The 96th NCB had been through basic training in Rhode Island and received its colors as a commissioned unit of the U.S. Navy on 17 June. Early in July the Battalion was alerted for overseas duty and shipped off to Gulfport POE. After returning to the POE from a ten-day embarkation leave and gung-ho to go into battle anywhere, the shipping orders were canceled and the "Travelling 96th" again boarded coaches for the three-day trip back to Rhode Island. Nothing can be found in either the Seabee or the National Archives to explain the mysterious wanderings but a reasonable explanation, given the round trip to Gulfport POE, is that a decision to send the 96th to the South Pacific was overruled when the Trident Conference set a high priority for Operation Alacrity. The goodbyes would have to wait until later in the year.

For the rest of their stay that year in Rhode Island, the battalion went through intensive training, including a week on the rifle range followed by a rigorous construction and maintenance program. Toward the end of the training period, a five-day leave was granted the Battalion. The Cruise Book notes that "About 180 men were A.W.O.L, and shortly thereafter approximately 180 "boot" haircuts appeared. The commander earned for himself the sobriquet "Clipper Packing Skipper."[59] This title became legend, even in the South Pacific.

SEVEN

CHURCHILL LOWERS THE BOOM, JUNE–SEPTEMBER 1943

> The tonnage war is the main task for the submarines, probably the most decisive contribution of submariners to winning the war. This war on merchant shipping must be carried out where the greatest successes can be achieved with the smallest losses.
>
> Dönitz's charge to U-boat fleet

The Azores Gap became the U-boats' favored hunting ground and, coincidentally, smack in the heavily trafficked Allied shipping lanes to North Africa and the Mediterranean. Until the convoy escort aircraft carriers (CVEs) became available, sailing in the central Atlantic without air protection was a formula for disaster and the principal source for the 2.1 million tons of shipping lost in the first half of 1943, a rate of destruction that was not sustainable. An Allied air base in the mid-Atlantic would plug the Azores Gap.

Admiral Dönitz, who had had so much success in the "tonnage war" against the United States found that his U-boats were being hit hard through the North and west Atlantic. With land-based Allied aircraft patrolling around the clock, U-boat losses were unsupportable. Shifting operations to the central Atlantic was important, for the better chances of survival and to interdict the heavy flow of Allied troop and matériel to North Africa and the Mediterranean.

Dönitz ordered U-boat operations in the North Atlantic discontinued; nuisance operations would be stepped up in the Caribbean and South Atlantic off the coasts of Brazil and West Africa; the major U-boat deployment was to be in the central Atlantic based on the Azores Gap. Until the new acoustic torpedoes and radar gear were ready, it was better to avoid combat where the odds were stacked too high against the subs.

Moving to the gap should do much to improve the efficiency and morale of the submariners. What Dönitz had not counted on was that aircraft flying off the CVEs would prove deadlier than he thought possible. The only saving virtue for the Germans was the fact that delivery of CVEs was slower than planned. Adm. Royal E. Ingersoll, operational commander naval forces in the central Atlantic, was promised twenty CVEs at the beginning of the year but had control of only one by the end of January. By August, when wolf pack Trutz was ordered to the central Atlantic, Allied command had finally assigned five CVEs to that zone.[1]

The situation started to improve in the second half of the year thanks to the CVEs. Instead of closely guarding convoys as was done by destroyers, destroyer escorts (DE), and frigates, the CVEs, accompanied by two or three DEs, would search for U-boats three hundred miles ahead of the convoy route. Any U-boats found would be immediately attacked by the carrier aircraft. The USS *Core*, one of the first CVEs to see action in the "black hole" of the Atlantic, was responsible for sinking two U-boats on its first mission. On 13 July aircraft on patrol from the *Core* 720 miles south-southwest of Faial spotted U-487. One plane, a Wildcat, was shot down by anti-aircraft fire but three other planes attacked and sunk the sub. Another encounter took place two days later when U-67 was spotted, attacked, and sunk 842 miles southwest of Flores.[2]

No matter how much the CVEs improved the chances for a safe passage for convoys, Churchill felt they could not substitute for the continuous day-to-day surveillance of sea lanes that only land-based aircraft could provide. A base in the Azores would provide that protection. Because the Portuguese government was not coming around to the Allied point of view quickly enough, Churchill, not one to stand on ceremony with the outcome of the war at stake, proposed Operation Alacrity whereby British troops would invade and occupy the Azores for the duration of the war. Cooler heads in his cabinet convinced him that one more crack at diplomacy might work, especially because Salazar appeared to be coming around to granting the base.

By June Churchill agreed that because an agreement appeared likely there was no need to invade. Eden was to open discussions with the Portuguese ambassador to London, Armindo Monteiro, while Ambassador Campbell was to continue direct negotiations with Salazar in Lisbon.[3]

8 June: Lisbon

Salazar was feeling the heat and realized that the time for equivocation and stalling was over, the Allies were going to occupy the Azores by any means, if not by diplomacy then by force. He wrote a cordial note to Ambassador Campbell promising cooperation "in name of the alliance that had existed nearly six hundred years between Portugal and Great Britain, the Portuguese Government would provide facilities in the Azores Islands."[4]

Campbell followed up this opening quickly in a meeting with Salazar. First, the prime minister recalled the consultations held two years earlier between the British and Portuguese military staffs in London at a time when Germany was all powerful and had the means and resources to invade the Iberian Peninsula. Despite this, the Portuguese offered to come to the aid of England strictly adhering to the provisions of the treaty of 1373 to provide support against "perceived threats." England politely declined the offer because the risk in opening up another front had to be avoided, but now the situation had changed, the Allies were in control of North Africa, and Germany no longer posed a serious threat to either Gibraltar or Portugal. No more thought had to be given to moving the government to the Azores.[5]

16 June: Lisbon

London cabled the ambassador back to raise "certain matters of the highest importance," specifically to approach Dr. Salazar to grant the facilities in the Azores. Campbell was authorized (a) to guarantee the withdrawal of our forces from the Azores at the end of hostilities, and (b) to give assurances regarding the maintenance of Portuguese sovereignty over all the Portuguese colonies.

South Africa associated itself with these assurances and "there is reason to believe that similar assurances will be forthcoming from the Government of the United States." As Salazar found out the United States would drag its feet on giving assurances.[6]

Knowing that Roosevelt wanted to obtain facilities for U.S. armed forces, Churchill cabled urging him to be associated with both the requests and the assurances of Portuguese sovereignty. Roosevelt's response was disheartening and, worse, soured Salazar's attitude towards the United States for many months. Roosevelt answered that the United

States would gladly join England to assist Portugal if German threats against her materialized either in the air or on the high seas, but said nothing about recognizing sovereignty over her territory. So for now the negotiations were solely between the two ancient allies: for Portugal to allow England to defend itself in the Atlantic with "succor" provided by the Portuguese, and for England to defend Portugal in case of a German attack.

Campbell wrote to Salazar, thanking him for considering to grant bases in the Azores. England was also grateful for his helping convince Franco to keep Spain from joining the Axis and noted that the possibility of a German invasion had virtually disappeared. However, a serious threat to the Allies was the U-boat offensive in the Atlantic, which impeded the buildup of United Nations forces and could seriously delay the final victory. The British government concluded that facilities in the Azores "for the operation of aircraft and surface vessels would be a decisive factor in the early defeat of the German submarine campaign in the Atlantic and, consequently, a vital contribution to an early victory of the United Nations."[7]

Campbell listed the facilities needed, and pointed out that the request was strictly under the terms of the six hundred year old Alliance: a) Facilities in São Miguel and Terceira for operating reconnaissance aircraft; b) Fueling facilities for naval escorts at either São Miguel or Faial.

Assistance would be provided against a possible German air attack on the Portuguese mainland and full protection for Portuguese shipping. At the end of hostilities all Allied forces would be withdrawn from the islands which would be returned to full Portuguese sovereignty.

Salazar, a stickler for formality, could not lightly turn Campbell down but had to agree to grant the bases or give good reasons why he would not. "They [His Majesty's Government—HMG] most earnestly trust that the Portuguese government will in principle agree to this, leaving for further discussion and mutual agreement the precise conditions governing the grant of such facilities."[8] If the Portuguese Government agrees, then His Majesty's Government will discuss the measures of assistance against a possible German attack on the Portuguese mainland and full protection for Portuguese shipping on the high seas. Campbell's note ended with the statement that the Union of South Africa had associated itself with these assurances and repeated that there was reason to believe that the U.S. government would as well.

Salazar assured Campbell that his request would receive immediate sympathetic consideration He called in his undersecretary for war,

Colonel Santos Costa who was dead set against allowing the bases, afraid that such an action would commit Portugal to the side of the Allies, end her neutrality, and invite a German attack. In Indonesia, they both knew the Japanese invaded East Timor under the pretext that Allied troops had landed there first and action was necessary to "protect Portuguese interests." If the Allies occupied the Azores the unpredictable Germans might decide to "protect" mainland Portugal because they lacked the resources to attack the islands.[9]

Salazar was not swayed by Santos Costa's arguments; the Alliance had been invoked, and Portugal was honor-bound to respect the British request. His ambassador in Berlin could face the German foreign minister with a perfectly reasonable excuse for allowing the British into the islands. The only information he wanted now from his undersecretary was: How long do you need to prepare and how much material do I ask of England to strengthen our defenses? Santos Costa had no trouble with these questions: three months and material enough for three divisions. Events were finally moving on a fast track.[10]

On 23 June Salazar answered the British ambassador, stating his government would approve an agreement negotiated by delegations and facilities would be granted according to the terms that were reached. "The Portuguese government considering the state of need invoked by His Majesty's government, and being conscious of the high service . . . they could render them . . . hereby declare their acceptance in principle." His letter ended with thanks to England and South Africa for agreeing to respect the sovereignty of all Portuguese territory and a reminder that he would also be happy to receive the same assurances from the United States and Australia. Negotiations were to start on 6 July, but Salazar first laid out some ground rules:

1. Portugal had to remain technically neutral. Any concessions granted to England would also take into account a duty to preserve the life and culture of the people of the Azores. The establishment of the facilities could have a potentially deleterious effect which had to be avoided at all costs. Before any concessions were granted, it was important for both governments to examine the political, military, and economic consequences involved. Another important consideration was that nothing in the agreement should violate the obligations of Portugal bound in the treaty signed with Spain in 1939 and 1940.

2. The Portuguese Government thanked H.M.G. for making a formal commitment to withdraw all forces from the Azores at the conclusion of hostilities. Salazar slyly points out that this promise is really not necessary since the original Treaty of Alliance specifically contains the requirement, but thanks anyway.

3. Thanks are also expressed to H.M.G. and the Government of South Africa for guaranteeing the integrity of Portuguese Sovereignty and all the territories of Portugal. It was understood that any facilities granted would be restricted to those who had a right to use them according to the treaty. That meant only British or Dominion troops could be on the islands.[11]

Eden was willing to accept the agreement even though it allowed only British forces to use the Azores; he was sure that once the British arrived, Americans could be worked in as well. British troops would arrive quietly and in modest numbers. The important thing was that Salazar finally allowed Allied bases in the Azores; this was no time to quibble over details. Churchill was elated. As he told Eden, "The great thing is to worm our way in and then, without raising any question of principles, swell ourselves out."[12] Salazar had already agreed that because British and U.S. warships operated jointly in the Atlantic, and convoys assembled with a mix of merchant ships of all nationalities, it would be difficult to discriminate against U.S. use of the marine bases. He allowed U.S. ships to use the port facilities but still held firm against U.S. air bases. As the War Cabinet predicted, Salazar eventually granted bases on the pretext of the 1373 treaty and and doing so was far better than destroying the good will built up over the past six centuries between the two countries.

Things finally appeared to be on track, but as predicted by people knowledgeable with the situation in Lisbon, which did not include anyone in Washington, negotiations for separate U.S. bases or even stationing Americans on British bases was not going to be easy. As Eden told Churchill, "Americans did not understand that modern Portugal was not a country from which they could get everything by threats or bribes, and that Dr. Salazar was not the kind of man who wanted to climb upon the Allied bandwagon in good time."[13]

On 10 June, two weeks before Salazar gave his approval to negotiate the agreement, an advance party flew out from Bristol decked out in civilian clothes as befitting undercover military officers going to a neutral country.[14] Secrecy was all-important and with it the need to remain anonymous. The party was headed by Air Marshal Sir Charles Edward Hastings Medhurst, assistant chief of Air Staff for Intelligence and Plans, and included Frank Roberts, Foreign Office adviser, Group Captain Vintras, and Lieutenant Colonel Denis Capel-Dunn. The mission was completed with the later arrival of three more including Rear Admiral R. M. Servaes and a representative from the Ministry of Economic Warfare. The Portuguese delegation was led by Adm. Botelho Sousa described as "a diminutive figure with short grey hair brushed forward over his forehead in a fringe and a grey moustache turned up fiercely at its ends" who held the title of major-general of the Armada, the same once held by the Duke of Medina Sidonia, commander of the ill-fated Spanish Armada of Philip II. The admiral was supported by General Craveiro Lopes (president of Portugal, 1951–58), representing the army, and Colonel Humberto Delgado, a staunch friend of England for the air force.[15]

The presence of the British mission in Lisbon was a well kept secret. The Germans never discovered its existence and the Americans finally learned on 26 June, a good two weeks after its arrival, that negotiations were about to start.[16]

29 June: Churchill to Roosevelt

Churchill informed Roosevelt that Salazar appeared ready to cede the Azores bases to the British but objected to U.S. participation until "the United States Government are willing to associate themselves with the assurances already given by His Majesty's Government." Then, almost pleading, he asked for authorization to inform the Portuguese that the United States was willing to assure Portugal's sovereignty over all her territories. Instead of agreeing, Roosevelt again raised his pet idea to involve Brazilian troops. The prime minister scotched the plan; it would jeopardize the success of the negotiations to try to persuade them to accept other than British forces.

Ending on a positive note, Churchill pointed out that discussions were about to begin and in fact the British delegation was leaving for Lisbon soon. Churchill assumed that the worst was over; Salazar was finally reconciled to the Allied bases and once the delegates sat down to negotiate, a final agreement would quickly follow. The Azores bases were a certainty. Not being a diplomat by choice he did not appreciate how complicated the negotiations would be; Salazar was in no rush to sign any agreement, feeling that much had to be ironed out before he would allow any British troops in the Azores.[17]

2 July: Roosevelt to Churchill

Roosevelt replied to Churchill his pleasure that the Allies were on the brink of having a base in the Azores but worried that the United States's best interests might not be taken care of in the negotiations. His latest plan was to send a defensive force to Portugal even though this would limit other actions in the Mediterranean and set back the timetable for Operation Overlord. The force would be strong enough to discourage a German invasion and might convince Salazar that he had nothing to fear by signing the agreement. The president pointed out that it was highly unlikely that the Axis would attempt a Peninsular campaign at this point so he had no qualms making the promise if it would help secure an agreement. To the COS, the president's new ideas were just as troublesome and hare-brained as his older ones. General Brooke describes the meeting to discuss Roosevelt's latest strategy:

> A long COS meeting to consider a long telegram from the president. The first suggested sending a whole division, plus four hundred AA [anti-aircraft] guns and some fourteen squadrons of fighters, to support Portugal in the event of Salazar granting us facilities in the Azores for submarine-hunting aircraft. Such action to my mind inevitably endangers our relations with Spain. . . . The whole situation is very dangerous and we may well find ourselves driven into a Peninsular war against our wishes . . . At 3 P.M. I went round to 10 Downing Street for a two-hour meeting with the P.M. [prime minister.] We warded off all the immediate dangers, but I am not certain that he realizes yet all the dangers that lie ahead of us in connection with our Azores policy.[18]

The COS agreed that it would be best to avoid specifics in the final agreement, just make Salazar happy with a generic promise that the Allies would come to the defense of Portugal should Germany invade.

On 7 July the Joint Chiefs asked the State Department to see if the

British would back up our ambassador's request to Salazar for a U.S. base. But on 22 July with the British negotiating directly with the Portuguese government and standing a good chance of success, they agreed that a direct approach by either the U.S. government or Pan Am might complicate the matter; better wait until the English finished playing their hand.[19]

July: Lisbon

Lisbon was teeming with Axis spies plus a great number of Portuguese officials and military sympathetic to the Axis, making it a full-time job for the British mission just to avoid scrutiny and not arouse questions on who they were and what they were doing in Portugal. One of the minor triumphs of the war was the fact that negotiations were about to begin for Allied bases in the Azores, which would tilt the battle against the U-boats and open up the Atlantic for unlimited convoy traffic; two teams of British officers and diplomats had flown incognito from London and none of this was discovered by the Germans until the agreement was announced. However, it was not too surprising considering that the Anglo-Portuguese agreement was only another failure in the long string of failures of German intelligence in the war. Despite the efforts of German secret agents and their Portuguese cohorts, the net effect of their espionage operations never rose above incompetence.

From the beginning of the conference on 5 July, it became clear that the Portuguese commission was in no hurry to conclude any kind of agreement. Many high-level Portuguese officers were sympathetic to the Axis and were members of the Legião, the Portuguese fascist Legion modeled after the Spanish Falange. Although most people at the highest levels of government, including Prime Minister Salazar and Foreign Minister Santos Costa, were pro-Allies, politicians were generally reluctant to intervene with the military on most issues.

At the meeting the British presented a list of their requirements in the Azores. Most important were facilities in São Miguel and Terceira for operating reconnaissance aircraft and unrestricted fueling facilities for naval escorts at either São Miguel or Faial. They also pointed out the presence of Axis nationals, both official and civil, on many islands and asked that they be removed by military or diplomatic means, offering their services to help remove them.

But the Portuguese negotiators had other ideas on exactly how much British involvement they would allow in the Azores. On 7 July Medhurst wrote to General Portal of the stumbling blocks found at the first two meetings: "It is quite clear they thought the 'facilities' we wanted would consist of a few aircraft landing in the Azores from time to time, with a few men to service them, and the occasional escort vessel to refuel. By granting such facilities nothing need be said to anyone and everything would be precisely as before. Therefore when we tabled our requirements in detail, their immediate reaction was 'but this will mean war for Portugal.'"[20]

On the same day, Vintras sent his first "Most Secret" report to Bill Elliot, director of plans at the Air Ministry, concerning an unexpected problem. The British wanted the Lagens Field runway on Terceira to be long enough to accommodate large bomber and transport aircraft, but in order to accomplish this, an alcohol factory sitting in the middle of the planned runway would have to be demolished. The locals found this unacceptable and were ready to resort to force to defend their distillery until the problem was resolved, presumably by a healthy payment from the Crown.

During the following two weeks of desultory negotiations with stalemate the keyword, the British did a lot of touring around the countryside and took advantage of the entertainment scene in Lisbon. They were warned by the embassy to stay out of good restaurants and *fado* bars, homes to the melancholy songs "of fate"—a Portuguese national obsession—but both warnings were largely ignored.

Enjoyable as the stay was in Portugal, the negotiations were going nowhere. After a long series of discouraging reports to General Portal, on 17 July Medhurst full of frustration ended one with "However I think that if H.E. is prepared to brandish a thick stick at Salazar, we shall probably achieve something in the end." By then not only the negotiating team had enough, but the British Empire as well.

Churchill took the suggestion seriously; if negotiations failed or continued to drag on much longer, he would resort to force. Since the start of the talks, he assumed that the deal was done, that only trivial details had to be worked out, and on 14 July he even told Roosevelt that the worst phase of the Battle of the Atlantic was over and that the air gap soon would be closed. He warned that the problem of U.S. air bases might not be resolved despite his promise to try to obtain the facility. However, "we have decided to insert the thin end of the wedge" and hoped to "despatch our occupation guests and some Hudson squadrons with a week. Mum's the word."[21]

On 3 August, while the British were still negotiating, the CCS reminded the president and prime minister of the United States's position vis-à-vis the Azores bases: any agreement limiting the use of facilities to British aircraft is not acceptable. Moreover, such limitation would not be in consonance with the Trident Agreement that "Land, air and sea facilities of the Azores will be available to all U.N. Forces."[22]

Although the British negotiators were failing to achieve U.S. entry into the Azores, Churchill urged patience; once the British had landed U.S. troops could "come in through the back door." Waiting out patiently might have suited the British and the State Department but only fed the Joint Chiefs' paranoia; they wanted their people in the Azores now and felt the negotiations were not going to help their cause.[23]

On 24 July Churchill sent a personal memorandum to Anthony Eden, which made it clear that the time for stalling in Lisbon was over. He left no room for alternative interpretations, extrapolation, or any roadblocks, but for the Portuguese to accept or else. The British proposal was to be put on the table, presented as an offer they could not refuse. Churchill's memorandum was relayed to Ambassador Campbell to be passed on to the negotiating team:

PRIME MINISTER'S PERSONAL MINUTE
SERIAL NO. M.514/3

10 Downing Street
Whitehall

Foreign Secretary:
1. This series of telegraphs shows clearly the policy of procrastination on the part of P. which is incompatible with our resolves. August 20 was fixed as the date when the ultimate sanction could be applied. But they came with this hope of parley, invoking the Alliance and so forth, and I certainly had the impression that the goods were going to be delivered in July.
2. Now, after all this vast verbiage and haggling, Ambassador Campbell talks of September 1 as being a date rather too early to be insisted upon, and the Portuguese have ample argumentative munitions to spread the matter out into the winter weather.

3. The time has come to let them know that this nonsense must cease. Every form of ceremony and civility has been exhausted. We must have the facilities in these islands by August 15. They ought to be told this, and the expedition should be prepared in accordance with what was agreed at Washington and what the Staff have worked out, and should sail so as to strike by August 20 or whatever is the earliest date now possible in consequence of the new forms of "Post-Husky."[24]

4. I do not think that time has been wasted in the discussions. Undoubtedly the Portuguese have committed themselves in principle to the occupation. This is a great advantage, especially as our forces could not have been ready earlier. But now we cannot go on waiting any longer, and we ought to tell them exactly what they are up against and that unless they agree to offer facilities freely and without fail by August 15 we will take our own measures in our own time,

W.S.C.

24.7.43[25]

Churchill's ultimatum was unexpected and left the British negotiating team in a great state of confusion. Vintras, however, was not confused and knew exactly what to do. He had served three years on the Joint Planning Staff—during which time he heard many proposals, some reasonable but many half-cocked from military, politicians, and diplomats on resolving the Azores dilemma—and he learned to understand Churchill's mind. Frustration was nothing new to Whitehall or to Washington but maybe now that England was prepared to lay down the law gridlock might finally be broken. Vintras was elated and decided on a private strategy to speed up the process.

Colonel Humberto Delgado was a good friend of Vintras, having worked closely with him on various Anglo-Portuguese commissions. Now, as a member of the Portuguese delegation Vintras felt that he could be counted on as completely pro-Allies and the one to take Churchill's ultimatum into confidence. The dramatic effect of the memorandum might just galvanize Delgado to take action, such as appealing to the highest level, to the prime minister himself, the one person who could get the negotiators to move on an agreement. Vintras told Delgado he had certain highly classified information that was of extreme importance and that could only be entrusted to him. The meeting could not take place in any official offices, either British or Portuguese, or in any of the public places they had commonly frequented such as bars or restaurants. They would meet by "accident" at the foot of a principal *Avenida*.

They met on an unusually wet day, and headed to an outdoor tavern: for all intents and purposes two well-to-do professional men in search of a beer. Both were dressed in civilian outfits: Delgado wearing a raincoat and sporting a soft felt hat with its brim turned down—a Hollywood spy outfit—and Vintras in his one and only civilian suit. Delgado was shown a copy of Churchill's note, which he found deeply disturbing: the rules of negotiations were going to change abruptly, a new ballgame was about to begin. Taking this action, Vintras felt he was placing his country before himself: an immediate decision was necessary from high officials in the Portuguese government and this approach was the best way to get negotiations moving. A favorable decision on the Azores bases could be reached quickly if Salazar or the foreign ministry were warned of the consequences of further delay. An order for action could not be ignored if it was passed down from the prime minister.

Delgado took action and negotiations suddenly started moving, but as the pace picked up the Portuguese produced a massive list of requirements. These meetings were described as "exasperating exercises" because many of the requirements were unrealistic or exasperatingly petty; the British were becoming frustrated again. Vintris himself argued directly with the vice-chief of the Air Staff questioning whether seventeen instructors were really needed to instruct the Portuguese on how to blow up balloons. Rear Admiral Servaes erupted into a screaming match with Admiral de Sousa over an unexpected requirement that the Portuguese Navy escort Allied convoys for the last six miles on their passage to the Azores. For Servaes this was the last straw: he told de Sousa he was sacrificing the six-hundred-year-old alliance for six miles of water. De Sousa had no idea of the hazards of sailing in a U-boat infested Atlantic, and that the Portuguese ships would only constitute an additional danger to themselves as well as the convoy. Because the Portuguese destroyers had no radar gear or training in U-boat tactical warfare, their assistance was definitely not welcome.

The unexpected obstructionist demands of the Portuguese negotiators was also a strain on London. When the British pressed Salazar to allow a start on building the bases, he insisted that the islands' defenses must be completed first and they could not be rushed. On 2 August Churchill and Eden had a "shouting match" over the endless delaying tactics of the Portuguese with Churchill insisting that he was right all along, the Azores should have been seized by force, and that Salazar was just stringing Eden along. Eden, with the support of Sir Alan Brooke, calmed Churchill down. The argument was moot because it was pointed out that no operation could be launched before the end of August, at the earliest. Churchill apologized but still insisted that Salazar was "intolerable." In the end, they agreed to give Salazar a deadline of 15 September later changed to 1 October and then 8 October, the date the British finally landed in the Azores.[26]

The delegates signed the agreement on the morning of 17 August, although Salazar did not sign on until about a month later. The British got just about everything they asked for including the use of ports and airfields.[27]

On 16 August the British sent a number of modern aircraft to beef-up the Portuguese Air Force, paid $30 million in cash, and agreed to aid Portugal in the event of an attack on the Portuguese mainland. The use of facilities on the Azores would commence on 8 October, as demanded by Churchill. A few days after the signing, Portuguese authorities removed all Axis nationals from the islands without any warning, even before their own governments had a clue about the agreement with England, and also lifted the sanctions against U.S. citizens, diplomats, and commercial enterprises in the Azores.[28]

Salazar's relations with Germany were aided unknowingly by Admiral Canaris's intelligence service, which had been portraying him as sympathetic to the Axis cause, and convinced Hitler to respect Portugal's neutrality. When word of the Portuguese "capitulation" reached Berlin that the British would shortly be operating in the Azores, Goebbels complained that "Salazar has lost his faith in us." To Hitler and his cabinet, who had believed the reports filed by their embassies in Spain and Portugal that the countries' sympathies lay with the Third Reich, this came as a profound shock. The alleged influence over Salazar and his government by the local fascists, the *legião*, turned out to be a fiction: the legião was nothing but a small fringe outfit of blowhards with little popular support. It was hard to accept the turn of events, to admit that the Portuguese government had always been on the side of England. German Intelligence reported one bit of unpleasant trivia: Salazar had removed Mussolini's signed portrait from his desk.

Any thoughts of punishing Portugal had to be tabled. Whatever stratagems the Nazis once considered, such as an invasion of Iberia or an attack on the Azores, were forgotten. No distractions could be permitted from the real problems of the disintegrating Russian front, the most costly bloodletting operation in German history, and the total collapse and surrender of their Italian ally. No question, Operation Felix had already been tabled indefinitely when Salazar honored the ancient alliance with England.

The fact that the agreement came as a surprise to the German High Command ranks high as a spectacular intelligence failure in the Abwehr's long history of failures in World War II. This one however demanded a harsh penalty: Ambassador Baron von Hoyningen-Hüne was recalled to Berlin and later executed.[29]

Considering that we had no fully functioning foreign intelligence service but relied on reports from our embassies, U.S. intelligence was vastly superior to the German. On 26 July, some seven weeks after the British team arrived in Lisbon, Colonel Robert A. Solberg, the U.S. military attaché in Lisbon, discovered that high level negotiations were taking place between the British and Portuguese. He cabled the Joint Chiefs:

> I was informed by a high officer of the Portuguese Staff, that for sometime past secret talks were being held between ranking British officers visiting here incognito and a selected group of Portuguese officers, the commission being headed by Admiral Botelboy [sic] Sousa.[30] There is a British rear admiral, an air vice marshal and an army brigadier at present in Lisbon and the subjects discussed are of military technical nature with regard to measures to be taken in case of British occupation of the Azores and Portugal's entry in the war.
>
> My interlocutor told me that the British Ambassador is seeing Salazar frequently and that results are being expected shortly. I was given to understand though that the Portuguese government is extremely anxious for American active participation and that they would be loath to enter into any commitments unless they were implemented by American guarantees. I ignore whether my informant was instructed to pass this information on to me or did it spontaneously, but I find it most significant. This sentiment is borne out by other reports from Portuguese sources

to the effect that before casting the die, the Portuguese will drive a hard bargain and will exact guarantees from the British endorsed by the U.S.[31]

Colonel Solberg's cable was a beacon for the Joint Chiefs. Unfortunately, if he was reporting exactly what he heard, then either he or the "interlocutor" were victims of wishful thinking. The Portuguese government was not eager for U.S. participation—especially without the guarantees—and had no desire to see U.S. forces anywhere in the Azores.

Kennan, who was closer to the pulse of the Portuguese government, was all for giving the guarantee. John Winant wanted to withhold it as a means of putting pressure on the Portuguese. The State Department, confronted with three very different approaches at odds with each other, the two diplomatic ones plus the Joint Chiefs who were ready to go to war with Portugal, did what it does so well, vacillate. Unwilling to seize the initiative, and afraid of the effects of hasty action, Winant was allowed simply to pass his ideas along to Churchill, which probably did not make the prime minister happy. Obviously no progress could be made on the U.S. bases while Salazar was worrying about U.S. designs to annex the Azores.

4 August: London

Anthony Eden, not understanding the refusal to acknowledge Portuguese sovereignty over her lands, pointed out to Winant that this one detail prejudiced Salazar's attitude towards the United States. On 29 June Eden asked the ambassador to warn President Roosevelt of the problem and emphasize that until sovereignty was recognized, Salazar would not allow U.S. forces in the Azores. Eden wrote out the message to send to Roosevelt:

> The President would authorize us to inform the Portuguese Government that in the event of a satisfactory agreement being reached the United States Government would be willing to associate themselves with the assurances already given by His Majesty's Government. . . .
>
> The negotiations are now reaching a decisive stage and it is becoming urgently necessary for us to . . . inform the Portu-

guese Government that the United States Government . . . associate themselves with the assurances.[32]

The memorandum stirred things up in Washington. A week after sending the memorandum Winant received a response signed by Cordell
Hull and initialed by Roosevelt: the United States was ready to assure
the Portuguese government that its troops would be withdrawn upon
the termination of hostilities, and it agreed to "respect—not maintain—
Portuguese sovereignty over all her colonies." However, Secretary Hull
went on, the Chiefs of Staff, with the approval of the president, "while
appreciative of the delicacy of conversations now in progress between
the British and Portuguese, nevertheless any agreement restricting facilities in Bracken[33] to British aircraft is unacceptable . . . and not in har-
mony with the Trident Agreement. They have further indicated the
vital importance that Bracken facilities be accorded air ferry, transport
and military operations for this country."[34]

5 August: U.S. Embassy, Rio de Janeiro

Oswaldo Aranha, Brazil's minister for Foreign Affairs passed on to the
U.S. ambassador disquieting news from the Brazilian ambassador in
Lisbon that: "British policy in Portugal is not calculated to be helpful
either to the United States or to Brazil" and emphasized the importance of having a capable Minister there. Caffery cabled the State
Department that "Aranha urges me to ask the Department to take care
of this" (underlined in pencil in original).[35]
    The memorandum seems to have broken some kind of record for
being passed around. Three different departments of the State Department stamped it: U.S. Liaison Office, Division of Political Studies, and
the Division of the American Republics; eight individuals initialed it
and a copy was sent to the Navy as well.

17 August: Joint Chiefs of Staff to Roosevelt

The Joint Chiefs were bitterly disappointed when they saw the final
agreement with the clear evidence that their ally could not be trusted.

They asked the president to forward their objections to the British prime
minister. After reviewing the need for U.S. facilities in the Azores, they
expressed their not-so-quiet fury:[36]

> The . . . agreement . . . does not provide adequate U.S. Navy
> facilities, or any facilities for United States air transport and air
> ferrying operations. . . . The British have assured us that they
> will make "every effort" to secure facilities for use by United
> States aircraft "as soon as possible." They have been unable,
> however, to give any assurance as to when, if ever, such facili-
> ties might become available . . . in any event, the source now
> being followed of indirect approach to the Portuguese will not
> provide facilities for a central Atlantic air route in time to
> relieve the existing shortage of high octane gasoline, or to be of
> value to the OVERLORD build-up during the winter months. . . .
>
> At the request of the British, the Combined Chiefs of Staff
> agreed on 22 July 1943, "that no further approach to the Por-
> tuguese authorities should be made by the United States Gov-
> ernment or by Pan American Airways until the negotiations
> now being carried on by the British and Portuguese Govern-
> ments are concluded." These negotiations were concluded on
> 17 August 1943 . . . and we are therefore free of our obligation
> not to approach the Portuguese authorities direct.
>
> Information received . . . from the U.S. military attaché at
> Lisbon indicates that the Portuguese government would wel-
> come American participation in negotiations concerning the
> use of the Azores and were "loath to enter into any agreements
> until they were implemented by American guarantees."
>
> We feel it is essential, in view of the grave military implica-
> tions of further delay in this matter, to pursue the course of
> action which appears best calculated to lead to the early acquisi-
> tion of the military facilities in the Azores that we so urgently
> require.
>
> We therefore recommend that you inform the Prime Minis-
> ter that the United States Government intends to open immedi-
> ate discussions with the Portuguese Government with a view to
> secure the desired facilities . . . and invite the British Govern-
> ment to participate in these discussions, if they so desire.

The letter prepared for the president's signature began with a reminder that the Anglo-Portuguese agreement (code name Ingot) failed to provide for the needs of the United States and ended with a challenge that the United States would go on alone to ensure its own best interests: "It is now apparent that course of indirect approach through you to Portuguese will not alone provide facilities for Central Atlantic air route in time. . . . I am therefore proposing . . . to open immediate discussions with Portuguese government to supplement . . . your continuing efforts on our behalf. I hope very much that your government will join us in these discussions."

18 August: London

The agreement on bases was signed. Churchill and his War Cabinet were pleased but wished Salazar had not been hung up so long. If the "black hole" had been closed years earlier thousands of lives and hundreds of thousands of tons of merchant shipping would have been saved and millions of good English citizens, including their prime minister, would have been spared many sleepless nights.

Churchill was inclined to fulfill the Joint Chiefs' request especially when Roosevelt informed him that a U.S. force of ten thousand men could be sent at a moment's notice to start work on the air base. His War Cabinet and his own Chiefs of Staff objected and convinced him to calm Washington down. First of all, such a large U.S. force would be a needless duplication of the British forces. Second, were the relations with Portugal: the English had finally made headway with Salazar and were getting what they asked for. Finally, Salazar still did not trust the United States.

14 September: Lisbon

The first secretary of the British Embassy informed Salazar that the Commonwealth of Australia and the Union of South Africa had now associated themselves with the assurances given by His Majesty's Government regarding Portuguese sovereignty over her colonial possessions. Salazar was happy to receive these assurances, but still was hoping to receive the same from the U.S. government.

September

Since 1 July, the Joint Chiefs had in hand a detailed report on the state of defenses and troop concentrations in the Azores with enough information needed to plan an operation. The report began: A keen observer, in 1935, wrote the following: "The nation that has possession of the Azores and can utilize the terrain of Terceira Island for fighters, bombers, and long range reconnaissance planes and can refuel submarines at Horta and Ponta Delgada holds the key to the North Atlantic." This survey would indicate that there is nothing substantially wrong with the preceding statement and added that the Portuguese defenses could not put up much of a resistance against a well-equipped modern army.[37]

A quarter of the active Portuguese Army was stationed in the Azores—ten times the normal peacetime garrison plus the largest contingent ever of naval forces. For the first time units of the Air Force were also posted on Terceira and São Miguel, so it was clear that Portugal planned to defend the islands. The Navy had a few escort vessels and destroyers stationed in the Azores that were judged to be of no great combat value but could be used to police coastal waters and fisheries and help rescue victims of U-boat attack. The Portuguese Air Force consisted of seventeen bombers, forty-three fighters, and twenty-five naval aircraft of which fourteen planes were stationed at Lagens, and thirty-one at Santa Ana airfield on São Miguel. Most of the planes were obsolete; standards of training, maintenance, and morale were judged to be low.

The report went into great detail on the organization and size of the Army and the Navy, and described the defensive fortifications of the islands. The disposition of the entire 16,565 troops stationed in the archipelago according to unit and exact location were given as were descriptions of the armament of all fixed artillery positions. Two fixed coastal gun positions on Terceira were at Angra do Heroísmo on Monte Brasil and at Nasceagua both consisting of four guns described as old, caliber unknown.

The personnel strength of the Portuguese Navy was estimated at about fifty-seven hundred men; the fleet consisted of seven sloops, five destroyers, ten gunboats, and three submarines as well as a number of miscellaneous support vessels. Most ships were stationed in Portuguese home waters but two destroyers, the *Tejo* and the *Douro*, both launched in 1935, displacing 1,239 tons, with a normal complement of 163 were at Ponta Delgada.

Formerly officers of all grades held a profound respect and admiration for the Germans, but with their recent military reverses this was changing. Reports indicated that influential people in the military as well as in the government were becoming more pro-Allies with fewer and fewer pro-Axis or even neutral. With the report in hand the Joint Chiefs dismissed any thought of serious resistance should they decide to go to the Azores with force.

September: The Tonnage War

Beginning this month the deficit caused by losses to shipping compared to new ships being launched was more than made up, finally alleviating Churchill's fear of losing the "tonnage war." The gap between ship losses and new construction started to disappear when the convoy system was finally adopted by the United States in mid-1942. By the end of the war sixty-two million tons of ocean-going ships were available to the Allies. Admiral Dönitz's U-boat fleet had had great success during the first four years of the war, but in the critical year preceding the invasion of Normandy it had almost no impact on the flow of convoys from North America to England.[38]

EIGHT

THE BRITISH ARRIVE, SEPTEMBER–OCTOBER 1943

i. Following is directive for ALACRITY.

This operation is implementation of 600-year-old alliance
between Britain and Portugal. Agreement has been mutually
and freely negotiated by British and Portuguese Governments
within terms and spirit of alliance, under which and in full
consultation and agreement with H.M.G. [His Majesty's
Government], Portugal has remained neutral since outbreak of
war and will continue to do so. It is H.M.G.'s hope that
Portuguese government will continue their policy of neutrality
on European mainland and maintain "zone of peace" in Iberian
Peninsula. We do not in our own interests wish to provoke
adverse German reactions which might involve us in
commitments in peninsula.

> Most secret directive from Joint Chiefs of Staff
> to Joint Staff Mission, 30 September 1943

On 20 August Churchill and Roosevelt, together with their military
and political advisers, met at the first Quebec Conference. The tide had
turned and the Allies were on the offensive almost everywhere, so planning could start on the next important step: the liberation of Europe.
Churchill, fearful of the high number of casualties expected in a cross-
channel invasion of France was still pumping for his operation of
choice: getting at Hitler through the "soft underbelly" of Europe. Allied
troops were in Italy, Mussolini had resigned, and with a pro-Ally government in place plus Italian partisans ready to rise up behind German
lines this seemed to be an excellent strategy. Other operations through
the Balkans or Iberia could start with unopposed landings anywhere
along the thousands of miles of undefended coastline and, at least in

the Balkans, Allied forces would move with strong support from guerrilla forces. Churchill had another good reason to go in through the
Balkans: foil Russian plans to subvert the postwar governments of Eastern Europe. Events proved Churchill correct, for as the war was ending
Russian troops poured into the Balkans destabilizing democratic movements everywhere but Greece, the only country to maintain a substantial Allied presence.[1]

It was agreed that the Anglo-American invasion would begin in
Northern France in the spring of 1944. Roosevelt vetoed the southern
Europe invasion strategy, pointing out to Churchill that the bulk of the
troops involved would be American and not British, so the United
States would suffer most of the expected casualties. Now it was even
more important to establish an air base in the Azores to ensure reliable
lines of communication between the United States and England. The
Air Transport Command would establish a regular schedule through
Lagens Field and naval air squadrons would fly protective cover for convoys.

At the meeting to discuss Operation Lifebelt, Eden said that arrangements had been approved by the CCS, the president, and the prime minister for British forces to move into the Azores, and that within two
weeks efforts would be made to obtain Portuguese consent for U.S.
forces to join them. Eden suggested that the United States should give
similar assurances, as already received from the British Government, to
withdraw forces from Portuguese territory after the war and to respect
Portuguese sovereignty in all her territories. Such assurances would
help obtain approval from Salazar for U.S. forces to join the operation.[2]

So a deal was struck in Quebec but the contention over the United
States's nonrecognition of Portuguese sovereignty was destined to be
played out to the last minute. If the commitment could be avoided,
then it would be; if it turned out to be a condition for entry into the
Azores, then it would be given, albeit reluctantly. The Joint Chiefs
were satisfied that they would finally have an air base and nothing was
going to stop it from happening.

19 September: North Atlantic

Admiral Dönitz never lost faith in his U-boats. He felt that the development of new technology would transform his fleet into super-
submarines, the Battle of the Atlantic would be won, and the Allies

would be forced to negotiate peace despite the fact that Germany was losing on every other front. The submarines going to sea were equipped with the state-of-the art weaponry and electronics: heavier anti-aircraft armament, improved radar-warning receivers for approaching aircraft, and now carried a deadly acoustic tracking torpedo code named *Zaunkönig* (wren). Dönitz felt sure that his newly equipped U-boats would tilt the balance back to Germany in the tonnage war. He was soon disabused.

The Allies knew these new developments were coming and had already taken counter-measures, including towed noise makers to confuse the acoustic torpedoes. British-American scientists developed the noisemaker, FXR (Foxer) gear, which put to sea starting in July and immediately proved highly successful in foiling torpedoes. FXR worked so well that many cases were recorded of torpedoes turning 180 degrees and chasing after their submarine masters. Dönitz complained that the kills estimated by U-boat captains firing the new torpedoes were far removed from reality. "The captains overestimated the number of escort vessels sunk. This was because when firing at short range, the boats were forced to dive immediately after discharging the torpedo to a depth of two hundred feet to avoid the danger of the acoustic torpedo being attracted by the noise of their own propellers."[3]

The Allies were exacting a high toll in U-boats with stepped-up air patrols from North Atlantic land bases as well as from merchant aircraft carriers (MAC) and CVEs. During August only ten Allied merchant ships were lost whereas twenty-one U-boats were sunk with most of the damage against wolf packs taking place in the Northern Atlantic. Dönitz ordered a drastic cut in wolf pack operations while the U-boat high command worked on a new strategy to restore the balance in their favor. After a lull in activity in August, Dönitz directed the U-boats to return to the offensive, but far away from the deadly North Atlantic bases, outside the VLR bomber effective range of five hundred miles, and close in and around the "black hole" of the Azores.

Dönitz ordered an all-out assault against the combined convoys ON-202 of thirty-eight ships and ONS-18 of twenty-seven ships outward bound from England with a total escort of fifteen antisubmarine vessels and one MAC. In ordering the attack he sent a personal signal, "The Führer is following every phase of your battle. Attack! Go to it! Sink them!"[4]

U-boat group *Leuthen* consisting of nineteen submarines armed with acoustic torpedoes was sent north of the Azores with orders to attack as soon as the convoys were out of range of Allied air bases and had entered into the Azores Gap. The battle lasted six days, 20–26 September, and ranged over three hundred nautical miles. The final count was three U-boats destroyed, two by British bombers operating at the extreme edge of their range and one by the CVE HMS *Keppel*. The convoy suffered six merchant ships and three escorts sunk; four additional escorts were damaged enough to be put out of action. The attack was broken off as the convoy reached within the range of VLR bombers based in Iceland and Greenland where a dense fog descended to cut visibility to zero and allowed the remaining U-boats to escape.

The U-boat captains reported sinking twelve escorts and nine merchantmen with loss of only two boats sunk and two damaged. The discrepancy between the U-boat report of damage inflicted and the actual number of ships sunk was typical of acoustic torpedo attacks. Dönitz complained about the habitual overestimate of vessels sunk but realized that nothing could be done until the torpedoes could be reprogrammed not to turn around and home in on the submarines.[5]

If there had been any doubt about the need for Allied bases in the Azores the answer was clearly demonstrated with the Leuthen attack. The lesson was not lost: aircraft must be based in the Azores and soon.

23 *September: Richmond Army Air Base*

An order arrived from Headquarters Army Air Forces, Washington, to the 928th EAR at the Richmond Air Base: "subject: warning orders . . . alerted the 928th Engineer Aviation regiment . . . for overseas shipment on or about 10 October 1943," or two days after the scheduled British landing in the Azores, even though the 928th had informed AAF headquarters it would not be ready for overseas duty until 1 December 1943. With the date rapidly approaching for overseas shipment, the Officers' School of Construction and Tactics and the Specialists Schools were reassigned to the 1907th Engineer Aviation Battalion. The 37 commissioned officers, 254 enlisted engineers, and 15 medics of the 928th now had just over two weeks to get ready for overseas. If diplomatic negotiating didn't work, the JCS decided it would just show up uninvited with or without anybody's permission. The British were not to be informed of American plans until the last minute.[6]

24 September: General Staff Meeting, Führer's Headquarters, Berlin

With disasters brewing or already brewed in every land theater in Europe, the OKM was happy to report that the U-boat campaign was a success. Hitler agreed and added "with unprecedented emphasis to the importance of submarine warfare against shipping which is the only bright spot at present in an otherwise dark war situation. Submarine warfare must therefore be stepped up by all available means."[7]

The success of the U-boat campaign was not entirely true, but considering how badly the other theaters were faring, it was acceptable. The Balkans had become precarious with strong partisan activity in Yugoslavia and Greece, no air force available for support anywhere, and the Axis navy in the Mediterranean left with only small vessels after the entire Italian fleet either surrendered or was scuttled. The crowning blow was the Allied invasion of Italy and the refusal of Italian forces to defend their country but rather organize partisan units behind German lines.

30 September: London

The British gave Salazar a deadline of 1 October to sign off on the agreement but while he was agonizing whether or not to sign, and as the deadline approached, Churchill decided to make up his mind for him. No more delays could be tolerated, the time for action was long overdue, ready or not Operation Alacrity would start. The British Chiefs directive with copy to the Joint Chiefs laid out the official Allied position that would follow Churchill's announcement for the start of the operation. The Office of War Information (OWI) was told that any information released about Alacrity should also protect Portugal to avoid provoking Germany into invading Portugal, possibly with the collaboration of Spain. The Directive read:

1. Full recognition should be given to 600-year-old alliance and to fact that Dr. Salazar's government has faithfully observed it.
2. Whilst claiming credit for this successful result by diplomatic negotiation we should not on any account imply that Portu-

gal is "climbing on to the band-wagon" or slapping Germany in the face. Initiative was entirely ours.

3. Do not suggest that Salazar Government has in any sense succumbed to pressure.

4. Nothing should be said which would imply that Portugal has abandoned her neutrality or which would give the Germans any further excuse for exerting increased pressure on Salazar Government.

5. Stress the temporary nature of facilities granted and fact that they constitute no infringement of Portuguese sovereign rights.

6. Describe more as being for protection of Central Atlantic route and entrance to Mediterranean and for better protection of Trans-Atlantic shipping of United Nations.

7. Bear in mind that while this arrangement is governed entirely by Anglo-Portuguese alliance the Americans have been fully consulted and are in accord.

8. Point out that Portuguese relations with Spain and our own attitude towards Spanish Government remain unaffected by this operation.[8]

30 September: Liverpool

Three small convoys secretly set sail from Liverpool carrying the newly formed 247th Air Group to the Azores, scheduled arrival 8 October in time to start building the air base on Terceira. The 247th was commanded by Air Vice Marshal G. R. Bromet, who had plenty of experience fighting U-boats; his previous command had been at Plymouth where his principal responsibility was the successful operation to hit the submarines in transit from the Bay of Biscay to their patrol grounds in the Atlantic.[9]

The task force was commanded by Commodore R. V. Holt and included the troop carrier HMT *Franconia* protected by a squadron of three destroyers, the CVE *Fencer*, antisubmarine trawlers, and landing craft. The press release that followed the landing stated they went "by invitation of the Portuguese Government." Additional air cover was supposed to be supplied by Flying Fortress bombers but never materialized because of the bad weather. Nevertheless rough weather plus the formidable escort combined to keep U-boats a safe distance away though they were detected and continually menaced the convoys as they approached the Azores. Operation Alacrity had started with some three thousand officers and enlisted men drawn from three services, Army Sappers, RAF, and Royal Navy. Bromet held command of the Combined British Forces Azores until 1945.[10]

Secrecy about the operation in the Azores had to be maintained for two good reasons: not to provoke the Germans into some action against Portugal, and the lack of suitable harbors. The ships were forced to lie offshore in deep water, unloading onto lighters where they made tempting targets for U-boats. To protect the operation, the announcement would be made well after the actual landings took place so it was of vital importance to prevent news leaks.

4 October: Hull Cable to Kennan

Now that the British were about to land in the Azores, the State Department decided to remove a principal obstacle to getting the United States into the Azores. Hull instructed Kennan to tell the prime minister that "this government undertakes to respect Portuguese sovereignty in all Portuguese colonies." However, he added, "if, and only if, Dr. Salazar should approach you with a request for such an undertaking."[11] The memorandum appears to be a compromise between the idealists in the State Department whose agenda included liberation of all European colonies after the war, and the realists who wanted to win the war first.

On Friday, the scheduled date of the landing, another telegram arrived from the State Department telling Kennan to go ahead and present the assurances of the United States at once, without waiting for any query from the Portuguese. If Salazar was curious why the change of heart in Washington, Kennan was supposed to offer this explanation: "Having regard to avoid unnecessary provocation to Germany, the United States Government on reflection thought that it might only embarrass [Dr. Salazar] to receive the United States assurances just before public announcement of the Azores agreement [with England]. United States Government were however ready to communicate these assurances now or at such time as Dr. Salazar considered most appropriate."[12] Still not knowing what it was all about, but orders being orders, off he went to the Foreign Office to arrange an interview with

Salazar. He was told that was impossible, the President was at the Spanish border conferring with General Franco, briefing him on what was about to take place in the Azores. By clever arm twisting, Kennan convinced the chief of the American Section of the Foreign Office that his message was very important and had to be delivered to Salazar in person. A telegram was sent to Salazar who answered immediately saying that he would return to Lisbon expressly to meet with Kennan at his private residence at 10 A.M. Sunday morning.

At 9:30 A.M. on Sunday 10 October, on his way to meet with the president of Portugal, Kennan first stopped by the embassy to see if any new messages had come in, hopefully one that would give him some clue on what this flurry of cables was all about. A top priority message had indeed come in and was decoded just ten minutes before his appointment. Sadly, the message was not enlightening but only stirred up the already badly muddled waters. Kennan tells the story:

> The decoding was completed only a few minutes before ten. A glance at the message filled me with consternation. I was, it said, under no circumstances to present the assurances; nothing was to be done pending further instructions. No explanations were offered for this sudden decision.
>
> What was I to do? I had persuaded the Prime Minister, the political leader of the country, to make a journey of two hundred and fifty miles, on a weekend, to see me. The appointment was now only five minutes off. I could not possibly cancel it at this late moment. Yet what could I say?

But then, being a consummate diplomat, he took a deep breath and decided to salvage something from the meeting. Salazar had after all broken off a conference with General Franco, his powerful fascist neighbor and for whom he had a healthy respect, just to meet with Kennan, and now suddenly the rationale for the meeting had gone up in smoke. Kennan proposed that they discuss Portuguese-American relationships in light of the wartime situation for as far as he was aware no one on the U.S. side had ever had such a discussion with him. Kennan pointed out what were common interests for both countries in maintaining the security of the Atlantic. When the interview was all over he felt the discussion had been fruitful which may have satisfied Salazar, but still left him very puzzled.[13]

6 October: Roosevelt to Churchill

Roosevelt transmitted the Joint Chiefs' complaints intact to Churchill:

> to Former Naval Person. I have just received the following recommendation from the Joint Chiefs of Staff:
>
> "The JCS desire to convey to you their serious concern regarding the situation which has developed with respect to the use of the Azores.
>
> The importance of the central Atlantic air transport and ferry route to the United Nations war effort cannot be overemphasized. Briefly summarized, it represents:
>
> 1. Potential saving over the six month period (November 1943–April 1944) of approximately [51.5] million gallons of high octane aviation fuel; sufficient to support 5,400 heavy bomber sorties per month for the same period or the rough equivalent of one month's consumption by the combined operations of the RAF and the USAAF in and from the United Kingdom.
> 2. Potential savings in engine hours of each bomber ferried to the United Kingdom, sufficient to permit six or more additional combat missions before engine over-haul.
> 3. The release of approximately 150 transport aircraft, which could thus become available for service in the India-Burma-China area where they are so urgently needed.
> 4. Some 15,000 trained ground personnel released for duty elsewhere.
>
> This gasoline consumption required by the longer southern route is at the direct expense of the U. S. Army Air Forces Training Program which has just been temporarily curtailed due to fuel shortage. Unless immediate action is taken to effect a saving, the flow of replacement combat crews to theaters of operation will soon be reduced. Alternatively the reserve levels of gasoline now maintained in theaters of operations will have to be lowered.
>
> The present British-Portuguese agreement covering facilities in the islands does not provide facilities for air transport and air ferrying operations. We have advised the British Chiefs of Staff of our requirements . . . , but we have little confidence that the

British will provide facilities for a central Atlantic air route in time to be of value to the OVERLORD build-up during the coming winter months.

We consider this matter to be so serious that we are suggesting that you bring it to the attention of the Prime Minister, emphasizing the grave implications of delay in securing facilities for air ferrying and air transport operations. Our suggestion is that a specific request be made to the Prime Minister to make Lagens Field, Terceira, available for air transport and air ferrying purposes immediately following our initial entry and that further negotiations with the Portuguese be instituted in which the United States will participate with Great Britain to secure the additional facilities so urgently required."

I agree that this is a very important matter.

Roosevelt[14]

8 October: Churchill to Roosevelt

Churchill answered the president immediately. He admitted that British forces were due to land in the Azores but to wait for the German reaction before deciding the next step. If it turns out to be merely abusive, as he suspected, then Salazar should be reassured and he would press to allow a U.S. air base in the Azores. Salazar should realize that he runs no greater risk having U.S. forces joining the British than he had before. Moreover, if he asks, he would have assurances from the United States that they will respect Portuguese sovereignty. If Salazar still refuses, being afraid that once allowed in the Americans would refuse to leave the Azores, then the president or Kennan should appeal and Churchill promised the full support of the British government.[15]

8 October: Terceira

After a week of sailing from England the three thousand RAF, Royal Navy, and Army Sappers landed without incident at Angra do Heroïsmo to start work on the Lagens air base. Though Salazar had not yet signed anything allowing them to be there, he would have to accept the fait accompli and sign after the fact. The British would start on the date set in the agreement.

9 October: Washington, D.C.

The Joint Chiefs could not understand how Roosevelt could tolerate being put off by the British and Portuguese. If they continued to play second fiddle to the British they would never see their U.S. air base in the Azores. Admiral Leahy signed a memo prepared by General Hap Arnold on behalf of the Joint Chiefs to Roosevelt laying out the history of the problem and the strenuous objections for the United States being left out of the Anglo-Portuguese agreement. The hang-up over recognizing the territorial integrity of Portugal was a diplomatic not a military concern and should properly be taken care of by the State Department. The Trident Agreement signed in June clearly stated that the United States would have its own air bases in the Azores; the Joint Chiefs felt the time was overdue to call the cards on that.[16]

Now that the British were getting their base in the Azores with an agreement that did not include their Allies, General Hap Arnold asked, "How could we trust either the Portuguese who won't grant us bases or the British who got what they wanted while urging us to keep quiet? They allegedly negotiated on our behalf but clearly did not." Arnold's memorandum laid out good reasons to negotiate directly with Portugal because the British were not doing it on behalf of the United States:

1. We have already brought to the attention of the British the grave implications of delay in securing facilities in the Azores for United States air ferrying and air transport operations. They have assured us that they would make "every effort" to extend to us the benefit of the desired facilities "as soon as possible."

2. I doubt whether any useful purpose would be served by again pointing out these implications to the British and again urging them to arrange to make these facilities available to us.

3. ... the course now being followed of indirect approach ... will not provide facilities for a Central Atlantic air route in time to relieve the existing shortage of high octane gasoline, or to be of value to the OVERLORD build-up during the winter months.

4. At the request of the British, the Combined Chiefs of Staff agreed on 22 July 1943 "that no further approach to the Portuguese authorities should be made ... <u>until the negotiations</u>

now being carried on . . . are concluded . . . These negotiations were concluded on 17 August 1943 . . . and we are
therefore free of our obligations not to approach the Portuguese authorities direct.

5. Information received from the U.S. military attaché at Lisbon
. . . indicates that the Portuguese Government would welcome American active participation in negotiations concerning the use of the Azores and were "loath to enter into any
commitments unless they were implemented by American
guarantees."

H. H. Arnold
General, U. S. Army
Commanding General, Army Air Forces.[17]

The Joint Chiefs agreed that a firm approach to Portugal was essential,
and that the British could not be counted on to represent our interests.
They recommended that the British COS be advised of the steps to be
taken following the initial token entry of U.S. air and naval forces on
Terceira, and the President be told of the advisability of the United
States's intervening directly in subsequent negotiations with Portugal.
The principal concern of the Portuguese government was the lack of
guarantees of territorial integrity, which should be taken care of immediately. The Chiefs considered the State Department spineless and
Kennan a traitor for not acting sooner and considered both to be serious
impediments to obtaining the bases.[18]

On 6 October the President sent Churchill the Joint Chiefs' memo,
"Plan of Entry of the U.S. into the Azores," which first recalled the
agreements at Quebec. U.S. forces would enter "into the Azores by two
or more United States escort vessels from UGS-22 sailing on 25 October 1943 and two aircraft from a CVE . . . The convoy will be routed so
as to pass the Azores on approximately 6 November and the carrier will
be within near aircraft range of Lagens Field, Terceira Island."

Subsequent to the initial entry of U.S. forces, the following steps
were proposed:

1. The Army Air Forces will make a complete photo reconnaissance of the Azores on or about 10 November.

2. Army and Navy Engineering and Communications personnel
will be sent to Fayal [Faial] and Terceira by air on or about

15 November to survey naval, air transport, air antisubmarine, and communications facilities.

3. VLR aircraft will be dispatched to Lagens Field . . . for antisubmarine work under temporary British operational control.

4. Equipment and personnel employed in development of facilities at Fayal [Faial] and at Lagens Field will be shipped by the 25 November convoy.[19]

In the proposal under 4, the Joint Chiefs would supply engineering and construction personnel, equipment, and materials to develop the facilities at Lagens for antisubmarine operations and make the field available for U.S. air transport and ferrying services as soon as facilities become available.

By presenting England with this plan of action the Joint Chiefs would not wait for approval to send forces to the Azores. Clearance had not been obtained with our allies nor was there any way to get Salazar's approval before 25 October when convoy UGS-22 was to sail from Newport News POE. The memo to the president asked that "approval by the British Chiefs of Staff of the proposals . . . is requested as a matter of urgency." Our troops would arrive less than a month after the British who would still be settling in and not be clued in to the U.S. plans until the last minute. It would be too late, in any case, for the British not to accept them.

11 October: London

Churchill was inclined to accept the proposed U.S. role especially when he learned that a force of ten thousand could be sent to work on a larger base, large enough to accommodate the heavy traffic for the coming invasion. The War Cabinet and his COS objected strenuously and convinced the prime minister to calm Washington down. First, such a large U.S. force would be a needless duplication of the British forces that were already headed to the Azores. Second, the English had made great headway with Salazar and were at last getting what they wanted. Finally, Salazar had reason to believe that once the Americans were in the Azores, they would not leave.

11 October: Richmond Army Air Base

Instead of packing for the trip to the Azores, the order of 23 September to the 928th EAR for overseas shipment was rescinded. Somebody high up in the chain of command overruled the Joint Chiefs. Accepting the appeal from London, either General Marshall or President Roosevelt must have passed the word to the Joint Chiefs to calm themselves and cancel the sailing orders, because such an action would not help the United Nations war effort. What kind of mess would the United States have gotten into with Americans suddenly landing in force in the Azores without warning Portugal or coordinating with England?

At this time the 928th Regimental Headquarters and Service Company was better prepared than when the first order for overseas shipment went out. Training was 100 percent complete for basic, specialist, and technical training and 75 percent for tactical training. A new readiness date was set for 25 November. Of course, nobody in the outfit had any idea from exactly how high in the Allied chain of command their orders had come: unquestionably, the president and the prime minister of England had had a hand in ordering them to unpack and stay.[20]

12 October: London

On this Columbus Day, 451 years after the admiral discovered the New World, Churchill revealed to the House of Commons that he had invoked the Windsor treaty of eternal alliance with Portugal and authorized an operation to protect the Azores. Churchill relished every moment of the historic event, taking great pleasure in springing on a surprised Parliament a treaty that few even knew existed and talking of places that none had ever heard of. As he described it:

> "I have to make to the House arising out of the treaty signed between this country and Portugal in the year 1373 between his Majesty King Edward III and King Ferdinand and Queen Eleanor of Portugal." I spoke in a level voice, and made a pause to allow the House to take in the date, 1373. As this soaked in there was something like a gasp. I do not suppose any such continuity of relations between two Powers had ever been, or ever will be, set forth in the ordinary day-to-day work of British Diplomacy . . .

His Majesty's Government in the United Kingdom basing themselves upon this ancient alliance, have now requested the Portuguese Government to accord them certain facilities in the Azores which will enable better protection to be provided for merchant shipping in the Atlantic. The Portuguese Government have agreed to grant this request.

Churchill felt the only sour note in the agreement was Salazar's insistence that under the terms of the 1373 treaty as a "benevolent non-belligerent," Portugal was granting only England the privilege of using the island of Terceira as a base for war operations. This was a clear violation of the understanding reached at the First Quebec Conference and also at Trident, which called for the Azores bases to be made available for all United Nations forces.[21]

That evening, the Lisbon newspapers carried the complete text of Churchill's statement to the House of Commons and added a communication from the Portuguese government explaining how this action did not compromise Portugal's professed neutrality in the war. The government "reiterated that while anxious and sincerely resolved to maintain neutrality the government regarded that neutrality as being conditional . . . upon the eventual entry into force of the Anglo Portuguese Alliance . . . As the Prime Minister so well said the grant of certain facilities in the Azores which has now been made by adding new force and vigor to the ancient alliance between Portugal and the United Kingdom . . . has resulted in the confirmation and strengthening of the political guarantees of the treaties apart from affording new proof of the existing friendship and a guarantee of its future development."

The statement included a reference to Spain, and all this had been cleared beforehand with Franco. Now the only question was Berlin's reaction to Portugal's declaration that she was still neutral, and that the Azores bases were given only to honor an ancient treaty.[22]

13 October: U.S. Embassy in Bern to Secretary of State

Leland Harrison, the U.S. minister to Switzerland reported to Secretary Hull "private reports September 12–13 state announcement British Portuguese Azores agreement caught Wilhelmstraße spokesman without any prepared comment."[23] After some time, the German government attempted damage control, asserting they had been aware of events all along:

1. Agreement caused no surprise. Berlin diplomatic circles which had observed for sometime increased activity by American and British agents at Lisbon and Oporto while reports of impending Allied action against Azores were current during past few days.
2. Wilhelmstraße refusal comment based on desire obtain more information especially from Lisbon nevertheless Berlin political circles express opinion Portugal probably forced by strong American British pressure make concessions which Allies now greet as important military advantage and seek exploit propagandistically.
3. Berlin acquainted with political and military background this development which now became urgent factor. Azores appear from strategic viewpoint of primary importance in present situation but it remains to be seen whether military actions are envisaged in connection therewith. Berlin awaits clarification this point of military and strategic significance.[24]

The Nazi lion was clearly toothless. Germany could no longer threaten outright invasion, but only a vague threat of military action, which given the disastrous circumstances on the battlefields of Italy, Russia, and North Africa could not be taken seriously. A land operation through Spain was impossible without cooperation from Franco; a strike through the air would result in an Allied occupation of Portugal and another Allied base on the European mainland.

The Germans finally responded to the British landing on the Azores with a menacing diplomatic note. The 1373 treaty was not an acceptable excuse for the breach of neutrality. The Lisbon papers reported that the German minister personally presented a note to Salazar "protesting energetically against Portugal's having granted to the British Government facilities in the Azores which the Government of the Reich describes in its note as a grave violation of Portuguese neutrality." The Berlin radio reporting the meeting in Portuguese said the conference lasted an hour and a half but gave no further details.[25]

For the remainder of the week the Portuguese were desperately worried that the Germans might attempt an invasion or begin unre-

stricted U-boat warfare against their ships at sea. When nothing happened, Salazar breathed a sigh of relief but the threat of a German reaction still weighed heavily, and kept him cautious over the next few
months in his dealings with the United States. With England he could
fall back on the ancient treaty; with the United States there was no
such excuse.

14 October: Roosevelt Cable to Churchill

Roosevelt had been told of Colonel Solberg's memo and cabled Churchill requesting him once more to inform Salazar that the United States
needed its own base in the Azores. Churchill assured Roosevelt that he
would fully support the request and would make every effort to have
that included in the agreement which was actually signed the following
day. The prime minister thought that the United States might come
under the "Friends to Friends" phrase in the treaty of 1373 but cautioned
Roosevelt to give the Portuguese a few more days to watch German
reaction over the agreement.[26]

Even with no German reaction, Salazar still refused to let the Americans in. The final agreement specifically stated "aircraft of the British
Commonwealth," so Anthony Eden argued that the Americans, with
their superior engineering capabilities, were needed to help build and
improve Lagens Field which would be left to Portugal after the war. A
longer, well-surfaced, weather-proofed landing strip was needed, in
addition to upgraded airport facilities to handle large VLR aircraft. The
new base was to serve not only the armada that would invade France
but also to liberate Portuguese colonies in southeast Asia. The forty
thousand Portuguese troops stationed in the Azores could be flown to
Indonesia together with Allied troops directly after the defeat of Germany.

Another worry was Spanish reaction. However, since Franco's warning to Salazar to preserve his country's neutrality the tide had changed
in the war. The British military attaché in Madrid reported that the
Spanish chief of staff felt that Germany was in no position to react militarily and for the first time Spain felt that Germany had lost the war.
Not wanting to be caught on the losing side, Franco notified the German
government that the Blue Division would be withdrawn from the Eastern Front. Without cooperation from Spain, and with the Allies in control of the Atlantic, Germany could not invade Portugal.[27]

17 October: Lisbon

Salazar finally signed the agreement on bases in the Azores but Operation Alacrity had started without his formal permission; events were moving faster than the formalities. Churchill held to the agreement setting 8 October as the date of execution.[28]

Salazar conceded the use of the airfield at Lagens on Terceira which had the longest beaten earth runway in the world, 3,281 meters (10,600 feet) by 91 meters (300 feet) wide. Using maps and information supplied by the Portuguese survey of December 1941, by the end of 1943 British Sappers and Portuguese laborers covered eighteen hundred meters of the runway with pierced steel planks. Not waiting for the luxury of take-off and landing on a firmer platform, barely a month after disembarking the 247th RAF Group was fully operational and scored its first kill. A U-boat was spotted, attacked, and sunk, all of which came as a distinct shock to Admiral Dönitz and a blow to his new strategy to shift operations to the "black hole." The central Atlantic was now covered by VLR bombers and would become just as dangerous for U-boats as the North Atlantic.

18 October: Lisbon

Kennan kept Washington informed of all that transpired in Lisbon, including rumors, negotiations, communications from the British, and Portuguese policy. Washington rarely reacted in any way to any of his messages; there were no answers to questions of policy nor any instructions on how to deal with the Portuguese, so he never was sure if anyone was even reading them. One Sunday morning he received a lengthy telegram that convinced him that his suspicions were true: no one in the State Department had read anything he sent. After Washington canceled its promise "to assure the prime minister that the United States was prepared to respect Portuguese sovereignty," Kennan worried that the Joint Chiefs might actually be preparing an armed operation against the Azores. The telegram confirmed his fears:

> The following instructions are given you by direction of the President, to be executed on October 18 or as soon thereafter as possible, if at such time no military action has been taken by Germany against Portugal. You are aware [not being clairvoy-

ant, he was not] that we have held in suspense certain negotiations in order to avoid interference with the negotiations leading up to the Anglo-Portuguese Agreement of August 17. Our
negotiations were designed to make available for us certain
facilities in the Azores for our Army and Navy. You are now
directed to seek an interview with Dr. Salazar and to request the
following facilities.[29]

Kennan's hair stood on end when he saw the list of facilities: the
United States was demanding bases on four separate islands, cable and
communications systems, observation posts, radar, and facilities for
troop accommodations; the entire plan was far more elaborate than all
that the British, invoking their ancient alliance, had requested. In addition to the naval and seaplane base on Faial and airplane bases on São
Miguel, Terceira, and Flores or Santa Maria (if Flores was unsatisfactory), in each port of the Azores, U.S. naval vessels should have "unrestricted port facilities and shore accommodations for necessary personnel." Kennan was to rely on the "Friends to Friends" statement in the
Anglo-Portuguese treaty of 1373 as his chief argument. Although the
British were expected to support him, the secretary of state made it
clear that "it is intended however that you shall take the lead in these
negotiations."

Kennan saw this as representing nothing other than a takeover of
the islands by our armed forces and the subsequent ruination of the
culture and traditional mode of life of the Azores. Salazar would be unprepared for demands of this nature; after all, the British must have
warned him only that we wanted to make use of their facilities. Salazar
might allow the United States into Terceira, but there was no way that
he would agree to let them take over the entire archipelago. In fact, the
prime minister considered that his concessions to the British closed the
books on Portugal's obligations, and that they were payment in full demanded by the 1373 treaty. The fact that the United States withheld
their guarantee of his country's sovereignty meant that he was negotiating under an implied threat of invasion. If the United States seized
the archipelago, Portugal would be back on the hot seat with Germany.
Because this time there would be no excuse of an ancient treaty, nor
any other kind of treaty but aggression pure and simple, Hitler's reaction might be more extreme than a diplomatic protest. He might decide
to occupy mainland Portugal or, more realistically, start unrestricted
submarine warfare against Portuguese shipping.

If the United States invaded the Azores, what would be Salazar's first recourse? He could turn to the British and invoke that same ancient treaty which Portugal had just honored. If he asked for protection against the United States, Churchill, with his strong sense of history and tradition, would find himself in a deeply embarrassing situation. Kennan would do his best to scotch the whole idea before it got off the ground.

Kennan was sure that no matter what Washington thought, the British ambassador to Lisbon, Sir Ronald Hugh Campbell, should be apprised of this latest message. Campbell had kept him informed of every detail of Anglo-Portuguese relations, keeping him better informed in fact than his own State Department, and now he too was shocked when he read the telegram. It was obvious to both that something had to be done to head off what could become a dangerous—or at least a deeply embarrassing—situation.

The critical question was: what to do? The order to see Salazar had come "by direction of the President." With the war raging, the president's orders were to be obeyed without question, especially those involving military matters. But if it was executed it would only create greater problems than it meant to solve. Kennan decided not to confront Salazar but to convince Washington the demands were unreasonable.

October: Berlin

The Germans were bitter about the British beating them into the Azores. Goebbels complained to Hitler that "Salazar has lost his faith in us," but could propose no solution, forceful or otherwise, to restore his faith.

The principal preoccupation for the German High Command was the Russian front, the threatened destruction of their forces in the Crimea, and the possible loss of Romanian oil. Although they very much wanted to take retaliatory action against Portugal, pragmatically there was little they could do. In fact, the subject of retaliation did not even come up during the October conferences with Hitler.[30] Admiral Dönitz ordered U-boats U-154 and U-616 to take stations off Ponta Delgada and Horta but they were forbidden to attack any warships or merchantmen within Portuguese territorial limits. Portuguese vessels would continue to be treated as neutrals; Portugal was still supplying tungsten—a critically needed metal for the German war machine.

While the U-boats patrolled offshore of the Azores, eastbound convoy UT-3 passed northwest of the islands under escort of no less than nineteen warships, including the battleship *Arkansas*. The commander of the convoy, Rear Admiral Henry D. Cooks, did not see any air support, nor did he see any signs of U-boat activity. Close behind convoy UT-3 was the fast CU-6, a troop-carrying convoy on a southerly route that passed within 380 miles of Flores. CU-6 also had no contacts with U-boats. Soon round-the-clock aerial surveillance would be operational from Lagens and all convoy leaders would breathe more easily.[31]

18 October: Lagens Field

The first RAF Flying Fortresses arrived and started antisubmarine operations the following day, relieving the nine Swordfish aircraft flown off the HMS *Fencer* that had been on patrol since the initial landing. The U.S. Air Transport Command inaugurated a new route to India with a refueling stop in the Azores with British—but not Portuguese—sanction. Now emergency shipments could be made in a timely manner and precious aircraft fuel would be conserved using the shortest transoceanic route.[32]

18 October: Washington, D.C.

The Joint Chiefs were convinced that chargé d'affaires George Kennan could not be trusted to negotiate on their behalf. He had been ordered to present their extravagant demands to Salazar, which he refused to do (and gave good reasons for not doing so). Although Roosevelt accepted his arguments, the Joint Chiefs maintained he was betraying the war effort and wanted him recalled to Washington to defend his actions. The Joint Chiefs asked the Department of State to accept "qualified army and Navy officers to set forth Army and Navy needs, and to give necessary technical assistance to him in negotiations he is beginning for the United States' use of the Azores." The military advisers were Navy commanders Gerald L. Huff and John E. Faigle, the army advisers were Col. G. G. Mason from the Air Transport Command and Col. J. H. Davidson from the Army Air Force. They were to go to Lisbon on 20

October but delayed their departure anticipating Kennan's appearance at the Pentagon.

A detailed document was prepared "for the guidance" of the Special Mission: first, they were told to familiarize themselves with fourteen references: seven memoranda and directives of the Joint Chiefs and four from the CCS. (Nothing from Kennan was included.) The requirements for bases which had horrified Kennan and the British ambassador to Lisbon, CCS 270/7, was foremost among the required readings. The Mission was admonished "to obtain the earliest possible implementation of these facilities." Other important guidelines included:

3. Long drawn-out negotiations are not desired. It is important that entry of adequate United States Forces to commence immediate construction be authorized without delay to obtain the benefits envisaged. If such preliminary construction can be approved in principle and be put in effect immediately this should be done without waiting for completion of the negotiations.

4. It is considered best not to go into too much detail as to requirements and expectations, but to secure the rights which will permit the United States eventually to establish the facilities required.

6. In connection with negotiations, the Portuguese may make demands for quid pro quo. You are not empowered to commit the Joint Chiefs of Staff. In case of any demands, they should be referred to proper agencies in the United States through appropriate channels for necessary action.[33]

20 October: Kennan to State Department

Kennan warned the State Department that there were compelling reasons not to confront Salazar with our demands. If Salazar was approached now, he would not only refuse them outright but would be suspicious about any other requests the United States might make in the future. No mention was made in the Anglo-Portuguese negotiations, and in fact the 1373 treaty did not allow participation by a third power. Salazar had already strained his relations with the Germans and felt he would be lucky if the only retaliation was sinking a ship or two or around the Azores. Kennan suggested that the best course of action would be "to slip quietly and gradually through the gap which the British have succeeded in opening for us," Churchill's message exactly. Because his orders came from the president rather than the State Department, would the Department allow him to return immediately to Washington and to explain his views personally to the president? He asked the British not to comment on their own before he had this opportunity because he had "no desire to evade the direct responsibility which I bear for the execution of these orders."[34]

Kennan received strong support from Churchill, who cabled Roosevelt on 19 October after learning of the Joint Chiefs' demands. There was no way that England could support the demands: "I cannot help feeling that we could not obtain these for you immediately, and I wonder whether you have any definite information from Lisbon that you would be able to obtain them by direct approach."[35]

Washington answered Kennan just two days later; the president saw no reason for him to return to Washington; a cable explanation would serve just as well. Kennan then drew up a long message listing reasons why carrying out the president's orders was a bad idea; it was not only counterproductive but there were reasons to think that it might be disastrous. He pointed out in particular that we had no quid pro quo to offer the Portuguese for abandoning their neutrality. To obtain facilities in the Azores the British had already promised away every possible benefit to Portugal, benefits related to economic warfare including most favored nation status, refurbishing their armed forces, and protection of shipping. Our ally had already played the diplomatic game skillfully and won; the cards were no longer in our hands, and we should now avoid actions that could foul up relations with Portugal.

Another prompt answer made Kennan believe that at last somebody was taking him seriously. The telegram stated that the president desired the negotiations with Salazar be left to his "judgment and discretion . . ." but that he "should just bear in mind that the need for the facilities was imperative and urgent." That was the good news. The bad news was that the State Department did not accept his argument that the United States had no quid pro quo to offer to the Portuguese in exchange for bases. The State Department pointed out that "we could assure them to respect the sovereignty of Portugal and its entire colonial empire, assurances that have thus far been withheld."

That last statement almost sounded ominous. Hitler specialized in ultimatums that read "if you allow our army to occupy your country peacefully we will respect your sovereignty; if not we will invade." In either case the country ends up without its sovereignty and being occupied. How else could the prime minister of Portugal interpret this message? No concessions, no "respect the sovereignty of Portugal," and U.S. occupation of the Azores in any case. Most probably, the British ambassador told Kennan, Salazar would respond in one of two possible ways. First he could appeal to England as a long standing ally for assistance in meeting the U.S. threat or he would resign the leadership of Portugal, neither course of action being palatable to the Allies.

23 October: Navy Headquarters, Pentagon, Washington, D.C.

The Intelligence Division of the Office of the Chief of Naval Operations issued a digest of information regarding the Azores containing political and geographical data, hydrographic charts, and other information to allow the Navy to complete a plan of action:

> the American Naval Aviation Group would serve as augmenting body to a large British unit and would be based . . . at LaGens [sic] Field. Under this arrangement the Allies would be able to hunt submarines around the clock, British patrols by day, American patrols by night. The American group, consisting mainly of B-24 four-engine Liberator Bomber Units, was assembled under the Commander, U.S. Naval Forces Azores. It is interesting to note that as early as mid-1942, the Bureau of Yards and Docks was completing . . . estimates for shipping equipment to be used by the Navy in establishing themselves in these islands.[36]

23 October: Lisbon and Washington, D.C.

Kennan discovered that Time-Life magazines were planning to feature the new Anglo-Portuguese agreement on the Azores in forthcoming issues. He was afraid that any publicity might prove disastrous, especially if it were reported in a prestigious newsmagazine with worldwide circulation. He sent off an urgent telegram to Ambassador Winant and the secretary of state:

> The success of these arrangements . . . depends partly on the extent to which they can be kept inconspicuous and not too provocative to German prestige. If we insist in rubbing it in publicly we can hardly fail to provoke some German reaction; and any such reaction could hardly fail to be disagreeable to the Joint Chiefs. As for Salazar he is sensitive to the extreme on this point. Some of our press reaction has already irritated him violently. Anything more of this sort can only increase this effect and serve to complicate seriously the delicate and responsible tasks which now lie before this mission.[37]

Acting Secretary of State Stettinius immediately went into action. He invited Charles Wertenbaker, the foreign editor of *Time,* to his apartment where they held "a frank and satisfactory talk" on the evening of 29 October. Wertenbaker was convinced it would be a bad idea to publicize the Azores agreement at this time and agreed to play down any matter concerning Portugal. In a month or so he said he would be back to discuss it again. Kennan and everyone else concerned could breathe easily.[38]

25 October: Lisbon

Kennan saw only one possible way to go in the negotiations with Salazar. First, he needed to assure him that the the United States would respect Portuguese sovereignty and then and only then ask for the bases in the Azores. Doing it this way was in direct violation of his orders from the State Department but Roosevelt was a higher authority. After all, the president had given him carte blanche to negotiate using his own "judgment and discretion," so why not ignore the State Department's impossible conditions, which would surely open up a Pandora's Box. On Saturday afternoon, alone at the U.S. Chancery, Kennan typed out this message to Salazar:

> Lisbon, October 25, 1943   No. 1:297
>   Excellency:
>   In pursuance to instructions from my Government, I have the honour to inform Your Excellency that in connection with

the agreement recently concluded between Portugal and Great Britain the Government of the United States of America undertakes to respect Portuguese sovereignty in all Portuguese colonies.

Please accept, Excellency, the renewed assurances of my highest consideration.

George Kennan

Kennan's letter did the trick. Finally Minister Bianchi could visit the secretary of state carrying a cheerful note from Salazar. The Portuguese government was officially elated, that it wished "to convey to the United States Government their appreciation and thanks for the guaranty thus given" to respect Portuguese sovereignty over her lands.[39]

The pleasure that Kennan must have felt, that finally Washington appreciated his efforts and he was making an impact on the highest levels of policy making, was short-lived. His letter to Salazar certainly cheered up the moody prime minister and dispelled any festering suicidal thoughts about an impending war with the United States. Then he composed a lengthy dispatch to Washington explaining in detail what he had just accomplished: a great triumph of foreign policy that would smooth our way into the Azores and in the long run hasten victory in the war. Portuguese policy towards the United States was bound to mellow and the United States would be allowed to build bases anywhere they were needed. Air bases by invitation without the need for an armed invasion were preferable to everyone but a few fire-breathing generals. At a minimum we would share the British bases with them.

Salazar was happy to receive the promise to recognize his country's sovereignty but, still felt that lacking a treaty of alliance, he could not grant the United States the same privileges given to England. Doing so would violate his country's neutrality. He suggested that if the U.S. units were "on loan" to the British and wore distinctive British insignia, then perhaps they could share Lagens with them. This would solve the need for additional air bases, but he still would not allow distinctive U.S. naval patrols to operate against U-boats. It was not until July 1944 that a U.S. Naval Air Squadron was officially permitted to operate from Lagens Airfield—on the condition that the flight crews wore both U.S. and RAF insignia.

The following day, Sunday, 24 October, the Portuguese Foreign Office informed Kennan that Salazar would be glad to receive him on Wednesday. The omens were good. No question that the interview would go well. But the embassy telegraph machine was still clacking ominously away, another telegram arriving from Washington. Gloom quickly replaced his short-lived elation. Before he could start preparing for the audience, which he was sure would resolve the problem of the bases and maintain the friendship of Portugal, the new message dispelled these hopes. It contained not a word of praise or even comment on how he so skillfully negotiated with the Portuguese. The message said nothing about a commendation; it ominously ordered him simply to return immediately, to take the next plane back to the United States. He had no idea what kind of reception awaited but almost certainly he was not returning to a hero's welcome.

Kennan's description of his journey home was dramatic enough evidence of the need to establish a first-class international air base in the Azores:

> These few planes, the original "Pan American Clippers" . . . , constituted the only civilian air link between North America and Europe . . . The planes were not normally capable of flying the Atlantic westbound, so the voyage from Lisbon to New York went via Africa, the east coast of South America, the Caribbean, and Bermuda. The trip took five days and nights. The crew was changed three times, but the same little group of passengers sat there day and night, getting off every few hours at refueling stops. The temperature at these stops varied wildly—in winter as much as one hundred degrees between certain of the African and South American stops and New York.[40]

Kennan took the first train to Washington from New York, arriving debilitated after his trip and still not sure of the kind of reception to expect—the renegade diplomat fitted out for a hanging or the triumphant hero returned as personal adviser to the president. It should not be too bad, he reckoned, there were limits to what the military could to him. As a civilian he probably could not be court-martialed and shot. However, he found out some years later, that some generals and admirals did entertain the idea that he should be tried for treason.

His telephone call to the State Department did not evoke any warm heartfelt homecoming greetings. He was told, without explanation or questioning, to show up at 8:15 A.M. next day. Still in the dark, the following morning he was driven to the Pentagon with Mr. Harrison Matthews, chief of the European Division of the State Department. Together with Acting Secretary of State Edward Stettinius they were ushered into a large room where the top military commanders of the country, including the Joint Chiefs of Staff, were already assembled.

Kennan quickly discovered that no one knew who he was, or his position, or that the ambassador to Portugal had died and nobody, needless to say, had read any of his dispatches. He was not introduced to anybody; the three civilians were merely ordered to take seats, "like prisoners in a dock" against a side wall of the room. Then followed a lengthy discussion among the high officials, all of which went over Kennan's head because he knew nothing of the country's plans and policies; he had never been enlightened by his bosses in the State Department.

Finally a question was posed to him: why did he not go ahead and present our demands to the Portuguese? From his previous experience with the Washington power structure he should have known better and not assumed as he did at first that those present had read his dispatches. He went over only the headings of his main arguments as a sort of review but this proved to be a complete waste of time. He had laid out in painstaking detail the rationale for his actions in communications with the State Department and the president but nobody present was even aware of the documents. His grand debut was rapidly turning into a fiasco.

Because he had not been introduced and nobody there had read anything he wrote it was clear that the makers of our country's policies and war strategy had been working in an information vacuum. They had lots of data on shipping losses and detailed maps of convoy routes in the Atlantic but no firsthand political or diplomatic information. Left to themselves and apparently not knowledgeable or caring about the diplomatic situation vis-à-vis Portugal, the Azores, or our ally England, unencumbered by facts the Joint Chiefs had devised their own stratagems.

Kennan pointed out that it would probably be possible for us to obtain permission to use the airfield the British were putting into shape. "'What field was that?' came the challenge. 'The Lagens field, on Terceira Island,' I replied. 'Hell,' bellowed the chief of the Air Force—General Henry ('Hap') Arnold—'that's nothing but a goddam swamp.'"

Kennan was afraid to argue the point with General Arnold, even though he was sure the statement was completely wrong; not even one decent swamp can be found on the entire island. In fact, just three weeks after this meeting, U.S. air transport planes started using Lagens on a regular basis. But when the commanding general of the Air Force makes a statement, even if it is completely wrong, no civilian would dare challenge it.

Kennan was having one of the worst days of his life. No root canal session could compare with the ordeal of being in a room with a bunch of generals and admirals who had been itching for a grand operation, but had been foiled by an unknown State Department lackey, a civilian still wet behind the ears who had dared to ignore their orders. He could not even justify his actions; shooting would be too good for him if only they could order it.

The discussion was rapidly falling into chaos. What was supposed to be an exchange of ideas had turned into a bitter denunciation of the entire State Department. Henry Stimson, the secretary of war, finally decided things were getting out of hand, and Kennan should leave before things got any worse. Stimson asked Stettinius, giving a nod in Kennan's direction, "Who is this young man?" Kennan was all of thirty-nine years old or a little more than half Stimson's age.

The acting secretary of state did not have the foggiest idea, so he turned to Matthews for help. After a minute or two of whispered prompting, Stettinius assured Stimson that the young man was George Kennan, our chargé d'affaires in Lisbon. Stimson reacted violently, "our what?" Stettinius explained that the ambassador had died and Kennan had been placed in charge.

Everything was now clear. The State Department had been derelict once again. It was amazing that the Joint Chiefs could even conduct a war considering the diplomatic and legal roadblocks that the State Department seemed to be forever erecting. "Well," said the secretary of war, "I think it's high time that we had a full-fledged ambassador who could give proper attention to our affairs at this important post. Will you see to that, Mr. Secretary?" Stettinius told Matthews to make a note of it, and then, turning to Kennan, now clearly a full-fledged pariah, he said, "I think you may go now."

Kennan found his way back to Washington from the Pentagon, his indignation just about at the boiling point. He had handled his post in Lisbon superbly by any standards, dealing with the Portuguese government and our British allies but rarely receiving a single word or even a hint of guidance. He had had no briefings from Washington yet he knew more about Portugal and the situation with the Azores than anyone in the capital. But to jump-start the Azores operation, a new ambassador to Lisbon was to be appointed. He would, of course be starting from scratch, with no real knowledge of the situation, but well-briefed on the Pentagon's plans.

Kennan convinced Matthews after the meeting that a dangerous but completely avoidable crisis was brewing and it was up to the State Department to head it off. Matthews telephoned Admiral William Leahy, President Roosevelt's chief of staff, to make an appointment for Kennan. When Leahy heard about the Pentagon fiasco he told Kennan to come over immediately to the White House. At last Kennan was to find a sympathetic audience. Leahy was "astonished" at the story and arranged an immediate meeting with Harry Hopkins, the president's senior adviser. Hopkins, as always, was all business, no time wasted on polite pleasantries, and cross examined Kennan for almost an hour. Kennan felt that if he failed this test, his future as a diplomat might be over. Hopkins questions were "sharp, skeptical, and menacing in tone," but when the inquisition was over he had clearly been won over to Kennan's side. He ordered Kennan to return to where he was staying, "and don't let yourself get out of reach of the telephone."[41]

He got back to the house and barely hung up his coat when the telephone rang. It was Hopkins telling him to return to the White House immediately. This was one of the most incredible days of Kennan's life, the depths of gloom at the Pentagon were to be followed by exhilaration in the White House and the day was not yet over. He was ushered into the White House, passed through a completely new set of corridors and asked to enter a different door than he had seen before. He opened the door not being sure what to expect, and found himself alone in a large room with only one other person—the president, Franklin Delano Roosevelt.

Roosevelt greeted him jovially, the first one that day who actually appeared glad to see him and told him to sit down on the other side of his great desk. The president had already been briefed by Harry Hopkins so there was no need to repeat the story and all its gory details, no questions were asked of Kennan, he only had to listen while Roosevelt expressed his thoughts. Kennan interjected that the military was planning to follow a hard line, first giving an ultimatum to Salazar followed by an invasion of the Azores. Roosevelt, completely unruffled, told Kennan not to worry "about all those people over there," in other words the Joint Chiefs of Staff, the secretaries of war and navy—the entire high command of our armed forces.

The president could not understand why Salazar would not trust him to return in good shape any island that we used now, and that any occupation was only for the duration of the war. After World War I he himself decommissioned the two naval bases that we had used in the Azores and returned them to Portugal in better shape than they ever had been. No diplomatic shenanigans, no ex post facto negotiations to maintain a presence: we just cleared out. All it might take this time is a letter to Salazar reminding him that there was a precedent for allowing us on the islands and that he had nothing to fear about our motives. "I'll tell you what I'll do," he said. "You come back here tomorrow morning and I'll give you a personal letter which you can take back to Portugal and present to Dr. Salazar; and then you just go ahead and do the best you can." Roosevelt's letter might not have the same legal force as the 1373 Anglo-Portuguese treaty but it might be all the convincing the Portuguese prime minister needed.

Things were working out better than Kennan had ever imagined. Far from facing a firing squad, he was actually going to make U.S. foreign policy and this time with the blessings of the president. He agreed completely with Roosevelt, thought this new approach would do the trick, and would be most happy to carry out the president's orders.

Now that Kennan had support from a higher level than the Joint Chiefs or even his bosses at the State Department, he felt more confident returning to his post in Lisbon. Because he would be working as a direct agent of the president, he had to know the Joint Chiefs' exact positions with respect to Portugal. The State Department complied, sending his request to the Joint Chiefs. There is no record of the reaction to the request. They had hoped to shoot Kennan for treason, or at least replace him with a more pliant diplomat, certainly not to see him return to Portugal more powerful than ever before.[42]

Matthews felt there was one additional prop Kennan needed in negotiations with Salazar: unblemished British support. He asked Roosevelt to write to Churchill stating, " I hope that he can depend on the full support of the British Ambassador to Lisbon in impressing upon the Portuguese the compelling importance to our common war effort of the early use of these facilities by United States forces and would appreciate your sending him instructions in that sense."[43]

Matthews suspected that Salazar was looking for excuses to reject a U.S. appeal for bases and would exploit any indication that the British were not in full accord with their ally. England's ambassador would insure there was no chance of that happening. Kennan picked up the president's letter to Salazar the following morning and returned to Portugal in a much better mood than when he left. Now he felt invincible, the president was on his side. From now on, nothing could possibly go wrong.[44]

31 October: Lisbon

While Kennan was in Washington, Crocker, the acting chargé d'affaires of the U.S. Embassy in Lisbon, reported a new and exciting development: Fernando dos Santos Costa, Portugal's undersecretary for war, invited Colonel Solberg, the U.S. military attaché, to call upon him for the first time. The invitation was clearly a result of Kennan's letter acknowledging Portuguese sovereignty and had been sent by order of Salazar. Solberg quoted Santos Costa as saying that "Portugal would favorably envisage, provided it remained both a pattern of the Anglo-Portuguese Agreement, to accord to the United States similar facilities, as for example in connection with convoys."

Crocker added that

> I am not unmindful of the difficulties of evaluating properly at such a distance the true import of this conversation. I am, however, persuaded that we would be on safe ground in concluding that the Under Secretary, probably reflecting Salazar's thoughts, wished to create the impression that he has at least an open mind in respect to an approach on the question of granting certain facilities to us. Neither Solberg nor myself have the impression that there was anything in the Under Secretary's statements which would justify the conclusion that we would necessarily be held within the precise limits of the British agreement.[45]

The big question, which could not be answered so easily, was whether or not the undersecretary had reached the same conclusions. However, the Joint Chiefs accepted Colonel Solberg's version, especially because it gave them a green light to go ahead. The Engineers and Seabees would soon be on their way.

The State Department next appointed Henry Norweb as ambassador to Portugal. Kennan was too junior a diplomat and had too many powerful enemies to allow him savor his great diplomatic triumph. But the State Department, which was "accustomed to sneezing whenever the Pentagon caught cold," was following the secretary of war's orders. Official Washington began to feel that finally the Azores bases were within easy grasp.

Although the Pentagon managed to get Kennan replaced as the United States's representative in Lisbon, he did stay on as first secretary of the Embassy. After all, it was his assessment and handling of negotiations that got the United States into the Azores, as well as avoiding a diplomatic crisis with England and preserving the good will of Portugal. Although Salazar might refuse to give written permission for U.S. troops to operate in the Azores, as Churchill predicted, once the British were established at Lagens Field he might wink at their "coming in through the back door."

What Kennan did not know was that the Joint Chiefs had started the wheels in motion to build a U.S. air base in the Azores months before he assumed his position in Lisbon. While diplomatic negotiations were still taking place, the 928th EAR at the Richmond, Virginia, Air Force Base and the 96th NCB had been formed and were in training for the operation. The task force would be ready whenever the United States figured out how to get it onto the islands.

NINE

SAILING ORDERS, NOVEMBER–DECEMBER 1943

> Suffice it to say, that with the inauguration of the Azores'[s] patrols, shipping losses fell off to such an extent as to become almost negligible; at the same time the men concerned wanted for little.
>
> Undated Report from the director, Atlantic Division, Bureau of Yards and Docks[1]

September–October

Immediately after landing in Terceira, the British airmen, sappers, and sailors, with help from local laborers, started work on the landing strip. The field had to be sturdy enough to serve VLR B-17 bombers and heavy transport aircraft waiting to fly the new, shorter transatlantic route. The construction technique was the same used on the many advanced landing fields built in theaters throughout the war. Marston-mat was the basic building block, a perforated steel plate ten feet long by fifteen inches wide with eighty-seven holes per plate. Normally sixty thousand mats were linked together to form an all-weather surface five thousand feet long by one hundred fifty feet wide, adequate to serve most types of Allied aircraft. The runway constructed at Lagens was made six thousand feet long and finished quickly to get operations started, but because of the expected heavy and long-lasting traffic, a more permanent hard-surface landing strip would soon be needed.[2]

Opening day for the new Lagens Air Field was a gala affair. A local Catholic priest delivered the blessing and the governor of the island cut the ceremonial ribbon held at each end respectively by RAF and Portuguese airmen. Adding some drama, a B-17 piloted by Squadron Commander P. E. Hadlow did a low-level flyover after which Air Vice Marshal Bromet ordered two flares to be fired, one red for England and the other green for Portugal. The colors were not due to any astute advance planning but were the only colors the Very pistols could fire. Brigadier João Tamagnini de Souza Barbosa, governor of the island, declared the Lagens Air Field officially opened.[3]

Despite the cool receptions for Americans and their proposals in Lisbon, the official attitude in the Azores was distinctly warm. On 8 November, less than a month after Air Vice Marshall Bromet moved three Coastal Command Hudson and Flying Fortress Squadrons into Lagens, two U.S. Wildcat pilots from the USS *Santos* made an "emergency landing" on the runway. The pilots were flying support for convoy UGS-22, then passing by the Azores as Roosevelt had promised, but respecting protocol reported themselves as lost. Brigadier Barbosa and Bromet were delighted to have their first U.S. guests and resolved to entertain them royally. Portuguese officials quickly organized an impromptu ball in their honor that night, and with warm speeches of welcome and friendship between the two countries, the Navy fliers were assured by the governor himself that Portugal stood by the side of the United States 100 percent.[4]

Friendly receptions were not restricted to Terceira. Two CVEs, the USS *Barker* and USS *Bulmer,* sailed into the port of Horta on Flores on the same day. The ships' captains alleged that they were short of fuel, which was readily provided by the Portuguese harbor captain with no untoward incident or protest. On the next day, three other convoy escorts, the USS *Hobby,* USS *Kalk,* and USS *Gillespie,* sailed into Ponta Delgada on São Miguel. They also found a friendly reception, despite Lisbon's insistence that Ponta Delgada was off-limits to Allied warships. These visits from UGS-22 were undoubtedly planned by the Joint Chiefs, testing the kind of reception a U.S. task force might expect when it arrived to stay in the Azores.

With VLR aircraft flying from airfields in the North Atlantic and the new RAF Azores base in the central Atlantic, plus Admiral Ingersoll's U.S. task groups, roles were beginning to be switched in the Atlantic. The ocean was no longer a graveyard for Allied ships; now it was the U-boats that were ending up on the bottom. During October twenty-three U-boats were sunk. In the months of November and

December, only 9 merchant ships were lost out of the 2,468 that sailed in sixty-four North Atlantic convoys, and at the same time, twenty-five U-boats were sunk in mid-ocean, including five by surface escorts, six by carrier aircraft flown off CVEs, and thirteen by land-based VLR bombers.[5]

As a result of horrendous losses in crews and submarines not compensated by Allied shipping losses, Admiral Dönitz called off his wolf-pack strategy and ordered the U-boats to disperse more widely. No longer could a wolf pack form a picket line, wait expectantly to ambush a passing convoy, and exact spectacular damage. The only encounters now would be by chance, solitary submarines meeting unescorted merchant ships. The war in the Atlantic had taken a decided turn for the worst for Germany.

5 November: Richmond Air Base, Virginia

A new alert for overseas shipment was passed down to the 928th, "the date to be specified." At least with this later date of sailing, the British would be well settled in and more time given for Salazar to change his mind about allowing Americans in the Islands. But whether Salazar approved or not, U.S. forces were coming to Terceira. This time the alert for overseas shipment would not be canceled; the liberation of Europe was only months away; the Azores air base had to be ready to play its role.[6]

6 November: North Atlantic

Group *Eisenhart*, a major operation of the U-boat command based in the North Atlantic off the Newfoundland Banks, lost two submarines this day: U-226 and U-842, both sunk by *Card*. U-boat losses in the area had become insupportable, which convinced Dönitz to abandon attacks against North Atlantic Halifax convoys and liquidate the group. The remnants of *Eisenhart* were to proceed individually to join group *Schill* patrolling the Liverpool–Gibraltar shipping lanes. Dönitz sadly noted in the U-boat War Diary that "we cannot stand these losses particularly with no successes to counterbalance them."[7]

7 November: Azores

The Joint Chiefs planned to station twelve Navy PB4Y Privateers at Lagens Air Field to join the RAF antisubmarine patrols and were even willing to place the units under titular British control. Salazar turned that idea down. The Joint Chiefs, not to be put off, sent out a secret reconnaissance party to Horta via Pan Am Clipper to reconnoiter air base sites. The party was led by Navy Captain W. G. Tomlinson accompanied by six officers, including Colonel David A. Morris of U.S. Army Corps of Engineers. Tomlinson was to become commander of the Navy units and Morris of the Army forces at Lagens Air Field.[8]

The party was told to contact Air Vice Marshal Bromet when they arrived, and he would provide additional personnel to help with their mission. Their objective was to "determine the requirements for carrying out the proposed United States plan for use of the Azores." In addition, they were ordered to "determine the general scope and nature of the British projects underway in the Azores and form an estimate of their intentions regarding U.S. participation." Acknowledging the delicacy of the mission, the orders included the warning: "No right to construct facilities have been obtained by the United States. In your contact with the British and Portuguese, use suitable discretion to avoid prejudicing negotiations now in progress."[9]

The party arrived at Horta but Portuguese authorities would not allow them to stay. Before leaving, they did note that the island was unsuitable for operating seaplanes or for air transport service and that it should receive no further consideration. They flew next to Terceira in two British airplanes where Air Vice Marshall Bromet advised them that the local officials would not allow them to proceed to any other island until—if ever—Lisbon approved. The reconnaissance party had seen enough, however, to conclude that as soon as arrangements could be made, a U.S. Navy antisubmarine squadron should be based at Lagens to back up the RAF.[10]

The antisubmarine squadron was ready and packed; the Navy appealed to the State Department to help get it into Lagens as soon as possible. Freeman Matthews suggested to Roosevelt that to accomplish this, the British would have to be in full accord or Salazar would turn down the request. Churchill should be asked to have the "British Ambassador to Lisbon [impress] upon the Portuguese the compelling importance to our war effort of the early use of these facilities by United States forces."[11]

9 November: Azores Operational Zone

Shortly after dawn, a Flying Fortress based in Lagens sunk U-707, a contact keeper and a linchpin for wolf-pack operations. The U-boat was to take part in a planned massive attack against convoy MKS-29A but its loss meant that the operation had to be called off. With the British base fully operational, it was apparent that the Azores Gap was closed and areas free of VLR bomber patrol severely diminished. Admiral Dönitz could no longer expect the high dividends around the Azores that he had once counted on.[12]

This was to become an oft-repeated story. By the end of the war, aircraft based on Lagens had detected thirty-eight submarines and attacked nineteen, which pretty much took the pleasure out of convoy-hunting for the U-boats. During the last quarter of 1943, with the Atlantic Ocean well patrolled and safer than it had been at any time during the war, nearly four hundred thousand troops were carried to England without suffering the loss of a single troopship. Before the end of hostilities, over three million had made the crossing.[13]

15 November: The Pentagon

The Joint Chiefs were only slightly deterred by the refusal to allow uniformed U.S. officers in the Azores; the Chiefs decided to send another group, this time in civilian clothes. After first clearing the operation with the British, ten Army and Navy personnel would be flown to Faial and Terceira to join an alleged British reconnaissance survey party. About the same time the Air Force was to carry out an aerial photo reconnaissance of all the islands, unless this could be provided by the British. Shipment of materials would be postponed until the full extent of U.S. participation in Operation Alacrity was clarified.[14]

Sir John Dill responded that the British Chiefs agreed with the proposals, but he pointed out—and it was a big "but"—it was first necessary to obtain visas and Portuguese permission for the party. Considering the restrictions put on the travel of foreigners in the Azores, this might be a major sticking point. Furthermore, the RAF was mapping the islands and detailed information on the state of affairs at Lagens Air Field would soon be passed on to General Marshall. If by some chance the Americans could get visas and travel to the Azores, then Air Vice Marshal Bromet would arrange their interisland transport. In any case, as soon as the RAF mapping was completed the Joint Chiefs would have a full set of maps.

Nothing came of the proposed undercover operation, but it clearly shows the mounting desperation felt by the Joint Chiefs. They were frustrated by what they felt was Portuguese intransigence and weak British advocacy of their cause. The state of affairs could not be allowed to continue much longer. If diplomacy failed to produce a U.S. air base, they would send a task force without approval from anybody.

November: Lisbon

Much of the Joint Chiefs' aggravation spilled out on Kennan, who was still the chargé d'affaires in Lisbon and trying to make sense out of the orders coming out of Washington. He had received and already deplored the Joint Chiefs' demands on the Azores but being a good diplomat was prepared to carry their list to Salazar. He expected the Chiefs to set their demands in some priority order but they never set one or at least never let Kennan know if such a list even existed. But he had to do something, so he decided to present the list to Salazar "in an informal and exploratory manner." Adding to his problems was the order not to consult with the British ambassador before seeing Salazar, so he avoided meeting with the ambassador after returning from Washington.[15]

Kennan needed some other questions answered before seeing Salazar. How could he explain the need for a separate airfield for submarine patrol when the CCS had agreed at ABC-1 that this fell within the British sphere of responsibility, and that the British were to be in charge of operations in the area of the Azores? He also pointed out that to have any chance of success the plan needed the full approval of the Combined Chiefs and not just the U.S. Joint Chiefs. He also decided that not only did the Joint Chiefs need British support, but that he did as well, so despite orders and as a matter of courtesy and to maintain good relations, he had to see the British ambassador. They met on 19 November to discuss strategies to take to Salazar.

R. Henry Norweb, appointed minister to Portugal with the rank of ambassador, arrived on the twenty-third, relieving Kennan as the United States's chief representative in Lisbon. However, when Kennan requested permission for Norweb to attend the meeting with Salazar, the Portuguese Foreign Office refused. Apparently Salazar's trust of Americans extended no further than the attaché.

Kennan's conversation with Salazar lasted two hours, starting brilliantly with the presentation of Roosevelt's personal letter to the prime minister. The president began by recalling the cooperation between the two countries in World War I, when as undersecretary of the Navy he visited Horta and Ponta Delgada which the Allies were using for repair, fueling, and antisubmarine facilities. "In those days there was never any question about the good faith of the United States in carrying out their pledge that as soon as possible after the war the bases would be dismantled . . . the relationship between the United States and Portugal was on a basis of mutual confidence and great friendship. In 1919 all of our forces were withdrawn."

Then Roosevelt went on to more personal matters, wishing "that I could have a chance to see you one of these days because I want to talk to you about another matter—the furtherance of cultural relations between the United States and Portugal . . . I do not need to tell you that the United States has no designs on the territory of Portugal and its possessions. I am thinking in long range terms because I do not think that our peoples have been in close enough touch in the past."

The letter did the trick, mellowing the prime minister with feelings of good will towards the United States. Salazar was clearly elated that guarantees had now been given by both England and the United States with respect to Portuguese sovereignty over her lands and publicized that fact on 26 November. That assurances had been given by "the two great maritime powers associated in war and committed to each other in peace" was stressed by italics and subtitles in press accounts in Lisbon newspapers. He contrasted this friendly gesture by the Allied powers to the action of Japan in occupying Portuguese Timor and, despite months of negotiations, refusing to leave. The unexplained puzzle is why the State Department powers-that-be kept waffling for so long. Both the English—their Allies—and Kennan informed the Department that giving the assurances could earn U.S. access to the Azores. The JCS were frustrated by the indecision, blaming Kennan although the problem lay with Washington. Once assurances to respect Portuguese sovereignty were given by President Roosevelt, as Kennan had predicted Salazar mellowed and allowed the Americans into the Azores without any need for intimidation or strong-arm tactics.[16]

He was now inclined to permit U.S. forces to use British facilities in the Azores on condition that "appearances were kept up," in other words acting as British troops, and as it also turned out, keeping their presence secret. Salazar saw nothing wrong with U.S. naval forces using the same facilities granted to the British Navy and that ferrying aircraft through the Azores to Europe was acceptable considering that they would become British after they arrived in England. He was not even against the idea of constructing a U.S. air base elsewhere in the archipelago, but having it done by Pan American Airways for the account of the Portuguese government. Portugal would award the contract to Pan Am to build and operate the air base but the military could use it— eventually—on terms to be negotiated.

Any other concessions would have to wait while he thought things over. Kennan was encouraged by the interview and felt that Salazar would let U.S. forces use the islands if he could "find a formula reconcilable with basic policy of neutrality which he is still trying to pursue." The British ambassador thought the United States's request for bases could be justified with the "Friends of Friends" argument in the 1373 treaty, and to sweeten the argument, Norweb was going to promise that the United States would be more willing to provide armaments and help defend Portugal. The gift of armaments was acceptable but Salazar was skeptical of Allied determination to defend Portugal in case of an attack. Lest the people in Washington get too optimistic about the chances of quickly concluding a deal with the Portuguese, Norweb threw in a word of caution: "We must remember that even if we can once overcome the qualms of principle in Dr. Salazar's mind we still have to face the usual Portuguese proclivity for horse trading over details."[17]

24 November: Lagens Air Field

Colonel Grant Mason of the U.S. Air Transport Command flying from Gander Newfoundland in a C-54 was the first American to fly directly from the United States to Lagens. Mason made an aerial reconnaissance of potential airfield sites and concluded that Flores was not suitable but suggested that the western part of Santa Maria would be an excellent place for the U.S. air base. The many advantages of Santa Maria over the other islands included better weather, level terrain, and a large unpopulated area unsuitable for agriculture but acceptable for airfield construction. The biggest disadvantage was the lack of a real harbor, but this was true for most of the other islands as well. This first landing was followed by a succession of U.S. aircraft, now arriving without protest from the Portuguese authorities. Navy Captain C. H. Sanders, a member of the Azores Reconnaissance Party, reported that Bromet appeared to be willing to share the facilities at the field and that Brigadier Tamagnini Barbosa was also satisfied with the arrangement.[18]

28 November–1 December: Tehran, Iran

At the Tehran Conference, Roosevelt, Churchill, and Stalin agreed on invasion plans for Western Europe. This was the first time the three leaders met, as well as the first time the Russian leader had been out of the country. The New York Times also reported the building of a thousand big bombers plus 7,789 other planes in November.[19] The record pace of construction meant that one plane was built every five minutes around the clock. The naval yards were also breaking records with a peak production of two hundred fifty thousand tons, largely combat ships, including the desperately needed CVEs. With U.S. industry producing war materials at this rate more U-boats would be destroyed, and with many more ships coming out of the yards than sunk, there was no way that Admiral Dönitz was going to win his tonnage war.

29 November: Lisbon

Minister Norweb learned through the British Embassy that on 23 June, at the outset of Anglo-Portuguese conversations, Salazar wanted Portuguese forces to take part in the liberation of Timor. On 4 October the Portuguese Foreign Office sent a memorandum to the British Embassy that in view of the long and unsatisfactory efforts to reach an agreement with Japan over Timor, the Portuguese government wished to participate in any effort to drive the Japanese out of the island. The British Foreign Office advised the State Department on 12 October of the Portuguese request and said the matter was being studied by British military authorities who would later submit it to the Joint Chiefs. But no response to the request had ever been received by the British Embassy and so Salazar, whom the Allies could little afford to cross, had been left stewing for the past four months. Salazar in fact told Kennan that if Portugal came into the war, he would not hesitate to grant facilities in the Azores to the United States. To avoid any violent reaction from the Germans, he emphasized in an interview with Henry Taylor of the Scripps-Howard press that relations with Japan had no connection with relations with Germany. Now it was the turn of the diplomats to wring a decision out of the military.[20]

1 December: Terceira

The time had come to "open the back door" and let the United States into Lagens Air Field. The first step was to negotiate an agreement regulating U.S. use of the airfield with no need to apprise the Portuguese government that this was being done. Three U.S. officers, including Captain D. H. Sanders for the U.S. Navy and Colonel D. A. Morris for the Army, landed at the field in a U.S. transport plane, and announced, to the consternation of the Portuguese authorities, that they were planning to stay without permission. Trouble came quickly. They had barely unpacked when Barbosa informed Bromet that the U.S. officers were persona non grata and not welcome on Portuguese territory. If they did not leave Terceira immediately, dire consequences would follow because they were foreign military officers who entered Portuguese territory without permission, without passports or visas, and thus they were legally incognito and technically considered as spies. This was not the reception expected and far different from Captain Sanders's previous visit to Lagens.[21]

Brigadier Tamagnini Barbosa had been appointed with seniority over the civil governor of Terceira and with orders to do whatever Vice Marshall Bromet requested but was given no advice on what to do if Americans landed, especially if they planned to stay. His only instructions were to make sure that the agreement with the British was followed to the letter. U.S. military showing up in the Azores was something that could only be settled by high-level diplomacy in Lisbon and not by field officers on Terceira. The Brigadier knew that Salazar did not want to let Americans in and be accorded the same privileges as the British lest Germany or Spain might consider that an act of aggression. His country's neutrality would be compromised, which might invite an invasion by the Axis.[22]

Before leaving the Azores, the U.S. officers signed an agreement prefaced with the statement that it was negotiated between Air Vice Marshal Bromet, Captain Sanders, and Colonel Morris, and was not to be considered final until approved by the proper higher authorities. The agreement included a "General Discussion":

> The objective is to provide as soon as possible the facilities for operating three V. L. R. squadrons of aircraft . . . in anti-submarine warfare and a monthly movement of about 1,200 U.S. and British aircraft.
>
> After a review of existing facilities at Lagens and showing they would be inadequate the agreement proposed two quite separate and distinct stages in the development of Lagens airfield:
>
> > a. Immediate completion of . . . facilities to handle three anti-submarine squadrons and 200 transient aircraft per month. This should be finished within two months if possible.
> >
> > b. subsequent expansion to take 1,200 transient aircraft per month . . .
>
> 4. . . . no acceleration of program can be achieved by the present small works force which will take up to March 1944 to fulfill its present commitment.
>
> 5. (in order to increase) the capacity of the airfield to 1,200 aircraft per month:
>
> > a. construction of a new main runway, 8,000 ft. x 200 ft. with 50 ft. shoulders and capable of taking the heaviest aircraft being designed.
> >
> > b. construction of a 6,000 ft. x 150 ft. transverse runway.
>
> 6. *Recommendations.*
>
> > a. First Proposals:—A U.S. Army Air Force composed as follows be forthwith sent to Lagens Aerodrome:—
> >
> > > i. Air Transport Command operating force approximately 600 . . . with all the necessary operating equipment. In order to initiate a monthly British/American movement of not to exceed 200 aircraft per month, a key force of not to exceed 100 personnel will arrive by air on or about 10th December . . . Remainder of force and equipment to come by sea.
> > >
> > > ii. Headquarters and Service Co. of Aviation Engineer Regiment, approximately 276 of all ranks, complete with standard equipment plus 150 tons per hour rock

crusher and screening plant and quarry set, percussion well drilling set, and other special equipment as deemed necessary.

iii. Aviation Engineer Battalion, approximately 775 of all ranks . . .

v. Except for personnel . . . to arrive by air, all personnel and cargo will come by sea, not more than one ship at a time; if possible in ships not to exceed 24' draft.

Alternative proposal:—

If, as seems likely at the moment, there is to be considerable delay in obtaining Portuguese approval for the first proposal, then the U. S. Army Air Force should be requested "under contract to the R.A.F.," to undertake the provision and operation of constructional equipment and material for the necessary expansion of existing R.A.F. facilities . . . In the meantime, the 100 key personnel . . . should be sent to Lagens, and a small flow of both U.S. and R.A.F. ferried aircraft, say 4 per day total, be started immediately to make this route a going concern.

7. Other Aerodrome Sites:—

For continued large movements, another aerodrome is necessary . . . The best indications are that the west side of Santa Maria offers the best site for an alternate aerodrome. Until the stormy sea season ends in April, it will be difficult and wasteful of vessels to discharge at Santa Maria. When the U.S. forces . . . are on Terceira, a small party would go by sea to Santa Maria, make a preliminary reconnaissance and hire native labour to prepare a landing strip for L-5 and C-47 airplanes. . . . A detailed ground survey would be made. Then, when the stormy season ends, the construction forces, equipment, materials, and supplies would be sent from the U.S. and discharged at Santa Maria. To do this, another Aviation Engineer Battalion would be needed. Similar consideration should be given for an emergency landing strip on Flores.

/s/ Air Vice Marshal Bromet
Senior British Officer
Azores

/s/ C. H. Sanders
Capt. U. S. N.
/s/ David A. Morris
Col. U. S. Army[23]

The agreement was technically only between three field grade officers but for the Joint Chiefs it was all the authorization they needed. Lagens Air Field would be improved by sending several thousand U.S. servicemen to the Azores. There was no need to wait for approval from the Portuguese government.

When the 928th Engineers embarked from the POE on 3 January 1944, their total strength was 267, including 9 attached U.S. Navy personnel. The advance party of 100 was reduced to 1 officer and 6 enlisted men of the survey section and did not fly out immediately. Having second thoughts about the operation, the Joint Chiefs must have felt that the party was too large and arriving too far in advance of the main body. The new date of arrival at Lagens Air Field was set at 12 January, five days before the arrival of the task force. The Santa Maria operation would wait until summer.[24]

A big mystery—or an incredible oversight—was the complete lack of mention of the U.S. Navy's role in the agreement, even though the Navy planned to send the five-hundred–man 96th Seabee Battalion and an antisubmarine bomber squadron to Terceira. When the Seabees appeared unheralded at the port of Angra over a week before the Army task force arrived, they came, as far as can be determined, without advance warning to anyone. Judging by the lack of documentary evidence, neither the State Department, the British, nor the Portuguese officials on Terceira or in Lisbon knew they were coming, or if they did have an inkling, they had no idea when.

1 December: Lisbon

On the same day Allied officers were in Terceira working out a deal over Lagens, George Kennan went to see Salazar to try to convince him to allow U.S. forces to move in. The prime minister probably had no idea how late in the game it was, and that events were moving ahead and could not be derailed by any action or inaction on his part. Although neither knew it at the time, Kennan was presenting Salazar "an offer he couldn't refuse," for whether or not he agreed, come January a U.S. task force would be landing on Terceira.

Kennan spent a long forenoon with the Portuguese prime minister. Although Norweb was now the official U.S. ambassador, Salazar felt most comfortable with Kennan and trusted him enough to discuss these important matters. Perhaps Kennan was also the only high official in the Embassy who could hold a conversation in Portuguese. Ambassador Norweb sent the secretary of state two telegrams the following day, the first, at noon, was a summary of the meeting; the second, at 5 P.M., his interpretation of Salazar's reactions to the proposals.[25] The first telegram stated that:

> a. Salazar still insists on maintaining neutrality so refuses to grant facilities to the United States outright.
> b. Salazar does not want to extend any further facilities to the British for their use or ours until he can be convinced the military situation has changed markedly with a decreased risk to Portugal. He cited Article Eight of the agreement which allowed "facilities in the Azores held to the absolute minimum" but subject to revision. This meant that no bases outside of Terceira could be given to the Allies. Norweb asked the British ambassador about this interpretation of the Article and was assured it was strictly Salazar's own.
> c. Salazar was prepared to allow U.S. use of the present British facilities on condition that an exterior appearance is maintained such as American aircraft having a nominal British marking. That would also mean only "technical" troops would be allowed who would serve under British command, preferably wearing British uniforms
> d. Salazar agreed to study arrangements for the construction of an air base on Santa Maria for the account of Portugal. The whole question of a Santa Maria air base also hung on his interpretation of the all-powerful Article Eight.

Norweb ended this first telegram on an optimistic note: "This signifies that we have acquired the camel's head and in addition a large part of his remaining anatomy into the tent and it is my belief that the opening should be fully exploited."

Norweb's second telegram was sent after he had more time to fathom exactly what the inscrutable Portuguese leader really meant when he said what he said to Kennan. This was a daunting task because no one was ever sure exactly what his pronouncements meant. In the copy in the National Archives, someone—Secretary Hull? General Arnold?

Admiral King?—underlined or outlined certain parts of the telegram;
these are indicated below:

1. [entire paragraph outlined] It is definitely agreed with Dr.
   Salazar that we shall use Terceira fully under any formula
   that can reconcile our use with the Anglo-Portuguese accord,
   but he wishes us to inform him . . . what that formula shall
   be. It would be quite adequate in the Prime Minister's opinion to have a nominal British marking of our planes . . . He
   was particularly concerned that we should *regard this as a
   facility granted us not by the British but by Portugal.* . . .

2. Salazar agreed to give careful study to the matter of American
   construction and use of a Santa Maria airport . . . Salazar was
   unable to see his way clear to granting us outright these facilities at once. The German Minister . . . has pursued him constantly with a variety of questions concerning a possible
   extension of facilities to us in the Azores. . . . Salazar seemed
   to think that we could construct an airfield for the account of
   the Portuguese government. After construction was completed, if we could demonstrate the added need for the base,
   plus the fact that the German threat to Portugal was diminished, then Salazar would turn over the Santa Maria field to
   the British under the infamous Article Eight and allow us to
   use it as we used Lagens airfield and the port of Horta. This
   way Salazar could make an official denial to the Germans
   that any special facilities had been granted to the United
   States. None of this was made as specific proposals but rather
   suggestions that Salazar was turning over in his own mind.

3. Regarding São Miguel: Salazar had already turned down the
   British request for use of the port and airfield . . . so Kennan
   did not hold out much hope that we would be allowed in.
   Kennan thought the island of Horta fit the needs of the fleet:
   an American tanker and a repair ship could be kept there and
   an airfield constructed for the use of our Navy aircraft. . . .

4. [paragraph outlined] The Prime Minister did not wish to consider any policy respecting Azores bases on the hypothesis of
   eventual Portuguese cobelligerency against Japan. However,
   he is anxious for an answer on Portuguese armed participation in liberating Timor . . . In my opinion it would be valuable for us to be helpful.

5. believe that on the basis of the foregoing the following action should now be taken by us:
   (a) Agreement should be reached by our Military authorities with the British as to precise nature of formula to be employed [in] Lagens. Such formula should then be placed in my hands for transmission to Salazar.
   (b) As regards constructing a Santa Maria airport, a preliminary proposal should be drafted at once . . . providing for our technicians to proceed to immediate survey of the Island. Most-favored-nation treatment should be covered, respecting a future use for commercial aviation, etc.

What the Embassy did not know was that our military were meeting with the British military at Lagens on the same day that Kennan met with Salazar. As far as keeping the embassy informed, everything henceforth would be after the fact. The military would act as they felt best; the embassy's role would not be to inform but to mollify Salazar. The ambassador however, was optimistic and ended his second telegram on a hopeful note: "It seems to me that the extent to which the Prime Minister has gone with us demonstrates real progress of which we should take full advantage. It will be particularly appreciated if our military and naval authorities will let me know the exact extent to which they expect to take this advantage."

4 December: Washington, D.C.

Hull was cheered by the telegrams—finally progress was being made—and informed the president that Salazar looked favorably on U.S. participation in both Lagens and on Santa Maria if certain conditions were met. But as the British had already learned things were not simple in dealing with the Portuguese prime minister, and that impressions Kennan or the ambassador might have from a conversation could turn out to be quite different from Salazar's. But at least the Americans were getting into the Azores "through the back door" now that the British were settled in.[26]

To start regular U.S. use of the Azores, Hull advised Norweb the Navy planned "to send a NATS [Naval Air Transport Service] C-54 to North Africa via Lagens scheduled to depart the following day, and that this will initiate an 'intermediate service.' The Army proposed to send shortly to Lagens three large planes with communications equipment and some ground personnel. In addition a ferry service B-17 will go through Lagens." The Joint Chiefs were moving ahead with operations in Lagens approved by the British hosts even if the Portuguese government, the owner of Terceira, had not been informed.

The secretary of state endorsed the actions of the Joint Chiefs and agreed to act more aggressively on the diplomatic front. He asked Ambassador Norweb to explain to Salazar that granting facilities to the United States was considered a concession from the Portuguese "and not (repeat not) from the British . . . especially in the light of his previous concern to place our concessions under Anglo-Portuguese agreement." Hull also wanted the restrictions on movements of U.S. consuls in the Azores lifted. Despite months of protest and an agreement to end them, they were still being enforced by local authorities and seriously interfered with activities of our representatives. This should be brought informally to Salazar's attention asking him to allow our representatives some freedom of movement in the islands.[27]

9 December: Lagens Air Field

A B-17, the first U.S. bomber to be ferried through the Azores following the Anglo-American agreement landed at Lagens. By the end of the month, the Navy and Army Air Transport Commands were operating a regularly scheduled transport service through the Azores. Finally, as the year ended, Salazar accepted the inevitable and gave permission, ex post facto, for the operation but with the understanding that it would be carried out under British control.[28]

11 December: Washington, D.C.

The relatively cheery attitude at the State Department was not reflected across the Potomac at the Pentagon. Where Secretary of State Hull saw a broken ice jam and progress in negotiations with Salazar, Secretary of the Navy Frank Knox still saw only an intractable log jam caused by gutless U.S. diplomats, a pig-headed Portuguese prime minister, and double-dealing British allies, all conspiring to keep us out of the Azores. Knox decided to lay down the law to the State Department people and let Hull how he wanted the Azores business to be conducted. Someone high up in the State Department underlined in pencil two items in the memo; the first concerned our relations with the British: "It is highly desirable that these negotiations be pressed, without regard to the extent of British support. The record of the negotiations to date does not indicate that British support can be expected to contribute materially to those of our objectives which are over and above the privileges granted to the British by the . . . agreement of 17 August 1943." The second item dealt with Kennan and his negotiations with Salazar: "Mr. Kennan, in despatch 2819, considers his position complicated by the question of strategic responsibility, United States or British, of the Azores area of the Atlantic. This matter should not be allowed to interfere with the negotiations." Knox ended on the note that "As a matter of military necessity it is to be hoped that the objectives of the subject negotiations will be realized at an early date."[29]

We can only imagine the personal effect Knox's letter had on Secretary Hull. He was asked to junk our British allies and to confront the Portuguese directly with our demands, either course spelling diplomatic disaster. The only way into the Azores, short of force, was via the coattails of the British, which was finally about to pay off, and that an ultimatum approach would not only alienate the British, our closest ally, but also Portugal, their oldest friend in Europe.

It took a couple of weeks before Secretary Hull answered the secretary of the Navy, presumably all the time he needed to cool off. On 29 December he wrote: "I . . . have noted that the Navy Department considers it desirable that these negotiations be pressed without regard . . . for British support and that the position of our negotiators should not be complicated by the question of strategic responsibility for the Azores area of the Atlantic." Hull continued with a reminder that Knox could not lay the entire guilt for the delay on the State Department: "This Department and the American Legation in Lisbon had been obliged to await a directive from our Chiefs of Staff respecting the formula under which current operations in the Azores would be conducted. In a communication dated December 4, 1943, the Department requested the views of the Joint Chiefs of Staff. It received a formula on December 23, 1943, which was communicated at once to the American Legation in Lisbon." The communication from the Joint Chiefs transmitted to Norweb and Kennan did not really answer the questions asked by Salazar who was not interested in generic statements but wanted to know the specific details of the formula.

12 December: Atlantic Ocean

A large British force landed on Terceira to augment the small one that had established the air base. As reported by LAC (Leading Air Crafts-man, equivalent to a Private First Class) Kenneth Garner, who took part in the landing, a week or so before at an ungodly early hour and without much warning his unit had been roused from warm beds in England, outfitted with full invasion packs, and marched onto a troop ship. This was obviously no two-bit operation. The convoy escort consisted of at least three warships, two destroyers, and a large cruiser. Of course, as an enlisted man, he had no idea where they were headed or why, and his piddling little carbine, not a weapon to instill any great degree of confidence in the bearer, seemed more appropriate for carnival target practice than as a weapon for an all-out honest-to-god war.[30]

After a fortunately uneventful cruise—German intelligence again had no idea of its existence or the U-boats were too intimidated to attack—all hands were relieved to land in a port where the street signs were not in German, French, or Italian, but, surprisingly, in Portuguese. The whole point of the operation was still not clear, but they were definitely not in North Africa or Italy nor were they the opening phalanx of an invasion of France and the Lowlands. Two months after Bromet's 247th Air Group, they came ashore in the same town of Angra do Heroísmo in the Azores in the middle of the Atlantic Ocean, and nowhere near the Mediterranean or the English Channel. Not helping to occupy Sicily and drive the Germans out of Italy might have disappointed some but at least they were not ambushed by a U-boat wolf pack en route and made it safely to an island (that, however, none had ever heard of before). They were starting a new adventure where the greatest dangers would come not from German shells but plague-bearing rats.

16 December: The Pentagon

Although Kennan's interview with Salazar did not make the entire Joint Chiefs happy, at least General Arnold interpreted it as a go-ahead to start the U.S. operation. Any more delay would prevent the air base in Terceira from being ready in time to serve the D-Day preparations. Arnold cabled RAF Air Marshall Portal: "I am planning to dispatch the first of the year one Liberty ship and 2 LSTs in convoy for Terceira in accordance with COS agreement, SEXTANT . . . These will be followed at approximately ten day intervals by two additional Liberty ships bearing material construction personnel, basic supply and house keeping personnel to 'expand' Lagens to handle 1200 transit aircraft monthly in according with local agreement dated 1 December 1943 . . . between Air Marshall Bromet and our War and Navy Departments."[31]

General Arnold must have also seen the report of Navy Captain J. E. Faigle to Captain Sanders "Additional Information Relative to Azores," dated 18 December 1943 and written up after his return from meeting with Kennan and Salazar in Lisbon. It was based on personal observations, RAF aerial reconnaissance, and information from Pan Am Clipper pilots and the station manager at Faial:

1. São Miguel airfield unsafe for heavy loaded aircraft and for night landings. The other field Rabo de Peixe, is a Portuguese military air base and ruled out.

2. Terceira has an excellent field at Lagens being developed by the RAF. It has an elevation of 180 feet and all air traffic is directed to it. Another site mentioned for a pure-American air base at Acerda is nothing but a rough cow pasture at an elevation of 1,080 [feet]. It should not be developed since it is covered by low hanging clouds and subject to strong winds.

3. Santa Maria information was taken from a report by the Office of Naval Intelligence (ONI) which favored establishing an air base on the island. The projected military airfield is at the southwest extremity of the island, at an elevation of 262.5 feet, on relatively flat terrain with a slight inclination from north to south obviating the need for an elaborate drainage system. The clay ground could take a weight of up to fifteen tons; the weather is the most favorable of all the Azores.

4. Fayal [Faial] is suitable only as an emergency field.[32]

Captain Faigle's report showed that the best way to get into the Azores now was through the RAF at the Lagens Air Field on Terceira. If a U.S. air base was needed later, it should be constructed on Santa Maria.

19–20 December: Hitler's Headquarters, Wolfsschanze

The final discussion on *Projekt Amerika* may have taken place on this date. With British troops already on Terceira and a U.S. Army convoy and a Navy Seabee battalion shortly headed that way, the *Amerika* bomber, even if it were manufactured, would not have a base from which to attack Boston, New York, or any other northeastern city. The Azores had become too remote to worry about what with more immediate problems in Russia, Italy, and just about everywhere else in Europe.

However, the OKM raised the question of Timor. Dönitz stressed the importance of winning over Salazar, which could be done by promising to help restore East Timor, Portugal's prize colony. Hitler admitted it would be in Germany's best interests to court the Portuguese president but he was caught in a no-win situation. Making friends with Portugal by promising to restore Timor would certainly alienate Japan, who happened to be Germany's most important remaining ally since Italy had surrendered to the United Nations. The Russians were advancing on the Eastern Front poised to take over the Romanian oil fields, cutting off Germany's only viable source of petroleum. Marshall Runstedt's answer to General Keitel's frantic appeal for advice summed it up: "What shall we do? Make peace you fools. What else can you do?" It was clear to everyone except Hitler that Germany was about to be beaten. Portugal and the Azores were too far down on his list of priorities to worry about. Dönitz's arguments for U-boat bases in the Azores were hardly discussed at the meeting, and were not even tabled for future discussion. The Azores were lost to Germany, the fate of the Atlantic Ocean and the lifeline to England were now in Allied hands.[33]

20 December: Army Air Force Base, Richmond, Virginia

Four days after Arnold advised the RAF that he was sending a task force to Terceira, orders arrived from Army Air Force headquarters to the 928th for imminent movement overseas, "to proceed by motor convoy to Camp Patrick Henry, POE, on December 24"[34] with Lieutenant Colonel Arthur Kemp to assume command of the regiment on 21 December. 928th Regimental Headquarters and Services Company strength was 14 officers and 241 enlisted men, including 16 from a well-drillers section who replaced the camouflage detail. This finally was *the* order, not to be canceled: the 928th was going to take an ocean trip whose destination was not to be revealed until they were well out to sea. Only some very high brass in Washington and London (and Colonel Kemp and his field officers) knew it was to the Azores. To everyone else, all they knew was that they were headed somewhere east across the Atlantic where camouflage would be irrelevant but well drilling critical.

23 December: Washington, D.C.

The State Department was awaiting the promised formula to present to Salazar explaining the kind of cover that would be used for the U.S. Forces to make them appear as quasi-RAF and, it was hoped, delude the Germans. With Salazar satisfied, permission would be granted for the Americans to land in the Azores. What the Department did not know was that the Joint Chiefs decided first to send the task force out to Terceira and then worry about a formula.

The Joint Chiefs answered the State Department with a lengthy review of the agreement signed at Lagens Air Field on 1 December that promised U.S. assistance to the British but still did not give any formula that could be presented to the Portuguese. Work on the formula was in progress with details to be settled by negotiation between General Arnold and Air Chief Marshal Portal.[35]

The 1 December agreement that covered the U.S. Army's coming to Terceira also stipulated that facilities for operating three British and a U.S. Navy VLR squadron for antisubmarine warfare would be provided as soon as possible. This was fundamental to the Navy's plans for the use of Lagens, although the details for provisioning and use of facilities by the VLR squadron had not been worked out. The Navy advised the Admiralty that Captain F. M. Hughes, who participated in the Azores survey, was proceeding to England to confer with appropriate British authorities concerning an operating formula for the use of Lagens by U.S. Navy antisubmarine aircraft. The formula was expected to provide:

1. the guise under which U.S. Navy personnel and aircraft could be stationed and operate from Lagens Air Field on antisubmarine activities;

2. . . . housing and operating facilities . . . provided by the U.S. Navy. . . .

3. entry of supporting personnel and equipment to provide for the operation and maintenance of a U.S. Navy squadron; and

4. entry as soon as practicable of a U.S. Navy VLR antisubmarine squadron to relieve a British Hudson squadron for duty elsewhere.[36]

The Navy found the justification it needed for sending the 96th NCB in the part of the agreement that stated that facilities for a VLR antisubmarine bomber squadron had to be prepared. The RAF certainly would not object because the VLR Navy planes would replace the medium-range Hudsons now stationed at Lagens, which could better serve for tactical support, a high priority for the coming Normandy invasion. Replacing the Hudsons with VLR bombers made sense because they would widen the zone of protection in the Azores gap by several hundred miles.

The Joint Chiefs' memorandum went on to remind the State Department that authority must still be found to send a survey party to survey Santa Maria and other islands to find a suitable site for an airfield. Flores was also mentioned, despite reports that it was unsuitable for a large air base, but nevertheless they wanted it surveyed as well. The westerly location of the island made it ideal at least as an emergency landing strip for U.S. aircraft.

However, this lengthy memorandum still did not answer the State Department concerns: in fact, it added another new one. The revelation that the Navy was to be involved in the Azores operation was just another cross the Lisbon embassy would have to bear. On 15 January 1944, the State Department went through an agonizing session on how to justify the involvement of a naval air squadron in the Azores operation. The squadron was not mentioned in the Anglo-Portuguese agreement of 17 August 1943, nor specifically in the 1 December agreement signed at Lagens, nor in the preliminary formula presented to Salazar on U.S. troop deployment in the Azores, and was even ruled out by AB-1 and the agreement at the Convoy Conference in Washington.[37]

On the other hand, competent U.S. and British officers had decided that a U.S. air squadron could use existing facilities with operations actually or nominally under British command. In addition, Norweb's cable of midnight 24 December stated "that we will be permitted full use of Lagens when we evolve a satisfactory formula covering such use under British aegis." There was also Kennan's conversation with Salazar on 1 December in which the prime minister "was willing to go the limit in making available to us existing British facilities providing external appearance of adherence to British agreement was maintained." Salazar seemed to think that a nominal marking of the planes as British would be sufficient.[38]

The Joint Chiefs' memorandum concluded with the statement that the United States would furnish a new formula to the prime minister providing for nominal markings of our planes but also reminded him that Portuguese participation would be welcome in a future operation against Timor if he cooperated now. The United States wanted him to recognize U.S. needs in the Azores and to stop exporting tungsten to Germany.

When Hull transmitted the Joint Chiefs' memorandum to the embassy in Lisbon, he eliminated any mention of Timor or tungsten and added that although the Navy would prefer to avoid even a nominal British marking, this requirement would be complied with, at least provisionally, if Salazar insisted.[39]

23–24 December: Hull Advises Norweb

On midnight of 23 December, Secretary Hull cabled instructions to present Salazar the preliminary formula agreed upon with the British:

1. to assist the British in expanding the facilities at Lagens, United States Army and Navy personnel and equipment will be transported to Terceira,
2. to assist the British in caring for United States and British transport and ferried aircraft through Lagens,
3. United States personnel activities will be directed toward assistance of the British, who will control those operations,
4. all United States personnel will be given thorough instructions respecting the nature of the Lagens operations, and
5. restrictions set forth in the Anglo-Portuguese agreements will be fully adhered to.

Norweb answered at midnight the following day. Before confronting Salazar, he wanted to make sure all his signals were straight, so he outlined his understanding of the situation based on directives from Washington and private conversations with the British embassy. Everything was straightforward enough except for two items: a new base was desirable on Santa Maria or another acceptable island and the United States was awaiting permission to construct and operate an airfield on Santa Maria.

Norweb's instructions on Santa Maria had been confusing, to say the least, authorizing him first to ask Salazar about building an exclusively U.S. base but if he refused, the British government would then ask for authority to build the base. Under the latter plan the airfield would be built with U.S. material and assistance under British control—but Norweb had also been told to negotiate without the knowledge of the British embassy. Then the ambassador was also told that the airfield was to be built under the same conditions as Lagens if the United States could not get in under the "friends to friends" clause in the 1373 treaty. In that case, it would be constructed according to the Anglo-Portuguese agreement signed earlier in the year and remain under British control. Colonel Mason informed Norweb that the whole matter had been thrashed out at the Cairo Conference on 22–26 November and 2–7 December, and clarification would come from the Joint Chiefs and the CCS within a few days. Then the ambassador would have the "background on this subject and help clarify any further instructions."[40]

24 December: POE, Hampton Roads, Virginia

Headquarters and Service Company 928th EAR arrived at the Port of Embarkation, Camp Patrick Henry, Newport News, Virginia. Later, on 30 December, one officer and eight enlisted men, a Navy crew for landing craft, "were attached to the 928th . . . for rations, quarters, administration and for such other functions as may be necessitated by circumstances." So wherever they were going, the 928th landing was to be amphibious but without camouflage.[41]

Shortly after Christmas the 96th NCB received their long awaited orders. The outfit was restricted to the naval base and the ship that would transport them to "Island X" was already being loaded. After five months of training, of train rides to Mississippi and back, the battalion was finally leaving for Operation Alacrity.

Some high-level planning had taken place at the Joint Chiefs' level to coordinate the combined Army-Navy operation. However, following standard operating procedure, except perhaps for the field officers, nobody in either unit had any idea that another was also involved. The duties of each had been carefully laid out long before they left the country, but this would only be discovered in Terceira.

24 December: The Pentagon

A delegation of six senior army officers led by General Nowland met for a briefing with George Kennan before his interview with Salazar. They were to make sure that, first, he clearly understood the needs of the Joint Chiefs, and, second, to keep them closely informed of the situation vis-à-vis the Portuguese government. They reported back that Kennan thought the statement worked out by the Joint Chiefs and the CCS that the Americans were in the Azores only to help the British would be acceptable with Salazar. He also thought that there was no longer any need for U.S. soldiers to be in civilian clothes. Kennan did not think the arrival of the Army engineers would cause any trouble so long as Air Vice Marshal Bromet himself notified the Portuguese authorities in plenty of time.[42]

Highlighted in the margin: Kennan noted Salazar's remark when the subject of Americans in the Azores came up that "You can thank me and not the British that you are here." Kennan interpreted this to mean that if the British had their way, Americans would never be allowed in the islands and that permission was only granted thanks to the United States's direct request to the prime minister. Now the paranoia was rampant; the Joint Chiefs' suspicion of double dealing by their ally was finally proven.

Regarding a U.S. airport on Santa Maria: Salazar would make no decision until it became clear that the Allies were going to win the war. Kennan felt that the only sure way to get into the island was through the Pan Am application filed with the Portuguese Council the past February. He thought "we would do much better to go in there under this application than to let the British assume control, and run away with this second airport." Pan Am could "request" the U.S. military to build it for them and also make the surveys of Santa Maria which needed to be done. Everybody would be happy, except possibly the British. Salazar would have a perfect cover—he was only allowing a commercial airport to be built under civilian control—and the Joint Chiefs could breathe a sigh of relief that the United States would not lose control. Kennan thought that the British would "faint" at the idea of the Pan Am plan if it went through.

Someone in the State Department was really upset with the next section of the memorandum, underlining and double marking it in the margin. In answer to the question on what further action should the War Department take, Kennan answered, "Put squeeze on the State Department," and take any other measures that will serve to assure favorable action. Presumably this advice did not earn him any "brownie points." Judging from the initials on the document, among those who read it were H. Freeman Matthews and W. P. George, who certainly must have passed it on to the secretary of state.

25 December: Washington, D.C.

With the imminent movement of U.S. forces to the Azores—and destined to be housed in an RAF base—General Arnold cabled Air Chief Marshall Sir John Portal advising him that his men were coming. Arnold stated that an understanding had been reached between the ambassador and Prime Minister Salazar allowing U.S. troops to enter Terceira immediately, although the precise formula under which aircraft and construction personnel would operate under British guise had not yet been worked out. Hull assured Arnold that the State Department was relaying this information to the U.S. ambassador for early presentation to Salazar in lieu of the precise formula that was yet to be devised.[43]

Arnold advised Portal that construction personnel and material needed for constructing a hard-surface runway, hard standings, and other necessary work on Lagens Air Field would be transported by a Liberty ship and two LSTs as part of convoy UGS-29, expected to depart from the United States about 1 January. Arnold also requested that the British furnish escort and antisubmarine protection for the task force when it reached Portuguese waters.

Based on British experience, Portal warned the Americans that "some further confirmation from Salazar may be necessary in advance of proceeding in Terceira." The secretary of state dismissed the warning: "This is not the understanding of the Department or of the Legation in Lisbon. Salazar made it clearly understood that we might go ahead *under cover of assisting the British* [inserted into the original typed message] but requested we simply engage ourselves to let him know frankly under what formula we would operate."[44] Hull added in a copy to the U.S. Embassy in London that this information could be mentioned informally to Portal.

Air Chief Marshall Portal was unhappy with Arnold's message. His answer, especially its tone, was sure to raise Arnold's hackles:

> That the State Department considers negotiations with the Portuguese have reached a stage which will allow you to proceed as you propose is indeed interesting to me. Especially so since the Foreign Office did not gain so definite an impression from conversations between your legation and our Ambassador in Lisbon. Our impression, on the contrary, was that before committing himself definitely, Dr. Salazar was awaiting the production of the formula.
>
> I feel I must repeat our view that the arrival of such large numbers of American personnel before the Portuguese have agreed may seriously impair the extension and operation of the facilities we want so much, because any false step at this time can react only unfavorably to our joint interests in the Azores.
>
> No difficulties, it is true, have the Portuguese so far raised over the arrival at Terceira of small numbers of American personnel, but notice will certainly be taken of the arrival of the large numbers now involved. . . . I should myself have preferred to delay the dispatch of your ships until your Minister has confirmed the position with Dr. Salazar, unless, of course, such confirmation can be obtained before January 1. I understand that your Minister will be seeing Dr. Salazar any day now.
>
> Most strongly would I press this course for your adoption, but if, however, the U.S. Government is convinced that Dr. Salazar will raise no difficulties, I am as anxious as yourself to expedite matters further, and confirmation is herewith given that British forces will supply your ships in Portuguese Territorial waters with the necessary escort and anti-submarine protection.[45]

At this late stage with both the Seabees and Army engineers packed and ready to sail awaiting only the armed escorts, nothing that Portal could say or do could call off the operation. General Arnold, who had been chafing to go ahead with or without British or Portuguese approval, must have found Portal's message particularly annoying. If anything it probably strengthened his resolve to go ahead. Ready or not, U.S. forces were headed to the Azores.

26 December: Arctic Ocean

The pride of the German Fleet, the battleship *Scharnhorst*, was sunk off Norway's North Cape. It had been assigned to play a principal role in a top priority for the German Navy: to help the war on the Eastern Front by preventing supply convoys from reaching Russia. This left the Germans with only one operational battleship, the *Tirpitz*.

29 December: Lagens Air Field

The Air Transport Command began a regularly scheduled eastbound service of C-54 transport planes through Lagens. By March 1944, all westbound transport aircraft returning from England or North Africa were stopping at the field.[46]

31 December: The Seabees Sail

An advance party of the 96th NCB consisting of the officer-in-charge of construction, two other officers, and an enlisted man arrived at Lagens, among the first passengers to use the newly inaugurated service to the Azores. The party immediately set to work mapping the site of the new Navy base and planning how to unload and store the gear of the battalion when it landed on 9 January. The Seabees were departing Davisville, Rhode Island, the day the party landed and would arrive as an unhappy surprise for the Portuguese authorities, who had no inkling that 13 Navy officers and 462 enlisted men were headed their way.[47]

Not only Portuguese officials were to be surprised when the Seabees landed. Neither the U.S. nor British ambassadors in Lisbon had been informed; no documents can be found to suggest that either knew anything about the Navy's plans or if they did, they had no idea just how soon the Seabees were due.

29–31 December: Lisbon

The wheels were in motion for Americans to head out to the Allied air base on Terceira and join Operation Alacrity, but the Joint Chiefs also wanted the air base on Santa Maria resolved. The State Department needed constant prodding if results were to be obtained. In addition to sharing the RAF base on Terceira, which they assumed was approved; despite the fact that Salazar still did not have the formula, they wanted their own air base. Secretary Hull passed on their concerns to Norweb, that the Joint Chiefs wanted to start construction on an air base as soon as possible and that he should press this in an early interview with the prime minister.[48]

Norweb had his marching orders, but was also given a fallback position. He was first to ask permission to start construction on Santa Maria, but if Salazar refused, then the Joint Chiefs wanted him "to press nevertheless for permission to go ahead without delay with reconnaissance and surveys on Santa Maria or other suitable island with the view to eventually coming back to the principal question."

Before seeing Salazar on New Year's Eve, Norweb proposed a strategy he thought had the best chance of success with Santa Maria. He would request the prime minister's approval for a survey by U.S. engineers accompanied by a couple of British engineers and "we would welcome the guidance and participation of any Portuguese officers he may assign to accompany the group." The British ambassador would see Salazar next and make known his government's concurrence with the whole arrangement. Norweb would follow in a few days requesting another interview to ask that the new airfield be built by and remain under the control of the United States. By then he also hoped to present to Salazar the Joint Chiefs' approval for Portuguese participation in the operation to liberate Timor and the statement that the new airport on Santa Maria was essential to transport men and materiel to the East Indies. Hull ostensibly went along with the plan by silent approval since no reaction was recorded at the U.S. legation.

On New Year's Eve, Ambassador Norweb had a long interview with Prime Minister Salazar and presented the formula under which U.S. personnel proposed to operate from the Lagens Air Field. Salazar apparently accepted the formula, according to the U.S. interpretation, thereby giving the green light to the Task Force, authorizing it to start operations on Terceira. Norweb then raised the question of sending a survey party to Santa Maria. The British had estimated that Lagens could not handle more than twenty-five aircraft a day, far less than the number needed to support the invasion of Europe. The problem could only be resolved by having a second air base in the Azores which the prime minister seemed to accept but with conditions. First, he would prefer the base to be on Horta but Santa Maria was acceptable if it was a superior site, as he already knew from his own engineers' reports. Second, he did not want any U.S. or British military personnel carrying out the proposed survey. Norweb, having in mind Salazar's "allergy to theory and imperviousness to practice," suggested a compromise whereby his government recommended a U.S. company to do the job. The Portuguese government would then invite the company to do so. Salazar remarked that his impression was that U.S. armed forces exercised some sort of control over all U.S. companies capable of carrying out such a survey anyway. Norweb interpreted the remarks that "in view of the spirit in which Salazar accepted this compromise we may feel free to induct members of the armed forces into company personnel provided a civilian character is preserved." Extrapolating what Salazar meant from his obscure or enigmatic remarks had proven to be a chancy exercise in the past; this time proved no exception.[49]

The interview ended with Salazar's asking if Portuguese troops would be involved in liberating Timor from the Japanese. He had repeatedly raised this question and hoped to receive an answer by now, but Norweb could only promise hopefully to have a response before their next meeting. Obviously a positive response would make the Portuguese prime minister more sympathetic to the U.S. proposals, from Lagens to Santa Maria. Norweb thought the prime minister's comments were "well-wishing for us and entire interview was in spirit of personal and official cordiality."[50]

On 7 January Norweb notified the Portuguese minister for foreign affairs—who also happened to be Salazar—that the U.S. Government selected Pan American Airways to carry out the survey on Santa Maria. Pan Am agreed it would accept the proposal if it was chosen by the Portuguese government, which in fact it was. Progress it appeared was being made on the diplomatic front.[51]

The year of war 1943 was ending on a different note than it began. The Germans had been winning the tonnage war, sinking ships faster than the shipyards could replaced them; now it was U-boats and crews that were being lost faster than they could be replaced. Even training the crews had become difficult as U-boat bases in the Baltic Sea were pounded by Allied bombing and threatened by Russian advances.

Dönitz, changing his strategies as fast as the situation in the Atlantic changed, and assigning U-boats where they could do the most damage and suffer the smallest losses, realized time was fast running out. With the Allies' base in the Azores, aerial surveillance was now afforded round the clock, protecting convoys in almost the entire North and central Atlantic. The cargo ships' "black hole" had turned into a hornet's nest for U-boats. Dönitz felt that the only chance he had to turn the Battle of the Atlantic around was by improved technology for the U-boats. That would be his highest priority for the new year.

Churchill and his War Cabinet were pleased with the agreement allowing the RAF base on Terceira but they wished Salazar had not been hung up for so long preserving his neutrality. If the Azores Gap had been closed earlier, England would not have come so perilously close to losing the Battle of the Atlantic; thousands of lives and hundreds of thousands of tons of merchant shipping would have been saved.

By the end of 1943, land-based air coverage extended to a radius of nine hundred miles from Newfoundland, five hundred miles from Iceland, nine hundred miles from the British Isles, and five hundred miles in the central Atlantic from Terceira. With land-based aircraft all around and now in the Atlantic, plus aircraft flying off the CVEs, life had become intolerable for the U-boats. In all of 1942, when Churchill worried about losing the war and Dönitz was boasting to Hitler that the U-boats alone could win it for Germany, 5,580,000 tons of shipping had been lost in the North Atlantic. In the last quarter of 1943, with the impact of the Lagens Air Field felt, only 146,000 tons were lost. In addition to making things more difficult for U-boats on patrol, the Germans lost their favorite rendezvous spot just west of the Azores where they met their milchkuhen and stocked up with diesel fuel, supplies, and even received mail. The milchkuhen were prime targets for the air patrols. In the last quarter of 1943, fifty-three U-boats were sunk in the North Atlantic, and as submarine losses mounted the ratio of Allied merchant tonnage sunk to U-boat losses turned against Germany. Dönitz would have to move his boats away from the death traps within the perimeter of the Allied air bases and have them seek out new, smaller, and less trafficked air gaps. When the Lagens air strip was upgraded by U.S. engineers the following spring, and heavier VLR bombers were stationed at Lagens, its perimeter was extended out to seven hundred miles and crossing the Atlantic, except for foul winter weather and endemic seasickness, fulfilled the dream of all convoys—an uneventful experience.[52]

However, Dönitz still did not want to give up on U-boat patrols in the central Atlantic for a very good reason: Allied operations had reached a fever pitch in the Mediterranean. After the liberation of North Africa, Tunisia, and Sicily, the Allies were working their way up the Italian peninsula and had started operations in the Balkans and Greece. Convoys from the United States supplying the Mediterranean theater had to pass through the central Atlantic, so traffic had increased enormously but the ships had to be attacked before they passed through the Gibraltar gate. With the demise of the Italian navy, U-boats had been swept clean from the Mediterranean.

From late 1941 and throughout 1942 North Atlantic convoys had been routed as much as possible to obtain protection from Iceland and Greenland air bases. With bases in Bermuda and the Azores after October 1943, the South Atlantic convoy routes came into being. U-boat hunting aircraft based at Lagens had a great advantage over the North Atlantic bases—better weather allowed more flying time as well as making U-boats easier to spot.[53]

No U-boat kills were recorded from mid-October to 31 December, 1943. During that time 2,326 ships sailed in fifty-five convoys from North America to England with only the loss of 2 cargo ships in mid-October. The New Year was dawning brightly for the United Nations. The big question for the State Department and the Joint Chiefs was what kind of reception awaited the task forces heading out to the Azores.[54]

TEN

ALMOST WAR WITH PORTUGAL, JANUARY–MARCH 1944

> On the last day of 1943, with Dr. Salazar's permission [which he later denied having given], an American airfield survey party, disguised as employees of a private concern arrived at Terceira. . . . The first commander, Captain William G. Tomlinson, on being briefed in Washington before his departure, was asked by Vice Admiral Edwards, "Now do you understand the Azores situation? . . . If you do, you are the only one in the Navy who does!"
>
> SAMUEL ELIOT MORISON

Although Portugal insisted on remaining neutral and putting off the United States's request to build an air base, she had been turning a blind eye to clandestine German operations in the Azores. Years before the war started, Admiral Canaris organized the *Etappendienst* destined to serve as a secret Supply Service to supply the hundred-odd warships the German Navy planned to keep at sea during the conflict. Agents of the Etappendienst were placed in or recruited from German shipping lines, and so had an easily explainable cover for their operations. One of the principal stations of the network was established in Horta on Faial, where Etappendienst agents were ostensibly employed by a German shipping line whose cargo business had dried up during the war. The cover worked well enough for them to continue the ship chandler business unmolested while they supported U-boat operations. Just before the British were allowed into Terceira, the business came to an abrupt end as all German and Italian citizens were expelled from the archipelago.[1]

Other organizations were also using Horta. It served as a regularly scheduled refueling stop for Pan Am transatlantic clipper flights from New York to Lisbon and as an important relay point for the transatlantic cable. Prevailing winds in the Atlantic made the harbor an ideal place for sailing vessels to put in and pick up provisions or to seek refuge from bad weather. This custom began with the earliest transatlantic explorers and continues for today's amateur sailors.[2] Horta was understandably a port the CCS wanted for refueling and provisioning convoys and warships. They must have been pleasantly surprised when Prime Minister Salazar granted the request for all Allied ships to use Horta, even though at the same time he would not permit the Joint Chiefs to build an U.S. air base anywhere in the Azores.

In December the Joint Chiefs received reports from the "Pan American Airways" party that had been sent to evaluate the islands as potential sites for air bases. Flores, the largest of the western islands, is about 180 miles closer to North America than Terceira, so was the first to be checked out. Although the reports do not appear to be in the U.S. National Archives, they must have pointed out the lack of suitable places and year-round bad weather for an air base in any of the western islands. The British had known this for at least two years from Major Delgado's survey of the archipelago, which concluded Terceira was the best place to build a large airport, with Santa Maria a good second choice.[3]

Because permission to refuel convoys had already been granted, U.S. naval bases would not be necessary—only an administrative unit. Admiral King established U.S. Naval Forces Azores Command or ComNavZor to take care of that and oversee convoy activities in the archipelago.

Negotiations over the air base were another story. Thus far they had produced what the Joint Chiefs thought was a verbal agreement, but as it turned out, was only another misunderstanding between the U.S. ambassador and the Portuguese prime minister. Norweb thought Salazar gave permission for U.S. troops to land in Terceira but the Portuguese maintained only that a discussion had taken place, Salazar was inclined to give his approval, but written permission had to wait while he thought it over. In fact, after he heard the GIs were coming anyway, the prime minister—very much upset—threatened to meet them with force if they attempted to land. The first two weeks of the New Year held out the theoretical possibility that the United States might find itself embroiled in an embarrassing conflict with Portugal.

31 December: Port of Embarkation, Davisville, Rhode Island

On the last day of the year, with the Seabees of the 96th anxiously waiting to board the *Abraham Lincoln,* new orders came down from Navy headquarters that only half the battalion would be going. The Navy decided to split the organization, sending companies B and C to the Marshall Islands in the Pacific, leaving the battalion with only companies A and D and what was left of Headquarters Company for the Atlantic operation. Obviously the Navy felt the job in the Azores could be handled by only half a Seabee Battalion and/or Seabees were just as urgently needed in the South Pacific. An announcement of the departure from Davisville appeared in the "Trailblazer," the 7 January edition of the battalion newspaper:

> PART OF 96TH PULLS OUT FOR NEW ASSIGNMENT
> With the "battle of the Narraganset" nearing a close and the situation "well in hand" a part of the 96th Battalion "shoved off" for a new assignment last week and left enough of the men in New England to take care of "mopping up operations" and any emergency that might arise.
> Most of Companies A and D and a part of Headquarters have been given a new assignment and moved from Camp Thomas last week. Comdr. E. H. Honnen, 96th Battalion skipper, accompanied the group on their new assignment . . . address Navy Post Office 815, 96th Naval Construction Battalion. c/o Fleet Post Office, New York.

On 31 December at 9:30 A.M. the 552 Seabees boarded the *Abraham Lincoln,* and at 11:15 A.M. departed Davisville for the Azores accompanied by 2,477 tons of construction supplies and equipment. The *Abraham Lincoln,* under the command of Captain C. G. Dietz, had previously belonged to the United Fruit Company and had changed from a banana trade ship to a naval armed guard troop carrier of the War Shipping Administration. The gross weight of the *Abraham Lincoln* was 7,191 tons, its speed 11.5 knots, and its armament one 5-inch .38 [caliber],[4] three 3-inch .50 [caliber], and eight 20-mm guns. The merchant marine crew numbered twenty-six with an additional thirteen in the armed guard unit under the command of Lieutenant (J.G.) Ross G. Partlow.[5]

On 3 January the armament pieces were test fired and found to be in fine working order except for the biggest gun, the 5-inch .38, which had to be recocked after each round. The following day they picked up the destroyer escorts *Ellis* and *Biddle*. Lieutenant Partlow had noted in the ship's log that "we are travelling alone," but now shepherded by two destroyers, he and the Seabees must have felt more secure than when they left Rhode Island to face the U-boat infested ocean all alone.[6]

At noon on 8 January the escort commander ordered the ships to start zig-zagging as radar must have picked up signals from a nearby U-boat. However, no U-boat encounter took place, either because the escorts scared them off, or the inferior German radar never found the mini-armada. At 8 P.M., about the time that zig-zagging ceased, a light was sighted on one of the islands of the Azores. In their final briefing before leaving the United States, the Seabees must have been told to expect a warm, friendly reception. They would get one but from the people not the officials, and they never knew how close they had come to receiving a distinctly hostile greeting from the officials.

3 January: U.S. Embassy, Lisbon

Word received by the Joint Chiefs in Washington from Colonel Sandberg stated that all was going well, and that Salazar had approved the operation:

> Our minister had interview with Salazar evening of 31st. Entire discussion on cordial and cooperative basis. Salazar informed that Navy VLR squadron would operate from Lagens under British control and under formula that squadron was on loan to British.
>
> Also informed early arrival Terceira American technical and construction personnel and in general terms of army program regarding ferrying aircraft.
>
> Salazar satisfied with all above. Definite interest shown in construction second air base. Salazar concedes Santa Maria best site but is more interested in air base on Fayal [Faial] for special reasons probably post war.
>
> Question of British or American control this second air base or of formula under which it might be constructed not raised

this interview. Salazar willing to permit survey party to visit islands but does not wish military personnel to comprise party. Suggested that US select reliable commercial company whereupon Portugal would invite that company to make survey. . . . He indicated indirectly that some members of party might be expected to be military or naval personnel under guise employees private concern inferring that he was merely seeking formula or cloak covering entry of party. . . . Suggest Pan American as most logical company because of their knowledge of Azores, previous preparations for similar survey, excellent standing in Portugal and fact that this survey if conducted by Panair would arouse least comment. . . . Question Portuguese participation in freeing Timor still of interest to Salazar. Both he and minister hope for early reply.[7]

Thus, according to Colonel Sandberg and the U.S. minister, a warm welcome was expected in the Azores. There was no apparent reason why the Seabees and the Army engineers could not start work immediately after landing. The Joint Chiefs were elated; Alacrity would soon become a U.N. effort and not solely British. However, given Salazar's penchant for vacillation, indecision, and frequent changes of heart, some surprises might lay ahead, but it was too late to call off the operation.

3 January: Hampton Roads, Virginia

The Navy Seabees were well under way to the Azores and the Army task force was only waiting sailing orders at Hampton Roads, Virginia, POE to link up with a convoy. Now UGS-29 had formed which they joined in three ships, the Liberty ship *John Clarke* and LSTs 44 and 228. The UGS nomenclature signified a slow convoy headed to the Mediterranean, one of the 189 UGS convoys that sailed starting in November 1942, averaging 58 ships with 9.3 escorts per convoy. Of the total of 11,119 ships convoyed, only nine were lost while in convoy formation, five stragglers lagging behind were sunk, and two damaged, so the chances of making it unscathed to the Azores were very good—98.87 percent in fact—as long as the ships kept up with the convoy. The voyage promised to be long, slow, and hopefully uneventful.[8]

Once a convoy left the POE, the individual ships made up a formation covering an enormous expanse of ocean. UGS-18, similar to UGS-
29 and which sailed shortly before, also averaged about 9 knots with its
ships arranged in twelve columns, keeping about a half mile between
columns. Approximately eight ships made up a column, each about a
mile apart. The commander sailed in the vessel leading the center column; tankers and ammunition ships took their position in the inner-
most columns. Thus the convoy was spread across forty-eight square
miles of ocean, which meant that any one ship would rarely catch sight
of the escort screen, except on those rare occasions when a destroyer
escort suddenly darted in between the columns. Suspicious signals
picked up on the destroyer radar had to be checked out because U-boats
had been known to suddenly pop up in the middle of a convoy, blaze
away at the cargo ships with its deck guns, then dive and disappear. If a
ship suffered a breakdown, a destroyer escort would be detached to
guard the unlucky individual until repairs could be made. But if the
repairs were not made quickly enough, it was abandoned and the escort
returned to the convoy. Survival of the majority was the paramount
rule of convoys, which meant that stragglers were left to their fate.[9]

UGS-18 would take advantage of the new Allied air base on Terceira.
The route to Gibraltar passed north of Bermuda, site of another Allied
base, and south of the Azores. The briefing officer before departure
warned the ships' captains not to feel too secure, recalling that UGS-6
was attacked off the Azores the past spring by a wolf pack of fifteen U-
boats and suffered four losses. But this happened before Lagens Field was
operational so hopefully it would not be repeated for this convoy.

The 928th was broken into three units for the trip, the two larger
ones boarding the Liberty ship and an LST, which judging by its ameni-
ties, the GIs swore was a converted garbage barge. The third unit, an
advanced party from the regimental surveying section consisting of one
officer and six enlisted men was to be flown out by MATS and due to
arrive on 12 January. The second LST carried Air Force and Transportation Corps personnel.[10]

The *John Clarke*, with a gross weight of 7,180 tons and a speed of 11
knots, was just an average ship in convoy UGS-29 commanded by
Commander R. S. Parr, made up of fifty-nine ships with twelve escort
vessels plus a CVE, the USS *Guadalcanal*. The convoy averaged 9.46
knots from Norfolk to Gibraltar, where it was turned over to a British
commander for its entry into the Mediterranean.[11]

The convoy was well out at sea when Colonel Kemp finally told the men of the 928th where they were going and why they needed so much specialized training. They were chosen for a secret operation; they would not be going with the rest of the convoy to the Mediterranean but would be landing instead in the Azores, a group of islands belonging to Portugal. After the convoy got closer to the islands they would know what kind of reception was waiting, but it was expected to be friendly. By the time the convoy left the POE, their British hosts in the Azores had approved the operation, but permission from the Portuguese, the real owners of the islands, was still unresolved. Kemp could not know that serious efforts to confirm Salazar's approval were still going on after the convoy was well on its way to the Azores. In case Salazar changed his mind again, the Joint Chiefs were prepared. If he had any thoughts of withdrawing permission to land, the Chiefs would make up his mind for him; the Seabees and Engineers were armed and backed up by two destroyers; they would land no matter what. The prime minister had just better bite the bullet and accept the fact that the Americans were coming.

5 January: Lisbon

The War Department finally got around to advising the State Department that a task force would be headed out to the Azores shortly. The notice ignored the important facts that the 928th Engineers had sailed two days earlier, and an even more serious omission was complete silence about the Seabees. The 96th NCB had been on the high seas for five days and due to land unexpected and unannounced on Terceira in only four more. The notice was received by Norweb, who of course had no idea that it was untrue but did his duty and quickly passed it on to Salazar: "I think you will be interested to know that I have today been advised by telegram that two 'Liberty Ships' and two landing barges are on the point of leaving the United States for Terceira carrying U.S. personnel and American equipment which are needed there by the British Government."[12]

That Norweb's memo was false and misleading was proven shortly when the 96th unexpectedly arrived. Salazar was outraged, accusing the U.S. minister of lying to him, and threatened to resist the landings with force.[13]

6 January: Terceira

Ninety-sixth NCB Commander Honnen and Capt. William G. Tomlinson, with the title "Commander, U.S. Forces, Azores," were flown to Lagens to await the arrival of the Seabees. Two days later their first charges arrived, a survey party headed by Captain Francis W. Hughes, flown in to select a site for the Navy installations, quickly followed the next day by the Task Force steaming unannounced into Angra harbor.

The engineers and Air Corps MATS personnel, more than twice the number of the Seabees, were expected to arrive in about two week's time. Commanding the U.S. Army forces was Colonel David A. Morris, who only received his orders on 28 December designating him "Acting Commander of all the U. S. Army Forces . . . at Lagens Airport, Terceira Island, Azores." Colonel Morris was an officer in MATS and his orders came from MATS commander Major General George, which made it clear that the primary purpose of the Army Air Force units was to build a base for transport and aircraft ferrying operations. U. S. antisubmarine patrol operations and harbor improvement would be left to the Seabees and a U.S. naval air squadron.[14]

7 January: Norweb to Secretary of State

Signs started to appear that trouble loomed ahead for the U.S. operation. British Ambassador Sir Ronald Campbell met with Salazar the day before and thought the meeting was going well until he mentioned his government was pleased to see permission finally granted for U.S. use of British facilities in the Azores. Salazar then raised an objection to one point, the inclusion of a U.S. naval squadron for antisubmarine patrol. He said that using the facilities for air transportation was legitimate but he could find no way to justify aggressive operations by U.S. naval forces. The German ambassador and the Spanish minister for foreign affairs had already put him on the spot regarding the RAF base on Terceira, which was openly engaged in antisubmarine operations. They demanded to know if Portugal should no longer be considered neutral. Salazar justified his collaboration with the British as a commitment of the 1373 treaty, but no such treaty existed with the United States. He was afraid that Germany might use the presence of U.S. troops as a pretext to invade his country as the Japanese had done in their invasion of

Portuguese Timor. Australian forces had landed on the island in an ill-fated attempt to defend it but were driven out by the Japanese who stayed "to protect the island against further Allied aggression."[15]

Campbell related all this to Norweb, who was very disturbed by Salazar's latest change of mind. When he informed the prime minister on New Year's Eve that a naval air squadron was arriving and would be based at Lagens Field. Salazar did not object at that time, in fact, he only asked how many planes comprised a squadron. Kennan discussed the same subject with him on 2 December and had the same impression that Salazar approved the squadron. When Kennan explained that the Americans could ostensibly serve under the titular command of the RAF, Salazar "showed no surprise and expressed no objection but pointed out that . . . a formula be found to reconcile . . . with the British Agreement." When Ambassador Campbell spoke to Salazar he also had the impression, which he had predicted beforehand, that the Allies could do anything they liked within the scope of the Anglo-Portuguese agreement but nothing outside of it. Salazar felt that the problem of affording facilities to the British was different than to the Americans.[16]

Norweb immediately alerted Colonel Solberg and Commander Kenneth Demarest, the naval attaché, of Salazar's unexpected decision. In his cable to Washington, Norweb added that he asked Salazar for an interview at his earliest convenience and "[U]ntil then I wish to reserve my comments on this curious and untoward happening." The ambassadors knew that dealing with Salazar called for infinite patience and to expect the unexpected. His latest change of heart was neither the first nor the last time he would foul up Allied planning and justify the Joint Chiefs' decision to do whatever had to be done to win the war, and let the diplomats explain it all ex post facto to the prime minister.[17]

8 January: Führer Headquarters, Wolfsschanze[18]

The OKM met with Hitler to report on the situation with respect to the Navy. Despite the many promises from Air Marshall Goering to assign Luftwaffe units to the Navy, no VLR reconnaissance aircraft had flown in support of U-boat operations. The U-boat commanders were severely frustrated hunting convoys with their now technologically improved boats, but still only finding targets of opportunity by chance, with no decent intelligence about convoy traffic from Admiral Canaris's Abwehr. The Kriegsmarine air reconnaissance wing suffered from a lack of planes and insufficient training of the crews in navigation and communications as well as low morale. Their unromantic missions were never rewarded by decorations, which Luftwaffe pilots garnered by the gross, although Hitler promised to remedy the situation with a liberal awarding of Iron Crosses to the naval pilots.

Without decent reconnaissance and with inferior radar, plus the risk of surprise attack from Allied aircraft flying off land bases in the Atlantic or from the CVEs, the U-boats kept surface cruising to an absolute minimum. Underwater operations however were inefficient with reduced visibility, extremely slow speeds, and a high cost in diesel fuel. Initially, the submarines felt they were safer submerged, but unknown to Admiral Dönitz, the Allies had developed short wave-length radar that detected the U-boats long before they realized they were spotted. Without any warning, an Allied destroyer would cross their bow or a bomber would drop depth charges. The war in the Atlantic was becoming more difficult for the submarines.

Hitler promised to talk to Goering about devoting the entire expanded output of the new VLR Ju-290 to the U-boat fleet and not the Luftwaffe. Considering the previous failed promises to commit other VLR bombers, such as the the Me-264 with a projected range of nine thousand miles or the He-177 with thirty-four hundred miles, to the Navy, Admiral Dönitz must have accepted the promise for the Ju-290 with some skepticism. Skepticism was warranted, for the new VLR aircraft never did show up for service with the U-boat fleet.

Admiral Dönitz, still with high hopes of getting U-boat and aircraft bases in the Azores, raised the question of relations with Portugal, ignoring the fact that an Allied base was under construction on Terceira. He thought Salazar could be won over by a promise to recover the island of Timor for Portugal, as the Allies had already promised. Dönitz was not too concerned about alienating Japan, which such an action would surely do; the Pacific theater was too far away for him to worry about. Hitler, recognizing that Japan was just about Germany's last reliable ally "showed little interest in having Germany step in to settle the Timor dispute even though he admitted that it would be in our interest to strengthen the position of Salazar, and that German intervention would accomplish this." Both the Allies and the Axis knew that Timor could be a crucial pawn in the race to get into the Azores but unfortunately for the admiral, the race was already won, the Allies had played that gambit.

This was the only mention of the Azores at the meeting. Nothing was said about the Allied air base on Terceira or the coming of the Americans, no discussion took place on what, if any, countermeasures could be taken. Two years earlier, the mere threat of an Allied occupation of the islands could trigger Operation Felix and the invasion of Portugal. Now, with the loss of the Sixth Army and all of its generals at Stalingrad, with the defeat and surrender of the crack Afrika Korps, and with Allied armies about to pour into Italy, the Führer had more to worry about than bombing Boston and the tonnage war in the Atlantic.

9 January, 6:43 A.M.: Lisbon

The Seabee task force was due in Angra in only a few hours, to be followed in two weeks by the Army Air Force units. The crisis had to be resolved quickly or else the consequences could be disastrous. Not only was Salazar upset by the U.S. "invasion force" landing in the Azores before he had given formal written permission, but he was also miffed by what he felt was the U.S. ambassador's deceit. The prime minister realized that the Seabees had left the Port of Embarkation before his New Year's Eve interview with Norweb had even begun. Adding insult to injury, Norweb's 5 January memorandum—that a task force was about to leave the United States—was a lie; the Navy engineers were more than halfway to the Azores by then. To give the ambassador credit, almost certainly he had no idea that the Seabees were even involved in the operation let alone having any information on their sailing date. Washington had misinformed him about the Army engineers, so in good faith and blissful ignorance of the situation he did not know that he was asking Salazar to approve a fait accompli. An incensed Salazar asked why the Americans should want his approval for landing on Portuguese soil if they were coming no matter how he answered. In a terrifying act of bravado he alerted the head of the Portuguese Forces in the Azores to get ready to resist the U.S. invasion "by force if necessary."

Anthony Eden told the British ambassador in Lisbon to see Salazar and get things straightened out quickly before any shooting started. Campbell had his work cut out; special pleading by the British to their ancient ally was needed to head off a potential disaster. At 6:43 A.M. Campbell sent a "Most Immediate" message to Anthony Eden with a copy to the Senior British Officer, Azores:

Doctor Leitão (of the Foreign Office) came round at 2 A.M. and gave me the message as described. He said that Dr. Salazar was at a complete loss as the American Minister had spoken only of technicians. Moreover, he had not yet given permission although he was on the point of doing so. He gave it now for technicians but if the troops attempted to land they would be prevented by force. Dr. Salazar moreover had been amazed to realize that the ships must have left the dock before the United States minister had spoken to him.

2. I said that I was equally at a loss as the United States Minister had understood that permission had been given for technicians and construction personnel and on the strength of what he had told me I had so informed my government. I could not say exactly what the force was composed of, but I could guarantee that it was not a combatant formation. I would send a telegram immediately to the Senior British officer in the terms of my telegram under reference and hoped that Dr. Salazar also would take appropriate steps to prevent any risk of hot-headed action such as would land us in an extremely grave situation.

3. I then went to see the United States Minister who told me that he had subsequently put into writing what he had said to Dr. Salazar and was completely mystified.

4. I can only suppose that Dr. Salazar whilst raising no objection at the United Sates Minister's interview was under the impression that he had understood that the permission would not be valid until it had been confirmed in writing. The misunderstanding as to the character of the force arose presumably from B.O.'s[19] use of the term "transports with troops" which I explained to Dr. Leitão might well have been used by an officer accustomed to dealing in such terms without realizing their significance in the present case.[20]

Norweb, alerted by Ambassador Campbell at 5 A.M., cabled the secretary of state at 7:36 warning of the impending disaster. The situation had been fouled up even more than necessary because Campbell himself did not know that Navy Seabees and Army Engineers were not only "troops" but also "technicians"—unlike the pure "technicians" found in most European armies. The Seabee motto—"*Construimus, Batuimus*" ("We Build, We Fight")—explains it all. Campbell only muddied the waters when Salazar asked him about "troops" coming to the Azores because he had given permission only for technicians and construction personnel. Campbell's answer professed ignorance of the nature of the U.S. force, which agitated the prime minister even more.[21]

Norweb was completely confused by Salazar's statements. He told Campbell that in his meeting on 31 December he had explained the nature and the purpose of the U.S. personnel and the equipment they were bringing in, all of which seemed to leave the prime minister satisfied. Then on 5 January he confirmed in writing the fact that two Liberty ships[22] and two landing barges loaded with personnel and equipment were leaving the POE for Terceira. Of course by 5 January both the Army and Seabee Task Forces were already well out at sea but that was only the date that Norweb was given. The Navy was reluctant to let the Portuguese or any third party know the exact dates of the convoy's departure from the United States and arrival in the Azores because of the good possibility that the information would be leaked to German intelligence.

Norweb asked Campbell to telegraph the SBO Azores requesting him to help arrange the landing of the Americans and their equipment. Campbell agreed and appealed to Leitão to get Salazar to take whatever steps were necessary to avoid "an extremely grave situation."

A second telegram was sent to SBO Azores at 7:20 A.M. with a copy to the Foreign Office in London:

> Dr. Salazar has just sent to tell me that he has learnt that you have informed local authorities that two American transports with troops will arrive in the course of tonight. He has given permission for technicians only and had therefore sent orders that if troops repeat troops attempt to disembark they are to be prevented by force.
>
> 2. With the approval of my American colleague I have sent message back to say that force is composed of technicians and construction personnel with equipment to match and not of troops in the sense of combatant formations. I begged him to send further instructions to local authorities in that sense and ordering them not to do anything rash.
>
> 3. Please explain to Perry and American commanders and endeavor to ensure that no untoward incident occurs.[23]

Thus, a potentially fatal misunderstanding between the Americans and the Portuguese centered on the nature of the units sent to construct the air base. Salazar's approval of "technicians" and not "troops" was based on a distinction made in the Portuguese army as well as in most of the armies of Europe which had no tradition of combat engineers. However U.S. Army Engineers and Navy Seabees were certainly "technicians" but they were also trained to fight if they found themselves in a situation where fighting was necessary to get the job done. If the United States was sending "troops" in the sense of infantry, they had no business entering Portuguese territory, but that was clearly not the case. If the origin of the Seabees as civilian construction workers had been explained to Salazar, they might have been acceptable, even though they were armed and had established a reputation in the South Pacific as a respectable fighting force.

An emergency diplomatic repair job was in order. A little war must not be allowed to erupt between Portugal, a small (proud/pig-headed) country, and the United States, a (rowdy bully/defender of free nations) (take your pick) each determined to have its own way. Compounding the problem was the fact that England, a long-term ally of both countries, had given its approval for the Americans to come to Terceira without clearing it with Portugal.

8–9 January: Terceira

Commander Bromet received the cables from the British embassy and immediately prepared to negotiate with Salazar's new envoy, General Passos e Sousa. The general had come to Terceira with specific orders to enforce the Anglo-Portuguese agreement to the letter.[24]

Bromet already had practice negotiating sticky situations with Portuguese officials thanks to his heavy-handed U.S. allies. The waters had been muddied a month earlier when the three U.S. officers came to sign the agreement on participation at the RAF air base. Not one word was exchanged with the Portuguese authorities, except perhaps for some unrecorded remarks when they were told they were persona non grata and subject to arrest if they stayed too long.

Bromet did a good job smoothing out the ruffled feathers of the Portuguese commander, Brigadier Tamagnini Barbosa, over the earlier incident. That was only a minor warm-up and not too difficult considering the Brigadier was very much pro-Allies. This time the problem was going to be much more difficult. He had to explain to a different Portuguese officer, who unfortunately was not pro-Allies, why a large U.S. force that arrived unexpectedly should be allowed to come ashore. Salazar had not approved the operation; his orders were to resist the landing with force.

In December Barbosa could warn the U.S. officers to leave and leave they did but only after signing the agreement with the British. This time there was no way short of force to keep the Americans from taking up their unwelcome residence on the island. Declaring the U.S. task force collectively and individually persona non grata would not work. A warning to turn around and not come back would have to be more than just a paper threat. To achieve the effect demanded by Salazar, an ultimatum to go away had to be backed up with the threat of force, but considering the diminutive size and poorly armed Portuguese garrison, serious resistance was impossible.

The new Portuguese commander in Terceira was a general and touchy about the Allies taking liberties with Portuguese sovereignty. As a special representative of Dr. Salazar he was the only person on the island, if not the entire archipelago, who had a copy of the Anglo-Portuguese agreement establishing the air base. He was sent to replace Brigadier Barbosa, who was judged too accommodating in dealing the Allies; someone was needed with the backbone to resist intimidation, to stand up to the United States, and to make sure the agreement was followed to the letter.

As soon as General Passos e Sousa received the request from Bromet to allow an U.S. party to land on Terceira for the purpose of working on the Lagens Airport, he contacted the General Officer Commanding, Azores (GCO), on Ponta Delgada. GCO responded that there was no objection to "working party landing but that landing of American Troops was not provided for under agreement and must be prevented." The GCO requested instructions from the Ministry of War in Lisbon and was answered by Salazar himself saying that he "authorized the landing of 522 Americans for the purpose stated."[25]

Not leaving well enough alone, Passos e Sousa sent a follow-up telegram to GCO that he had just learned "that working party was to construct huts, installations, etc., for American air crews and air force personnel." GCO requested urgent instructions from Dr. Salazar but in the meantime "informed Officer Commanding Terceira that such

American forces, as opposed to working parties, could not be allowed to land on the island and if they did so should be treated as enemies."26

General Passos e Souza received this disquieting order and, very upset, he telephoned Bromet that no men or materials would be allowed to land and if they attempted to do so they would be fired upon. Nowhere in the agreement was there any mention of U.S. troops being allowed to land in the Azores so they better just stay in their ships, turn around, and go home. Passos e Sousa was in a state verging somewhere between panic and hysteria when he telephoned Bromet threatening that his troops were prepared to resist the Yankee invasion. Bromet clearly had his work cut out for him. Too hell with "succor," there was no way the RAF was going to uphold the treaty of 1373 and help their ancient Portuguese allies defend the Azores against a U.S. invasion. This called for high-level direct face-to-face negotiations before Passos e Sousa started another war all on his own.

Bromet invited the general to come over to his place for a heart-to-heart talk. Passos e Sousa's intelligence officer warned of an Allied plot to kidnap him, so he first refused to accept the invitation. Eventually he relented, and arrived at Bromet's headquarters still in a highly nervous state accompanied by an armed motorcycle escort. The night has been described as foggy making it a perfect theatrical setting to the high-level crisis meeting of the island's top military commanders.

Commander Bromet had to improvise which he did brilliantly. No guidelines were ever issued by RAF headquarters on how to deal with this or any other diplomatic crisis that might arise. In fact in one of the more classic boners of the war, Bromet had been ordered to pack up and was sent off to the Azores with his task force and no one with any authority had remembered to give him a copy of the Anglo-Portuguese agreement. He never had a detailed briefing and had no inkling that such an agreement even existed. He must have assumed from what he heard over the BBC broadcast that Churchill invoked the Windsor Treaty of 1373 and that he and his task force were headed out to the Azores in accordance with the terms of that ancient treaty, to provide "succor" for Portugal against a perceived German threat. He certainly could not have known about the existence of the 1373 treaty before hearing Churchill's speech, nor did he have a copy. To justify the Azores operation Churchill quoted chapter and verse in the Windsor Treaty, but that was signed a good four centuries before the United States existed so had no proviso about Americans being invited to give "succor." Included in the briefings that Bromet never received was the fact that the United States was involved in Operation Alacrity and that Salazar, always a stickler for the literal interpretation had refused to allow any U.S. troops on Portuguese territory.

Bromet must have looked Sousa in the eye and then proceed to fabricate a perfectly reasonable story to calm the excited general down. First of all, he informed Sousa, he had been appointed Commander of the Combined British Forces in the Azores, which was true. He also had the full authority of the British Chiefs of Staff for the landing of the Americans, which could have been true if any one of the Chiefs had remembered to grant it. The Americans were to serve in concert with the RAF so Bromet himself would act for them with the Portuguese authorities and Sousa could, for all intents and purposes, make believe they weren't there but just another arm of the RAF. Either the story worked, or General Passos e Sousa chose the safer course of discretion over valor. Portuguese forces did not resist the landing and the U.S. contribution to Operation Alacrity/Lifeline could proceed. Once again the classic British—now also Allied—tradition of "muddling through" triumphed. For his sterling performance in damage control, preventing an embarrassing incident, and running the Lagens operation, President Harry Truman later awarded Commander Bromet the Legion of Merit, Degree of Commander.

Bromet also convinced Sousa that the 96th Seabees and the 928th EAR were not "troops" as Salazar feared, but "technicians." Because Sousa had no experience with these peculiarly U.S. organizations, Bromet could use any rationale he thought of and the general would not contradict him. The British army is one of the few military organizations that also have fighting engineers, the Royal Sappers, soldier technicians who carry carbines for defense but also theodolites for surveying. In fact, a unit of Royal Sappers had been detached to serve in Terceira and was responsible for laying the pierced-plank landing strip used by the RAF. General Sousa was convinced he had better ignore the orders from Lisbon, keep his troops in the barracks and, if necessary, explain it all to the prime minister after the fact. The general gave his approval—the destroyer escorts had enough fire power to outshoot anything he had and it was clear that the Seabees were going to land with or without his permission.

After nine days at sea, at 9 A.M. the USS *Abraham Lincoln* and its escorts pulled into Angra Bay. The Seabees had no idea that their arrival was unexpected, had precipitated a major diplomatic crisis, and the deceptively peaceful reception was thanks to the outstanding efforts of Commander Bromet. The Cruise Book of the 96th contains not the slightest hint that the Seabees were aware of the crisis precipitated by their arrival, but only mentions their pleasant surprise at how beautiful the island looked after nine days at sea:[27]

> The *Abraham Lincoln* dropped anchor in the picturesque harbor of Angra do Heroïsmo, largest town on the island of Terceira, in the Azores group. The closely clustered stone and stucco buildings with their red tile roofs, the two-century-old forts which flanked the town and harbor entrance, and the background of smooth, green mountainsides criss-crossed by low stone fences, presented a beautiful picture to the land-hungry Seabees who crowded the ship's rail.
>
> The Seabees were coming to improve the port facilities at Praia da Vitória, the nearest town to the air base, to build bulk fuel installations and lay a submarine pipe line, to construct a camp for themselves and for the Navy airmen and to prepare airfield facilities for the bomber squadron. The site selected was called Santa Rita, after a small village on the east side of the airfield and closer to the port of Praia than Lagens.[28]

The enlisted men and officers were unloaded by two U.S. LCMs that had been carried over on the deck of the *Abraham Lincoln*, and two British LCMs that were waiting for them in the harbor. Following orders from Lisbon the official reception by the Portuguese authorities was cool, but the local populace was under no such constraint. The Seabees greeting was distinctly friendly:

> It was a Sunday morning, a fine warm day, and the whole town had turned out to witness the landing. From early morning they had lined the streets and roads overlooking the harbor and now, viewing the smart appearing Americans at closer range, they smiled, waved, and shouted greetings and words of welcome. Many of the natives had lived in the United States and had relatives still there . . . One woman sitting in a window, kept repeating in halting, labored English, "Allo! Allo! I'm glad—the Americans—are here. I like Americans."[29]

Offloading the ship required nine days. Cargo and personnel were brought ashore by the LCMs and local Portuguese lighters. On several occasions, the weather was rough enough to require the *Abraham Lincoln* to leave the unprotected harbor and cruise out to sea but by 18 January the unloading was complete.

The landing was peaceful but what if Salazar had insisted on holding out against the Seabees? The scenario conjured up in that case would have the destroyers in Angra harbor blasting away at the town, and the RAF flying in support of their Allies bombing Portuguese forts and garrisons on the island. If the Portuguese military had been ordered to resist the invasion, common sense and the intimidating U.S. destroyers loaded as they were with more firepower than everything the Portuguese had on the island might have convinced them to do otherwise.

If there had been a shooting reception in Angra harbor, generations of historians would have had a field day with Operation Alacrity. Instead of being buried in secret archives of the British and U.S. governments, the operation would have earned a stellar role in the history of World War II, and reams of books would have argued its pros and cons. It's just as well this scenario never was played out.

Norweb must have breathed a big sigh of relief as he cabled the secretary of state at 1 P.M.: "Understand landing completed without incident this morning."[30]

9 January: Washington, D.C.

Cordell Hull cabled Norweb with pointers to bring to Salazar's attention just to make sure the landing crisis of the Seabees would not be repeated with the 928th Engineers, expected in about two weeks. Norweb was told to point out that the Seabee's departure on 31 December was approximately simultaneous with Salazar's granting permission to come. Also to make sure Salazar knew that the Engineers were not "troops" in the sense envisaged by the prime minister and to have him advise his officials in the Azores that the landing was approved.

Something went wrong when Norweb met with Salazar. The prime minister had gotten his hackles up. He complained that the large force now on its way to the Azores was larger than he thought necessary to build an air base. Always worried that the United States might want to stay in the islands after the war, he needed time to think it over before granting permission for the new task force to land. Hull was accepting none of that, cabling Norweb on 12 January that a delay was out of the question, the first ship was due near the end of the week. "This expedition has no combat character and is composed solely of technical personnel and equipment. This appears to come within the formula agreed to . . . December 31. If . . . there is still opposition to this expedition, please inform the Department immediately."[31]

12 January: London

Churchill received word from Eden that the Portuguese were threatening to resist the Engineers' landing with force.[32] He was predictably furious and told Eden that the Americans were to be supported "vigorously." His words were direct and to the point, his patience had long since gone: "There is no need for us to be apologetic in dealing with any of these neutrals who hope to get out of Armageddon with no trouble and a good profit." At any event there was nothing the Allies could do now to assuage Portuguese feelings. The Seabees had already arrived and were busy unloading their gear and the Army, due to land in only five more days, was coming ashore with or without Salazar's approval.

12 January: Terceira

Commander Honnen assigned about three hundred officers and men to duties including stevedoring and other jobs connected with the port and setting up a supply dump, with the remaining one-hundred-sixty sent ahead to Lagens Field "to begin the building of a permanent camp for occupancy by a Liberator squadron. This was the original assignment for which the battalion was sent overseas."[33]

The Seabees were thankful for their peaceful entry into Terceira and the warm greetings they received. Something else they did not realize was that the lovely clear day of landing was an anomaly. The sun and warmth disappeared the following day, replaced by heavy rain, high winds, and chilly nights that stayed to plague them and the Engineers for the next few months. A sixty-mile-per-hour gale blew away their pup tents and brought the galley tent at Lagens crashing down on the heads of the cooks. Because of the fierce stormy weather, it took nine days to unload the ship. The mud was knee-deep but nobody complained, considering the other half of the battalion was probably in the South Seas fighting the Japanese and catching weird tropical diseases.

12 January: Lisbon

One hour before Norweb was scheduled to meet with Salazar, he cabled Cordell Hull with more disquieting news and rumors. The naval attaché reported that a British plane had been fired upon by Portuguese anti-aircraft at Ponta Delgada. The source of the rumor, Commander Henriques of the Maritime Police, added that something must have happened which irritated or frightened Salazar, who met with the chiefs of the police forces and the Republican guard, apparently urging the officials to avoid showing too many signs of friendliness to the Allies. Henriques had been told he was too friendly and should correct his attitude. Brigadier Barbosa was ordered back to Lisbon, "that his health required his return but this is not believed to be the main reason. The British naval and military attaché agree on this."[34]

After encoding and sending the above cable to Washington, the British embassy sent Norweb a copy of a telegram from the British consul general at Ponta Delgada. In a conversation with the Portuguese military commander he learned that Salazar sent a message that he had not agreed "to the establishment of United States aircraft or forces in Terceira, as opposed to construction units even if under British Command." It appeared that Salazar thought the Seabees in Terceira were enough Americans and he would not permit any more. "Salazar's instructions . . . would not permit the landing of American ground personnel, etc., and may well cause a serious incident if the situation is not clarified before the arrival. I am seeing Salazar at five o'clock this afternoon."[35]

The forebodings were of disaster; Norweb once again had his work cut out, or else the 928th landing might turn out to be more along the lines of Anzio than Iceland.

12–13 January: Lisbon

Norweb could finally breathe more easily.[36] He had seen Salazar the evening before and found him in a more conciliatory mood than he had been at any time in the past week. Two possible explanations for his change of heart: Campbell's meeting might have softened him up or intimidated him, either one having the same effect; or with bravado gone and common sense restored he resigned himself to the inevitable: the Americans were going to land whether or not he permitted it. The prime minister sent instructions to General Passos e Sousa that the new U.S. task force had official permission to come ashore.

Norweb also tried to convince Salazar to permit the U.S. Navy bomber squadron to operate out of Lagens under RAF control and reminded him that he had approved such an arrangement only two weeks earlier. The prime minister was now adamantly opposed to any kind of combatant role for the United States in the Azores and no argument could change his mind. He did imply that he would get in touch with Mr. Richard C. Long, regional director of Pan American Airways, to see if his company could carry out a survey for the projected new airfield on Santa Maria. Considering the crises of the past two weeks, re-solving two out of three problems with Salazar must have been a morale-booster for the harried U.S. minister.

When the Joint Chiefs learned of Salazar's refusal for the Navy squadron, they chose not to accept it but opted to confront the prime minister on the issue. The decision was made to inform Salazar "that since his objections to the operation of an American navy squadron were made at such a late date, it was not practicable . . . to countermand the arrangements made by the Combined Chiefs of Staff but that to meet his objections, this American squadron had been incorporated into the RAF, the incorporation being a fiction, not a fact."[37]

This was how the Joint Chiefs wanted it. The United States had lost its patience and if overt action was required, so be it. The prime minister had to realize that these were proposals he could not afford to turn down. In any case, the British could always explain away any problems that might develop. In the end cooler heads prevailed, the Joint Chiefs were talked out of taking precipitate action, and the squadron of twelve Navy PB4Y Privateers, which had been alerted for assignment to Lagens, would have to cool its heels for a few more months awaiting a change of heart by the Portuguese prime minister.[38]

12 January: Terceira

After having been kept on board since their arrival in Terceira, shore liberty finally started for the crew of the *Abraham Lincoln*. Each day one-third of crew were allowed ashore from 10 A.M. to 8 P.M., but their choice of diversions were severely limited—they were only given five dollars worth of Portuguese escudos, barely enough for a dinner and a glass of *vinho* (wine), but not enough to cavort with the ladies of the night.[39]

12 January: Azorean Waters

A Leigh-Light Wellington bomber of British Squadron 172 flying from the new RAF Azores base at Lagens sank the U-231 about 465 miles north of the archipelago (44°15'N, 20°38'W). The U-boat may have been the same one detected on 8 January stalking the Navy task force when the order was given to execute zig-zagging maneuvers and could have been out now prowling for the Army flotilla.[40]

14 January: Terceira

The weather was particularly brutal this day, so the *Abraham Lincoln* raised anchor and slipped outside Angra harbor, hoping to find a better shelter to discharge its cargo. Angra, being very deep and open up to the south in the direction of the stormy Atlantic, was not one of the most desirable ports, but as the ship would soon find out, the other choices were not much better. In fact, in the entire archipelago, outside of Horta there were no truly first-rate natural harbors. In addition to its other problems, Angra lacked docking facilities for a ship the size of the *Abraham Lincoln*. At Praia da Victória, a small port closer to Lagens, the ship dropped anchor just offshore and discharged some cargo into small lighters operated by British stevedores. But soon a decision was made that Angra was the better of the two bad choices so next day the ship returned there to finish unloading. Improving the port at Praia would be a high priority for the 96th.[41]

15 January: Atlantic Ocean, South of the Azores

At 8 A.M. at 33°N, 33°21'W, the *John Clarke* and the two LSTs plus four naval escort vessels were detached from convoy UGS-29 and turned northeast to Terceira. The first port of call shown on the *John Clarke* ship movement card after it departed Hampton Roads was Gibraltar with a due date of 22 January. Gibraltar was crossed out and Terceira entered on the line below with no due date but showing an arrival of 17 January. The change in sailing orders raises a few questions. Did the captain of the *John Clarke* actually believe he was headed to the Mediterranean when he left Virginia? Was it so critical to maintain the secrecy of the Azores operation that he was only told of his ship's true destination after he was well out to sea? Could Colonel Kemp have been the only person on the *John Clarke* who knew the secret or were his orders sealed and opened only after leaving the POE? There are no ready answers to these questions and no documents in the National Archives that shed any light on them.[42]

None of the GIs of the 928th had any idea, of course, of the crises that took place on shore and the delicate diplomatic negotiations that went on while they were out at sea. They were somewhat confused when they were warned one day without any explanation to check out their carbines and that they might have to fight their way ashore. This was strange considering that Portugal was not supposed to be at war, and even if it were, it would certainly not be on the side of the Axis. When the reception for the Seabees turned out to be a warm, friendly one the crisis simmered down, and in fact before landing Colonel Kemp guessed that they might expect a similarly warm reception rather than a firefight. After all, nearly every Azorean family had close relatives in New England, California, or Hawaii. They also established themselves in the New World with bakeries and sausage makers producing spicy *linguiça* and *choriço*, and even broadcast radio and television programs in their unique Azores dialect.

Meanwhile seemingly alone at sea, the GIs awoke, looked out over the decks, and were not encouraged by the sight. What they saw was terrifying: drenching rain, dark gray skies, fifty foot waves, and wild white-caps, but worst of all their small ships appeared to be abandoned in the vast unfriendly ocean. The powerful looking destroyers and CVE escort had left with the main convoy to Gibraltar and left them with a few diminutive—and mostly invisible—subchasers. The GIs did not have the luxury of the Seabees who sailed in (relative) comfort on the *Abraham Lincoln*, privately escorted by destroyers, which brought them safely in high style to Terceira.

Each small troop ship could occasionally catch sight of another small ship and nothing else but giant waves, nothing designed to instill confidence in a safe arrival in the Azores. The GIs did not know that their mini-armada did have an escort, even if they could not see it. Their small escort ships were doing their job, ranging far out scouting for U-boats. For the GIs, the saving thought was the fact that their ships bobbing up and down, seemingly out of control, would make difficult targets for torpedoes to hit as they disappeared into troughs and reappeared on wave crests higher than the ships' bridges. It was just as well none of the GIs had heard about acoustic torpedoes.

By the time the Army task force reached Terceira, Commander Bromet had made peace with General Passos e Sousa. He convinced the general that the Americans should be considered a part of the RAF, and therefore as honorary Englishmen they had to be allowed to join their compatriots at Lagens.

17 January: Terceira

The Seabees had unloaded in a conventional style, utilizing lighters, LCMs, and the primitive docking facilities at Angra. The Army mini-fleet offloaded on a small beach on the eastern side of the island, nearer the air base. Although Murphy's Law—that if anything can go wrong, it will—had not yet been formulated, it was already working for the 928th. The Liberty ship discharged its passengers as soon as it arrived.[43] At 8:30 P.M., while the two LSTs were standing by waiting for the bigger ship to finish unloading its cargo, the anchor chains snapped on the LST carrying most of the heavy equipment. As every good sailor knows, a ship left to itself will seek out an opportunity to create havoc and this LST was no different—it drifted ashore and crashed onto a beach of boulders at the foot of a cliff.

The GIs evacuated the LST without any casualties. Being engineers, the incident was accepted as only another challenge, so they went ahead and built a new access road to the beached LST. About forty-five enlisted men and two hundred hired laborers were detailed to construct a road through a farm down to the base of the cliff and build a causeway out to the bow of the ship. After four days of progress on the access road, a severe storm came up battering the LST even more, and, as the last straw of Murphy's curse, the ship caught fire. After extinguishing the blaze and waiting for the storm to subside, the sole undamaged vehicle found on board was a D-8 tractor-bulldozer. The only saving virtue in this disastrous incident was the hospitality and care the RAF and the Royal Navy showed their Yankee "guests" at Lagens Field. Transportation was furnished to the airfield where a temporary campsite had been prepared, ready for use by the Americans until they could build their own camp when new gear arrived from the States.

The heavy equipment badly damaged in the wreck was either not salvageable or was in desperate need of spare parts. The weapons that had been issued were functional even though they had no further use in the operation, except for the salvaged 40-mm antitank gun that all EAR must proudly display in front of their command tents. Thanks to Commander Bromet the Portuguese garrison had remained in their barracks during the entire landing operation.

The U.S. landings were the first uninvited ones on Terceira by an army since 25 July 1581. This time folks from the nearby villages hurried to watch the Americans pass through on the RAF lorries en route to the air base and greeted them with smiles and some bolder ones even waved back at the GIs. The locals might have been straining their eyes to spot a close relative, a descendent from the wave of emigration that took their grandparents and great grandparents to New England.

Arriving at Lagens, the engineers were awed by the sight, most notably the 545-meter ridge that overlooked the airfield to the west, the Serra do Cume, a shoulder of a large volcanic caldera. To the east was the Atlantic, wild and gusty and always churning up large whitecaps. You had to feel sympathy for pilots, for in addition to these natural problems, they had two other serious worries each time they landed during that first winter. The unfinished landing strip left little room for pilot error and most of the time the entire region suffered under the most miserable weather conditions, with strong winds and blinding rainstorms. But this was the best site on Terceira, one of the two best in the entire volcanic archipelago, the one General Arnold called nothing but a mud puddle. The Joint Chiefs accepted the role of second fiddle to the RAF at Lagens, but they knew there was no way they would follow the other conditions mandated by Salazar. They would not allow U.S. troops to disguise themselves as members of His Britannic Majesty's Royal Air Force nor would they have U.S. aircraft sport RAF insignia. Because the Joint Chiefs had invited themselves onto the island, they were going to set their own ground rules despite any British-Portuguese agreement to the contrary.

As more equipment arrived construction at the base proceeded smoothly and rapidly. The Seabees and the Engineers worked around the clock. The tents and administrative offices were snug, or as snug as could be expected considering the rains never stopped during the first two months. Streets and corners and plots were laid out where individual tents were to be erected. Before the 928th left Virginia, sign-boards had been made up with labels "CO HQ," "REGT HQ," "928 MESS," and "S-3" duly emblazoned with the twin tower emblem of the Corps of Engineers. In a few days, the camp was laid out, complete with flag-pole and fluttering GI-issue forty-eight-star Old Glory. Drainage ditches had to be dug around each tent to keep them from washing away in the torrential rain. Surveying for the extended runway for Lagens Field was the top priority after the quarters were erected, so each morning the survey crew would go out—rain or shine (usually the former)—to map and set out grade stakes to guide the bulldozers. If the dozers followed the markings on each stake—"cut 0.4'" or "fill 0.3'"—then an ideal runway surface would result, with an elevated crown at the center line and a slight gradient down towards the shoulders. There would be no surprises for landing aircraft and good drainage off the tar-mac, a serious problem in the rainy Azores.

Meanwhile, at Santa Rita, the Seabees were busy making a decent harbor at Praia, and erecting a permanent camp with facilities to house themselves and the Navy bomber squadron expected to arrive shortly. The first day they began removing the ubiquitous stone fences and other obstructions. The stone fences were a favorite home for the large rat population and their infected fleas, responsible for the endemic bubonic plague on the island, and responsible for most of the few deaths among the Allied forces. Before leaving the United States, the task forces had been inoculated against the plague, but unfortunately the serum was the wrong variety. The only vaccines in stock back home were for the East Indian plague, which did not help at all against the Azorean rats and their pneumonic-variety fleas. But Seabee con-struction took note of the plague menace:

> In the erection of all buildings, the presence of bubonic-plague-bearing rats had to be taken into consideration, so that in addi-tion to making doubly sure that the buildings were tight, con-crete decks were laid throughout.
>
> The men first lived under pup tents and later erected pyra-midals, all the while standing knee-deep in mud, eating British rations. Quonset huts were erected for galleys, BOQ [Bachelor Officers Quarters] and Battalion Headquarters, as well as ware-house huts; mess hall tents followed. Work progressed rapidly despite the rains and before too long Camp Santa Rita took on the aspect of a typically well ordered and well functioning Seabee base.[44]

18–19 January: C-in-C Navy and the Führer at Wolfsschanze

An ominous sign of how badly the war was going was the disclosure that a Croatian colonel, a liaison officer to the German staff in Yugoslavia, had deserted. But not merely deserted, he took off together with his wife in a Do-217 ("which we gave to Croatia"[45]), and flew directly to a British airfield in Italy. Because he was not harassed by Allied aircraft that were in control of the air space at that point, it was clear that the desertion and the delivery of the brand new Dornier had been carefully coordinated with the enemy. Other more serious items on the agenda included:

> OKM reported the possibility of attacking a large convoy in the North Atlantic in the near future by subs equipped with 3.7-cm anti-aircraft guns. The weak air reconnaissance will have to be concentrated at the proper time and place, over the expected shipping lanes. On the other hand, as a follow up to the invasion of the Azores, there was an imminent danger of an Anglo-Saxon landing in Portugal for which U-boats would be too late to prevent. The subs would be occupied approximately three weeks by the operation against the convoy and would require about nine days to reach Portuguese waters. [The] Führer believes there will be more obvious signs when the enemy intends to land and gave his consent for the convoy attack. OKM was also pleased to report that the surface speed of new subs when electric motors are used was 15 knots and even faster underwater because of the newly designed fish-like shape.[46]

19 January: Washington, D.C., and Lisbon

The Joint Chiefs finally got around to warning the secretary of state that a task force was going to land in the Azores. The only problem with the message was that both the Seabees and the Army task force had already disembarked yet Secretary Hull was informed that the first of two ships was due in the islands at the beginning of the following week. A new ship with supplies and equipment for the engineers did arrive, but not until the first week of February. Norweb was told to arrange "with minimum delay" complete clearance for the ships and advised to keep reminding Salazar that first, we wanted a U.S. airfield on Santa Maria, and second, a Navy bomber squadron at Lagens.[47]

Nothing was found in the State Department or National Archives files to explain the reason for the time gap between the actual landings and the Joint Chiefs notifying the State Department. Word was sent to Norweb, who informed Salazar on 21 January that a U.S. ship with the first contingent of U.S. troops would land during the coming weekend and another ship was due during the week of 7–13 February. This incident appears to have been an exercise in extreme diplomacy because both Salazar and the minister knew that U.S. forces had already arrived and were installed on Terceira. On 24 January Salazar thanked Norweb for his message and let him know the military authorities on the island had been duly informed. The prime minister, still worried that the United States might have undisclosed sinister intentions, asked if more troops were being sent than actually needed to work on the air base. In order to stroke the prime minister, Norweb was told to remind him that a first-class air base was being built on Terceira, that another one could be built on Santa Maria, and both would revert to Portuguese control when the war was over. Salazar in turn reminded Norweb that he was still awaiting approval to his request for Portuguese troops to accompany the United Nations forces in an operation to liberate Timor. The State Department's stock answer to that question was that "a more substantial contribution to the war in the Pacific can be furnished by Portugal in providing us a site for the proposed additional air base." This was a quid pro quo waiting for the first quid to happen. At any rate, the Joint Chiefs were not too sure that they would like poorly armed and trained Portuguese fighting alongside their troops in the South Pacific.[48]

19 January: Angra

After four days of unloading the *Abraham Lincoln*, the job was finally finished. At 1200 the ex-banana boat lifted anchor and, escorted by the U.S. destroyer *Ellis*, arrived in Baltimore on 29 January at 6:50 A.M.[49]

21 January: Terceira

A new military commander of the island, Brigadier Álvaro Teles Ferriera de Passos, arrived. He had been in charge of mobilizing the Portuguese army to counter a possible German invasion and was expected to present a hard line to the Allies. However it turned out otherwise as he proved to be a good friend to both the British and Americans.[50]

12 February: Lagens Field

Salvage of the LST was completed with the last of any usable equipment unloaded and put to use. Only a few other pieces of equipment, including a concrete mixer, road grader, and air compressor, had been received by this date—handicapped by the lack of heavy equipment, construction work on the field had gone slowly. However, the survey crews were out every day; detailed engineering maps would be ready whenever final construction began.[51]

The number of U.S. personnel on Terceira reached 1,874, or four times that of their British hosts. The idea of the Americans being in the service of the RAF remained pure fiction and was never implemented. However, to maintain their "secret" presence it was felt that, for the first few weeks at least, the GIs should be restricted to the air base. By now every person on the island of Terceira and probably most everyone else in the archipelago—as well as the Abwehr—knew that the Yanks had landed. Exactly how effective this restriction to base was highly questionable, so the order was lifted and the Americans could finally make morale-boosting R-and-R trips to town. They could head out on a long truck ride to the capital, Angra do Heroísmo, or make a shorter hop to the nearby village of Praia da Vitória. Almost anywhere they went they could sample the good life, Azores fashion, with all the joys of garlic-laden cooking and spicy meals washed down with local wine, and sample the good Portuguese brandy in *tavernas*.

16 February: Terceira

A second LST arrived a few days later than expected by the embassy and Salazar. The misstatement about the arrival date was deliberate because of the need to preserve secrecy and the well-grounded fear that such information could be passed on to German agents. This time there were no unexpected crises as the LST was unloaded, the needed heavy equipment brought to the air base and immediately put to use. Now the task of runway construction could go full speed ahead, rain or no rain.[52]

Some unexplained incidents suggested that someone on the island was out to sabotage the operation. The most serious was at the rock crusher plant, which was critical for the entire operation and where an explosive device caused some minor damage. The device may have come in accidentally or deliberately in a load of rock picked up at the quarry and dumped into the jaws of the crusher. Because of the tight security around the plant, explosive charges could only get into the crusher through the rock feed from the quarries. Closer oversight of the laborers at the quarries was ordered, and the incident was not repeated, nor was the person responsible ever apprehended.

Another incident for which I found no mention concerned the arrest and return to the United States of a sergeant for a general court-martial. The sergeant spoke fluent Portuguese and was listed in the Table of Organization as the official regimental translator. One day he was carted off on an ATS plane accompanied by an armed guard never to be heard from again. Colonel Kemp does not note the incident in his history nor were the charges against the sergeant ever revealed to his fellow GIs. Because of the lack of information—outside of the guard revealing that the subject was headed for a court-martial—the incident remains unexplained.

17 February: Santa Rita, Terceira

The Seabee detachment sent ahead to Santa Rita finished erecting the new naval station. About one hundred huts of various sizes were ready, complete with all essential appurtenances. As equipment and stores from the Seabee dump at Angra kept filling the newly constructed warehouses, personnel were transferred in small groups almost daily to the new base. Finally on 27 March the last of the material arrived, the dump was closed, and all the remaining personnel logged in to the new Navy base.[53]

However more suitable Angra was for unloading ships, it was seventeen kilometers from Lagens over a miserable dirt road made even more miserable when the rains came. Praia was just next door to the air base so had to be the preferred port. On 21 February Captain Tomlinson asked that necessary dredging and the construction of a pier at Praia be done to provide an anchorage for four LCMs and a pontoon barge, as well as to facilitate ship unloading operations.

February: Azores

By now the 247th RAF Group had made a major impact on U-boat operations in the Atlantic. Practically all the U-boat sightings, including thirteen attacks and two confirmed kills, had been to the east and northeast of the Azores, where wolf packs were deployed across central Atlantic shipping lanes. U-boats that once felt free to operate anywhere in the Azores Gap found that sailing within five hundred miles of Lagens air base was extremely hazardous. Admiral Dönitz ordered U-boats to operate in the restricted gap left between the Azores zone and operational zones of the North Atlantic bases.[54]

The submarine fleet now suffered a two-pronged problem—morale and efficiency. First, they had to make it out of the pens on the French coast. That formerly simple task had become a nightmare with Allied air patrols constantly searching and attacking any U-boat leaving or returning. If the submarines did get out of the Bay of Biscay, finding a large open area of the Atlantic where they could safely maneuver was the next problem. Their once "happy hunting grounds" were gone and now they would actually have to avoid the target-laden transatlantic shipping routes. Second, they could no longer rendezvous with the milchkuhen supply submarines around the Azores where they picked up not only fuel and supplies but also mail and news from home. The primary concern of U-boat captains was now to stay alive during their prescribed Atlantic patrol, and then to make it through the Bay of Biscay gauntlet back to safe harbor. The numbers were stacked against them; there was a close to zero statistical chance of surviving three consecutive patrols. By the end of the war, of a total of 1,170 U-boats built, only 863 had become operational and of them 753 were sunk. In raw figures the U-boat fleet suffered 87 percent losses with comparative casualties among the crews as well. It was no surprise with the submariners spending most of the time just trying to stay alive that their enthusiasm for sinking Allied ships was at an all-time low.[55]

The Atlantic was effectively covered and sailing to Southampton from Newport News was almost as safe as cruising on a Swan Boat on the Boston Commons. Operation Felix, with German troops swarming ashore from submarines and overwhelming the Portuguese army, was scratched. The VLR *Amerika* bombers would not use the Azores as a base. New York, Washington, and Boston could breathe a sigh of relief—if they knew—and would survive the war without knowing the terror and destruction of aerial bombardment.

This month the ATC started to use Lagens as a scheduled refueling stop for aircraft headed to the China–Burma–India theater. Personnel and equipment could be sent out from Washington and arrive in CBI in a timely manner with transit time measured in hours rather than days. In March the ATC changed the routing of ferrying aircraft flying to Europe. In case of bad weather or an emergency, Bermuda was also available. A transport schedule went into effect connecting the United States and England, served by eleven C-54 flights daily each way. In January MATS carried 350 tons of cargo and 785 passengers eastbound to the European and Mediterranean theaters. By July those numbers had increased to over nineteen hundred tons and 2,570 passengers. The new Azores route now made it possible to rush critical supplies and personnel to where needed and with the assurance that they would arrive in a timely fashion.[56]

The first emergency air cargo shipment to fly via Lagens carried five sets of bridging pontoons shipped at the urgent request of Gen. Mark Clark for the war in Italy. Later, in June and July another emergency shipment came through Lagens, carrying 125 tons of equipment specially designed to combat the German rocket bombs devastating London and other English cities. Compared to the older air transport routes, in addition to being faster, Lagens allowed heavier loads to be carried because there was no need for spare fuel tanks. There is no question that providing for the rapid shipment of emergency equipment and supplies saved thousands of lives and millions of gallons of aviation fuel.

The Joint Chiefs were pleased with the arrangements at Lagens but still wanted to station a naval air squadron there and needed an air base on Santa Maria. They wanted our minister to pursue the question of Santa Maria more energetically with Salazar and make sure he understood that the base was to be under U.S. control, that this was a quid pro quo for Portuguese participation in the liberation of Timor. The State Department still felt strongly that the British must bring up the question of basing the naval air squadron at Lagens because justification had to be found in the Anglo-Portuguese agreement.[57]

The British COS came up with a formula to present to Salazar justi-
fying an U.S. squadron on Lagens Field. The formula was a masterpiece
of diplomatic rationale:

1. The Anglo-Portuguese agreement authorized operations in the
   Azores under the British Coastal Command.
2. The U.S. squadron will be a unit of the British Coastal Command, which directs operations both in England and the Azores.
3. The U.S. squadrons are operating similarly as units of the British
   Coastal Command in England.
4. The U.S. squadron will be transferred to the Azores by the British
   Coastal Command from the European theatre and not from the
   United States.[58]

Ambassador Campbell agreed to present the formula to Salazar.
When the prime minister started to equivocate, Campbell pinned him
down by threatening to report to London that despite repeated representations by both the British and U.S. ministers permission was still
being withheld. Salazar finally relented and suggested he might reconsider provided some sort of British markings were placed on the U.S.
planes. This was the break needed to send the naval air squadron at
Lagens. At last the Seabees would get their tenants for the camp at
Santa Rita that had been constructed with such great care.

Norweb sent the good news to Washington. The British fully supported the U.S. position. A naval air squadron would be stationed at
Lagens and an airfield constructed on Santa Maria, built and operated
solely on a U.S. account.[59]

Dr. António de Oliveira Salazar and British Ambassador Sir Ronald Campbell negotiate for Allied use of facilities in the Azores in 1943.
UK Foreign Ministry photo

*Brig. João Tamagnini de Sousa Barbosa, military commander of
Terceira, and Air Vice Marshal Geoffrey R. Bromet, British air
officer commanding in the Azores, meet in Angra do Heroísmo,
8 October 1943.*
Photo courtesy of James H. Guill

The pierced plank runway at Lagens is inaugurated with a benediction and ribbon cutting by Brigadier João Tamagnini de Sousa Barbosa and a speech by Air Vice Marshal Geoffrey R. Bromet.
Portuguese Air Force photo

The 928th Engineer Aviation Regiment LST on the rocks. A fire following this wreck destroyed most of the 928th Engineers' equipment.
From Kemp, *History of the 928th Engineer Aviation Regiment,* National Archives

First anniversary party for the 928th EAR. **From left,** *Capt. Harris Gitlin, company commander, Lt. Col. Arthur Kemp, regiment commander, Brig. Gen. A. D. Smith, theater commander, and an air force base engineer colonel.*
From Kemp, *History of the 928th Engineer Aviation Regiment,* National Archives

Angra 96th NCB dump. Supplies and equipment were unloaded and deposited here temporarily and were later shipped to Santa Rita naval base.
Official U.S. Navy photo

Praia dock under construction.
Official U.S. Navy photo

U.S. Naval Camp Santa Rita on Terceira Island under construction. Native transportation equipment in foreground.
Official U.S. Navy photo

The author in Pan-American Airways gear, Santa Maria.
Author's collection

Construction on Santa Maria, improvement of the aerovaca *landing strip by native labor. Sons are there to run errands.*
Author's collection

Aerial view of Santa Maria, August 1945.
Official U.S. Air Force photo

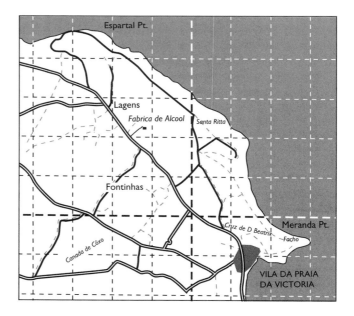

Enlargement of the northeast corner of Terceira showing (1)
the "Fabrica de Alcool" (Alcohol Factory) in the middle of the
planned northwest-southeast trending runway, (2) Santa Rita
misspelled Santa Ritta, the Seabee/naval base, (3) Lagens
RAF/U.S. Air Force HQ called Lajes today and NATO/U.S.
base HQ. Scale is shown by the 1 km. grid lines.
Modified from British Intelligence sources

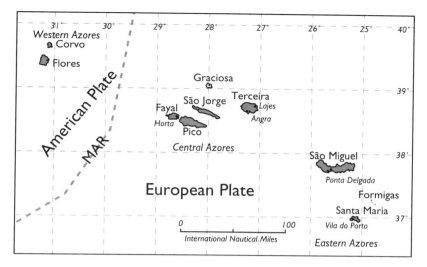

Azores Archipelago showing the islands and the Mid-Atlantic
Ridge (MAR) boundary between the American and the European plates.

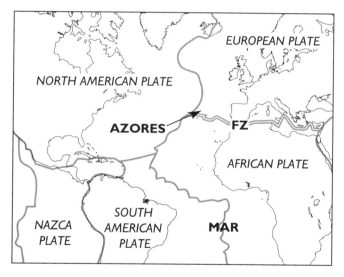

World plates showing the position of the Azores at the junction of the Mid-Atlantic Ridge (MAR) and the east-west
trending Azores-Gibraltar Fracture Zone (FZ).

Modified from U. S. Geological Survey

ELEVEN

NEGOTIATING SANTA MARIA, APRIL–JULY 1944

Late in the spring of 1944, even as half a dozen U-boats slipped through the Azores-Cape Verdes gantlet for operations in the Indian Ocean, Admiral Dönitz had dispatched the first of a small but troublesome succession of schnorchel-equipped 740-ton submarines to North American coastal waters, evidently in hopes of distracting Allied antisubmarine forces from an all-out assault on his vulnerable West France flotillas, currently preparing for their transfer to Norwegian bases.

P. K. LUNDEBERG, "American Anti-Submarine Operations"

April

On 6 April, U-boat U-302, commanded by Captain Sickel, sunk the last two merchant ships of World War II to go down in the vicinity of the Azores. But that was the only good news for Admiral Dönitz, who was losing U-boats and their crews at a faster rate than they could be replaced. He decided to abandon attacks on convoys and withdraw the U-boats completely from the North Atlantic until new submarines with improved technology became available. Besides, he wanted to conserve his fleet to defend against the expected Allied invasion of the continent, which the German High Command was sure was about to begin. Newly designed submarines equipped with state-of-the-art radar and heavier armament had to be produced to allow the U-boat fleet to do battle against the convoys on even terms. Allied countermeasures, especially aerial surveillance by VLR bombers and CVE aircraft, were highly successful, routinely detecting and attacking submarines long before they could even approach their targets. Dönitz thought the newly outfitted

submarines would restore the balance in Germany's favor, returning to
the earlier days when Allied losses greatly exceeded new ship production. It still was not too late to cut the Allied lifeline to Europe, and force
the Allies to agree to a negotiated peace.[1]

Three innovations had given him especially high hopes: the acoustic
torpedo, schnorchel,[2] and newly designed submarines. The Walter submarine had hulls and engines that were capable of higher underwater
speed and increased maneuverability than the older U-boats. Comparing
the data on the older and the newly designed U-boats shows why the
Allies had much to worry about: the Mark XXI U-boats would have a
faster speed underwater than most convoys and could stay submerged
for long periods to evade any aircraft out hunting for them. The Mark
XXIII, the midget submarine, was especially designed for operations
around the British Isles, where it could work in relatively shallow water
and was hard to detect by radar because of its small size.[3]

The Allies knew about the new U-boats on the drawing boards and
planned their own countermeasure: keep them from being launched.
U-boat production centers of Hamburg, Bremen, and Danzig were sub-
jected to extremely heavy Allied "carpet" bombardment, enough so
that none of the new submarines were produced by D-Day. At the Yalta
Conference the following year the British delegation urged Stalin to
capture Danzig as soon as possible because thirty percent of the U-
boats were being built there. The British told the Russians that "It
would be very difficult for the Allied air and surface forces to combat
these new types of U-boats because they have a high underwater speed
and are equipped with the latest technical devices."[4]

Admiral Dönitz had another important reason to worry about losing the port to the Russians. Danzig, sitting on the Baltic Sea and not
across the threatening North Sea from England, was the only naval base
available to train U-boat crews.

5 April: Camp Santa Rita, Terceira

With most basic structures finished at Santa Rita, and with a little time
on their hands, the Seabees began adding refinements to the camp. Three
miles of pierced plank surfacing had been added, nose hangars and count-
less hard stands constructed, and fresh water storage tanks holding
seventy-nine thousand gallons of water were erected. Work that started
on 27 March on an 8-inch submarine pipeline to unload aviation fuel
directly from tankers over a distance of thirty-eight hundred feet into

storage tanks was completed on 21 May. The port of Praia could start to receive cargo with its new dock and dredged marina.

The entire camp was landscaped, roads were graded and surfaced with crushed lava, culverts installed and drainage perfected, sod was laid and grass was sowed, and the huts given a second coat of paint. A drill field and rifle range were laid out, a baseball diamond marked off and outfitted. Still not satisfied after finishing these projects and behaving as if they planned an extended stay, tennis, handball, basketball, and badminton courts were laid out, as well as horseshoe, shuffleboard, boxing, and wrestling facilities. There was truly nothing on the island or probably in the entire archipelago to compare to this elegant Navy installation, not even the local country club and certainly not the RAF or the Army engineers camps. The total value of these and other improvements was calculated at the time to add up to about 1.6 million dollars.[5]

Open house was held to show off to the other military and locals the new base with its exact geometric pattern, straight red roads against a background of new green grass, and gleaming huts. Camp Santa Rita was duly christened, and quickly became the great showplace of the island.

10 April: Lagens Field

This day was designated 928th Regimental Day with a half-holiday declared to commemorate its first anniversary. A banquet was held with beer and soft drinks, and guest speakers were flown in for the occasion, the principal one being Brigadier General A. D. Smith, MATS theater commander. Other highlights were the awarding of thirty-seven Good Conduct Ribbons to enlisted men and the publication of "A Short History. First Anniversary, 928th Engineer Aviation Regiment, Headquarters and Services Company, APO 100, New York," with text by Staff Sergeant Womer and illustrated by PFC Roy Fox (who went on to become a well-known cartoonist after the war).[6]

May: North Atlantic

The CCS, British and U.S. combined Chiefs of Staff, declared the North Atlantic almost completely free of U-boats.[7]

17 May: Secretary of State
to Minister Norweb

Hull transmitted a memorandum prepared by the CCS on the necessity for an additional air base in the Azores which emphasized that "although some sort of favorable action is expected we cannot further delay on this account before successfully concluding negotiations for additional airfield." Lagens Field was already working near full capacity, and would not be able to handle the expected great increase in air traffic. Operations of the Air Transport Command alone called for 1,350 landings by September but by the following January that figure would jump to 2,100 monthly, not including diversions from the southern route and the substantial British operations. Santa Maria was desperately needed before the end of the year.

Another argument for the second field was as a suitable weather and emergency alternate to Lagens during its long periods of foul weather. With no emergency field available, loss of equipment and life was inevitable. Lagens and Santa Maria together could adequately handle all the traffic plus diversions from the Caribbean, South Atlantic, and Central African Wings of the Air Transport Command. The long southern air route would become a backup only, allowing the release of thousands of trained personnel to combat zones.

Even if the war in Europe ended before the new base was fully functioning, operations would still increase because the central Atlantic route was the most direct way to the Far East. The CCS felt the survey for the Santa Maria base must be started by 15 June followed immediately by actual construction if the new field was to be ready before winter set in. By autumn rough weather comes to the Azores and a delay of only one month might force postponing construction for another year.

The memorandum from the Chiefs to the State Department ends on an "offer you cannot refuse" theme: "Please seek an immediate interview with the Prime Minister on the subject of the additional airfield alone and insist upon approval, final and definite, for prompt survey of Santa Maria. Should you encounter further difficulty please advise at once and furnish your recommendations."[8]

Minister Norweb clearly had his work cut out.

Hull cabled Norweb later the same day with news that the Portuguese government had contacted Pan Am responding to its application—filed over a year previously—and had asked if the company was still interested in building the airfield. Presumably the pressure on

Salazar by the Allied ambassadors in Lisbon was paying off. The War Department asked Pan Am to follow up, which it did by sending Mr. Long, their chief of European operations, to Lisbon. The State Department assured the airline that it had no objections to their negotiating directly with the Portuguese government but Hull also told Norweb not to let up the pressure to approve a military air base on Santa Maria. Knowing the prime minister, it made sense to have more than one approach because there was a better chance of approval if he had a choice between the U.S. government and Pan Am rather than being confronted with one take it or else option.⁹

19 May: Minister Norweb to Secretary of State

Norweb started the ball rolling with an exploratory conversation with Portuguese Minister Sampaio before going to see Salazar. The minister knew about the U.S. request for an air base on Santa Maria and guessed that Salazar would be mostly interested in such an airfield if construction were undertaken by Portugal with assistance from U.S. technicians. Salazar was still afraid that official U.S. government involvement would compromise Portugal's neutrality and might bring on some sort of German retaliation. Norweb reminded him that the proposed Pan Am project would not officially involve the government and thus could not compromise Portuguese neutrality. "Salazar was also concerned with how and when Portuguese troops would be involved in the Timor operation. The Prime Minister wanted to preserve the colonial empire intact after the war which the early arrival of Portuguese troops on the island would help insure. Although the quid pro quo had been presented to Salazar that if he allowed an American base on Santa Maria, the Allies would have Portuguese troops accompany them into Indonesia, he wanted the Timor question settled before he approved anything."¹⁰

Washington's reaction was immediate. The State Department prepared an *aide mémoire* dated 20 May to the British embassy in Washington advising that the CCS would welcome any step taken by Portugal to become an active ally in the war against Japan as well as against the European Axis powers. The note concluded with the statement that the British and U.S. governments should direct their ambassadors in Lisbon "without delay to concert their action and acquaint the Por-

tuguese government with this grave decision." The following day Norweb was told to communicate the CCS decision to Salazar and to
remind him that the Santa Maria air base was needed to fly Portuguese
troops to the war in the Pacific.[11]

23 May: Norweb to Secretary of State

Happy news for the secretary of state. Norweb went to see Salazar and
found him in an unusually conciliatory mood. He agreed to invite Pan
Am to make a survey of Santa Maria and allow construction of the airfield to start immediately after, as long as it appeared that Portugal was
building and paying and that the field was needed for postwar communications. The question of Allied use would be deferred, presumably
until Salazar was sure that Germany had no chance to retaliate. Norweb suggested that a small survey party under Pan Am guise be sent
without delay to the Azores where they would be joined by Portuguese
officials to take care of such things as the expropriation of land and
planning housing.

The wheels of progress actually appeared to be grinding. Pan Am
answered Salazar's invitation saying that they could start work on
Santa Maria before 15 June. Six technicians would be sent from the
United States on a Pan Am flight to Horta where they would meet up
with another technician leaving from Lisbon on 9 or 10 June. It was
hoped that the Portuguese mission could depart on the same Pan Am
plane to Horta.[12]

23 May: Camp Santa Rita, Terceira

Commander Honnen received orders taking him away from the island
on temporary duty. For the remainder of the stay of the 96th NCB
on Terceira and for the movement back home Lieutenant Michael A.
Dandry took over the duties of acting officer-in-charge. With nothing
left to do on the camp, the battalion mainly kept busy improving the
dock and harbor facilities at Praia.

The quay was improved and enlarged; a small craft basin created;
and approaches to both were dredged. With the improved facilities,
ships had no need to anchor at Angra with its problems of inefficient
unloading and distance from the airfield. During their stay on Terceira,

the 96th Battalion stevedore crew unloaded a record forty thousand tons of cargo, much of it also in record time. For their work in improving the harbor at Praia, constructing the Camp Rita facilities, and stevedoring, Commander Honnen and others received letters of commendation from the Navy.[13]

29 May: Azorean Waters

U-549 was the last U-boat sunk in World War II around the former "black hole." During the entire year, only four other U-boats ventured into the Azores strategic zone and were also destroyed: one on 13 January by British aircraft stationed at Lagens and the other three on 16 January, and 9 and 10 April by the USS *Guadalcanal* (CVE 60). Compared to the thirty-two U-boats sunk around the Azores in 1943, it was clear that U-boats were now avoiding the islands and in fact that the Atlantic was almost free of submarines. Dönitz agonized over the sad fact that in ordering his U-boats out to patrol he was sending the crews to an almost certain death. He debated with his conscience and consulted with his fleet commanders whether it would be better to suspend all operations and wait until the new improved boats came out of the naval yards, promised for the end of 1944. Considering how the other German armed forces and the country itself was suffering, the commanders agreed with Dönitz that despite the overwhelming odds against them, the crews should continue to go out to do battle rather than completely withdraw the fleet from the Atlantic. To better the odds of survival, Dönitz and his staff set their highest priorities:

1. Develop better radar so the U-boats would know when they were being stalked.
2. Stronger anti-aircraft armament so the boats could defend themselves against aerial attack.
3. Mass production of an improved acoustic torpedo.

Until these proposals could be implemented, transatlantic sailing lost its fear for the convoys as they passed through the Azores gap unmolested with supplies and troops for the imminent invasion of France. Operation Overlord was being readied with no loss of manpower or materiel; the ocean journey was close to stress-free.[14]

5 June: South Atlantic

U-boats stopped the Portuguese merchant ship *Serpa Pinto* in mid-Atlantic and sunk it with some loss of life. This incident prompted Salazar to order the embargo of all tungsten shipments to Germany, not only the products of British-owned mines as he had previously ordered. Of the three thousand tons of tungsten needed annually for the German war machine, two thousand came from the Iberian Peninsula, the bulk from Portugal. Spain, responding more quickly to Allied pressure than her neighbor, had embargoed all her tungsten shipments to Germany the year before. With most of her tungsten supply lost, Germany would have to settle for softer steel alloys for its war machine.

Acting Secretary of State Stettinius made an official announcement of the embargo on 8 June, acknowledging the support of the Brazilian and British governments in convincing Portugal to take this action. Brazil's support was especially important, for according to Norweb "the Brazilian Ambassador's approach . . . took Salazar completely by surprise and the injection by the Brazilians of the thought that Portuguese blood was being shed because of the wolfram together with the psychological effect of being appealed to by the daughter nation—a member of the family—at the very moment it was preparing an expeditionary force proved to be extraordinarily effective."[15]

6 June: D-Day, Allied Landing in Normandy

The *New York Times* reported "Thousands of American, Canadian and British soldiers under cover of the greatest air and sea bombardment of history, have broken through the 'impregnable' perimeter of Germany's 'European fortress' in the first phase of the invasion and liberation of the Continent."

8 June: Norweb to Secretary of State

A cable came in from the CCS to the military attaché that might have upset any progress made in the negotiations over Santa Maria. The decision that was approved regarding participation of Portuguese forces in the Far Eastern theater was now postponed pending more consultations. Norweb was distinctly unhappy with this latest turn of events and feared they put a Santa Maria agreement at risk.

Hull thought Norweb should try to get the Santa Maria base without conceding the point, but added that if it was absolutely necessary, he could tell Salazar that the U.S. government would not object to Portuguese participation in an eventual Timor expedition. Norweb was also cautioned against letting the British know of these negotiations and that "it was imperative to avoid permitting the British to bring the additional field within their agreement with the Portuguese in any way." The Joint Chiefs wanted complete control over Santa Maria, a 100 percent U.S. air base in the Azores.[16]

22 June: Secretary of State to Ambassador Norweb

First the good news: the State Department raised the status of the U.S. legation in Lisbon to an embassy, which made Norweb a full-fledged ambassador. Then the bad news: Washington was concerned that the British were trying to get their hands on Santa Maria airport. Knowing Salazar's preference for legalities and that given the choice he would go along with England rather than the United States, Hull decided to try to keep that from happening. A problem was that Campbell considered himself the logical and legal—through both the 1373 treaty and the Lagens Field agreement—representative to negotiate with Salazar and it was his responsibility to present decisions of the CCS. Norweb was told that if the British ambassador should try to do that, to make sure he was with him and to present the U.S. proposal for Santa Maria. If such an arrangement was not practical, then Norweb himself was to take the earliest first step and just present the proposal to Salazar.

The Joint Chiefs were also having second thoughts about allowing Pan Am to construct the Santa Maria air base. The only way to have it built in time and control its use was for the Corps of Engineers to do it. The 928th Engineers were on Terceira, which was not that far away, and had already constructed a first-class airfield in record time, so it made perfect sense for them to tackle this new field rather than send over a crew of civilians from the United States. Norweb was told to make it clear to Salazar that no private commercial company had the facilities or know-how to execute so large an undertaking. Considering the time element, it would be preferable to permit construction by U.S. Army Engineers in uniform. The main reasons for this were that, first, delay would be caused by the need to furnish members of the military with civilian clothes and in civilianizing all the equipment and materials; second, work would move much more rapidly under full military discipline and control rather than by civilian cover or supervision. Therefore, it was essential to obtain this concession from Salazar and let the 928th come over from Terceira.

A third objection not mentioned was purely political. In previous dealings with Pan Am Secretary Hull felt that the company would always slip clauses into contracts which acted primarily for its own benefit and not that of the country. This had to stop; no one company should be the exclusive beneficiary of any transaction with the Portuguese government over the Azores air base. Congress was also upset with the virtual monopoly of U.S. aviation given to Pan Am. The Senate Special Committee to Investigate the National Defense Program, chaired by then-Senator Harry S. Truman, was looking into the policy of granting exclusive concessions to private companies. Hull felt that a majority in both houses of Congress were strongly against this policy and did not want the State Department to be a party to any such arrangement.

There was one serious problem with the new scenario. Salazar might consider that using the military brought the arrangement under the aegis of the Anglo-Portuguese agreement, which once more eliminated U.S. control. A way out of the dilemma might be to have Pan Am involved in the initial survey followed by Army engineers when actual airfield construction started. If this arrangement were approved, then the civilian cover would be dropped as soon as practicable.

Hull emphasized that an understanding regarding a modus operandi for Santa Maria must be approved as early as possible. Norweb was to keep the State Department and Colonel Love, the new military attaché, in Lisbon closely informed.[17]

24 June: Secretary of State to Ambassador Norweb

Hull was told that the British government was delaying the presentation of the CCS decision because it felt necessary to consult with the Australian government. Hull cabled the London embassy to urge action out of the British, but resolved that inaction was not going to slow the United States. The Joint Chiefs would not accept any more delay so Hull cabled Norweb: "it is our feeling and that of the War Department that unless you find serious objection to such a move you should seek an early appointment with Salazar in order to acquaint him with the CCS decision . . . Campbell could be informed and invited to join you. If Campbell declines, your presentation of the matter would presumably be limited to the American point of view."[18]

Hull felt that there was a good chance of success dealing with the Portuguese prime minister. A supply purchase agreement had been signed with Portugal—very much in their favor—with a first shipment of one hundred jeeps expected early next month. Time was a critical factor. With the approach of winter the Joint Chiefs would not tolerate any more delays.

On hour after he sent the cable to Norweb, Hull sent one to Ambassador Winant. The British Foreign Office felt that in addition to approval from the Australians, the British Chiefs of Staff needed to be consulted once more. The U.S. Joint Chiefs were furious; why yet another review when as members of the Combined Chiefs the British chiefs had already approved? As far as Washington was concerned, the decision was made: one way or another a Portuguese expeditionary force would accompany the attack on Timor. It was clear to the State Department that the British were temporizing, finding one excuse after another for inaction. Hull directed Norweb that unless he perceived "serious objection, press Salazar for an immediate and final answer." The ambassador was also directed to urge Campbell to press for a decision in regard to stationing the Navy squadron at Lagens Field. If an immediate answer was not received, the Navy might have to reconsider the entire matter. Not a hint what the Navy might do; perhaps confront the Portuguese with another fait accompli?[19]

3 July: Secretary of State
to Ambassador Norweb

The British lion finally moved, just enough to please the secretary of state. Ambassador Campbell was authorized by his foreign office to present jointly with Norweb a statement that the Allies would welcome Portuguese participation in an expedition to liberate Timor. The U.S. ambassador's instructions from Washington were still the same, only if pressed to promise that possibility which meant he had to be circumspect in the meeting with Salazar. A conference should first be held under the U.S. and British ambassadors to determine Portuguese capabilities in connection with such an expedition and to study logistical and other related problems. Campbell was not authorized to discuss the Santa Maria project, "but this need not restrict your action and you may go ahead in the light of instructions already furnished and of your own best judgment . . . it is essential definite agreement be reached this week on . . . Santa Maria."[20] Norweb thought he now had smooth sailing, his confused instructions had been cleared up, and an agreement was almost certain. He requested an appointment to see Salazar at his earliest convenience.

Then followed an incredible exchange of cables between the embassy in Lisbon and the secretary of state. Hopes would be raised then dashed as Salazar continued to raise objections to proposals that were thought to be settled. Norweb's optimism vanished, replaced by frustration dealing with issues that never seemed to get resolved. Simple straightforward problems such as the need for an emergency airstrip on Santa Maria which could be constructed within ten days were put off for decision. Lieutenant Colonel Hermínio José Serrano, senior member of the Portuguese survey party in the Azores, left a crew on the island to await authorization from Lisbon to build the strip but authorization did not come. To lay it out, Serrano used the preliminary maps of the Pan Am engineers, which impressed him with their high quality. Norweb also reminded Salazar that the port facilities would have to be upgraded so that the three ten-thousand-ton Liberty ships needed to transport the materials for the base could be unloaded. As ever, Salazar promised to think over the requests seriously, and to come back with answers. Norweb might not have been surprised with the way the negotiations were going if he had checked with his British colleagues on their own experience negotiating the base on Terceira. [21]

7 July: Ambassador Norweb to Secretary of State

Nothing was coming easy in Lisbon; it seemed as if negotiations were unraveling. The Timor issue was fouled up for suddenly the Portuguese and British who had been insisting on armed participation were having second (third, fourth, ad infinitum) thoughts. England and Portugal were now worried about the status of Macao, a small Portuguese island just off the coast of China and a virtual hostage of Japan. Many British citizens were fugitives on the island and would be interned if the Japanese came. Portugal was afraid that if it declared war, Macao might be occupied by Japan and then claimed by China after the war. The German ambassador warned Salazar that his country would react harshly if Portugal declared war on Japan. The Japanese ambassador also called and asked if an agreement had been made "with the Americans" for Portugal to join in an expedition to Timor. Salazar only replied "not yet." It never took much to unnerve Salazar; these visits were enough to do the trick. Finally, after much soul-searching the prime minister decided he would not change his mind about Timor, he would not worry about the British hostages, and rationalizing that Germany had already lost the war, he would take his chances with Macao.[22]

13 July: Ambassador Norweb to Secretary of State

Subject to constant pressure from Washington and questioned whether he was really doing his best with Salazar, Norweb must have appreciated just how Kennan felt the year before. Because Norweb's telegrams were not getting a sympathetic reception in Washington, he decided to set the record straight with a description of the political environment in Lisbon and a defense of his actions. Some of his more pointed comments:

> It may have been difficult for us to convey in telegrams with what urgency and stress we are viewing developments but on other hand at no time do we feel we have given grounds for the note of discouragement. . . . On contrary although we are far from satisfied and are driven almost to point of exasperation by tempo of developments they are not abnormal from Portuguese point of view. For the past weeks the movement has been definitely progressive and in the week since survey was completed . . . the matter is moving forward. . . . In dealing with the Prime Minister one has to learn to read the signs and interpret the language endeavoring to draw correct conclusions therefrom. At this point we do not doubt eventual attainment of our long range objectives since we are confident that he himself not only

is attracted by the prospect of a first class transatlantic airfield for Portugal but also had in mind a contribution which will redound to Portugal's advantage in the Far East.

He is wise and farsighted and at the same time a prudent man and there is evidence that he is considering every angle on this project including Portuguese neutrality in Europe. . . . Sampaio assured me that Salazar was giving his attention to our Azores and that as soon as his mind was made up he would receive me. . . . I repeated I was deeply disturbed by the time factor . . . our main concern is lest he sacrifice this unique opportunity by his constitutional incapacity to move fast.[23]

Another example of Salazar's "constitutional incapacity to move fast" was his finally granting permission for the U.S. naval air squadron to operate at Lagens Field. The squadron would act under the British Coastal Command and use RAF emblems on the aircraft which had had been proposed almost a year earlier. Santa Rita would finally receive its guests.[24]

15 July: Terceira

Earlier in the month, orders were received for the major part of the Seabee Battalion to return to the United States with roughly one hundred men remaining on the base to form a new CBMU-613 (Seabee Maintenance Unit). The 96th was returning for reassignment to the Pacific Theater.[25]

22 July: Washington, D.C., and Lisbon

The Joint Chiefs kept up an almost constant pressure on Cordell Hull to speed up the negotiations for the Santa Maria air base. Hull, in turn, passed their concerns on to Norweb: "Following receipt of a memorandum from the Joint Chiefs of Staff, whom we were keeping minutely informed of the negotiations in Lisbon, we cabled Norweb that the Joint Chiefs . . . were increasingly anxious to obtain these facilities. . . . The president prepared a letter expressing Allied concerns on the delay over Santa Maria to Salazar, this time carried personally by an emissary, Paul Culbertson, Assistant Chief of European Affairs to Lisbon."[26]

Culbertson and Ambassador Norweb presented the message to Salazar on 22 July ".earnestly requesting authorization for the immediate sending to Santa Maria of the materials to construct the air base."[27] Roosevelt pointed out that because of the bad winter weather problem, construction should start immediately or the project would have to be abandoned.

Salazar was once again won over by a letter from Roosevelt and agreed but on condition that Pan American would do the job. He agreed that Pan Am could start immediately, and that their engineers could start a survey to pick a location for the civilian airfield. He realized that Pan Am might be a cover for the U.S. military but insisted that he could deal only with Pan Am to keep up appearances of neutrality. He gave orders to Colonel Serrano to start work immediately on the temporary landing strip on Santa Maria. When the subject of Timor came up, Salazar said that he was negotiating with the Japanese directly asking them to return the island so he did not want to discuss military use of Santa Maria just yet. He was still reluctant to let U.S. service personnel into the Azores, and following his usual modus operandi, postponed a final decision awaiting the Pan Am bid.

Norweb stayed up that night preparing the bid. The total tender offer for the construction of the air base on Santa Maria was for $3,130,000, which was accepted almost immediately and approved by Washington just as quickly. Salazar cabled Roosevelt on 27 July, "It appears to me that the fundamental accord with the construction company has been satisfactorily made so that work can commence immediately."[28]

The Joint Chiefs accepted the concession as a positive start towards having their own base. Even though it took many months of diplomatic wrangling and hard negotiating, the timing was still acceptable for construction. The Chiefs had followed on the coattails of the British into Terceira, and now that the arrangement had been virtually approved they could just as easily hop on to those of Pan Am. The Pentagon already planned to use the Pan Am cover to send Army engineers into Santa Maria, insisting that a professional job be guaranteed only if the military did the job, carried out under tight discipline and control. The 928th Engineers, a short hop by air or ship away from Santa Maria, could start immediately; no need to mount an operation from the United States. All they had to do was anoint a crew from S-3 (Plans and Operations) as Pan Am employees and send them on their way.

On 28 November Salazar finally gave written approval for work on Santa Maria to proceed. By then construction of the base was well under way and it was already serving as a back-up airfield for Lagens.[29]

27 July: Terceira POE

Early in the morning, the men of the 96th NCB and their gear were moved to the dock that they built at Praia. While they had been on Terceira their accomplishments exceeded all expectations, enabling anti-submarine aircraft and the Air Transport Services to operate at peak efficiency, with all the service and care expected from a first-class air-field.

Promptly at 11 A.M. the Navy supply ship USS *Ariel* dropped anchor and 345 enlisted men and 11 officers of the Battalion went aboard. The 613th Seabee Maintenance Unit stayed on Terceira to maintain the port and installations at Lagens and Santa Rita until 1 February 1946 when they were rotated back to the United States. The *Ariel* up-anchored at 5 P.M. and sailed to Horta where it joined a convoy of seventeen ships shielded by ten escort vessels. After seven days of placid sailing through sunny days and moonlit nights—a contrast to the stormy voyage over—they tied up at Bayonne, New Jersey, where they boarded a waiting train which brought them back to Camp Endicott, Rhode Island, arriving just before dawn, 4 August, exactly one year after the infamous Gulfport junket.

However, arriving home did not mean that the war was over for the 96th. On 15 November they departed Davisville and after a week's cross-country trip 27 officers and 1,075 enlisted men arrived at Port Hueneme, ready for their second tour of overseas duty. The battalion reached their destination, Manicani Island, on 13 March 1945 in time to take part in the earliest phase to liberate the Philippines. It is interesting to note that a 1945 press release referred to their previous assignment as on "other islands X." Apparently mere mention of the Azores was still off limits.[30]

TWELVE

PAN AM GOES TO SANTA MARIA, AUGUST—DECEMBER 1944

> We were surprised and disappointed over the hesitancy of the Portuguese government to make available the necessary lands and to permit construction to begin . . . unless the Portuguese government immediately authorized all necessary land expropriations and the completion of the air base on Santa Maria, we would be obliged to discontinue the staff conversations at once. . . .
>
> The President having approved, this message was conveyed to Salazar by Ambassador Norweb. It led within a few weeks to an agreement, signed November 28, 1944, for the construction and use of the Santa Maria air base.
>
> CORDELL HULL, Memoirs

Santa Maria is the island closest to Europe, with Portugal only 869 miles (1390 kilometers) away. It is also one of the smallest with a total area of 37 square miles (97 square kilometers), a population today of about six thousand, and a simple economy based chiefly on fishing and raising cattle. The island's capital, Vila do Porto, was founded in the 1430s and is the oldest town in the Azores, with a beautiful fifteenth-century parish church and a commemorative stele, dedicated in 1432 to "the discoverers." Columbus returning from his first voyage to New World in 1493 called in at what is now the hamlet of Anjos on the northern coast. The airfield is now an international airport and was an important stop for transatlantic flights until the 1970s, when newer commercial jets could make it nonstop across the Atlantic. The *Encyclopedia Britannica* states that the airfield was originally constructed as a U.S. air base in 1944. That statement can be made now but the official government position at the time was that Pan Am constructed the base and anything else was denied.[1]

At the end of July 1944 the Joint Chiefs would not tolerate any more delay. Roosevelt had asked Salazar on 22 July to allow engineering work to start immediately and Salazar did approve a civilian air base to be constructed by Pan Am. The Joint Chiefs decided to wink at the civilian requirement. If Salazar wanted Pan Am to do the job, a detachment from the 928th would be the "Pan American engineers."

August: Terceira

Unbeknownst to themselves, a group of five enlisted men, including myself, were selected from the Engineering Section of S-3 of the 928th to form a survey crew for the nineteen-man Pan-Am team that was to go to Santa Maria. The mission was so secret that no reference could be found in the declassified files of the State Department, the Joint Chiefs, or of the 928th EAR in the National Archives. The events leading up to and carrying out the mission are told from my best recollection of them.

An officer from intelligence flew out from Washington to Lagens Field to brief the members of the Pan-Am team, to tell them exactly what they were getting into and remind them that the mission was voluntary. If anyone wanted out, to do so before the briefing. Nobody wanted out. The meeting began with an explanation of what the operation was all about and why we were selected to carry it out:

> You have been chosen for a special important mission. Reasons for selecting you were that
> 1. You engineered the airfield and runway at Lagens in record time and with high precision[2]
> 2. Your personnel records are unblemished and
> 3. Your company officers have expressed confidence that you can carry it out.
> Lagens Field is doing the job it was designed for. Aircraft based here are monitoring submarines, cleaning up the last haven left for the U-boats in the Atlantic. However, traffic to and from Europe as well as to the Far East will increase making it imperative that the United States build a new air base, one with better weather conditions and larger than Lagens, with sturdy and

longer runways to accommodate the heavier traffic, and one that is under American control. The first step towards building such an air base has been taken, that is a tentative site has been found. Now a team is needed to travel to the site, check it out, map it in detail, and construct a temporary camp and landing strip. The area mapped must be large enough to lay out buildings, hard standings, and runways. Surveying stakes should be set so that an Engineer battalion could come in behind you and immediately begin construction work on the airfield.

None of this can be revealed to anyone, at least not until you receive clearance from the Air Force. You will travel to the island of Santa Maria on a Portuguese commercial ferry wearing civilian clothes, and carrying U.S. passports that identify you as engineers working for Pan American World Airways. You will not wear dogtags, or any kind of identification that might give you away as U.S. Army personnel.

We questioned the need for civilian clothes and why we couldn't wear Army gear. The response did not answer anything: it's very important to travel in civilian clothes. You must believe that whatever the reasons, this operation is for the good of the country and the war effort.

Why the operation had to be undercover and not overtly military, which was not revealed then, was of course the fact that Salazar's permission was only to Pan Am. As far as the outside world was concerned we were civilians working for Pan Am.

A question on several people's minds: what happens if the Portuguese discover that we're GIs and not civilians? The briefing officer was reassuring—to a degree—first telling us that what had been done until then was not bad. Although the Geneva Convention gave Portugal the right in wartime to execute any foreign soldiers captured out of uniform on its soil—in other words technically spies—that would not happen to judge by a recent incident. Some U.S. airmen made a forced landing in Portugal and were interned in the Ritz Hotel in Lisbon for the duration, held in their own recognizance. They had the run of the hotel and the city on their word that they would not try to escape from the country. If our cover was blown, then presumably something similar would happen and the Army would leave it to the State Department and the U.S. Embassy to look after us as internees. Not a bad fate for soldiers serving their country at war.

So the Joint Chiefs would have it their way, albeit downscaled. No covert OSS operation, no Marine-Navy amphibious landing, just a Corps of Engineers detachment dressed as civilians going to Santa Maria with the official blessings of the Portuguese government.

Our gear arrived a few days later on a C-47 that flew out of Presque Isle, Maine. It was packed in three large wooden crates and full of the latest L.L. Bean fashions for the field man, accompanied by another officer who came along to give us a final briefing and pep talk to the effect that: "Santa Maria will henceforth be referred to only as Station 'X,' APO 406. The words Santa Maria are not to appear on any piece of paper, official or otherwise. Passports are genuine State Department issue, even though some of the information is made up. Names, dates of birth, and photos, the fact that you are American citizens are all correct, only the statement where your title and employer are shown is not. You are now Pan American Airways engineers."[3] He emphasized the fact that it was important for the success of this operation to keep the Portuguese authorities thinking Pan Am and not U.S. Army. We had to forget about being in the army; as far as the outside world was concerned we were traveling on company business. When we returned to Lagens, a debriefing officer would tell us what we could say about the operation—probably nothing, at least not until after the war.

We were given our passports, plus passage on the *Emprêsa Insulana de Navigação* sailing from Terceira to Santa Maria and some escudo spending money. The tickets were for deckside accommodations, not staterooms, so we slept on deck. We were advised to get deck chairs in a protected spot as soon as we boarded, away from the wind and rain and to keep together. Fraternization with the passengers was to be avoided. Part of the "Pan Am" detail had gone ahead to get permits, scout out the land, and inform the local politicos that we were coming.

3 August: Terceira

This entry appears in Colonel Kemp's *History:* "A detachment of two officers and 17 enlisted men have been employed in making surveys, erecting a 500 man tent camp, building roads and landing strips on the island of Santa Maria since 3 August."[4]

The *Emprésa Insulana* was on its return voyage to Santa Maria, completing the loop which included the islands of Pico, Faial, Graciosa, Terceira, and São Miguel. Our gear was stowed in barracks bags and left behind; traveling now was with new suitcases loaded with the latest men's fashions from the States.

Of course, none of us knew anything of the events that made the trip necessary. We were sailing barely one week after Salazar had granted permission to "Pan American" to build an air base on Santa Maria but four months before official permission was given for any U.S. forces to be on the island. The invasion of Normandy had begun two months earlier on 6 June, and vast amounts of men and materiel had to arrive in France fast, which meant flying via the Azores especially during the winter. With two air bases in the Azores, the Air Transport Commands could expand flight schedules with connections to every theater command on earth.

5 August: Santa Maria

After an uneventful trip the *Emprêsa Insulana* ship docked in Santa Maria. The "Pan Am" engineers debarked and headed out to the site, to establish camp, start surveying, and get a landing strip finished. When we arrived, the Portuguese flag was already flying over a tent housing airport and customs control.

The site chosen was an *aerovaca,* a meadow that was suitable for landings and take-offs: flat, obstacle-free, and relatively free of strong crosswinds. *Aerovacas* had been established all over the Azores by the military for their own or civilian emergency use and acted as runways whenever the cows were chased away. Not much of an attempt was made to improve them so their chief use remained for pasture rather than aircraft. The Santa Maria *aerovaca* had been well sited in the western part of the island. It had every advantage for an airfield: 360 degrees clear view for aircraft and underlain by easily excavated sedimentary rocks rather than the tough volcanics omnipresent elsewhere in the archipelago. The task was going to be easy—no trees or houses on the site so no interference with survey lines or bulldozers; grade stakes set easily; a civil engineer's dream come true.

Although not one plane landed all the time we were there, the airport controllers were still kept busy. Their powerful radio transmitter was an important link in the mid-Atlantic network of marine rescue operations, although it may have served more often as a "Western Union" for local residents.

The work went smoothly and rapidly. With the good clear Santa

Maria weather, we shot the longest, clearest telescopic sights since we arrived in the Azores. Locals hired as laborers did the rough grading and removal of large obstacles on the runway allowing for the next step, laying of a pierced plank landing strip. The survey had to produce a detailed topographic map at a two foot contour interval to allow laying out the seven-thousand-foot by five-hundred-foot runway by the Corps of Engineers planners. Once men and construction materiel arrived from the States and work began, surprises had to be avoided if the air-field was to be finished quickly—no unexpected big holes to fill, no large rock outcrops to dynamite.

12 August: Terceira

By now the Portuguese authorities who, under orders from Lisbon, had been trying not to acknowledge the presence of U.S. forces in the Azores began to loosen up. Despite their government's intransigence, they knew that without the Americans the air base and port of Praia would never have been built. To break the ice and establish good relations, at least socially, the U.S. officials invited their Portuguese counterparts to a big party. Whether Salazar knew it or not, his representatives on Terceira were fraternizing and getting along beautifully with the Americans.[5]

Although relations with the Portuguese were improving, the commander of U.S. naval forces reported that personal relations between the Allies were not going smoothly. The report stated that relations were a bit strained at first, that those U.S. officers "who gave advice rather consistently suggested that the British would 'try to pull the wool over our eyes' and to be on guard." There were no confrontations because U.S. military personnel "were instructed to keep all conversation on a light level and to smile broadly at anyone who tried to start an argument that might become heated." My own personal experience—admittedly at a much lower level—was otherwise. Contacts with the British were always amiable; I do not recall ever being told to avoid an argument or warned to keep the conversation light. We had RAF guests at our mess hall and they in turn brought us to their NAAFI (PX equivalent). At a higher level, some high ranking U.S. officers might have felt "wool being pulled over their eyes" by the RAF who in turn felt their purported guests were trying to take over the air base. After all, by diplomatic and military agreement this was supposed to be theirs.[6]

Runway 29-11 was finished and made available for aircraft landings. Colonel Kemp reported that "the runway was paved 6,000 [feet long] by 150 [feet] wide with an asphalt penetration surface consisting of a 4 [inch] compacted thickness base course and a wearing course of approximately 2 [inches] in thickness, placed on a sub-base of gray volcanic ash of a minimum thickness of 6."[7]

"Runway 34-16 the main runway will have a paved section of 10,400 [feet long] by 200 [feet] wide. Grading work was nearing completion. . . . It is estimated that on or about 21 September a 5,500 [foot] paved section will be completed and ready for use. With the approaching rainy season and the removal of the rock quarry, the completion date for the runway is estimated to be 30 November."

The 928th Engineers were building an airfield that would be the envy of any in the world at the time. Lagens and Santa Maria would both be in operation by the end of the year.

14 August: Santa Maria

We had our first and only visitor in camp, Sr. Silveira (not his real name), a high functionary of the *município* who paid a courtesy call on behalf of the governor of the island. Most likely his motives were other than just courtesy; he wanted to know exactly what we were up to and our real relationship—if any—with Pan Am.

The first problem with the visitor was that he spoke no English and none of us spoke any Portuguese. He was, however, fluent in French. As the only one in the party who spoke French I became the unofficial tour guide. We showed Sr. Silveira our maps and sketches, and how the runway would eventually appear. Then came the allegedly social part of his visit: he wanted to know everything about us, where we each were from, all about our families, where we went to school, and what engineering credentials we had. He seemed to be properly impressed that we were qualified to lay out an airfield, that we knew what we were doing, and thanked us for showing him such a courteous visit. Then he invited me to visit him that Sunday in his home for dinner, a *jantar* with his family. I thanked him and said I would be there.

Sr. Silveira's family was charming, his diminutive Senhora, son, and lovely daughter. The dinner and wine were excellent with many Portuguese culinary delights that I could only imagine at the G.I. mess. After dinner, Silveira cornered me for some brandy and a private tête-àtête. He showed me the recent *Diário dos Açores,* which described how Hitler's Reich was rapidly approaching armageddon. The first French column, General Leclerc's Second Armored Division, entered Paris, reaching the Luxembourg Gardens near the city center at 10:20 A.M. The U.S. Third Army fought its way to Nôtre Dame Cathedral in time to hear the ancient bells pealing the liberation of Paris. Bridges across the Seine that had been wired with explosives by the SS were dismantled. The German commander defied Hitler, and refusing to burn Paris, ordered his forces to stack their arms and not resist the Allies.

Sr. Silveira observed that it must be exciting for those Americans fighting to free France and asked if I had any friends or relatives in the army of liberation. I told him I did indeed. Next was a question we all half expected, to be prepared to think quickly and answer forthrightly, lying for the good of the operation and our country, remembering always that we worked for Pan Am building a commercial airfield.

Silveira asked something to the effect: "Don't you ever feel that perhaps as a patriotic young man you should be in the Army, fighting alongside your cousins and friends. How will you ever explain when this Great War is over that you were a civilian, that you did not serve in the American army along with your countrymen who shed their blood in a great cause?"

I allowed that if I had my way, I would be in France marching down the Champs Elysée liberating Paris, or in Rome, or on a Pacific island with General MacArthur fighting the Japanese, liberating Timor, and not here in the Azores enjoying the good life, *a vida boa.* Minor ailments—sinusitis and a third degree malocclusion—kept me out of service. There was a slight element of truth in the statement: the ailments kept me from a commission in the Navy, so I might have passed a lie detector test if one had been available. Still wanting to do something for the war effort I decided to join Pan American.

The rest of the afternoon was more relaxing, sitting on the patio, sipping local *vinho,* and being entertained by Sr. Silveira's daughter playing her twelve-string Portuguese guitar and singing a few melancholy *fados.* Sr. Silveira must have been satisfied with my visit, for no more officials came to the camp nor was anyone else invited for *jantar;* we must have been officially vetted as Pan American engineers.

The survey was finished in record time—three weeks—the airstrip was staked out; the map was drawn. The next phase was up to Engineer Headquarters: design of the airfield, calculating the materials and equipment needed and the date the field would be finished and ready for operations. With nothing else for the survey crew to do a DC-3 landed on our new strip on 31 August and brought us back to Lagens.

August–September: Terceira

Events moved swiftly after our return. In our first debriefing we were told in plain, unequivocal language not to reveal where we had been and what we had been doing there. We would eventually get the "all-clear" after it was certain that no secrets could be compromised and no high officials embarrassed. Then and only then could we say anything about operations in the Azores.

Shortly after the debriefing, we each received a commendation from the theater commander, Brigadier General A. D. Smith. In peacetime Smith had been CEO of United Airlines and was now theater commander of the Military Air Transport Command. The commendation was fascinating for what it did not say, not the vaguest hint on what we were being commended for:

> In returning Cpl Norman Herz . . . from the temporary duty he has been performing since August 1944 I commend him for the part he shared in this enterprise. He at all times performed assignments willingly and in a superior manner. His attitude, efficiency, conduct and bearing, both while working and in contacts with the local populace, tended toward the success of this detail.
> [signed] A. D. Smith
> Brigadier General USA
> Commanding[8]

A board was convened to have the Pan Am crew appointed to Officer Candidate School (OCS) and out of the Azores. We all passed with flying colors and were flown back to the United States to Fort Belvoir, Virginia, for Engineer OCS, or to San Antonio for Air Force. We each still wondered about the Santa Maria operation: why was it so important that it earned us officer's commissions? The questions were only answered fifty years later.

Before being flown back to OCS on October 31, we signed a document promising that "I will not make public any information gained at this base . . . and I will not divulge to anyone not entitled to receive the information any details about location of bases, routes taken, arrival and departure times, weather, location of units, strength, materiel, equipment, plans, or any other information of a classified nature."[9]

Although the big questions about Operation Alacrity have been answered in the National and Seabee Archives, many little questions will never be answered, such as: Was the afternoon with Sr. Silveira and his family purely social or was he fishing to learn the "Pan Am" engineers' true identity? Was Portuguese security really taken in by the cover or did they ignore it to avoid embarrassing problems with America? Anwers to these and many other questions cannot be found in any official U.S. government files. If such information existed it might have been in the "cosmic top secret files" of World War II—the "burn before reading" stuff.

6 October: Washington, D.C.

Even though Salazar was still temporizing and withholding permission to begin construction, the Joint Chiefs were ready to start work on an air base on Santa Maria, especially now with the preliminary work done, and the maps and plans of the "Pan Am" detail in hand. The prime minister asked for a quid pro quo, that the United States first agree to accept his list of supplies and services in the strategic shipping and economic fields before he would consider approving Santa Maria. Secretary of State Hull did not feel the United States was in a position to commit itself and instead drafted a response pointing out that the greatest contribution Portugal could make to the war in the Pacific, especially liberating Timor, would be to allow the building of an airfield on Santa Maria.[10]

Hull went on that the United States interpreted the hesitancy of the Portuguese government to make available the necessary lands and permit construction to start as a grave obstruction to the war in the Pacific and a direct aid to Japan. Unless the Portuguese government immediately authorized the land expropriations and completion of the air base on Santa Maria, we would be obliged to discontinue the staff conversations at once, to decline to engage in any negotiations concerning economic or other matters, and immediately curtail the economic aid we were furnishing. The memorandum was enthusiastically endorsed by the CCS as well as Roosevelt and was conveyed to Salazar by Ambassador Norweb.

28 November

An agreement was finally signed for the construction and use of the Santa Maria air base by the United States. But like everything else that occurred in Portuguese-Allied negotiations, things had not gone exactly smoothly. There was a quid pro quo involved: we would have complete use and control of the base for the duration of the war and six months thereafter, and in return Portuguese armed forces could take part in the liberation of Timor. A furious exchange of secret correspondence between the British and U.S. embassies with Salazar preceded the agreement, because of the problem of U.S. insistence on using the word "control" (*"contrôle"*) referring to who was to run the air base.[11]

When the British negotiated their air base on Terceira, they acted more discretely. Knowing full well that de facto they would control the base, but acknowledging that the island was part of Portugal and preserving Portuguese sensitivity, they gave up the satisfaction of being the de jure overseers as well. The highest officer on the island was to be Portuguese, so theoretically, the lower ranked British officer in charge would have to take orders from him. None of this politeness apparently for the Americans; everything had to be spelled out their way. With the furious exchange of letters that ensued, secretaries and couriers must have been kept very busy. There is no record of the time that each letter was written and delivered, but all are dated November 28:

1. Sir Ronald H. Campbell to Dr. Oliveira Salazar: His Majesty's government recognizes the right of the Portuguese government to participate in operations to expel the Japanese occupiers and restore Timor to full Portuguese sovereignty. This participation can be carried out in direct and indirect form: direct participation by the use of Portuguese forces and "indirect participation by the concession to the Government of the United States of facilities for the construction, use and control of an air base on the Island of Santa Maria, for the purpose of facilitating the movement of American forces to the theatre of war in the Pacific . . . under . . . a special agreement between the Portuguese Government and the Government of the United States."

2. Dr. Oliveira Salazar to Sir Ronald H. Campbell: Acknowledges receipt of Campbell's letter and repeats back a transla-

tion into Portuguese. In his translation of the section "indirect participation . . ." it is obvious that he found the word "control" very upsetting; it appears in italics, "*contrôle*," the only word so treated in any of this correspondence. He ends the letter with the statement that the Portuguese Government agrees with the content of the note and considers the document as his answer and constituting an agreement between the two governments.

3. Mr. R. Henry Norweb to Dr. Oliveira Salazar: Repeats verbatim most of the original letter of Ambassador Campbell. The United States "accepts . . . the participation of Portugal in such operations as may be conducted eventually to expel the Japanese from Portuguese Timor in order that that territory may be restored to full Portuguese sovereignty." As part of the deal Portugal will grant "the concession to the Government of the United States or facilities for the construction, use and control of an air base on the Island of Santa Maria." Norweb did not italicize "control."

4. Dr. Oliveira Salazar to Mr. R. Henry Norweb: The secretaries had it easy this time. The letter is identical to the one sent earlier in the day to the British Ambassador, and still includes the italicized "*contrôle*." Salazar must have been hoping that the Americans would get the point without belaboring it, expressing it in a subtle form rather than as a loud protest. He was unhappy surrendering a piece of Portuguese territory to a country that until recently refused to give any assurance that it would return the land after the war.

Later that same day an agreement was drawn up and signed by Ambassador Norweb and Prime Minister Salazar, first permitting the United States to build its air base on Santa Maria and second for Portuguese forces to take part in the liberation of Timor from Japan. Protecting Portuguese sensitivities and also to maintain the illusion for Germany that this was only meant as a belligerent act against Japan, the agreement is entitled "Agreement between the Portuguese Government and the Government of the United States establishing the form of indirect participation of Portugal in Pacific operations."

The first Article of the Agreement stipulated that the Portuguese and U.S. governments would construct an airfield on Santa Maria, that when all construction was completed it would be considered the property of the Portuguese State. In Article 2 Portugal conceded the use without restrictions of the base which will remain both for operations and administration and *contrôle* (still in italics in the Portuguese version) under the command of the U.S. Air Force. The British Community, as allies of the United States and Portugal will also be allowed to use the airfield.

Article 3 stated that the United States would return the base to Portugal within six months after the termination of hostilities. Article 4 that the base could eventually be used for both Portuguese commercial and military aircraft. Article 5 called for the agreement "to be considered secret while one of the Governments judges it inconvenient to reveal its contents." Then Salazar and Norweb signed the agreement, dated Lisbon, 28 November 1944.

Salazar's insistence on italicizing the terrible word "control" finally got through to Norweb and the State Department. In the final communication of the day Norweb assured the prime minister that "under instructions, that the employment of the word 'control' in the texts in no way suggests any thought on the part of the United States government to seek jurisdiction in matters within the sovereign prerogatives of Portugal." How much or if this nebulous statement mollified Salazar we do not know, but it was written in classic diplomatic jargon, committing nothing specific and not answering the question of exactly what the United States's intentions were. Because Article 3 committed the United States to return the base to Portugal, Salazar must have felt the question had become moot, that Norweb's explanation was the best he could expect.

On 4 August a new outfit, the 1391st Army Air Force Base Unit, was formed within the Air Transport Command, Mid-Atlantic Division, and assigned to operate Santa Maria Airfield. Although the detachment from the 928th Engineers did not know it when they would sail to Santa Maria, they were inaugurating this embryonic outfit. In September, shortly after they had finished the survey and returned to Lajes, construction began on what became one of the best overseas facilities of the Military Air Transport Command. The Army Corps of Engineers hired a civilian construction company to build the airfield under its supervision in what was called Project 111. To maintain the base's secrecy and going by the letter of the agreement with Salazar, Pan American was the titular manager in charge of construction for the U.S. Army Air Force. The base along with three A-shaped runways was completed on 15 May 1945, but Air Transport Command operations had already started to move to Santa Maria from Lajes in April.[12]

December

The Air Transport Command established a guaranteed schedule—three times weekly air service starting in the winter of 1944–45 and following the new, shorter, and good-weather route via Washington–Newfoundland–Azores–Paris. With the Allies moving ahead through France and Germany still a dangerous enemy, an express air service to fly personnel and emergency supplies and equipment from the States was more important than ever. U-boats sent out at the end of December sank nine merchant ships totaling fifty-nine thousand tons for the loss of seven U-boats in action and five sunk through other causes. When the U-boats lost their bases in the Bay of Biscay to the Allied advance and were moved to Norwegian ports, one thousand miles was added to the passage to operational areas around the British Isles. With a high rate of U-boat losses and neither boats nor crews easily replaced, plus the loss of operational time at sea, Admiral Dönitz's plan to interdict Allied transatlantic shipping and force the United States and England to seek a negotiated peace with Germany was clearly not to be.

Dönitz's U-boat fleet suffered losses not only in combat but even more were destroyed in the shipyards. The admiral was expecting 290 new submarines to come out of the yards but heavy Allied bombing attacks cut the number down to 65 that were actually delivered. In June there were 181 boats in commission; by the end of the year the fleet could only count on 140. Dönitz, the perennial optimist, the last one left in Hitler's command circle, still thought a final assault with his newly designed schnorchel-equipped Walter-class U-boats plus a horde of midget submarines could wreak havoc in the seas around the British Isles. While the Wehrmacht was collapsing on all fronts, the decision was made for one last gasp attack on Allied forces defending the western front. The Ardennes offensive (the Battle of the Bulge) was to begin on 1 January. If the ground offensive in Belgium succeeded, plus a successful U-boat offensive in the North Sea, perhaps Germany might still be able to salvage an armistice. Hitler never gave up the idea that Britain and the United States would make peace with Germany so all three could take on Russia, which he considered the common enemy. If the planned offensives failed, and events continued going as they were, then it would be all over for the Nazis.[13]

The Battle of the Bulge was eventually contained and the Allies resumed the offensive, carrying the war into Germany. The war in the Atlantic might not have been conceded by the OKM, but the U-boat crews had. Sir John Slessor, Marshall of the RAF, wrote that

> It must always be one of the mysteries of the war that the enemy should have waited to stage a serious attack on the Gibraltar convoys until we were established in the Azores and were thus in the position to give them effective air cover throughout their passage. In mid-November a very formidable pack deployed across the route of S.L. 139 and K.M.S. 30.[14] But the form had changed from that of October. There was no attempt to follow up by day, no evidence of an inclination to stay up and fight it out, and a marked lack of determination in the attacks by night. It is very difficult to resist the conclusion that the primary preoccupation of the U-boat crews is now not to kill but to avoid being killed—and that is the beginning of the end in a service which must rely entirely for its effect on a bold, offensive spirit.[15]

THIRTEEN

ALLIED VICTORY
AND BEYOND, 1945—

> The U-boat attack was our worst evil. It would have been wise
> for the Germans to stake all upon it.
>
> WINSTON CHURCHILL, *Second World War*

With the liberation of France, the U-boats could no longer be based in
the Bay of Biscay. Dönitz abandoned the submarine pens and moved
the entire fleet to Norway. The British Admiralty now had two new
things to worry about: first, the U-boats had been technologically upgraded with improved radar, heavier armament, and schnorchels to
vent their diesel exhaust and, second, they would operate from Norwegian bases closer to British waters than the Bay of Biscay. Coastal Command Air Groups were switched from Bay of Biscay patrol, which they
could cover easily to the vast expanse of ocean between the Shetlands
and Iceland. There was no gauntlet of RAF bombers for the submarines
to pass now sailing directly from Norwegian ports into the open ocean.
They started to come out in the middle of August 1944 and by the end
of the month no less than sixteen had gone into the Atlantic by the
northern route. Only two were sighted from the air and none were
attacked. This was a new and frightening development, "an unpalat-
able change" according to Captain Roskill.[1]

The new submarines immediately showed they were going to be a
serious threat. U-482 on patrol north of Ireland sank the corvette HMS
Hurst Castle and four merchantmen. In the last quarter of 1944, the
ratio of U-boats lost to Allied ships sunk returned briefly to the frightening days of August 1942. The OKM was pleased, for despite Hitler
and his General Staff constantly denigrating the role of U-boats, the
Atlantic suddenly appeared to be the only battle going in Germany's

Merchant Ships Lost through Enemy Action, 1940–1945

| | ESCORTED LOSSES | | | | UNESCORTED LOSSES | | | |
| | IN CONVOY | | STRAGGLERS | | EX-CONVOY | | INDEPENDENT | |
YEAR	NUMBER	TONS	NUMBER	TONS	NUMBER	TONS	NUMBER	TONS
1939	12	65,000	5	35,000	10	76,000	186	568,000
1940	203	939,000	91	357,000	95	522,000	444	1,551,000
1941	290	1,198,000	90	362,000	161	787,000	300	1,080,000
1942	344	1,859,000	66	326,000	86	528,000	876	4,468,000
1943	275	1,629,000	54	299,000	8	42,000	207	976,000
1944	85	470,000	8	44,000	4	26,000	78	404,000
1945	56	292,000	4	20,000	3	11,000	24	66,000
TOTALS	1,265	6,452,000	318	1,443,000	367	1,992,000	2,115	9,163,000

Source: Grove, Defeat of the Enemy Attack on Shipping, table 14.

favor. If the war could be turned around at this late date, the U-boats had the only chance to do it.

But then in December the ratio abruptly changed. U-boats sunk nine merchantmen totaling fifty-nine thousand tons but lost seven of their own in action and five by other causes. In January 1945 eleven merchant ships were sunk totaling fifty-seven thousand tons but the same number of U-boats were lost. Offsetting much of the technological advantage gained by the newly equipped U-boats was the serious loss of operational time at sea. In 1942 when the U-boats sailed from the Bay of Biscay they remained at sea sixty days, twenty days in transit and forty operational. In December 1944, adding one thousand miles to the trip just to reach operational zones, and without their milchkuhen for resupply, they could be at sea for only thirty-seven days, twenty-eight days in transit, and nine operational. The milchkuhen had become a favorite target for VLR bombers and effectively ceased to exist by this time. To maximize the amount of damage they could do, the submarines were restricted to the North Atlantic, operating as closely as possible to their Norwegian bases.[2]

Now the North became more dangerous than the central and South Atlantic, so the Admiralty reorganized shipping routes. This was a dramatic reversal of the former scenario when convoys hugged the northernmost Atlantic, sailing under the protective cover of Allied bases in Iceland and Greenland, avoiding the riskier passages through the central Atlantic and the notorious "black hole." The southern transatlantic convoy routes to England were opened for the first time since the fall of France in June 1940 and became the favored routes.

The air group based at Lagens was reinforced with Liberator bombers transferred from Iceland and Greenland. At the end of August the first large ocean convoy homeward bound from the South Atlantic arrived in England. This one was quickly followed by another large convoy in mid-September sailing from Halifax, Nova Scotia. Both convoys arrived safely and encountered no U-boats. Orders went out from the Admiralty that all convoys were to pass to the south of Ireland. "The wheels of war had indeed turned full cycle": the "black hole" of the Atlantic was now a golden carpet.

The superiority of air patrol over surface vessel reconnaissance was clearly demonstrated against the new schnorchel-equipped U-boats. Because the submarines no longer had to surface to air out their diesel exhaust, they expected to avoid detection by constantly moving underwater. The fumes were now continuously exhausted through the

schnorchel as they cruised submerged, hidden from surface observation. However, the diesel exhaust left a long distinctive trail easily
spotted from the air, but normally difficult to see from great distances
at sea. When the expanded air patrols from the Azores drew their first
blood on 26 September 1944, they owed it to diesel exhaust. One of the
newly transferred Liberator bombers flying in support of a convoy spotted the long smoky trail being emitted by U-871. A few well aimed
depth charges and the U-boat was quickly dispatched to the bottom.
The Allies had an unexpected advantage to counter the new German
technology; there was no way to conceal diesel exhaust from the air.

The air base on Santa Maria fulfilled all Allied expectations. Air
Transport Command operations were transferred from Lajes in April
1945 and remained in Santa Maria until 1 September 1946 when, in an
agreement with the Portuguese government, they returned to Lajes. The
Santa Maria air base proved to be one of the final nails in the coffin for
U-boat operations in the Atlantic and was, as promised, of great strategic value for the war in southeast Asia. The promise to make it a civilian
air base was also kept after the war. Today, however, the only scheduled
flights from the United States to use Azores air bases are of SATA, the
Azores airline, from Boston to Terceira, São Miguel, and Santa Maria.
Santa Maria, with the longest runway in the central Atlantic, affords aircraft such as the Concorde the only place to put down, which it did on
more than one occasion.

3 January: OKM Meeting with Hitler, Führer Headquarters

Admiral Dönitz, always the optimist, reviewed the dismal state of the
battle against Allied shipping but also held out the bright promise of a
new technology. After reporting on the unfavorable record of U-boat
versus enemy cargo sinkings, he discussed plans for the new *Seehund*
midget submarines. In his calculations he assumed that out of the
eighty scheduled to operate per month, fifty would be able to attack,
launching two torpedoes each for a total of one hundred torpedoes
against Allied shipping. Continuing the statistical fantasy, if twenty
percent of the torpedoes hit their targets, about one hundred thousand
tons would be sunk. With enough Seehunds in operation Allied tonnage destroyed would approach the levels of four years ago and might
just drive the enemy to seek a negotiated peace.

Dönitz also cheered up Hitler with encouraging reports from the schnorchel-equipped U-boats. They had found success in waters where the older U-boats had been driven out, such as the Irish Sea and the Bay of Biscay. His biggest headache now was Allied air attacks against submarine bases and shipyards and on U-boats en route to their distant zones of operations. Hitler promised to see to it himself that anti-aircraft reinforcements were sent to harbors where the submarines were based or being produced.

25 January: OKM Meeting with Hitler, Führer Headquarters

Dönitz was forced to admit his great disappointment, the Seehund midget submarines were not living up to expectations. Of the first ten that left Ijmuiden in Holland on 21 January, nine returned so far without having successfully launched their torpedoes. Although they operated well in tests carried out in the Baltic Sea, because of the severe weather conditions of the North Sea plus undisclosed technical defects "their mission was unsuccessful." Again putting the best spin he could on the obvious failure of the midget submarines, Dönitz emphasized the great discovery that enemy aircraft and naval forces, even with their superlative radar, could not see nor locate them. Further, he discovered that they were also "relatively immune to depth charges because they offer so little resistance because of their shape, that they are tossed aside like a cork instead of being damaged."[3]

Unfortunately for the German Navy, despite Hitler's promise to protect the U-boat yards with better anti-aircraft artillery, they were still pounded almost daily by Allied bombing. Skilled mechanical workers were not available, most had been drafted into the infantry as part of the last ditch effort to reinforce the decimated ground forces. Many working in the shipyards were "volunteer" laborers from the occupied countries and could be counted on to sabotage as much equipment on the submarines as they could get away with.[4]

28 January: OKM Meeting with Hitler, Führer Headquarters

This meeting pointed out the grim fact that Hitler was losing, or had already lost, all sense of reality. With the Navy down to its last battleship, with U-boat losses unsustainable, with Allied forces already across German frontiers everywhere and punching their way through the remnants of the Reichswehr, the twilight of the Thousand-Year Reich was obvious to almost everyone but the Führer. Admiral Dönitz brought up the need for icebreakers with winter coming on in full blast; they were needed to keep the sea lanes open to bring troops back to Germany from occupied northern Europe. The *Schliesen* was the last ship left in the Navy that was heavy enough to act as an icebreaker but Hitler wanted to use her to attack land targets in support of ground troops, so he ordered the 28-cm guns replaced with heavier guns. The Reichswehr at that point needed all the help it could get. The admiral reported the conversation with the Führer without comment: "The C-in-C Navy replies that since the loss of the *Schleswig-Holstein,* the *Schliesen* is the only ship in the Navy which can be used as a heavy ice-breaker. The Führer replies that after the war the Navy must build heavy icebreakers at once so that the German Reich will not be dependent again on begging icebreakers from Russia for use in German waters as before the war, or will have to use naval vessels for this task in wartime." At this low point in the war, the Führer's promise of ice-breakers in the postwar German Navy must have had a low priority on the admiral's list of things to worry about.[5]

The Azores were now a shining Allied beacon in the Atlantic. The protection afforded by the airfields kept the convoys coming, supplies and troops for the invasion were reaching England in massive quantities. With the maps of Santa Maria in hand and permission from Salazar to go ahead, the new airfield was built without problems, immediately fulfilling its promised role as a backup for Lagens and accommodating aircraft in transit to southeast Asia.

7 *May: North Atlantic*

A new U-boat, model XXI, was being assembled in Bremen, Hamburg, and Kiel but production was slowed by Allied bombing. Some thirty to fifty were allegedly nearly finished, and on 30 April U-2511 entered the North Atlantic, the only one ever released for active duty. It sailed from Bergen in Norway under the command of Lieutenant Commander Schnee, "an exceptionally brilliant captain" and with "an equally experienced Chief Engineer, Lieutenant Commander Suhren." Commander Schnee's final report of those few days at sea show that the technologically superior model XXI might have made things uncomfortable for the Allies had the war continued much longer. The problem for Germany was that on the day of the simulated battle test of the XXI, V-E Day (Victory in Europe) was declared. With Admiral Dönitz now acting Chancellor of Germany and about to sign an unconditional surrender, hostilities were ordered to end and all U-boats told to return to harbor. Schnee's optimistic report reads:

> First contact with the enemy was in the North Sea with a hunter killer–group. It was obvious that with its high underwater speed, the boat could not come to harm at the hands of these killer-groups. With a minor course alteration of 30°, proceeding submerged I evaded the group with the greatest ease. On receipt of order to cease fire on May 4 I turned back for Bergen; a few hours later I made contact with a British cruiser and several destroyers. I delivered a dummy underwater attack and in complete safety came within 500 yards of the cruiser. As I found out later during a conversation when I was being interrogated by the British in Bergen, my action had passed completely unnoticed. From my own experience, the boat was first class in attack and in defense; it was something completely new to any submariner.[6]

June–July 1945

Air traffic through the Azores did not taper off when hostilities ended in Europe, but if anything, became heavier than before. Aircraft and personnel were being redeployed to the United States for transfer to the Pacific for what was expected to be a long and bloody operation against Japan. The ATC organized two massive ferry operations, Operation White Project to bring aircraft back from Europe and the Mediterranean Theater of Operations (MTO) and Operation Green Project to bring personnel home.[7]

In one version of Operation White Project, fifty to sixty planes a day were to fly the northern Atlantic route from Valley in Wales through Iceland; twelve a day from Europe and five to twenty from MTO through Lajes; and twenty-five via the South Atlantic through Africa and Brazil. In June–July, 4,182 heavy bombers flew home, 459 via the Azores. Operation Green Project called for fifty thousand men a month to return home from Europe: 40 percent by the South Atlantic, 50 percent via Santa Maria, and 10 percent through Iceland and the North Atlantic. Those fortunate enough to follow the central Atlantic route from Casablanca took thirty-six hours to reach the United States, less than half the time required for their cohorts flying via the South Atlantic.

One of the better known returnees to follow the middle route was George McGovern, who went on to a distinguished career in politics as U.S. senator from South Dakota and Democratic presidential candidate against Richard Nixon. He had been awarded the Distinguished Flying Cross for service in Italy as a B-24 command pilot with the 15th Air Force. On 18 June with the war in Europe over and Japan still to be reckoned with, he was returning to the United States for R & R and redeployment to the Pacific theater.

McGovern left Cerignola Air Base near Rome with a full plane load headed to Marrakech, North Africa, then on to the Azores. About a hundred miles from Santa Maria, the navigator confessed that he was lost: "I think it's just temporary, I'll get a fix." When the B-24 arrived where the air base was supposed to be there was nothing but pure blue Atlantic Ocean. McGovern's thoughts were grim—he had survived thirty-five combat missions and was about to end his life because his navigator could not find the Azores. All was saved however when he raised the tower, got the correct heading, and soon spotted the islands. But what an airfield! "Here's this eleven thousand foot runway. We hadn't seen a runway like this since we left the States." McGovern, greatly relieved put the plane down, refueled for the long trip to Gander, and took off again headed west. Many other combat crews must have also been pleasantly surprised to spot this oasis in the Atlantic with a runway twice as long as anything they had flown out of in Europe.[8]

September 1945: Terceira

With the surrender of Germany in May, U.S. Navy antisubmarine operations in the Azores were ended. With only routine weather and police duties, units were slowly withdrawn and, finally, on 1 February 1946 CBMU-613, the last remnant of the 96th NCB, sailed home. By May 1946, only a token force remained on the island to sustain communications and the air facility, considerably fewer than the contingent of Air Force and Army Transportation Corps personnel who are still stationed at Lajes to maintain the air base.[9]

30 May 1946

A little more than a year after the termination of hostilities in Europe, an exchange of correspondence between Salazar and Ambassadors Herman Baruch of the United States and Sir Owen O'Malley of England set 3 June as the date of formal transfer of Lajes and Santa Maria to Portugal, but U.S. and British aircraft in transit serving the forces of occupation in Germany and Japan could continue to use the field for the next eighteen months. The following year, all military operations at the Santa Maria air base were transferred to Lajes, and Santa Maria became a purely commercial airfield, used by Pan American and TWA as a mid-Atlantic fueling stop.[10]

Postscript

The critical role played by the Azores bases in the defense of the free world did not end with the victory in the Battle of the Atlantic. After the war, Lajes started a new role serving first as an air base for U.S. and Portuguese forces, and now for NATO as well. The importance of the airfield as a link in the worldwide network which allows supplies, materiel, and personnel to be moved rapidly to trouble zones was first demonstrated during the Berlin Airlift—Operation Vittles—which ran from 24 June 1948 until 31 October 1949. A steady stream of food, coal, and other necessities were flown into the beleaguered city by 441 aircraft, 309 of which were U.S., made possible by the network of airfields. A rigid timetable was established allowing for nearly two million tons of cargo to be flown into Berlin, eventually breaking the Soviet blockade. The success of the airlift impressed upon Washington decision makers the importance of maintaining a U.S. presence in the Azores to support our armed forces worldwide and to sustain our readiness to quickly confront threats to world peace.[11]

Major General Laurence S. Kuter urged negotiating the long-term use of Lajes Air Base to insure its availability to NATO forces. Because Portugal was a member of NATO, in fact one of its founding members, he thought the agreement could be considered an important Portuguese contribution to the pact:

> Lajes Field is now and will continue to be the hub of air transport activities across the Atlantic. In the event of an emergency,

that transport load would be greatly increased and the requirement to support movements of combat aircraft would be considerable . . . Under any development which might arise in the
event of war, the overwhelming importance of this station is at
once apparent. It assumes almost as vital an air link between the
United States and Europe and/or Africa as did the Hawaiian
Islands to the Far East Theater in WW II. At the same time, the
vulnerability of its exposed position must be recognized. For
these reasons it is the opinion of this command that not only
should the present base at Lajes be improved so as to be fully
capable of supporting on short notice a greatly increased and
continuing load on its facilities, but that arrangement be made
for emergency use of Santa Maria and that every possibility be
explored to further develop the air supportability and defensibil-
ity of the island group as a whole.[12]

6 September 1951: Lisbon

On this date a long-term agreement was negotiated between the U.S.
secretary of defense and the Portuguese minister of national defense
whereby Lajes officially became a NATO air base shared by its member
nations. Portugal and the United States are full partners in the use of
the base, recognizing that Portugal is sovereign and owns the territory
and facilities. The United States did not actually sign on until 18 May
1984 but in 1957 Portugal announced it would continue to honor the
agreement. In 1984 about one thousand Americans and an equal number of Portuguese were stationed at Lajes under the overall command of
a Portuguese officer.

The agreement granted the United States full permission to utilize
both the Santa Maria and Lajes bases and to operate a communication
facility on São Miguel. Article II of the agreement had shades of the
great sticking point of World War II: sovereignty. Paragraph 1 stated
that "This agreement is concluded in recognition of Portugal's full sovereignty," that the defense of the Azores is the responsibility of the Portuguese Armed Forces, and that U.S. forces will, as a courtesy, fly the
flags of Portugal and the United States side by side in front of their
headquarters building. As allies forty years after the war, cooperation
and friendship were the key words—no more Portuguese dissimulating
or Yankee bullying.[13]

13 December 1971: Terceira

History continued to be made on the island of Terceira. Twenty-eight years after the landing of the 928th EAR and the 96th NCB, the president of Portugal, Marcello Caetano, presided over a meeting at Angra between President Nixon, President Pompidou of France, Mr. Andronikof of the USSR, and Major General Walters, national security adviser to President Nixon. The French delegation flew out from France on a Concorde landing in Santa Maria, the only airfield with a strip long enough for the supersonic jet. Although to judge by later events, the meeting diplomatically was a failure, the airfield of Santa Maria proved that the engineer planners did build it ahead of its time, that it would accommodate supersonic aircraft which did not even exist at the time it was built—the only airfield in the Atlantic that could do so.[14]

August 1990: Desert Storm

By 1990 U.S. representation at Lajes had grown considerably: 1,659 Army, Air Force, and Navy personnel and an equal number of civilians assigned to the base. The Portuguese contingent consisted of approximately fifteen hundred civilians under contract plus a number of Portuguese Air Force and support personnel. Although no U.S. airlines were flying into Lajes, the Portuguese National Airline (TAP) and the Azorean Airline (SATA) provided regular service from Lajes throughout the archipelago and overseas to Boston and Lisbon.[15]

Lajes supported Operation Desert Storm which started on 7 August to liberate Kuwait from Iraqi invaders. During the Operation as many as fifty-six aircraft were at the field at any one time in addition to the thirty-three tanker aircraft based there. Gen. Norman Schwarzkopf commanding Desert Storm passed through the base, as did many other distinguished persons including U.S. Senators and Congressmen. The commander of U.S. Forces Azores and the 1605th Military Airlift Support Wing, Brig. Gen. Charles C. Branhill Jr., stated, "At Lajes Field we were the first in action. We'll be the last ones done."

14 August 2001: Lajes

On 14 August 2001, the headline in the *New York Times* read, "Canadian Jet, Engines Dead, Lands Safely in the Azores." Air Transat Flight

236, carrying 291 passengers and 13 crew members from Toronto to Lisbon was prepared to put down in the Atlantic but managed to land instead at 5:46 A.M. at Lajes. The Airbus had lost all its power but glided to a safe landing, fortunate that trouble developed exactly over the only salvation available in the middle of the Atlantic.[16]

Two months later, on 9 October, Lisbon radio RDP Antenna 1 reported that the United States asked Portugal and other members of NATO for intelligence and security support in operations against the Taliban Regime in Afghanistan and Osama Bin-Laden's terrorist organization. In making the request, the United States specifically noted the need for expanded use of the Lajes Air Base and for unspecified intelligence cooperation. Defense Minister Rui Pena assured the United States of the full cooperation of Portugal and that the country was ready to participate in military operations, if requested to do so.[17]

A Government Accounting Office report on U.S. readiness summed up the importance today of Lajes and the need to maintain overseas air bases: "Previous mobility studies and actual experience in OPERATIONS DESERT SHIELD AND DESERT STORM demonstrate the importance of all six European bases to supporting contingency operations. Access to these bases is critical to maintain the Air Force ability to conduct mobility operations at planned wartime levels . . . in particular . . . Rhein Main, Torrejon and Lajes to both airlift and air refueling operations."[18]

15–16 March 2003: Terceira

U.S. President George W. Bush, British Prime Minister Tony Blair, and Spanish Prime Minister José Maria Aznar met on Terceira as guests of the prime minister of Portugal to discuss the crisis in Iraq. The leaders of the three countries issued an ultimatum to the UN Security Council, declaring diplomacy to win support for disarming Iraq would end on 17 March and that military action to depose Saddam Hussein, Iraq's president, would begin immediately with or without UN endorsement. In a front-page article, the *New York Times* described it as a "hurried meeting at an air base here on lush Terceira island in the eastern Atlantic."

Following the example of thirty years earlier by then President Richard Nixon, world leaders from both sides of the Atlantic found Terceira an ideal place geographically to meet. The Azores with its large airfields linking the Eastern and Western Hemispheres are only a relatively short hop from either side of the Atlantic.[19]

Postscript

Most books and movies on World War II have depicted its brutal and bloody land battles and have not paid much attention to the longest conflict of all—the battle against the U-boats. Not only was it fought every day of the war without let-up until V-E Day, but had it been lost, victory almost certainly would have gone to the Axis. Churchill set the record straight: "The battle of the Atlantic was the dominating factor all through the war. Never for one moment could we forget that everything happening elsewhere, on land, at sea, or in the air, depended ultimately on its outcome, and amid all other cares we viewed its changing fortunes day by day with hope or apprehension."[20] Winston Churchill was certain Hitler did not play his strongest hand, that if he had listened to his admirals, Germany might have won. By constantly promising to build up the U-boat fleet, but not following through; by ordering the Norwegian coast heavily patrolled awaiting an English invasion that never came; by choosing Operation Sea Lion and then Barbarossa over Felix; and by putting off landing in the Azores until it was too late, Hitler prevented Admirals Raeder and Dönitz from implementing their grand strategy. A naval blockade of England and an assault on Allied shipping in the Atlantic might have been enough to win the war for Germany.

An unappreciated hero in all this was Generalissimo Francisco Franco, dictator of Spain. He was the only national leader on the Continent to stand face to face with Hitler and reject his proposals. If Franco had given in to intimidation German armies would have marched into Iberia, laid siege to Gibraltar, and invaded North Africa and Portugal. His standing up to Hitler forced the German General Staff to go ahead with Operation Barbarossa and see their Reichswehr decimated on a grand scale. If Spain had agreed with the Nazis and Operation Felix succeeded, then the Mediterranean would have been closed, North Africa would have been in Axis hands long before the Allies arrived on the scene, and the Atlantic islands would have been U-boat and Luftwaffe bases. This would have added up to victory for Germany in the war at sea and possibly World War II itself.

An important factor in Germany's losing the Battle of the Atlantic was clearly Hitler's refusal to allocate more resources to the U-boat fleet. Of the 101 U-boats assigned to operations against convoys at any one time forty-one were in port for outfitting and repairs. Of the fifty-nine on duty at sea, most were in transit to or from their home pens, leaving a total of only nineteen actually on operations. Keeping in mind the enormous scale of destruction wreaked on Allied warships and cargo ships by only nineteen U-boats makes it hard to understand why Hitler did not listen to his admirals. If Dönitz had been given the submarine fleet he wanted, Allied shipping might have been wiped out of the seas considering that this small handful of boats sunk 2,449 cargo ship totaling 14,119,413 tons, sunk or damaged 193 warships including 8 aircraft and escort carriers, 15 battleships and light cruisers, and 77 destroyers and destroyer escorts.[21]

Losses to the U-boat fleet were also enormous, the greatest suffered by any arm of the combatant powers. According to Lundeberg, 772 U-boats were sunk in Atlantic-Arctic-British waters, 305 by shore-based aircraft alone, 28 by joint air-naval, 52 by bombing bases in port, and 17 by RAF mines, making a total of 49.9 percent destroyed by aircraft, mostly flying off land bases. At the war's end 156 U-boats surrendered to the Allies, and 221 were scuttled by their crews. Of the two remaining "pocket battleships," the *Prinz Eugen* was sunk in the atom bomb tests at Bikini whereas the *Nürnberg* was given to Russia in indemnity.[22]

Concerning the crews who served in the U-boats: of the 39,000 men, 27,491 went down with their ships and 5,000 more were taken prisoner. Although relatively few in number, Dönitz's men suffered what must be the greatest mortal losses of any single arm of any nation. Towards the end of the war, when Allied technology overwhelmed that of the Germans, when VLR bombers were blanketing almost the entire Atlantic and it was nearly suicidal for a U-boat even to show its schnorchel, crew after crew willingly stood out to sea, without hesitation or complaint.[23]

The Azores Islands played a key role in the battle against the U-boats. Although this is barely acknowledged in most official and unofficial histories of World War II, the facts speak otherwise. The final "Report of the United States Naval Facilities in the Azores" states:

> Allied acquisition of the Azores as a base was a decisive blow against German submarine warfare. This little cluster of Portuguese islands, two thirds of the way between our east coast ports and Gibraltar, when coupled with Bermuda and Newfoundland, put the North Atlantic convoy route within range of land-based bomber protection over the entire transoceanic journey. The development of auxiliary aircraft carriers which could release planes for convoy protection overcame the submarine

menace to some extent and for a time after their appearance there was a lull in the undersea attacks. Then, however, Nazi U-boats returned in force and proved that they could still inflict heavy damage on our shipping. True, they lost a prohibitive number of undersea vessels, but that was cold comfort when our own losses were totaled. Carrier aviation, moreover, was subject to a three-fold enemy threat: from the air, from underseas, and from the surface of the sea when German raiders were on the loose. Land-based planes in antisubmarine warfare were, on the other hand, to all intents and purposes menaced only by opposing aviation. Finally, and most important of all, the number of planes that could be sent into the air from our new mid-ocean landing field far exceeded that which could be sent up from any carrier group.[24]

ABBREVIATIONS

Note: "Homeward" refers to England.

ABC	American-British Commonwealth Conversations containing a "United States–British Commonwealth Joint Basic War Plan"
ATC	Army Air Forces Transport Command
CCS or CCOS	Combined Chiefs of Staff, Anglo-American military chiefs
C-in-C	Commander in Chief, usually of the German Navy
COS	British Chiefs of Staff
CVE	Small aircraft carrier convoy escorts
EAB	Engineer Aviation Battalion
EAR	Engineer Aviation Regiment
FRUS	Foreign Relations United States
GUF	United States fast and slow troop convoys to and from North Africa
GUS	United States freight convoys to and from North Africa
HG	Homeward Gibraltar convoys
HX	Main homeward convoys from North America
HXF, HXM, HXS	Home fast, medium, and slow North Atlantic convoys replacing SC April 1944. SC convoys restarted October 1944.
JCS or JCOS	American Joint Chiefs of Staff
KMS UK	Convoys to and from Gibraltar and through the Mediterranean
LCM	Landing Craft, Mechanized
LCV	Landing Craft, Vehicle
LSA	Landing Ship, Assault
LSI	Landing Ship, Infantry

LSI-L	See LSA
LST	Landing Ship, Tank
MAR	Mid-Atlantic Ridge
MKS	Convoys to and from Gibraltar and through the Mediterranean
NARA	National Archives and Records Administration, United States
NATS	Naval Air Transport Service
NCB	Naval Construction Battalion, "Seabees"
OB	Main outward-bound North American convoys from Liverpool
OKM	*Oberkommando der Marina,* Supreme Commander in Chief German Navy
OKW	*Oberkommando der Wehrmacht,* Supreme Commander in Chief German Army and Chief of Staff of the Armed Forces
ONF	Main outward bound fast convoys with through A/S escort, replacing OB July 1941
ONS	Main outward bound slow convoys with through A/S escort, replacing OB July 1941
POE	Port of Embarkation
SC	Slow homeward Atlantic convoys, started August 1940
SL	Homeward West Africa convoys
UGF	United States fast and slow troop convoys to and from North Africa
UGS	United States freight convoys to and from North Africa
VLR	Very long range aircraft

NOTES

CHAPTER 1. THE BLACK HOLE IN THE ATLANTIC

1. The term *United Nations* was originally used during World War II to denote those countries that were allied against the Axis powers (Germany, Japan, Italy). A conference at Dumbarton Oaks in Washington, D.C. (21 August–7 October 1944) was the earliest attempt to permanently establish the current United Nations. The proposals, later discussed and more clearly outlined at the Yalta Conference in February 1945 by Winston Churchill, Joseph Stalin, and Franklin Delano Roosevelt, formed the basis of negotiations at the United Nations Conference on International Organization, held in San Francisco. The United Nations Charter was signed at the conference and came into force on 24 October 1945. The term *United Nations* in this book is used in its original sense. See *Encyclopedia Britannica*, CD97, version 1.1., s.v. "United Nations."

2. During World War II the Allies referred to the field as Lagens or LaGens but in Portuguese today it is *Lajes*.

3. Craven and Cate, *Services Around the World*, 307.

4. Lundeberg, "American Anti-Submarine Operations," 262.

5. http://www.cbcph.navy.mil/museum/Seabee History/battalions.html.

6. National Archives and Records Administration, Modern Military Records and State Department Files 811.34553, "Efforts of the United States to Obtain from Portugal Certain Military Privileges in the Azores."

7. Guill, *History of the Azores*, 1–31.

8. Azores Islands Web site; Beaver, *Activities of the NCBs in the Azores*, 2.

9. Guill, *History of the Azores*, 22–28.

10. Zitellini, "Lisbon Earthquake."

11. Guill, *History of the Azores*, 19.

12. Ibid., 17–22.

13. Atkinson, *British Contributions*, 6.

14. Vintras, *Portuguese Connection*, 109–115.
15. *Encyclopedia Britannica*, CD97, version 1.1, s.v. "Portugal."
16. Bryans, *Azores*, 19–22.
17. Mees, *Histoire de la découverte des iles Açores*.
18. Angra was later renamed Angra do Heroïmo to commemorate the island's heroic resistance to invading Spaniards in 1580–82. Praia was also renamed Praia da Victória, now spelled Praia da Vitória, in honor of the victorious battle by local Portuguese farmers over the Spanish invaders.
19. Bryans, *Azores*, 19–22.
20. Wignall, *Project Revenge*, 19.
21. Bryans, *Azores*, 41–42.
22. Guill, *History of the Azores*, 504–9.
23. Herwig, *Politics of Frustration*, 42–54.

CHAPTER 2. THE WAR BEGINS:
PORTUGAL OFFERS SUCCOR, 1930–1940

1. Although commonly referred to as prime minister, António de Oliveira Salazar's official titles were President of the Council of Ministers and Minister for Foreign Affairs of Portugal.
2. Kay, *Salazar*, 128.
3. Ibid., 176.
4. Ibid., 123.
5. Matloft and Snell, *United States Army in World War II*, 5.
6. Ibid., 44–45.
7. Leighton and Coakley, *United States Army in World War II*, 28.
8. Ibid., 56–57, 73–74.
9. Jacobsen and Smith, *World War II Policy*, 65–68.
10. Four army columns marched on Madrid during the Spanish Revolution; the fifth was named for the pro-Franco Nationalists operating covertly within the city.
11. As the British did in the War of 1812.
12. Jacobsen and Smith, *World War II Policy*, 65–68.
13. Churchill, *Second World War*, 2:567.
14. *Führer Conferences*, 110–12.
15. Ibid., 65–66, 73–79.
16. Conn and Fairchild, *United States Army in World War II*, 71.
17. Churchill, *Second World War*, 2:654.
18. *Führer Conferences*, 131.
19. Waller, *Unseen War in Europe*.
20. Dönitz, *Memoirs*, 277; Vintras, *Portuguese Connection*, 57.
21. Churchill, *Second World War*, 2:654, n. 677.

22. *Führer Conferences*, 81; Conn and Fairchild, *United States Army in World War II*, 73.
23. Churchill, *Second World War*, 2:654, n. 677.
24. Vintras, *Portuguese Connection*, 59–60.
25. Churchill, *Second World War*, 2:654, n. 677.
26. Waller, *Unseen War*, 155–58.
27. Ibid.
28. Guill, *History of the Azores*, 512.
29. Dönitz, *Memoirs*, 151. The UA had been built for the Turkish navy but was not delivered when war broke out.
30. Guill, *History of the Azores*, 513.
31. Herwig, *Politics of Frustration*, 211–13.
32. Conn and Fairchild, *United States Army in World War II*, 83–84.
33. Churchill, *War Papers*, 765.
34. *Führer Conferences*, 141–43.
35. Conn and Fairchild, *United States in World War II*, 76–80.
36. Ibid.
37. Herwig, *Politics of Frustration*, 222–23.
38. Compton, *Swastika and the Eagle*, 214.
39. Leighton and Coakley, *United States Army in World War II*, 42–43.
40. Conn and Fairchild, *United States Army in World War II*, 83–88.
41. Herwig, *Politics of Frustration*, 212.
42. Ibid., 212–14.
43. *Führer Conferences*, 146–47.
44. Ibid., 149–50.
45. Ibid.
46. Ibid.
47. Churchill, *Second World War*, 2:933.
48. Ibid.
49. Ibid., 1011.
50. He estimated two years.
51. Hull, *Memoirs*, 921.
52. *Führer Conferences*, 160–63.
53. Jacobsen and Smith, *World War II Policy*, 132–35.
54. Ibid.

CHAPTER 3. THE VIEW FROM WASHINGTON,
JANUARY–MAY 1941

1. Hull, *Memoirs*, 919.
2. *Führer Conferences*, 134.
3. Jacobsen and Smith, *World War II Policy*, 193.

4. Hull, *Memoirs*, 922–23.

5. National Archives and Records Administration, State Department Doc. 741.53/110 PS/GC.

6. Herwig, *Politics of Frustration*, 222.

7. Kay, *Salazar*, 161.

8. Guill, *History of the Azores*, 514.

9. Personal communication from local fishermen.

10. Vintras, *Portuguese Connection*, chapter 2.

11. National Archives and Records Administration, State Department Doc. 853B.00/35 PS/DB.

12. A month later, on 10 April, Roosevelt ordered naval forces to patrol the waters around the Azores.

13. National Archives and Records Administration, State Department Doc. 853B.00/35 PS/DB.

14. Leighton and Coakley, *United States Army in World War II*, 60.

15. Chester, *Azores*, 167.

16. Jacobsen and Smith, *World War II Policy*, 149–50.

17. Ibid.

18. Ibid.

19. Hull, *Memoirs*, 935–36.

20. Guill, *History of the Azores*, 514.

21. Leighton and Coakley, *United States Army in World War II*, 60–61.

22. Ibid.

23. Getúlio Vargas, president of Brazil.

24. Hull, *Memoirs*, 940–41.

25. FRUS 1941, Europe, 2:836–37, Doc. 1930.

26. Ibid.

27. Stevens, "Franklin Delano Roosevelt and the Azores Dilemma," 649–50.

28. *Encyclopedia Britannica*, CD97, version 1.1.

29. Hull, *Memoirs*, 940–41.

30. Kay, *Salazar*, 161.

31. FRUS 1941, Europe, 2:837–39, Doc. 1599.

32. Ibid.

33. Hull, *Memoirs*, 941.

34. FRUS 1941, Europe, 2:839–40, Doc. 1471.

35. Ibid., 840–41.

36. Stevens, "Franklin Delano Roosevelt and the Azores Dilemma," 647.

37. *New York Times*, 7 May 1941, 12. (Quoted in Stevens, "Franklin D. Roosevelt and the Azores Dilemma.")

38. Craven and Cate, *Services Around the World*, 87.

39. FRUS 1941, Europe, 2:841, Doc. 853B.014/16.

40. FRUS 1941, Europe, 2:841–42, Doc. 253.

41. National Archives and Records Administration, State Department Doc. 853B.014/13 PS/HH.

42. Kennan, *Memoirs*, 143–44.

43. Gannon, *Operation Drumbeat*, 95.

44. FRUS 1941, Europe, 2:842–43; European War 1939/11895.

CHAPTER 4. THE UNITED STATES GOES TO WAR,
MAY–DECEMBER 1941

1. Dönitz, *Memoirs*, 296–98.

2. Roskill, *Offensive*, pt. 2, 364.

3. Stevens, "Franklin Delano Roosevelt and the Azores Dilemma," 641–56.

4. Leighton and Coakley, *United States Army in World War II*, 52. Chief Naval Operations and Chief of Staff statement, 27 January 1941, WPD4402–94, quoted in idem.

5. Leighton and Coakley, *United States Army in World War II*, 82.

6. Conn and Fairchild, *United States Army in World War II*, 5–15; Leighton and Coakley, *United States Army in World War II*, 60.

7. Dönitz, *Memoirs*, 188.

8. Chester, *Azores*, 162.

9. National Archives and Records Administration, War Plans Division WPD 4422–3, WPD 4422–4.

10. Conn and Fairchild, *United States Army in World War II*, 16–26.

11. D-Day is the unnamed day of which a military operation is launched. Although 6 June 1944, the date the Allied forces invaded France, is the most famous, every World War II operation had its own D-Day.

12. National Archives and Records Administration, State Department Doc. 381, Azores JCOS, letter, Admiral Stark to General Marshall, 23 May 1941, G-4/31832.

13. Leighton and Coakley, *United States Army in World War II*, 70.

14. Churchill, *Second World War*, 2:1077.

15. Hull, *Memoirs*, 944–45.

16. Ibid., 946–47.

17. *Führer Conferences*, 219.

18. Ibid., 196–200.

19. Dönitz, *Memoirs*, 228–29.

20. Dallek, *Franklin Delano Roosevelt and American Foreign Policy*, 264–65.

21. FRUS 1941, Europe, 2:843–44.

22. The Portuguese Crown Prince Dom Pedro liked the country so much that he refused to return to Lisbon after the war and stayed in Brazil to become the country's first emperor.

23. FRUS 1941, Europe, 2:844–45, Doc. 853B.014/36.

24. Ibid., 846.
25. Ibid., 847.
26. National Archives and Records Administration, State Department Doc. FW853B.014/27 PS/HH.
27. That is, during the entire tenure of Franklin D. Roosevelt as president.
28. National Archives and Records Administration, State Department Doc. FW853B.014/27 PS/HH.
29. Ibid.
30. National Archives and Records Administration, State Department Doc. 853B.014/42 PS/LDP.
31. Leighton and Coakley, *United States Army in World War II*, 75.
32. National Archives and Records Administration, War Plans Division, 3 November 1941, WPD 4161–21, Memorandum General Maloney for War Plans Division.
33. National Archives and Records Administration, State Department Doc. 853B.014/30 PS/PJ, 18 June 1941, "Defense of the Azores," participants: British Minister, Mr. N. M. Butler; Undersecretary, Mr. Welles.
34. FRUS 1941, Europe, 2:850–51; State Department Doc. 853B.014/30.
35. Herwig, *Politics of Frustration*, 224.
36. Stevens, "Franklin Delano Roosevelt and the Azores Dilemma," 651.
37. FRUS 1941, Europe, 2:851; Telegram 853B.014/40a.
38. *Führer Conferences*, 221.
39. Ibid.
40. Stevens, "Franklin Delano Roosevelt and the Azores Dilemma," 652.
41. Ibid.
42. FRUS 1941, Europe, 2:851–53; State Department Doc. 853B.014/41a.
43. Ibid., 853–56; State Department Doc. 853B.014/414/5.
44. *Führer Conferences*, 222–25.
45. Herwig, *Politics of Frustration*, 221–23.
46. Hull, *Memoirs*, 974–76.
47. Stevens, "Franklin Delano Roosevelt and the Azores Dilemma," 653; Herwig, *Politics of Frustration*, 160–61.
48. Herwig, *Politics of Frustration*, 196.
49. *Führer Conferences*, 166–67.
50. Ibid.
51. Leighton and Coakley, *United States Army in World War II*, 117–18.
52. Michael Gannon, in *Operation Drumbeat*, argues that the U-boat assault during 1942 "constituted a greater strategic setback for the Allied war effort than did the defeat at Pearl Harbor—particularly in that the loss of naval vessels destroyed . . . at Hawaii [did not affect the decisive carrier battles at Coral Sea and Midway] whereas the loss of nearly 400 hulls and cargoes . . . threatened both to sever Great Britain's lifeline and to cripple American war industries" (xviii).

53. *Führer Conferences*, 245.
54. Guill, *History of the Azores*, 514.
55. National Archives and Records Administration, State Department Doc. 741.53/8-2442 CS/D.
56. Randolph Churchill, *Road to Victory*, 23; Churchill, *War Papers*, chapter 2.
57. Churchill, *Second World War*, 3:588.
58. Herwig, *Politics of Frustration*, 230.
59. National Archives and Records Administration, Azores JCOS Doc. 381, memorandum to Franklin Delano Roosevelt #A82205–A2206.
60. FRUS 1941, Europe, 2:856–59.
61. Ibid.
62. Jacobsen and Smith, *World War II Policy*, 193–94.
63. Hinsley and Simkins, *Security and Counter Intelligence*, 176.

CHAPTER 5. THE U-BOATS' HAPPY WAR, 1942

1. Dönitz, *Memoirs*, 202–4.
2. Gannon, *Operation Drumbeat*.
3. Hinsley et al., *Influence and Strategy Operations*, 176; Roskill, *Offensive*, pt. 2, 101–2.
4. *Führer Conferences*, 263.
5. National Archives and Records Administration, State Department Doc. 853H.00/5 PS/MM.
6. Ibid.
7. Ibid.
8. Ibid.
9. FRUS 1942, 2:232–41.
10. National Archives and Records Administration, State Department file 853H.00/5 PS/MM.
11. Ibid.
12. Stratton, "Germany's Secret Naval Supply Service," 1085.
13. *Führer Conferences*, 279–80.
14. Kennedy, "Victory at Sea," 70.
15. Grove, *Defeat of the Enemy Attack*, 38–39.
16. Dönitz, *Memoirs*, 205–7.
17. Hinsley and Simkins, *Security and Counter Intelligence*, 159–62.
18. *Führer Conferences*, 284–85.
19. Dönitz, *Memoirs*, 228–29.
20. Vintras, *Portuguese Connection*, 41–42.
21. FRUS 1942, 5:664–65, telegram 7792.
22. Hinsley et al., *Influence and Strategy Operations*, 2:232.
23. FRUS 1942, 5:665.
24. Dönitz, *Memoirs*, 288–93; *Führer Conferences*, 290–93.

25. Guill, *History of the Azores*, 515–19.
26. FRUS 1942, 2:239–41.
27. Ibid.
28. Ibid.
29. *Führer Conferences*, 294.
30. Hinsley et al., *Influence and Strategy Operations*, 2:476.
31. Ibid.
32. Dönitz, *Memoirs*, 272.
33. National Archives and Records Administration, State Department file 853B.20/68 PS/PN.
34. Gannon, *Black May*, 103; Hull, *Memoirs*, 1190–94; *Führer Conferences*, 298–306; Waller, *Unseen War*, 27, 242–70.
35. Hinsley et al., *Influence and Strategy Operations*, 2:481.
36. *Führer Conferences*, 298–301.
37. Ibid.
38. Ibid.
39. Ibid.
40. Ibid.
41. Ibid., 302–5.
42. Hough, *Longest Battle*, 268–69.
43. Ibid.
44. Hinsley et al., *Influence and Strategy Operations*, 2:553.

CHAPTER 6. THE TRIDENT CONFERENCE,
JANUARY–JULY 1943

1. Eden, *Reckoning*, 390; Hull, *Memoirs*, 1195.
2. Lundeberg, "American Anti-Submarine Operations," 449–52.
3. Dönitz, *Memoirs*, 427.
4. Roskill, *Offensive*, pt. 2, 370.
5. Churchill, *War Papers*, 2:529.
6. Ibid., 218.
7. *Encyclopedia Britannica*, CD97, s.v., "world wars"; Hinsley et al., *Influence and Strategy Operations*, 2:565.
8. Gannon, *Black May*, 2.
9. FRUS 1943, 5:653, telegram #65.
10. Ibid., 654.
11. Hull, *Memoirs*; Gannon, *Black May*, 109; Chester, "The Azores," 170–71.
12. *Führer Conferences*, 306–8, 35; Gannon, *Black May*, 107.
13. Dönitz, *Memoirs*, 299–300.
14. Ibid., 166–67.
15. FRUS 1943, 5:654, telegram 401.
16. FRUS 1943, 5:654–56, telegrams 463, 491; 2:548.

17. Vintras, *Portuguese Connection*, 163–66.

18. Ibid., 43. Emphases in original.

19. Lundeberg, "American Anti-Submarine Operations," 5–8; Gannon, *Black May*, 158; Morison, *Atlantic Battle Won*, 27–28.

20. Ibid.

21. Gannon, *Black May*, 2.

22. Randolph Churchill, *War Papers*, 7:412. 21 March 1943, Trident, Minutes of the fourth meeting held at the White House. Most Secret Cabinet Papers 99/22, "Operation Lifebelt, Occupation of the Portuguese islands of the Azores. Essential to the conduct of the U-boat war" also set target date for cross-Channel landings as 1 May 1944.

23. A regiment normally consists of four battalions. For this operation, for the 928th one was deemed sufficient.

24. Kemp, *History of the 928th Engineer Aviation Regiment*, 1.

25. Craven and Cate, *Services Around the World*, 239–75.

26. *Führer Conferences*, 316–19.

27. National Archives and Records Administration, "History of the 928th Engineer Aviation Regiment."

28. Gannon, *Black May*, 282, 348.

29. Craven and Cate, *Services Around the World*, 88.

30. Vintras, *Portuguese Connection*, 45–46.

31. FRUS 1943, 2:527–28. Algiers Cable 735 written by Robert D. Murphy, U.S. political adviser, staff of supreme allied commander, Mediterranean theater and personal representative of Franklin Delano Roosevelt in North Africa with the rank of minister.

32. *Führer Conferences*, 320–27.

33. Trident—National Archives and Records Administration, CCS #225, 15 May 1943, JCS Azores files A37522-A37527; Minutes of the fourth meeting held in the White House, 21 May 1943. Most Secret Cabinet Papers 99/22; Churchill, *War Papers*, 412; Guill, *History of the Azores*, 521–24.

34. Code name for the invasion of Sicily.

35. Vintras, *Portuguese Connection*, 163–66.

36. Bryant, *Turn of the Tide*, 665–67.

37. Coakley and Leighton, *United States Army in World War II*, 175.

38. National Archives and Records Administration, JCS/Azores file A38337.

39. Ibid.

40. Eden, *Memoirs*, 392.

41. Hinsley et al., *British Intelligence*, vol. 3, pt. 1, 211; Gannon, *Black May*, 330.

42. Ibid.

43. Ibid.

44. Dönitz, *Memoirs*, 233.

45. Ibid.

46. *Führer Conferences*, 334–35.
47. The "embassy" was technically a Legation, several steps lower in prestige, and headed by a minister and not a true "ambassador."
48. Kennan, *Memoirs*, 143; FRUS 1943, 2:547–48, 1964.
49. Ibid.
50. FRUS 1943, item # 6116, 4 October 1943, 547.
51. Author's note: from personal experience, anyone arriving on a new military base without inoculation records, an unfortunately frequent occurrence, had to repeat the complete inoculation series.
52. *96th NCB Cruise Book*.
53. Germinsky, *Fighting Seabees*.
54. Lundeberg, "American Anti-Submarine Operations," 63; Roskill, *Offensive*, pt. 1, 2–3.
55. Hinsley et al., *British Intelligence*, vol. 3, pt. 1, 211–12.
56. Roskill, *Offensive*, pt. 1, 16.
57. *Führer Conferences*, 329–30.
58. Ibid., 338–39.
59. A parody on "Pistol Packing Mama," a popular song of the day.

CHAPTER 7. CHURCHILL LOWERS THE BOOM,
JUNE–SEPTEMBER 1943

1. Lundeberg, "American Anti-Submarine Operations," 62–64.
2. Guill, *History of the Azores*, 519–29.
3. Woodward, *British Foreign Policy*, 379f.
4. Guill, *History of the Azores*, 523–24.
5. Portugal, *Documentos Relativos*, 1–9, author's translation from the Portuguese.
6. Ibid.
7. Ibid.
8. Ibid.
9. Ibid.
10. Kay, *Salazar*, 168.
11. Portugal, *Documentos Relativos*, 10–12, author's translation.
12. Portugal, *Documentos Relativos*, 13; Woodward, *British Foreign Policy*, 382.
13. Ibid.
14. The principal reference for much of this section is Vintras, *Portuguese Connection*, pt. 1.
15. National Archives and Records Administration, State Department file 741.53/118.
16. FRUS 1943, 533; #741.53/137: Telegram.
17. Ibid., 534–35; #741.53/118: Telegram.

18. Ibid., 535–36; 30 June 1943, item 299; Bryant, *Turn of the Tide*, 666–67.
19. National Archives and Records Administration, JCOS-Azores file A82203, A84558, 15 October 1943; A37522, 15 May 1943.
20. Vintras, *Portuguese Connection*, 61–62.
21. Churchill, *War Papers*, 7:441; National Archives and Records Administration, State Department Doc. 741.53/7*f*1543 O/LE, telegrams #363, 364, 450. PM Personal Minute M. 514/3, 24 July 1943.
22. National Archives and Records Administration, JCOS-Azores File 381.
23. National Archives and Records Administration, State Department file 741.53/120.
24. Post-Sicily.
25. Vintras, *Portuguese Connection*, 68.
26. Eden, *Reckoning*, 400.
27. Portugal, *Documentos Relativos*, 19–23, author's translation.
28. Guill, *History of the Azores*, 525.
29. Vintras, *Portuguese Connection*, 72–73.
30. Admiral Botelho Sousa, the major-general Armada.
31. National Archives and Records Administration, JCOS Azores file A82204.
32. National Archives and Records Administration, State Department file 741.53/121 PS/SF; file 741.53/121 PS/LF.
33. Code word for the Azores.
34. National Archives and Records Administration, State Department file 741.53/121 PS/SF; file 741.53/121 PS/LF.
35. National Archives and Records Administration, State Department file 741.53/123 PS/DF.
36. National Archives and Records Administration, JCOS Azores file A83305. Memorandum is shown as it appears in the file.
37. National Archives and Records Administration, JCOS Azores file, Azores National Defense prepared by the Western European Branch, Europe-African Group, I. G. (Inspector General).
38. Grove, *Defeat of the Enemy Attack*, 42, plan 15; Lundeberg, "American Anti-Submarine Operations," 62–63.

CHAPTER 8. THE BRITISH ARRIVE,
SEPTEMBER–OCTOBER 1943

1. Hull, *Memoirs*, 1231–33.
2. Ibid., 1232–35; National Archives and Records Administration, State Department file 741.53/8*f*2043 OS/LE.
3. Lundeberg, "American Anti-Submarine Operations," 253; Grove, *Defeat of the Enemy Attack*, 118–19.
4. Guill, *History of the Azores*, 524–25.
5. Roskill, *Offensive*, pt. 1, 4, 33; Guill, *History of the Azores*, 524–25.

6. Kemp, *History of the 928th Engineer Aviation Regiment*, 5.

7. *Führer Conferences*, 368–69.

8. National Archives and Records Administration, JCOS Azores file, Directive J. S. M. 1182.

9. Roskill, *Offensive*, pt. 1, 47; Slessor, *Central Blue*, 488.

10. Vintras, *Portuguese Connection*, 86–87.

11. National Archives and Records Administration, State Department file 741.53/124B PS/BK; Kennan, *Memoirs*, 147–48; FRUS 1943, 2:551–52.

12. Ibid.

13. National Archives and Records Administration, State Department file 741.53/128 PS/ATB.

14. FRUS 1943, 2:547–48.

15. Ibid., 550–51.

16. National Archives and Records Administration, JCOS Azores file, A81305-A81308, JCS 319/5.

17. Ibid., A82202.

18. Ibid., A82204.

19. Ibid., A81309–A81310.

20. Kemp, *History of the 928th Engineer Aviation Regiment*, 6.

21. Hull, *Memoirs*, 1231.

22. National Archives and Records Administration, State Department file 741.53/133 PC/CF.

23. Harrison must have meant October.

24. National Archives and Records Administration, State Department file 741.53/137 PC/CF.

25. National Archives and Records Administration, State Department file 741.53/140 PS/ATB.

26. The statement in the treaty reads, "as true and faithful Friends they shall henceforth reciprocally be Friends to Friends and Enemies to Enemies and shall assist, maintain, and uphold each other mutually by sea and by land against all Men that may live or die."

27. National Archives and Records Administration, State Department file 741.53/142 PS/RA.

28. Hull, *Memoirs*, 1340.

29. FRUS 1943, 2:554–56.

30. *Führer Conferences*, 142–49.

31. Lundeberg, "American Anti-Submarine Operations," 263–64.

32. Craven and Cate, *Services Round the World*, 87–88.

33. National Archives and Records Administration, JCOS Azores file A84558, JCS Secret Memorandum 319/7.

34. FRUS 1943, 2:556–61, 558.

35. Ibid.

36. Undated report "Naval Facilities in the Azores" in the Command Histo-

rian's Office, Naval Construction Battalion Center, Port Hueneme, California, from the Director, Atlantic Division, Bureau of Yards and Docks.

37. National Archives and Records Administration, State Department file 741.53/145 PS/CF.

38. Ibid.

39. Kennan, *Memoirs*, ch. 6; Portugal, *Documentos Relativos*, 30–31 (English and Portuguese).

40. Kennan, *Memoirs*, 156.

41. Ibid., 160.

42. National Archives and Records Administration, JCOS/Azores file 381.

43. National Archives and Records Administration, State Department file 811.34553B/41c.

44. Ibid.

45. FRUS 1943, 2:562–64.

CHAPTER 9. SAILING ORDERS,
NOVEMBER–DECEMBER 1943

1. Undated report, Command Historian's Office, Naval Construction Battalion Center, Port Hueneme, California, 4.

2. Guill, *History of the Azores*, 526–27.

3. Vintras, *Portuguese Connection*, 93.

4. Lundeberg, "American Anti-Submarine Operations," 260–62.

5. Roskill, *Offensive*, pt. 1, 37–56.

6. Kemp, *History of the 928th Engineering Aviation Regiment*.

7. Grove, *Defeat of the Enemy Attack*, 118.

8. Guill, *History of the Azores*, 527–29.

9. Ibid.

10. National Archives and Records Administration, State Department file 811.34553B/39, O. S. Colclough, Office of the Chief of Naval Operations to Mr. George, State Department, 26 November 1943.

11. National Archives and Records Administration, State Department file 811.34553B/41c, Freeman to Franklin Delano Roosevelt, 8 November 1943.

12. Lundeberg, " American Anti-Submarine Operations," 274.

13. National Archives and Records Administration, JCOS Azores file A84558; Lundeberg, "American Anti-Submarine Operations," 249–50.

14. National Archives and Records Administration, War Department General Staff, Operations Division Memo re: Land Airport Facilities in the Azores to Colonel McBride from Lieutenant Colonel J. K. Woolnouth, Chief Policy Section.

15. FRUS 1943, 2:566–67.

16. National Archives and Records Administration, State Department Azores file 811.34553B/32.

17. FRUS 1943, 2:564–65, 569–70.
18. Guill, *History of the Azores*, 530–31; National Archives and Records Administration, State Department file 811.34553E/32C PS/RIR.
19. *New York Times*, 28 November 1943, 1.
20. National Archives and Records Administration, State Department file 811.34553B/33.
21. National Archives and Records Administration, JCOS Azores file A99798, 1 December 1943.
22. Vintras, *Portuguese Connection*, 91.
23. National Archives and Records Administration, JCOS Azores file A99798, 1 December 1943.
24. Kemp, *History of the 928th Engineering Aviation Regiment*, 8.
25. National Archives and Records Administration, JCOS Azores file A99811-A99812; FRUS 1943, 2:573–76.
26. FRUS 1943, 2:576–77.
27. National Archives and Records Administration, State Department file 811.34553B/36.
28. Craven and Cate, *Services Around the World*, 88, 102–3; National Archives and Records Administration, State Department file message 3151 Norweb to Secretary of State, 31 December 1943.
29. National Archives and Records Administration, State Department Azores file 811.34553B/48.
30. Verbal communication to author.
31. National Archives and Records Administration, JCOS Azores File 381.
32. Naval Construction Battalion Center Command Historian's Office, Port Hueneme, California.
33. *Führer Conferences*, 373–74.
34. Kemp, *History of the 928th Engineering Aviation Regiment*, 10.
35. National Archives and Records Administration, JCOS Azores file 811.34553R/46 1/2.
37. National Archives and Records Administration, State Department Records Memorandum, 15 January 1944 Division of European Affairs.
38. Ibid.
39. National Archives and Records Administration, State Department file 811.34553B/36.
40. FRUS 1943, 2:577–79.
41. Kemp, *History of the 928th Engineering Aviation Regiment*, 7.
42. National Archives and Records Administration, State Department file 811.34553B/46 3/4. Words underlined are underlined in the original.
43. National Archives and Records Administration, State Department file 811.34553B/420. Arnold's original message to Portal #A-5070 was sent on 23 December. This copy transmitted by Secretary Hull to the Legation is dated two days later.

44. Ibid.
45. National Archives and Records Administration, State Department file 811.34553B/47 1/2.
46. Guill, *History of the Azores*, 532.
47. Report Lieutenant J. F. Beaver to Director, North Atlantic Division, Bureau of Yards and Docks, 5 June 1946, #24234, ATL-4 2, entitled "A Report of the activities of the Construction Battalions in the Azores . . ." in Naval Construction Battalion Historian's Office, Port Hueneme, California.
48. FRUS 1943, 2:579–81.
49. Ibid., 580–81.
50. Ibid.
51. FRUS 1944, 4:2.
52. Vintras, *Portuguese Connection*, 94.
53. Groves, *Defeat of the Enemy Attack*, plot 32, plans 16–6, 7; 17–6, 7.
54. Lundeberg, " American Anti-Submarine Operations," 264.

CHAPTER 10. ALMOST WAR WITH PORTUGAL,
JANUARY–MARCH 1944

1. Stratton, "Germany's Secret Supply Service," 1953; Lundeberg, "American Anti-Submarine Operations," 510.
2. *New York Times*, 2 May 2001, 10TR.
3. Lundeberg, "American Anti-Submarine Operations," 262.
4. The numbers refer to the barrel diameter, 5″ and length, 38″.
5. RG24, Records of Bureau of Naval Personnel, Smooth log of Naval Armed Guard aboard the USS *Abraham Lincoln*, 4 April 1944, Lieutenant (JG) Ross G. Partlow Jr., USNR; RG38 Records of U.S. Tenth Fleet Ship Movement Card for USS *Abraham Lincoln*. Lieutenant Beaver's report to Director, North Atlantic Division, Bureau of Yards and Docks, 5 June 1946, #24234, ATL-4 2, entitled "A Report of the activities of the Construction Battalions in the Azores . . ." states only 475 Seabees debarked.
6. *96th NCB Cruise Book.*
7. National Archives and Records Administration, Navy Department B966ƒ968, NCR 7563 3 January 1944.
8. Grove, *Defeat of the Enemy Attack*, 36.
9. Hoehling, *Fighting Liberty Ships*, 34–35.
10. Kemp, *History of the 928th Engineering Aviation Regiment*, 8.
11. National Archives and Records Administration, RG 38, Records U.S. Tenth Fleet Convoy file UGS-29.
12. National Archives and Records Administration, State Department file 811.34553B/49 1/2.
13. Ibid.
14. Guill, *History of the Azores*, 530–31.

15. FRUS 1944, 4:2–4. Although the document, #100 of the Embassy in Lisbon, is dated 7 January 1944, it was only received by the State Department in Washington on 18 January. National Archives and Records Administration, State Department file 811.34553B/47 1/2.

16. FRUS 1943, 2:573.

17. António de Oliveira Salazar's actual titles were president of the Portuguese Council of Ministers, minister of war and minister of foreign affairs of Portugal.

18. *Führer Conferences*, 373–75.

19. Senior British Officer, Azores.

20. National Archives and Records Administration, JCOS Azores File, cable B3552.

21. FRUS 1944, 4:4–5.

22. The USS *John Clarke* was a liberty ship, but the USS *Abraham Lincoln*, although with similar specifications, was not.

23. National Archives and Records Administration, JCOS Azores File, cable B-3553.

24. Vintras, *Portuguese Connection*, 91–92.

25. National Archives and Records Administration, State Department Azores file "Text of message from His Majesty's Consul at Ponta Delgada dated January 9th."

26. Vintras, *Portuguese Connection*, 91–92.

27. *96th NCB Cruise Book*, 10–13.

28. Santa Rita is spelled "Santa Ritta" on older maps and sometimes on JCS documents. Praia is actually Praia da Vitória.

29. Vintras, *Portuguese Connection*, 91–92.

30. National Archives and Records Administration, State Department file 811.34553B/51.

31. National Archives and Records Administration, State Department file 811.34553B/55.

32. Churchill, *War Papers*, 7:647.

33. *96th NCB Cruise Book*, 14–15.

34. National Archives and Records Administration, State Department file 34553B/47½.

35. Ibid.

36. FRUS 1944, 4:5–7.

37. Ibid., 7–8.

38. Guill, *History of the Azores*, 527.

39. National Archives and Records Administration, RG24, Records of Bureau of Naval Personnel, Smooth log of Naval Armed Guard aboard the USS *Abraham Lincoln*, 4 April 1944, Lieutenant (JG) Ross G. Partlow Jr., USNR; RG38 Records of U.S. Tenth Fleet Ship Movement Card for USS *Abraham Lincoln*.

40. Roskill, *Offensive*, 248; Grove, *Defeat of the Enemy Attack*, 261.

41. National Archives and Records Administration, RG24, Records.

42. National Archives and Records Administration, RG 38, Records U.S. Tenth Fleet Convoy file UGS-29.

43. Kemp, *History of the 928th Engineer Aviation Regiment*, 8–9.

44. Report Lieutenant J. F. Beaver to Director, North Atlantic Division, Bureau of Yards and Docks, 5 June 1946, #24234, ATL-4 2, titled "A Report of the activities of the Construction Battalions in the Azores . . ." in Naval Construction Battalion Historian's Office, Port Hueneme, California; *96th NCB Cruise Book*, 16.

45. *Führer Conferences*, 382.

46. Ibid.

47. FRUS 1944, 4:8–9.

48. Ibid., 15, Cable, Stettinius to Norweb 29 February 1944 #621; FRUS 1944, 4:9–10.

49. National Archives and Records Administration, RG24, Records.

50. Guill, *History of the Azores*, 534–35.

51. Kemp, *History of the 928th Engineering Aviation Regiment*, 13; Guill, *History of the Azores*, 534.

52. Kemp, *History of the 928th Engineering Aviation Regiment*, 13.

53. Early Construction Battalion reports and maps spell the site "Santa Ritta"; *96th NCB Cruise Book*, 16–17.

54. Vintras, *Portuguese Connections*, 94.

55. Dönitz, *Memoirs*, 488–89.

56. Craven and Cate, *Services Around the World*, 148, 102–3.

57. FRUS 1944, 4:17–21.

58. Ibid., 18–19.

59. Ibid., 22–23; Cable #1282, 28 April 1944, Norweb to State Department.

CHAPTER 11. NEGOTIATING SANTA MARIA,
APRIL–JULY 1944

1. Guill, *History of the Azores*, 532–33; *Führer Conferences*, 377.

2. Spelled in various ways; Dönitz, *Memoirs*, 424.

3. Ibid., 479.

4. Ibid., 428, quoting U.S. State Department Yalta Documents.

5. *96th NCB Cruise Book*, 18; Beaver, *Activities of the CBs in the Azores*, 3.

6. Kemp, *History of the 928th Engineering Aviation Regiment*, enclosures 19, 20.

7. Roskill, *Offensive*, 242–43.

8. FRUS 1944, 4:23–24, State Department, #1389, 1390.

9. Ibid.

10. Ibid., 25–27; 711.53/41d, Embassy #1526.

11. Ibid.
12. FRUS 1944, 4:27–31, Embassy #1676, 1570, 1581.
13. *96th NCB Cruise Book*, 18–19.
14. Guill, *History of the Azores*, 528–29; Dönitz, *Memoirs*, 406.
15. FRUS 1944, 4:101–2; 1944, 2:120, 131–32; "wolfram" is a synonym for tungsten.
16. FRUS 1944, 2:33; State Department #1703, 12 June 1944.
17. FRUS 1944, 2:40–41; State Department #1888, 1 July 1944; State #1795, 22 June 1944, 36–37.
18. FRUS 1944, 2:37–39; State Department #4969, #1848, #1816, 24 June 1944.
19. Ibid.
20. FRUS 1944, 2:41–51; State Department #1889, 3 July 1944.
21. Ibid.
22. FRUS 1944, 2:43–45.
23. FRUS 1944, 2:48–51; Embassy #2162, #2213.
24. Ibid.
25. *96th NCB Cruise Book*, 20.
26. Hull, *Memoirs*, 1342; FRUS 1944, 2:51–56.
27. Ibid.
28. Ibid.
29. Ibid.
30. *96th NCB Cruise Book*, 20; Naval Facilitator in the Azores.

CHAPTER 12. PAN AM GOES TO SANTA MARIA,
AUGUST–DECEMBER 1944

1. Guill, *History of the Azores*, 1–6.
2. A survey carried out later by the Corps of Engineers with high precision instruments detected a slight curvature on the center line of the runway. It was measured in a few minutes of arc, much beyond the capabilities of the surveying instruments used by the 928th.
3. Author's personal recollection.
4. Kemp, *History of the 928th Engineer Aviation Regiment*, 18.
5. Chester, *Azores*, 175.
6. "Establishing U.S. Naval Activities in the Azores, January to August 1944," 3; Chester, *Azores*, 175.
7. Kemp, *History of the 928th Engineer Aviation Regiment*, 17.
8. Author's personal files.
9. Ibid.
10. Hull, *Memoirs*, 1343.
11. Portugal, *Documentos Relativos*, 35–51.
12. Lajes Air Base Web site http://www.lajes.at.mil.

13. Craven and Cate, *Services Around the World,* 106; *Führer Conferences,* 421–23.

14. 1. Homeward (England) West African Convoy; 2. Slow convoy: England to North Africa.

15. Slessor, *Central Blue,* 476.

CHAPTER 13. ALLIED VICTORY AND BEYOND, 1945–

1. Roskill, *Offensive,* pt. 2, 175–77.

2. Dönitz, *Memoirs,* 423–25; *Führer Conferences,* ch. 1.

3. Ibid., 432.

4. Ibid.

5. Ibid., 433.

6. Dönitz, *Memoirs,* 355–57, 427–29.

7. Craven and Cate, *Services Around the World,* 213–22.

8. Stephen E. Ambrose, *The Wild Blue,* 258–60.

9. The spelling of the town and the air base were officially changed from Lagens to Lajes after the war; Beaver, *Activities of the CBs in the Azores,* 6.

10. Craven and Cate, *Services Around the World,* 52–65.

11. Guill, *History of the Azores,* 538–39.

12. Ibid.

13. FRUS 1984, 2:7–11.

14. *New York Times* Archives, "Kissinger Transcripts."

15. Guill, *History of the Azores,* 540–41.

16. "Canadian Jet, Engines Dead, Lands Safely in the Azores," *New York Times,* 25 August 2001, A5.

17. BBC, "Portuguese ministers says USA asked NATO countries for more intelligence resources," 9 October 2001.

18. General Accounting Office, Report GAO/NSIAD-94_138, 16.

19. Sanger and Hoge, *New York Times,* 17 March 2003, "Threats and Responses: Diplomacy;" "Bush and Two Allies Seem Set for War to Depose Hussein."

20. Churchill, *Second World War,* 5:6.

21. Dönitz, *Memoirs,* 489–90.

22. Dönitz, *Memoirs,* 392; *Führer Conferences,* 489.

23. Cannon, *Operation Drumbeat,* xxi.

24. Undated report on file, Command Historian's Office, Naval Construction Battalion Center, Port Hueneme, California, from the Director, Atlantic Division, Bureau of Yards and Docks.

BIBLIOGRAPHY

Almada, José de. *Aliança Inglesa: subsídios para o seu estudo.* Lisbon: Imprensa Nacional, 1946–48.

Ambrose, Stephen E. *The Wild Blue: The Men and Boys Who Flew the B-24s Over Germany.* New York: Simon and Schuster, 2001.

Atkinson, W. C. *British Contributions to Portuguese and Brazilian Studies.* London: British Council, 1974.

Beaver, J. J. *A Report of the Activities of the Construction Battalions in the Azores During the Recent Conflict.* Department of the Navy, Office of the Director, Atlantic Division, Bureau of Yards and Docks, New York, 5 June 1946.

Booth, B., R. Croasdale, and G. P. L. Walker. "A Quantitative Study of Five Thousand Years of Volcanism On São Miguel, Azores." *Philosophical Transactions of the Royal Society of London* 288 (1978): 271–319.

Brazão, Eduardo. *The Anglo-Portuguese Alliance.* London: Sylvan Press, 1957.

Bryans, Robin. *The Azores.* London: Faber and Faber, 1963.

Bryant, Arthur. *The Turn of the Tide.* London: Ivan Collins Sons, 1957.

Chester, Edward W. "The Azores: The Hesperides Golden Apples." in *The United States and Six Atlantic Outposts.* New York: Kennikat Press, 1980.

Churchill, Randolph. *Road to Victory.* Boston: Houghton Mifflin, 1986.

Churchill, Winston S. *The Churchill War Papers.* Martin Gilbert, ed. New York: W.W. Norton, 1993.

———. *The Second World War.* 6 vols. Boston: Houghton Mifflin, 1950–54.

Coakley, R. W., and F. M. Leighton. *The United States Army in World War II: Global Logistics and Strategy 1943–45.* Washington, D.C: Department of the Army, Office of the Chief of Military History, 1968.

Compton, J. V. *The Swastika and the Eagle: Hitler, the United States, and the Origins of World War II.* Boston: Houghton Mifflin, 1967.

Conn, S., E. R. Engelman, and B. Fairchild. *The Western Hemisphere: Guarding the United States and Its Outposts.* Vol. 12, pt. 2 of *The United States Army in World War II.* Washington, D.C.: Department of the Army, Office of the Chief of Military History, 1964.

Conn, S., and B. Fairchild. *The Western Hemisphere: The Framework of Hemisphere Defense.* Vol. 12, pt. 1 of *The United States Army in World War II.* Washington, D.C.: Department of the Army, Office of the Chief of Military History, 1960.

Craven, W. F., and J. L. Cate, eds. *Services Around the World.* Vol. 7 of *The Army Air Forces in World War II.* Chicago: University of Chicago Press, 1958.

Dallek, Robert. *Franklin Delano Roosevelt and American Foreign Policy, 1932–1945.* New York: Oxford University Press, 1979.

Dönitz, Karl. *Memoirs: Ten Years and Twenty Days.* Annapolis, Md.: U.S. Naval Institute Press, 1990.

Dorwart, J. M. *Conflict of Duty.* Annapolis, Md.: U.S. Naval Institute Press, 1983.

Dutton, D. *Anthony Eden.* London: Arnold, 1997.

Eden, Anthony. *Reckoning: The Memoirs of Anthony Eden, Earl of Avon.* London: Cassell, 1960–65.

Establishing U.S. Naval Activities in the Azores, January to August 1944. Command File World War II Report. Washington, D.C.: Navy Yard.

Foreign Relations of the United States (FRUS) 1941. *Diplomatic Papers.* Europe. Vol. 2. Washington, D.C.: Government Printing Office, 1959.

———— 1943. *Diplomatic Papers.* Europe. Vol. 2. Washington, D.C.: Government Printing Office, 1964.

———— 1943. *Diplomatic Papers.* American Republics. Vol. 5. Washington, D.C.: Government Printing Office, 1965.

———— 1944. *Diplomatic Papers.* Europe. Vol. 4. Washington, D.C.: Government Printing Office, 1966.

———— 1984. *Diplomatic Papers.* Europe. Vol. 2. Washington, D.C.: Government Printing Office, 1984.

Führer Conferences on Naval Affairs, 1939–1945. Annapolis, Md.: U.S. Naval Institute Press, 1990.

Gannon, Michael. *Black May.* New York: HarperCollins, 1998.

————. *Operation Drumbeat.* New York: Harper and Row, 1990.

Germinsky, Robert A. *The Fighting Seabees.* Washington, D.C: Navy Office of Information, 1994.

Grove, E. J. *The Defeat of the Enemy Attack on Shipping, 1939–1945.* Rev. edition. Aldershot, UK: Ashgate, 1957.

Guill, James H. *A History of the Azores Islands.* Tulare, Calif.: Golden Shield Institute, 1993.

————. "Nine Keys to Atlantic Defense." U.S. Naval Institute *Proceedings* 79 (1953): 1076–83.

Herwig, H. H. *Politics of Frustration.* New York: Little Brown, 1976.

Hinsley, F. H., and A. G. Simkins. *Security and Counter Intelligence.* Vol. 4 of

British Intelligence in the Second World War. New York: Cambridge University Press, 1990.

Hinsley, F. H., E. E. Thomas, C. F. G. Ransom, and R. C. Knight. *Influence on Strategy and Operations.* Vol. 2 of *British Intelligence in the Second World War.* New York: Cambridge University Press, 1986.

Hoehling, A. A. *Fighting Liberty Ships: A Memoir.* Columbus: Ohio State University Press, 1990.

Hough, Richard. *The Longest Battle: The War at Sea 1939–45.* New York: Morrow, 1986.

Hull, Cordell. *The Memoirs of Cordell Hull.* Vol. 2. New York: Macmillan, 1948.

Jacobsen, H. A., and A. C. Smith Jr., eds. *World War II Policy and Strategy: Selected Documents.* New York: Clio Books, 1979.

Kay, Hugh. *Salazar and Modern Portugal.* London: Eyre & Spottiswoode, 1970.

Kemp, A. H. *History of the 928th Engineer Aviation Regiment (Less Three Battalions).* College Park, Md.: National Archives and Records Administration, n.d.

Kennan, George. *Memoirs.* Vol. 1. Boston: Little Brown, 1967.

Kennedy, David M. "Victory at Sea." *Atlantic Monthly,* March 1999, 51–76.

Kissinger Transcripts. Meeting at Junta Geral, Angra do Heroïsmo, Terceira, Azores. Top Secret Memorandum of Conversation, *New York Times* Archives, 13 December 1971.

Leighton, R. M., and R. W. Coakley. *The United States Army in World War II: Global Logistics and Strategy, 1940–43.* Washington, D.C: Department of the Army, Office of the Chief of Military History, 1955.

Lundeberg, P. K. "American Anti-Submarine Operations in the Atlantic, May 1943–May 1945." Ph. D. diss., Harvard University, 1954.

Matloft, M., and E. M. Snell. *The United States Army in World War II: Strategic Planning for Coalition Warfare, 1941–42.* Washington, D.C.: Department of the Army, Office of the Chief of Military History, 1953.

Mees, Jules. *Histoire de la découverte des iles Açores et de l'origine de Leur Dénomination d'Iles Flamandes.* Ghent, Belgium: Université de Gand Recueil de Travaux, Faculté de Philosophie et Lettres, 27 fascicule 1901.

Morison, Samuel Eliot. *The Atlantic Battle Won.* Boston: Little, Brown, 1956.

National Archives and Records Administration. Modern Military Records, "Declassified files of the Joint Chiefs of Staff relating to the Azores Bases." College Park, Md.

———. State Department Declassified Files 811.34553, "Efforts of the United Sates to Obtain from Portugal certain military privileges in the Azores." College Park, Md.

Naval Facilities in the Azores. Report from the Director, Atlantic Division, Bureau of Yards and Docks. Port Hueneme, Calif.: Naval Construction Battalion, n.d.

Ninety-Sixth NCB Cruise Book World War II. CD-Rom. Port Hueneme, Calif.: CEC/Seabee Historical Foundation, 2002.

Portugal, Ministério dos Negócios Estrangeiros. *Documentos relativos aos acordos entre Portugal, Inglaterra e Estados Unidos da America para a conçessão* . . . Lisbon: Imprensa Nacional, 1946.

Roosevelt, Franklin D. *The Public Papers and Addresses of Franklin D. Roosevelt.* Vol. 10. Edited by Samuel I. Rosenman. New York: Random House, 1941.

Roskill, S. W. *The Offensive.* Vol. 3 of *The War at Sea 1939–45.* 3 parts. London: Her Majesty's Stationery Office, 1960.

Saemundson, Kristján. "Subaerial Volcanism in the Western North Atlantic." In *The Western North Atlantic Region,* edited by P. R. Vogt and R. E. Tucholke. Vol. M of *The Geology of North America.* Boulder, Colo.: Geological Society of America, 1986.

Seabee History Web site. Available at http://www.cbcph.navy.mil/museum/ Seabee History/battalions.html.

Slessor, J. C. *The Central Blue.* New York: Praeger, 1957.

Stevens, Donald. "Franklin D. Roosevelt and the Azores Dilemma, 1941." *Historian* 54 (1992): 641–56.

Stratton, R.O. "Germany's Secret Naval Supply Service." U.S. Naval Institute *Proceedings* 79 (1953): 1085–90.

U.S. House of Representatives. *Strategic Airlift: Further Air Base Reductions in Europe Could Jeopardize Capability.* Report to the Chairman, Subcommittee on Readiness, Committee on Armed Services, GAO/NSIAD-94-138.

Vintras, R. E. *Portuguese Connection: The Secret History of the Azores Base.* London: Bachman and Turner, 1974.

Waller, John H. *The Unseen War in Europe: Espionage and Conspiracy in the Second World War.* New York: Random House, 1996.

Wignall, Sydney. *Project Revenge: Azores International Marine Archaeological Expedition.* St. Helens, UK: Casey Technical, 1971.

Woodward, F. L. *British Foreign Policy in the Second World War.* New York: Oxford University Press, 1952.

Zitellini, N., et al. "Source of the 1755 Lisbon Earthquake and Tsunami Investigated." *EOS* 82 (2001): 285–91.

INDEX

ABOUT THE AUTHOR

Norman Herz was born and educated in New York City. During World War II he served as a corporal in the Army Corps of Engineers in Operation Alacrity. He won a commendation for his role in the operation and an appointment to Air Force Officer Candidate School. After the war he was awarded a doctorate in geology from Johns Hopkins University and went on to a distinguished career as a geologist, including eighteen years with the U.S. Geological Survey (USGS). While he was with the USGS, Herz spent eight years in Brazil, and for his work there he was elected to the Brazilian Academy of Sciences. In 1970 he was appointed professor and head of the geology department at the University of Georgia, where he remained until his retirement in 1995. He has been a visiting professor at universities in Brazil, France, and the United States and has carried out research in archaeological geology in Greece, Romania, India, and many other countries. He has also been recognized for his work with archaeologists and has authored or edited six books and well over one hundred articles in the field. For these contributions in 1995 the Archaeological Institute of America awarded him its highest honor, the Pomerance Award for Scientific Contributions to Archaeology.

The Naval Institute Press is the book-publishing arm of the U.S. Naval Institute, a private, nonprofit, membership society for sea service professionals and others who share an interest in naval and maritime affairs. Established in 1873 at the U.S. Naval Academy in Annapolis, Maryland, where its offices remain today, the Naval Institute has members worldwide.

Members of the Naval Institute support the education programs of the society and receive the influential monthly magazine *Proceedings* and discounts on fine nautical prints and on ship and aircraft photos. They also have access to the transcripts of the Institute's Oral History Program and get discounted admission to any of the Institute-sponsored seminars offered around the country.

The Naval Institute also publishes *Naval History* magazine. This colorful bimonthly is filled with entertaining and thought-provoking articles, first-person reminiscences, and dramatic art and photography. Members receive a discount on *Naval History* subscriptions.

The Naval Institute's book-publishing program, begun in 1898 with basic guides to naval practices, has broadened its scope to include books of more general interest. Now the Naval Institute Press publishes about one hundred titles each year, ranging from how-to books on boating and navigation to battle histories, biographies, ship and aircraft guides, and novels. Institute members receive significant discounts on the Press's more than eight hundred books in print.

Full-time students are eligible for special half-price membership rates. Life memberships are also available.

For a free catalog describing Naval Institute Press books currently available, and for further information about subscribing to *Naval History* magazine or about joining the U.S. Naval Institute, please write to:

Membership Department
U.S. Naval Institute
291 Wood Road
Annapolis, MD 21402-5034
Telephone: (800) 233-8764
Fax: (410) 269-7940
Web address: www.navalinstitute.org